Frommer's®
Montréal & Québec City

My Montréal & Québec City

by Herbert Bailey Livesey

A SNAPSHOT: QUÉBEC CITY, FEBRUARY, CARNAVAL DE QUÉBEC IN FULL
swing. Dog sleds clatter down cobblestone streets turned into snowy race lanes in the shadow of the city's grand castle, the Château Frontenac. Children of every age press against temporary metal fencing to take in the howling rush. It's −26°F, but, astonishingly, absurdly, the cold seems to have zero effect on the cheer of the Québécois.

Another snapshot: Montréal, a sidewalk table, a much warmer summer day. Locals chat over bowls of café au lait in the unique patois of the region that meshes French into English. These are people born into a city where French and British traditions and languages still exist side by side, with both peppered by an internationalism that reflects Canada's liberal immigration policies.

An infectiously relaxed zest for living coupled with a palpable reverence for the past—these are the defining characteristics of this singular province. Smartly done preservation efforts over the past two decades have created two cities where visitors can sink deeply into old-world Europe, able to imagine what life might have been like in the 17th and 18th centuries. And yet there also are pockets of architecture, food, and fashion as wildly design-forward as you'll find anywhere.

The photographs on the following pages give a taste of the many reasons to put Montréal and Québec City on your list of must-see destinations.

MONTMORENCY FALLS (left) are higher than Niagara—as anyone is sure to be told, several times, upon visiting. Back in the 18th century, British and French forces lobbed cannonballs at each other from entrenchments on both banks. These days, fireworks, sometimes seen above the falls, are strictly for fun, and launched during annual festivals.

MONTREAL'S VIEUX-PORT (above) features the silver-domed 1847 Bonsecours building seen here in the foreground, with the cobblestone streets and preserved buildings of Colonial-era Vieux- Montréal surrounding it. In the distance, modern-day office towers rise above the landscape. A wide park along the water's edge hosts cyclists, rollerbladers, concerts, sunbathers, and others out for *le pique-nique* in the warmer months.

The high altar of the **BASILIQUE NOTRE-DAME (left)**, easily the most beautifully embellished of Montréal's hundreds of churches, is richly carved linden wood, as is most of the interior. The bell in the tower weighs 12 tons, and the floor rumbles when it rings. Orchestras perform here, drawn by the magnificent acoustics. The church's Protestant Irish-American architect, James O'Donnell, was so stirred by what he had wrought that he converted to Catholicism.

Pedestrian-only **RUE DU TRESOR (above)** in Québec City is an obligatory stop on every stroll through the old Upper Town. Artists line both sides of the narrow lane, their watercolors, prints, and drawings on display. There's no pressure to buy. Subject matter is mostly various vistas and details of their city, but some artists set up easels beside nearby outdoor cafes and offer to do portraits.

The historic district of Québec City is the only walled city north of Mexico. It's divided into two parts: Basse-Ville, the older part down by the river where the first European settlers built and farmed, and Haute-Ville, atop the steep-sided cliff to which the French citizens withdrew for greater safety from invaders. This **FUNICULAIRE (left)** connects the two, affording spectacular views and escape from the Breakneck Stairs, the other pedestrian route down the hill.

SUGARING-OFF (below) season is February through March, when sap is drawn from the vast stands of sugar maples with which the province is blessed. At first, the sap was merely processed, transformed into syrup and candies, and sent off to eager buyers. Then some canny Québécois decided to offer meals in his *cabane à sucre*—sugar shack. That evolved into an industry, and some sugar shacks stay open all year, providing gargantuan farm meals, live folkloric entertainment, simple lodgings, and even sleigh rides.

Boosters call Montréal the "City of Festivals," and justifiably so. Apart from a few bereft weeks here and there in the coldest months, it takes specific intent and careful planning to avoid celebratory events of one kind or another. Festivals throughout the year highlight comedy, film, cuisine, theater, cycling, motor racing, and fireworks. The greatest explosion of energy and talent, however, is during the annual **JAZZ FESTIVAL (above)**, with hundreds of performances in scores of venues, many of them free.

Montréal's **HÔTEL DE VILLE (right)** stands at the top of the Place Jacques-Cartier, which was the open-air market square of 19th-century Montréal. The extravagantly detailed French Second Empire style of the building is seen to best effect at night, and a dozen other impressive structures are similarly illuminated, constituting a rewarding—and safe—after-dark walking tour.

Québec's magnificent **CHATEAU FRON-TENAC (above)** is the signature symbol of the city. In style, it's a Loire castle on steroids, one of a chain of luxury hotels strung along the route of the Trans-Canada railway to encourage tourism at the start of the 20th century.

The long staircase leading down from the elevated La Citadelle to the promenade known as Terrace Dufferin is transformed into a **BOBSLED RUN (right)** during Québec City's annual winter carnival. No special skills or particular athleticism is required for the short but thrilling run, unless you count climbing up to the starting point.

Opposite page: © Walter Bibikow/Getty Images

Routinely designated the top ski resort east of the Mississippi, **TREMBLANT** marches up the slope of its namesake mountain 75 miles north of Montréal. While winter is its prime season, it has a full array of activities in the warm months. Accommodations and dining options range from economical to deluxe. And while kids are catered to, there are plenty of places for parents, teens, and couples to hide away.

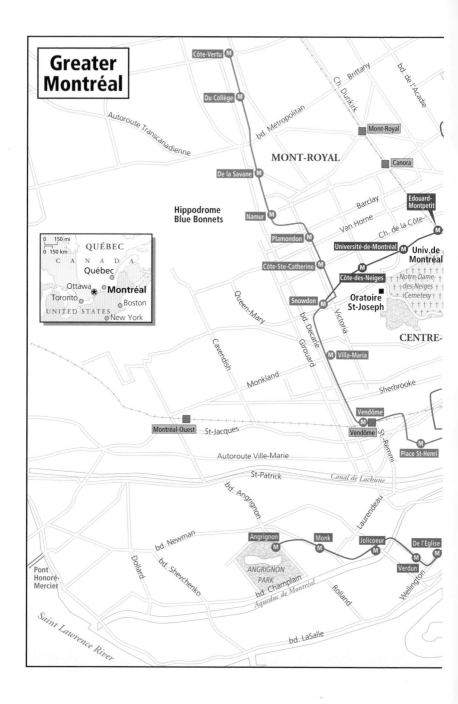

Greater Montréal

Côte-Vertu M

Du Collège M

Ch. Dunkirk

Brittany

bd. de l'Acadie

Autoroute Transcanadienne

bd. Métropolitan

Mont-Royal

MONT-ROYAL

Canora

De la Savane M

Barclay

Edouard-Montpetit M

Hippodrome
Blue Bonnets

Namur M

Van Horne

Ch. de la Côte

Plamondon M

Université-de-Montréal M

Univ.de
Montréal

Côte-Ste-Catherine M

Côte-des-Neiges M

*Notre-Dame-
des-Neiges
Cemetery*

Oratoire
St-Joseph

QUÉBEC

CANADA

Québec

Snowdon M

Ottawa

Montréal

Toronto

Boston

UNITED STATES

New York

Queen-Mary

bd. Decarie

Victoria

CENTRE-

Villa-Maria M

Cavendish

Girouard

Monkland

Sherbrooke

Montréal-Ouest

St-Jacques

Vendôme M

Vendôme

St-Remmi

Place St-Henri M

Autoroute Ville-Marie

St-Patrick

Canal de Lachine

bd. Angrignon

Laurendeau

Pont
Honoré-
Mercier

bd. Newman

bd. Shevchenko

Dollard

Angrignon M

Monk M

Jolicoeur M

De l'Eglise M

Verdun

ANGRIGNON
PARK

bd. Champlain

Aqueduc de Montréal

Rolland

Wellington

Saint Lawrence River

bd. LaSalle

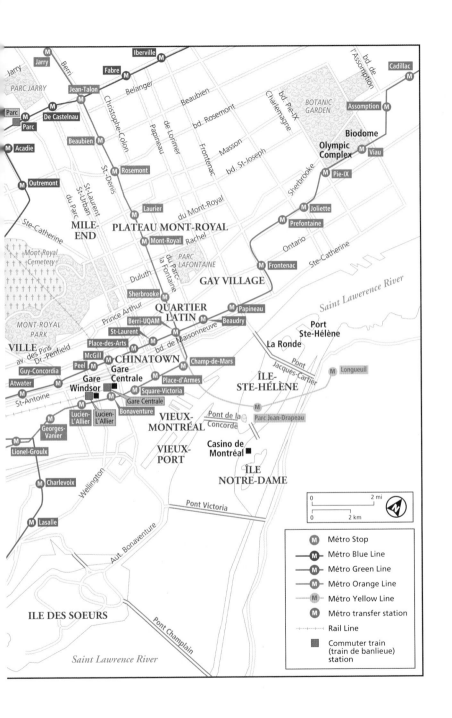

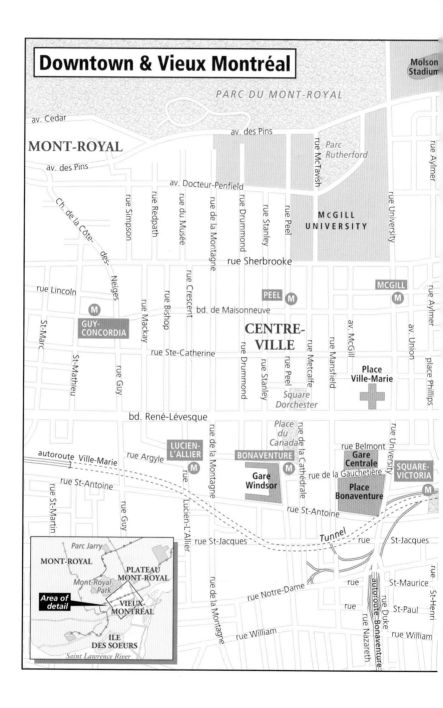

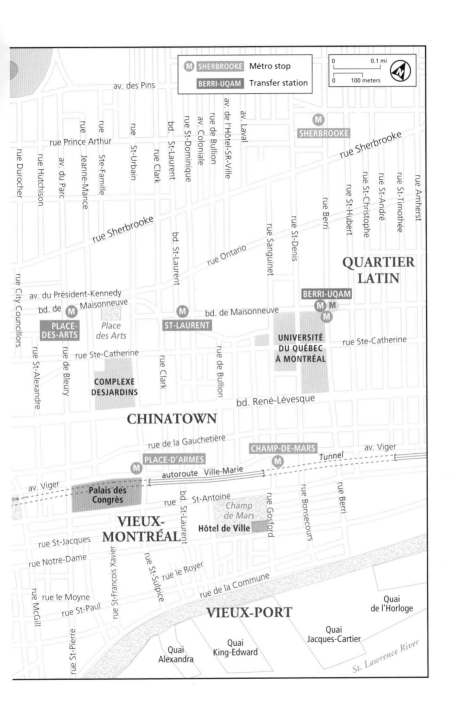

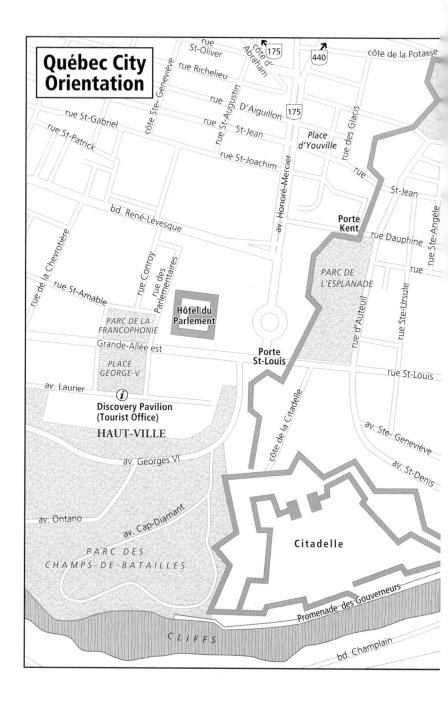

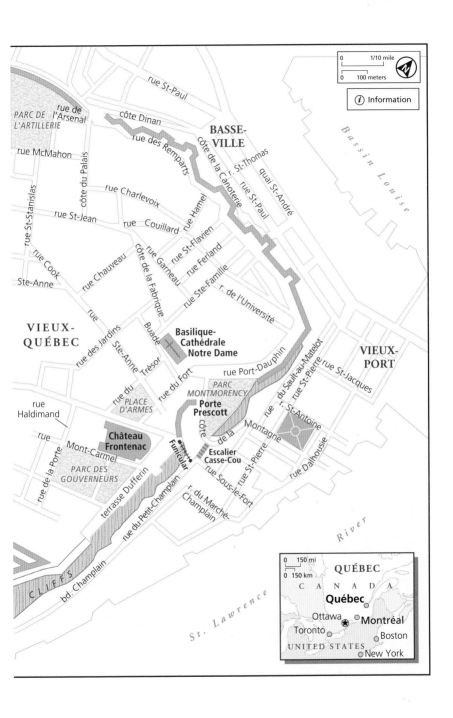

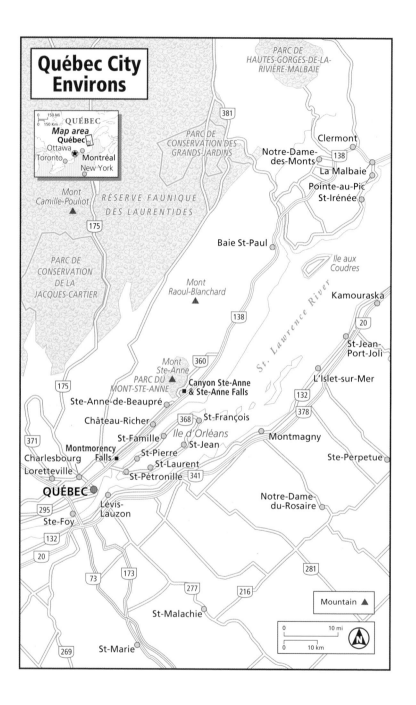

Québec City Environs

PARC DE HAUTES-GORGES-DE-LA-RIVIÈRE-MALBAIE

QUÉBEC

Map area
Québec

Ottawa

Toronto   **Montréal**
New York

0   150 Mi
0   150 Km.

Mont Camille-Pouliot ▲

RÉSERVE FAUNIQUE DES LAURENTIDES

175

PARC DE CONSERVATION DE LA JACQUES-CARTIER

PARC DE CONSERVATION DES GRANDS-JARDINS

381

Clermont

Notre-Dame-des-Monts   138

La Malbaie

Pointe-au-Pic
St-Irénée

Baie St-Paul

Ile aux Coudres

Mont Raoul-Blanchard ▲

138

Kamouraska

20

St-Jean-Port-Joli

St. Lawrence River

360   *Mont Ste-Anne* ▲

PARC DU MONT-STE-ANNE

Canyon Ste-Anne & Ste-Anne Falls ■

175

Ste-Anne-de-Beaupré

L'Islet-sur-Mer

132

378

Château-Richer

368   St-François

St-Famille   *Ile d'Orléans*

371   **Montmorency Falls** ■   St-Jean

St-Pierre

Charlesbourg

Loretteville   St-Laurent

St-Pétronille   341

Montmagny

Ste-Perpetue

QUÉBEC

Lévis-Lauzon

295

Ste-Foy

Notre-Dame-du-Rosaire

132

20

281

73   173

277   216

St-Malachie

269   St-Marie

Mountain ▲

0   10 mi
0   10 km

Frommer's®

Montréal & Québec City 2009

by Leslie Brokaw

Here's what the critics say about Frommer's:

"Amazingly easy to use. Very portable, very complete."
—BOOKLIST

"Detailed, accurate, and easy-to-read information
for all price ranges."
—GLAMOUR MAGAZINE

"Hotel information is close to encyclopedic."
—DES MOINES SUNDAY REGISTER

"Frommer's Guides have a way of giving you
a real feel for a place."
—KNIGHT RIDDER NEWSPAPERS

WILEY
Wiley Publishing, Inc.

ABOUT THE AUTHOR

Leslie Brokaw travels frequently to Montréal and Québec City from her home base in Boston. She has contributed to recent editions of *Frommer's Canada* and *Frommer's New England*. Brokaw is the editor of *Leader*, a publication of the Girl Scouts of the USA, and is a film columnist for *The Boston Globe*. She's also on the faculty of Emerson College.

Published by:

WILEY PUBLISHING, INC.

111 River St.
Hoboken, NJ 07030-5774

ISBN 978-0-470-38223-3

Editor: Avital Binshtock with Linda Barth
Production Editor: Michael Brumitt
Cartographer: Roberta Stockwell
Photo Editor: Richard Fox
Production by Wiley Indianapolis Composition Services

Front cover photo: Place Jacques Cartier and Town Hall in Montréal
Back cover photo: Two waiters outside a Québec restaurant window

For information about our other products and services or to obtain technical support, please contact our Customer Care Department within the U.S. at 800/762-2974, outside the U.S. at 317/572-3993 or fax 317/572-4002.

Wiley also publishes its books in a variety of electronic formats. Some content that appears in print may not be available in electronic formats.

Manufactured in the United States of America

5   4   3   2   1

CONTENTS

9 MONTRÉAL STROLLS 130

10 MONTRÉAL SHOPPING 150

11 MONTRÉAL AFTER DARK 160

12 SIDE TRIPS FROM MONTRÉAL 172

13 GETTING TO KNOW QUÉBEC CITY 202

14 WHERE TO STAY IN QUÉBEC CITY 209

APPENDIX: FAST FACTS, TOLL-FREE NUMBERS & WEBSITES 289

INDEX 297

LIST OF MAPS

AN INVITATION TO THE READER

In researching this book, we discovered many wonderful places—hotels, restaurants, shops, and more. We're sure you'll find others. Please tell us about them so that we can share the information with your fellow travelers in upcoming editions. If you were disappointed with a recommendation, we'd love to know that, too. Please write to:

Frommer's Montréal & Québec City 2009
Wiley Publishing, Inc. • 111 River St. • Hoboken, NJ 07030-5774

AN ADDITIONAL NOTE

Please be advised that travel information is subject to change at any time—and this is especially true of prices. We therefore suggest that you write or call ahead for confirmation when making your travel plans. The authors, editors, and publisher cannot be held responsible for the experiences of readers while traveling. Your safety is important to us, however, so we encourage you to stay alert and be aware of your surroundings. Keep a close eye on cameras, purses, and wallets, all favorite targets of thieves and pickpockets.

ACKNOWLEDGMENTS

This edition of the book continues to draw from more than 10 years of earlier versions that were written by Herbert Bailey Livesey, the author's stepfather. She wishes to acknowledge her debt to The Geezer for his fine taste, keen research, and deft work. Livesey continues to write about travel and food at www.geezerwisdom.blogspot.com. Matthew Barber, whom the author was fortunate enough to marry during the months this book was being written, took judicious notes at many of the meals and helped write the restaurant chapters of this book.

Other Great Guides for Your Trip:

Frommer's Canada

Montréal & Québec City For Dummies

Frommer's Montréal Day by Day

Frommer's Nova Scotia, New Brunswick & Prince Edward Island

FROMMER'S STAR RATINGS, ICONS & ABBREVIATIONS

Every hotel, restaurant, and attraction listing in this guide has been ranked for quality, value, service, amenities, and special features using a **star-rating system.** In country, state, and regional guides, we also rate towns and regions to help you narrow down your choices and budget your time accordingly. Hotels and restaurants are rated on a scale of zero (recommended) to three stars (exceptional). Attractions, shopping, nightlife, towns, and regions are rated according to the following scale: zero stars (recommended), one star (highly recommended), two stars (very highly recommended), and three stars (must-see).

In addition to the star-rating system, we also use **seven feature icons** that point you to the great deals, in-the-know advice, and unique experiences that separate travelers from tourists. Throughout the book, look for:

Finds	Special finds—those places only insiders know about
Fun Facts	Fun facts—details that make travelers more informed and their trips more fun
Kids	Best bets for kids, and advice for the whole family
Moments	Special moments—those experiences that memories are made of
Overrated	Places or experiences not worth your time or money
Tips	Insider tips—great ways to save time and money
Value	Great values—where to get the best deals

The following **abbreviations** are used for credit cards:

AE	American Express	DISC	Discover	V	Visa
DC	Diners Club	MC	MasterCard		

FROMMERS.COM

Now that you have this guidebook to help you plan a great trip, visit our website at **www.frommers.com** for additional travel information on more than 4,000 destinations. We update features regularly to give you instant access to the most current trip-planning information available. At Frommers.com, you'll find scoops on the best airfares, lodging rates, and car rental bargains. You can even book your travel online through our reliable travel booking partners. Other popular features include:

- Online updates of our most popular guidebooks
- Vacation sweepstakes and contest giveaways
- Newsletters highlighting the hottest travel trends
- Podcasts, interactive maps, and up-to-the-minute events listings
- Opinionated blog entries by Arthur Frommer himself
- Online travel message boards with featured travel discussions

What's New in Montréal & Québec City

Like a teenager after a New Year's Eve blowout, Québec City is recovering this year from its 400th anniversary celebrations of 2008. On July 3, church bells rang across the city as they haven't since the end of World War II.

There were the parties, of course, with the likes of Céline Dion and Paul McCartney playing free concerts. There were grand art extravaganzas, including famed Québec theater artist Robert Lepage's multimedia show projected on silos in Québec's Old Port, eliciting high praise along with oohs and aahs. A rare traveling exhibition from Paris's Louvre came to town, too. And, of course, there were politics, with the history of the province's long struggle over separatism from the rest of Canada both downplayed and cheered.

Canadian Prime Minister Stephen Harper did the downplaying, saying that the founding of the city by French discoverer Samuel de Champlain also marked the founding of a "great Canadian country, strong and free." He was countered by French Prime Minister François Fillon, who said that Québec was an extension of France on the North American continent, and that "French has never been extinguished in America"; Fillon also repeatedly referred to Québec as a "country," and locals seemed to side more with him. The fête, it seemed, wasn't about Canada at all, but a party celebrating, as one resident put it in the *Globe and Mail*, "400 years of French pride in this land of America."

So some conflict and division got churned up again along with all the good will, but things have settled down and now the party's over. For tourists, no bother: There's a whole city, freshly repainted and polished up, to explore, and it's more relaxed than it was last year.

The big issue looming large for foreign travelers is the incredible strength of the Canadian dollar (known to all as the "loonie," thanks to its relief image of a common loon). After a long, slow creep, the loonie reached parity with the U.S. dollar on September 20, 2007, and has stayed there.

Mostly, that's bad news for visitors. A Canadian dollar that cost US87¢ and 43p to purchase in early 2007 now costs about US$1 and 50p—an eyebrow-raising 15% increase. That means a C$200 hotel room that cost US$174 (£86) in January 2007 now costs US$200 £100—a spike of US$26 (£14). A C$50 meal that cost US$43 (£22) now costs US$50 (£25)—an additional US$7 (£3.50).

On the other hand, a tourism industry anxious to attract tourist dollars, euros, yen, rupees, pounds, and other currencies is sweetening the deals where it can. Bargain hunters can find a wider variety of travel packages than ever at hotel and tourism websites, including www.bonjourquebec.com and www.tourisme-montreal.org, and through discount services like Priceline.

PLANNING YOUR TRIP Passport rules continue to be in flux. All air travelers between the U.S. and Canada have been required since January 2007 to present a passport both coming and going. It looked like U.S. and Canadian citizens traveling by land or by sea would also need a passport starting sometime in 2008, but that hasn't happened, in large part because of concerns about the impact the new rule would have on tourism. For now, a government-issued photo ID, such as a driver's license, plus proof of citizenship, is ample if you're traveling by car, but if you've got a passport, bring it. Check **http://travel.state.gov** for the most up-to-date information about traveling from the U.S.

WHERE TO STAY　The esteemed **Ritz-Carlton Montréal** has started a $100-million renovation and will be closed for 15 months, until October 2009. The hotel's 229 rooms and suites will be transformed into 130 rooms and suites, plus 50 condo-residences. The front façade and much-loved back garden will reportedly be preserved.

Other notable changes on the Montréal hotel landscape include a new **Westin** (© 514/380-3333; www.westinmontreal. com) slated to open sometime in 2009 at 250 rue St. Antoine ouest, directly across the street from the fine **Hôtel InterContinental Montréal** (p. 78) and the Palais des Congrès convention center, at Vieux-Montréal's north end. The new **Opus Hotel Montréal,** 10 Sherbrooke ouest (© 866/744-6346; www.opushotel. com), took over the chic but dark Hôtel Godin in late 2007. Also, the all-suite, luxury **Hôtel Le Crystal,** 1100 rue de la Montagne (© 514/861-5550; www. hotellecrystal.com), opened in downtown in spring 2008. We'll review these in future editions of the book after they've had a chance to get their sea legs.

In Québec City, new owners gave a total overhaul to **Hôtel Champlain,** 115 rue Ste-Anne (© **800/567-2106;** www. champlainhotel.com), and even the smallest rooms now have silk curtains, king or queen beds, 300-count cotton sheets, and flatscreen TVs.

WHERE TO DINE　In Montréal, Hôtel Le Germain added some sizzle to its operation with the November 2007 opening of **Laurie Raphaël Montréal,** 2050 rue Mansfield (© **514/849-2050;** www. hotelgermain.com/en/laurieraphael.asp), in the hotel's restaurant space. It's the first offshoot of Québec City's most famous restaurant.

The founders of the well-liked seafood-and-meat joint **Joe Beef** have opened an Italian eatery, **Liverpool House,** just a few doors away at 2501 rue Notre-Dame ouest (© **514/313-6049**), as well as the **McKiernan** luncheonette and wine bar (no. 2485; © **514/759-6677**).

A favorite Plateau Mont-Royal restaurant, Brunoise, shut down in November 2007. The owners had expanded in early 2007 to the less expensive **La Brasserie Brunoise,** 1012 rue de la Montagne (© **514/933-3885;** www.brunoise.ca), next to the Bell Centre, and are continuing with the new operation.

In Québec City's St-Roch neighborhood, the estimable **Utopie** restaurant has expanded with to a tapas and wine bar right next door, **Le Cercle,** 228 rue St-Joseph est; © **418/948-8648.**

WHAT TO SEE & DO　After hosting an avant-garde opening exhibit as part of Québec City's 400th celebrations, **Espace 400e** (p. 241) will become a Parks Canada discovery center right on the waterfront, with exhibits to be determined.

The must-see **Musée de la Civilisation** (© **866/710-8031;** www.mcq.org; p. 234) has a major new exhibit called *"Territories," which highlights* Québec's culture through the lens of territory occupation and natural-resource use.

If you're going to be in Québec City in August 2009, try to be there the 6th through the 9th to see what's in store for the 250-year anniversary of the Battle of the Plains of Abraham. More than 2,000 historical reenactors will set up encampments in the manner of 1759 British and French soldiers on the huge grassy park at the edge of the city. They'll participate in a re-creation of the battles that resulted in France's loss of the territory and British rule of Canada. More information is available at **www.quebec09.com**.

In the epicenter of Québec City's tourist district, excavation under **Terrasse Dufferin,** the promenade alongside the Château Frontenac that overlooks the St. Lawrence River, is now complete, and you can view the work by way of walk-through tours (no reservation required) and Plexiglas flooring and walls.

In Montréal, nothing will be able to top the 2008 appearance of native son Leonard Cohen at the annual **Festival International de Jazz,** though planners are sure to try to come up with something almost as impressive for the July event.

Both Montréal and Québec City continue to tinker with their **museum cards,** which are a great deal if you're gunning to see a lot in a short amount of time: They grant entry to dozens of museums and attractions, as well as to public transit. See p. 109 and p. 234.

One final note: Like the Québecois themselves, this guidebook goes back and forth a bit between using the English and French names for areas and attractions. Most often, we use the French-language titles, as Québec's state-mandated language is French and most signs, brochures, and maps list the names in French. Occasionally, however, we'll use the English name or translation as well if that makes the meaning clearer.

The Best of Montréal & Québec City

If Montréal had a tagline, it could well be "Any excuse for a party." An enormous *joie de vivre* pervades the way the city presents itself, organizes itself, and goes about its business. The calendar is packed with festivals and events that bring out natives and guests from around the world.

To boot, a billion-dollar building boom has filled most of the vacant downtown lots. Over the past 40 years, and especially in the most recent 15, Montréal has become a modern city in every regard, with skyscrapers in unexpected shapes and bright, noncorporate colors; a beautifully preserved historic district; and a large area of artists' lofts, boutiques, cafes, and miles of restaurants.

American and European travelers will likely find Montréal an urban near-paradise. The subway system, called the Métro, is modern and swift. Streets are safe. Montréal's best restaurants are the equals of their south-of-the-border compatriots in every way.

Québec City, more traditional and more French, is replacing its former conservatism with an ever-expanding aura of sophistication. With its impressive location above the St. Lawrence River and its virtually unblemished Old Town filled with 18th- and 19th-century houses, this city looks like France and is almost impossibly romantic—it's unlike any other city in North America.

1 UNFORGETTABLE TRAVEL EXPERIENCES

MONTREAL

- **Listen to Jazz:** In downtown, Old Town, the Plateau, and all over, this is a favorite pastime of locals and visitors, especially in late June and early July during the renowned Festival International de Jazz. See p. 29.
- **Savor Top-Notch Cuisine at Affordable Prices:** Experience all of French cuisine's interpretations—traditional, haute, bistro, Québécois—the way the locals do: by ordering the *table d'hôte* specials. You'll get to indulge in three or more courses for a fixed price that is only slightly more than the cost of a single a la carte main course. Most full-service restaurants offer the option, if only at midday. See p. 81 for more information.

- **Explore Vieux-Montréal:** The old quarter has an overwhelmingly European flavor. Wander Place Jacques-Cartier, the district's most popular outdoor square; explore museums and the churches' stunning architecture; stroll or bike along the revitalized waterfront. See chapter 8 for more information, as well as the walking tour of Vieux-Montréal on p. 112.

QUEBEC CITY

- **Linger at an Outdoor Cafe:** Tables are set out at Place d'Armes in Upper Town, in the Quartier du Petit-Champlain in Lower Town, and along the Grande-Allée—a quality-of-life invention the French and their Québécois

(Moments) **Romantic Québec City**

"Romance" could be Québec City's middle name. Every narrow street, leafy plaza, sidewalk cafe, horse-drawn *calèche,* pitched roof, and church spire breathes recollections of France's provincial towns. But to get the full Québec City treatment, amble those streets under a full moon and find a bench on **Terrasse Dufferin,** the promenade alongside the Château Frontenac in Upper Town. The river below will be the color of liquid mercury in the moon's glow, and there will be more stars than you can ever remember seeing. Streaks of comets and music faintly heard from the *boîtes* in Lower Town are possibilities. Romance is a certainty.

brethren have perfected. See chapter 15 for more information.

- **Soak Up the Blossoming Lower Town:** Once all but abandoned to the grubby edges of the shipping industry, the riverside neighborhood of Basse-Ville/ Vieux-Port has been reborn, with antiques shops, bistros, and boutique hotels filling its rehabilitated 18th- and 19th-century buildings. See chapter 16 for more information, as well as the walking tour of Lower Town on p. 255.

- **Relax in Battlefields Park (Parc des Champs-de-Bataille):** This beautifully situated green space overlooks the St. Lawrence River. It's particularly lively on weekends, when families and lovers come to picnic and play. See p. 239 for more information.

2 THE BEST SPLURGE HOTELS

MONTREAL

- **Hôtel Le St-James,** 355 rue St-Jacques ouest (© **866/841-3111**): Setting the standard against which any boutique hotel in town must measure itself, this former 19th-century bank in Vieux-Montréal lets no luxurious detail escape its attention. From its opulent main hall to the sybaritic subterranean spa to its immaculately trained staff, Hôtel Le St-James provides an experience that may well be the highlight of your visit. See p. 76.

- **W Montréal,** 901 rue Square-Victoria (© **888/627-7081**): If you qualify as hip, aware, and on the fast track, waste no time booking a suite at this local branch of the spreading chain. It won't hurt if your platinum card is paid up and you don't need much sleep. There

are three bars and lounges, a hyperchic restaurant, and a clientele composed of knockouts of both sexes. See p. 77.

QUEBEC CITY

- **Auberge Saint-Antoine,** 8 rue St-Antoine (© **888/692-2211**): Sure, there's the Château Frontenac, looming up above, the very symbol of the city. But for a more intimate, less overwhelming visit, stay in Basse-Ville, or Lower Town. This auberge started as a stylish but largely unexceptional B&B and has grown in calculated phases into one of Québec's most desirable lodgings, with a chic lounge and a top restaurant to boot. See p. 215.

- **Dominion 1912,** 126 rue St-Pierre (© **888/833-5253**): Also a key player in the redevelopment of the once dreary

House Swapping

House swapping is becoming a more popular and viable means of travel; you stay in their place, they stay in yours, and you both get an authentic and personal view of the area—the opposite experience of the escapist retreat that many hotels offer. Try **HomeLink International** (www.homelink.org), the largest and oldest home-swapping organization, with more than 13,000 listings worldwide; it costs $75 for a yearly membership. **InterVac.com** ($69 for more than 20,000 listings) is also reliable. Many travelers find great housing swaps on Craigslist (www.craigslist.org) too, though the offerings are not vetted or vouched for, so swap there at your own risk.

Basse-Ville/Vieux-Port, the Dominion has rooms so large and bedding so cozily enveloping that you may not want to go out. Do, though, at least for the fireplace, croissants, and café au lait in the lobby. See p. 216.

3 THE BEST MODERATELY PRICED HOTELS

MONTREAL

- **Auberge Bonaparte,** 447 rue St-François-Xavier (© **514/844-1448**): When the long-established restaurant on the ground floor, Bonaparte (p. 92), was accorded a massive rehab and expansion, its owners built the comely inn upstairs. Rooms are simply furnished, but they're clean and roomy enough, and a rooftop terrace overlooks Vieux-Montréal's Basilique Notre-Dame. See p. 80.

- **Auberge Les Passants du Sans Soucy,** 171 rue St-Paul ouest (© **514/842-2634**): Just around the corner from Bonaparte, this charming little B&B helped pioneer Vieux-Montréal's recovery to its current status as the must-see quarter of the city. Fireplaces and jet tubs are standard in all nine bedrooms. See p. 80.

QUEBEC CITY

- **Hôtel Sainte-Anne,** 32 rue Ste-Anne (© **877/222-9422**): Practically in the shadow of the Château Frontenac (p. 210), this Euro-design hotel occupies a row house in the middle of Upper Town's most touristy district. Rooms are stripped to the minimum, but as equipped as can be reasonably expected at these relatively gentle prices. See p. 215.

- **Hôtel Champlain,** 115 rue Ste-Anne (© **800/567-2106**): Even the smallest rooms boast silk curtains, king or queen beds, and 300-thread-count sheets. A self-serve espresso machine by the front desk ensures free cappuccinos at any time of day or night. See p. 214.

4 THE MOST UNFORGETTABLE DINING EXPERIENCES

MONTREAL

- **Nuances,** 1 av. du Casino, in the Casino de Montréal (© **514/392-2708**): This

gourmet resto at the top of the city's casino got an impressive face-lift in 2007 that made the decor as contemporary and elegant as the food—all creamy walls and pale leather banquettes. It's a room with real star power. See p. 105.

- **Toqué!,** 900 Place Jean-Paul-Riopelle (*©* **514/499-2084**): Superstar chef/owner Norman Laprise has been thrilling Montréal gourmands for years. In dishes of startling innovation, he brings together diverse ingredients that have rarely appeared before on restaurant plates. There's little point in describing individual dishes, for he replaces them with some new invention before any of his entrees achieve signature status. See p. 90.

- **Initiale,** 54 rue St-Pierre (*©* **418/694-1818**): From its gracious tone and subdued lighting to its carefully paced multicourse menus, Initiale exudes silky polish from greeting to adieu. You will dine gloriously. See p. 225.
- **Laurie Raphaël,** 117 rue Dalhousie (*©* **418/692-4555**): Dazzling. Given the growing local competition, the owners transformed their setting and shook up the menu. Service is spot-on and the food creative and artfully presented. See p. 228.

5 THE BEST MUSEUMS

MONTREAL

- **Musée des Beaux-Arts,** 1379–80 rue Sherbrooke ouest (*©* **514/285-2000**): Canada's first museum devoted exclusively to the visual arts started out in 1912 in a neoclassical space on Sherbrooke's north side. A newer pavilion on the opposite side is now connected by an underground series of galleries. Temporary exhibits are strong, and the permanent collection is largely devoted to international contemporary art and Canadian works. See p. 108.
- **Pointe-à-Callière (Montréal Museum of Archaeology and History),** 350 Place Royale (*©* **514/872-9150**): A first visit to Montréal might best begin here. This strikingly modernistic structure at the edge of Vieux-Montréal marks the spot where the first European settlement put down roots in the city. It

stands atop extensive excavations that unearthed not only remains of the French newcomers, but also of the native bands that preceded them. On the self-guided tour, you'll wind your way through the subterranean complex. See p. 113.

QUEBEC CITY

- **Musée de la Civilisation,** 85 rue Dalhousie (*©* **418/643-2158**): Here is that rarity among museums: a collection of cleverly mounted temporary and permanent exhibitions that both children and adults find engrossing, without talking down or metaphysical maunderings. Make sure to make time for *"People of Québec . . . Then and Now,"* a permanent exhibit that is a sprawling examination of Québec history. See p. 234.

6 THE BEST OUTDOOR ACTIVITIES

MONTREAL

- **Traverse the Lachine Canal:** First constructed to detour around the rapids of the same name, Lachine fell into disuse after the St. Lawrence Seaway was built.

Over the last few years, however, it has been renovated to serve as a recreational resource. It connects the Vieux-Port with Atwater Market, a little more than a mile away. You can explore the canal and its surroundings by guided boat tour or on foot—or you can rent a bicycle or in-line skates at Vieux-Port. See chapter 8.

- **Bike the City:** Montréalers' enthusiasm for bicycling has provided the impetus for the ongoing development of bicycle paths that wind through downtown areas and out to the countryside. Cyclists are allowed to take their bikes onto designated Métro cars, and some taxis and buses sport special racks for them. Rentals are available from several outlets. See "Outdoor Activities" in chapter 8.

QUEBEC CITY

- **Take a Walking Tour:** Combine immersion in Québec's rich history with a good stretch of the legs among the battlements and along the ancient city's cobblestoned streets. Use the walking tours in chapter 17 or go on a group tour; information about meeting points, times, and routes is at the information center at Terrace Dufferin, opposite Château Frontenac.

- **Visit Montmorency Falls:** A 15-minute car or bus ride north of the city is this spectacular iron-tinged cascade—it's higher than Niagara Falls, as you will frequently be reminded. You can walk to the base and, if sufficiently motivated, to the top. You can also take a cable car to the other side. Incredibly, there's a footbridge, open to anyone brave-hearted enough to walk it, crossing directly over the plunging water. In summer, this is the site of an international fireworks festival. See "Montmorency Falls" in chapter 20.

7 THE BEST ACTIVITIES FOR FAMILIES

MONTREAL

- **Visit the Biodôme de Montréal:** This is perhaps the city's most engaging attraction for children of any age. The Biodôme houses replications of four ecosystems: a Laurentian forest, the St. Lawrence marine system, a polar environment, and, most appealingly, a tropical rainforest. See p. 114.

- **Explore the Jardin Botanique and Insectarium:** Montréal's Botanical Garden features Chinese and Japanese gardens and greenhouses, while the Insectarium next door is home to praying mantises, tarantulas, a Butterfly House, and a gift shop that sells lollipops with scorpions inside. See p. 115.

QUEBEC CITY

- **Watch the Changing of the Guard:** La Citadelle is the fortress built by the British to repel an American invasion that never came. It's still an active military post, and the ceremonial changing of the guard and beating the retreat are colorful and don't take too much time. See p. 238.

- **Thrill to the Canyon Ste-Anne:** The massive canyon and its thundering Ste-Anne waterfalls feature footbridges that go directly across the water. This attraction is about a 45-minute drive from the city. See chapter 20.

8 THE BEST OF MONTREAL & QUEBEC CITY ONLINE

There's lots of information on Montréal and Québec City on the Internet. Here are a few of our favorite resources:

- **Bonjour Québec** (www.tourisme.gouv. qc.ca): The official site of Québec province's government is a comprehensive information bank about all things Québec. You'll find information about upcoming events and ongoing attractions, and you can search for hotels and reserve online.

- **Midnight Poutine** (www.midnight poutine.ca): This terrific blog—with more than a dozen contributors—describes itself as "a personal ongoing account of the city's happenings" and "a delicious high-fat source of rants, raves, and musings. It provides the insight you never find in newspapers and the details and tangents that would never fit in a weekly."

- *Hour* (www.hour.ca): *Hour* is a Montréal culture magazine that highlights local happenings. It's available in print and online, and includes entertainingly grumpy and often profane takes on current events. Restaurant and arts reviews are regularly updated.

Montréal & Québec City in Depth

As the twin cities of the province of Québec, Montréal and Québec City have a stronger European flavor than Canada's other municipalities. Most residents' first language is French, and a strong affiliation with France continues to be a central facet of the region's personality.

The defining dialectic of Canadian life, in fact, is language, and it's a thorny issue that has long threatened to tear the country apart. Many Québécois have long believed that making Québec a separate, independent state is the only way to maintain their rich French culture in the face of the Anglophone (English-speaking) ocean that surrounds them. Québec's role within the Canadian federation has been the most debated and volatile topic of conversation in Canadian politics.

There were reasons for the festering intransigence, of course—about 250 years' worth. After France lost power in Québec to the British in the 18th century, a kind of linguistic exclusionism developed, with wealthy Scottish and English bankers and merchants denying French-Canadians access to upper levels of business and government. This bias continued well into the 20th century.

Many in Québec, though, stayed committed to the French language after British rule was imposed. Even with later waves of other immigrant populations pouring in over the cities, there is still a kind of bedrock loyalty held by many to the province's Gallic roots. France may have relinquished control of Québec to Great Britain in 1763, but France's influence, after its 150 years of rule, remained powerful—and still does. Many Québécois continue to look across the Atlantic for inspiration in fashion, food, and the arts. Culturally and linguistically, it is that tenacious French connection that gives the province its special character.

Two other cultural phenomena have emerged over the past 10 years. The first is an institutional acceptance of homosexuality: By changing the definition of "spouse" in 39 laws and regulations in 1999, Québec's government eliminated all legal distinctions between same-sex and heterosexual couples and became Canada's first province to recognize the legal status of same-sex civil unions. Gay marriage became legal in all of Canada's provinces and territories in 2005. Montréal, in particular, has transformed into one of North America's most welcoming cities for gay people.

The second phenomenon is an influx of even more immigrants into the province's melting pot. "Québec is at a turning point," declared an early 2008 report about the province's angst over the so-called reasonable accommodation of minority religious practices, particularly those of Muslims and Orthodox Jews. "The identity inherited from the French-Canadian past is perfectly legitimate and it must survive," the report continued, "but it can no longer occupy alone the Québec identity space."

Together with 70,000 aboriginal people from 11 First Nation tribes who live in the province, immigrants help make the region as vibrant and alive as any on the continent.

The ancient walls that protected Québec City over the centuries are still in place today, and the town within their embrace has changed little, preserving for posterity the heart of New France.

Not so for Montréal. It was "wet" when the U.S. was "dry" due to Prohibition from 1920 to 1933. Bootleggers, hard drinkers, and prostitutes flocked to this large city situated so conveniently close to the American border, mixing with rowdy people from the port, much to the distress of Montréal's mostly upstanding citizenry. For 50 years, the city's image was decidedly racy, but in the 1950s, a cleanup began alongside a boom in high-rise construction and the restoration of much of the derelict Old Town. In 1967, Montréal welcomed the world to Expo 67, the world's fair.

Today, much of what makes Montréal special is either very old or very new. The city's great, gleaming skyscrapers and towering hotels; the superb Métro system; and the highly practical underground city date mostly from the 40 years since the Expo. The renaissance of much of the oldest part of the city, Vieux-Montréal, only began blossoming in the 1990s.

To understand the province's politics, you need to back up a few years. A phenomenon later labeled the "Quiet Revolution" began bubbling up in the 1960s. The movement focused on transforming the largely rural, agricultural province into an urbanized, industrial entity with a pronounced secular outlook. French-Canadians, long denied access to the upper echelons of desirable corporate careers, started to insist on equal opportunity with the powerful Anglophone minority.

In 1968, Pierre Trudeau, a bilingual Québécois, became Canada's prime minister, a post he held for 18 years. More flamboyant, eccentric, and brilliant than any of his predecessors, he devoted much time to trying to placate voters on both sides of the French-English issue.

Also in 1968, the Parti Québécois was founded by Reneé Lévesque, and the separatist movement began in earnest. Inevitably, there was a radical fringe, and it signaled its intentions by bombing Anglophone businesses. The FLQ (Front de Libération du Québec, or Québec Liberation Front), as it was known, was behind most of the terrorist attacks. Most Québécois separatists, of course, were not violent.

For decades, secession remained a dream for many Québécois; as recently as 1995, a referendum on sovereignty lost by a mere 1% of the vote.

During the 1990s, an unsettled mood prevailed in the province. Large businesses left town, anxious that if the province actually did secede, they would find themselves in a new country instead of Canada. Money was tight, rent was cheap, and opportunities were limited.

But by 2000, things began to change. The Canadian dollar strengthened against the U.S. dollar. Unemployment, long in double digits, shrank to less than 6%, the lowest percentage in more than 20 years. Crime in Montréal, which was already one of the continent's safest cities, hit a 20-year low. The presence of skilled workers made Canada a favored destination for Hollywood film and TV production. The rash of for rent and for-sale signs that disfigured Montréal in the 1990s was replaced by a welcome shortage of retail and office space.

In 2002, the 28 towns and cities on the island of Montréal merged into one megacity with a population of 1.8 million.

Today, the quest for separatism seems to be fading. Conversations with ordinary Québécois suggest they're weary of the argument. In March 2007, the Liberal

Party, headed by Jean Charest, won just a minority government, with an out-of-nowhere second-place victory for the new Action Démocratique du Québec party and its young leader, Mario Dumont. The separatist Parti Québécois placed a distant third with just 28% of the vote. The moment marked, many think, the beginning of the end of the campaign for independence.

Just as significantly, the proportion of foreign-born Québec citizens continues to grow. After the arrival of 1.1 million immigrants to the country between 2001 and 2006, foreign-born nationals now make up 20% of Canada's population, with Montréal, Toronto, Vancouver, and Calgary as their prime destinations. In some areas, Chinese dialects are outpacing French as the second most commonly spoken language; visitors to Montréal will notice that the city has large pockets of neighborhoods where the primary languages spoken are Mandarin and Cantonese.

2 LOOKING BACK AT MONTREAL & QUEBEC CITY

FIRST NATIONS & FIRST EUROPEANS

The first "immigrants" to the region were the Iroquois, who settled in what's now called Québec long before the Europeans arrived. The Vikings landed in Canada more than 1,000 years ago, probably followed by Irish and Basque fishermen. English explorer John Cabot stepped ashore briefly on the east coast in 1497, but it was the French who managed the first meaningful European toehold.

When Jacques Cartier sailed up the St. Lawrence in 1534, he recognized at once the tremendous strategic potential of Québec City's Cap Diamant (Cape Diamond), the high bluff overlooking the river. But he was exploring, not building an empire, and after stopping briefly on land, he continued on his trip.

Montréal, at the time, was home to a fortified Iroquois village called Hochelaga, composed of 50 longhouses. Cartier was on a sea route to China but was halted by the fierce rapids just west of what is now the Island of Montréal. (In a demonstration of mingled optimism and frustration, he dubbed the rapids "La Chine," assuming that China was just beyond them; even today, they're known as "the Lachine.") He then visited the Indian settlement, landing in what's now Old Montréal and paying his respects to the natives before moving on.

Samuel de Champlain arrived 73 years later, in 1608, motivated by the burgeoning fur trade, obsessed with finding a route to China, and determined to settle Québec. He was perhaps emboldened after the Virginia Company founded its fledgling colony of Jamestown, hundreds of miles to the south, just a year before.

Called "Kebec," Champlain's first settlement, or habitation, grew to become Québec City's Basse-Ville, or Lower Town, and then spread across the flat riverbank beneath the cliffs of Cap Diamant. In 2008, Québec City hosted major celebrations of the 400th anniversary of this outpost's founding.

Champlain would make frequent trips back to France to reassure anxious investors that the project, which he said would eventually "equal the states of greatest kings," was going apace. (He also married a 12-year-old girl during one of those trips.) But the first years were, in truth, bleak. Food was scarce and scurvy ravaged many of the settlers. Demanding winters were far colder than in France. And almost from the beginning, there were hostilities, first between the French and the Iroquois, then between the French and the English (and, later, the Americans). Champlain aligned himself with the Montagnais and Algonquin tribes, participating in battles with the Iroquois. At issue was control of the lucrative trade of the fur of beavers, raccoons, and bears, and the hides of deer; the pelts were shipped off to Paris fashion houses. The commercial battle lasted nearly a century.

To better defend themselves, the Québécois constructed a fortress atop the cape, and gradually the center of urban life moved to the top of the cliffs.

The British and French struggle for dominance in the new continent focused on their explorations, and in this regard, France outdid England. Their far-ranging fur trappers, navigators, soldiers, and missionaries opened up not only Canada but also most of what eventually became the United States, moving all the way south to the future New Orleans and claiming most of the territory to the west, a vast region which later comprised the Louisiana Purchase. At least 35 of the subsequent 50 states were mapped or settled by Frenchmen, who left behind thousands of city names to prove it, including Detroit, St. Louis, New Orleans, Duluth, and Des Moines.

Paul de Chomedey, Sieur de Maisonneuve, arrived in 1642 to establish a colony and to plant a crucifix atop the hill he called Mont-Royal. He and his band of settlers came ashore and founded Ville-Marie, dedicated to the Virgin Mary, at the spot now marked by Place-Royale in the old part of the city. They built a fort, a chapel, stores, and houses. One settler, the energetic Jeanne Mance, made her indelible mark by founding the Hotel-Dieu-de-Montréal hospital, which still exists today. Pointe-à-Callière, the terrific Montréal Museum of Archaeology and History, is built on the site where the original colony was established.

Life was not easy for the settlers. Unlike the friendly Algonquins who lived in nearby regions, the Iroquois in Montréal had no intention of giving up their land so easily to the new settlers. Fierce battles raged for years. At Place d'Armes today, there's a statue of de Maisonneuve, marking the spot where the settlers defeated the Iroquois in bloody hand-to-hand fighting.

Still, the settlement prospered. Until the 1800s, Montréal was contained in the area known today as Vieux-Montréal. Its ancient walls no longer stand, but its long and colorful past is preserved in the streets, houses, and churches of the Old City.

ENGLAND CONQUERS NEW FRANCE

In the 1750s, the struggle between Britain and France had escalated. The latest episode was known as the French and Indian War (an extension of Europe's Seven Years' War), and strategic Québec became a valued prize. The French appointed Louis Joseph, marquis de Montcalm, to command their forces in the town. The British sent an expedition of 4,500 men in a fleet under the command of a 32-year-old general, James Wolfe. The British troops surprised the French by coming up and over the cliffs of Cap Diamant, and the ensuing skirmish for Québec, fought on September 13, 1759, became one of the most important battles in North American history: It resulted in a continent that would be under British influence for more than a century.

Fought on the Plains of Abraham, today a beautiful and much-used city park, the battle lasted just 18 to 25 minutes, depending on whose account you read. It resulted in 600 casualties, including both generals, who died as a result of wounds received. Wolfe lived just long enough to hear that the British had won. Montcalm died a few hours later. Today, a memorial to both men overlooks Terrasse Dufferin in Québec City and is the world's only statue to commemorate both victor and vanquished of the same battle. The inscription, in neither French nor English but Latin, is translated as, simply, "Courage was fatal to them."

The capture of Québec determined the war's course, and the Treaty of Paris in 1763 ceded all of French Canada to England. In a sense, this victory was a bane to Britain: If France had held Canada, the British government might have been more judicious in its treatment of the American colonists. As it was, the British decided to make the colonists pay the costs of the French and Indian War, on the principle that it was their home being defended. Britain slapped so many taxes on all imports that the infuriated U.S. colonists openly rebelled against the crown.

George Washington felt sure that French-Canadians would want to join the American revolt against the British crown, or at least be supportive. He was mistaken on both counts. The Québécois detested their British conquerors, but they were also devout Catholics and saw their contentious neighbors as godless republicans. Only a handful supported the Americans, and three of Washington's most competent commanders came to grief in attacks against Québec and were forced to retreat.

Thirty-eight years later, during the War of 1812, the U.S. army marched up the banks of the Richelieu River where it flows from Lake Champlain to the St. Lawrence. Once again, the French-Canadians stuck by the British and drove back the Americans. The war ended essentially in a draw, but it had at least one encouraging result: Britain and the young United States agreed to demilitarize the Great Lakes and to extend their mutual border along the 49th parallel to the Rockies.

THE RISE OF SEPARATISM IN QUEBEC

In 1867, the British North America Act created the federation of the provinces of

Québec, Ontario, Nova Scotia, and New Brunswick. It was a kind of independence for the region from Britain, but was unsettling for many French-Canadians, who wanted autonomy. In 1883, *"Je me souviens"*—an ominous "I remember"—became the province's official motto. From 1900 to 1910, 325,000 French-Canadians emigrated to the United States.

In 1968, the Parti Québécois was founded by Reneé Lévesque, and the separatist movement began in earnest. One attempt to smooth ruffled Francophones (French speakers) was made in 1969, when federal legislation stipulated that all services across Canada were henceforth to be offered in both English and French, in effect declaring the nation bilingual.

That didn't assuage militant Québécois, however. They undertook to guarantee the primacy of French in their own province. To prevent dilution by newcomers, the children of immigrants were required to enroll in French-language schools, even if English or a third language was spoken in the home; this is still the case today.

"When I lived in Montréal in the '60s," wrote Ruth Reichl, the editor of *Gourmet* magazine, in the March 2006 issue, it "was strangely segregated. The Anglophones I trailed through the staid streets were a proper lot, more English than the English, with their umbrellas and briefcases. They may not have been hurrying home to early tea, but I imagined they were. . . The Jewish community I found in another part of town was an entirely different experience. The people were boisterous, and their streets were rich with the scent of garlic, cloves, and allspice emanating from the mountains of pickles and deliciously rich smoked meat that I spied each time a restaurant door swung open. The French-Canadians had their own territory, too, and they stuck to themselves, speaking their own robust and expressive language. . . What struck me most, as a New Yorker accustomed to the hodgepodge

March of the Language Police (or La Police de Langue)

When the separatist Parti Québécois took power in the province in 1976, it wasted no time in attempting to make Québec unilingual. Bill 101 made French the provincial government's sole official language and sharply restricted the use of other languages in education and commerce.

While the party's fortunes have fallen and risen and fallen (the 2007 elections saw its worst showing ever), the primacy of Française has remained.

In the early days, agents of L'Office de la Langue Française fanned out across the territory, scouring the landscape for linguistic insults to the state and her people. Merry Christmas signs were removed from storefronts, and department stores had to come up with a new name for Harris Tweed.

Because about 20% of the population spoke English as a primary language, one out of five Québécois felt instantly declared second-class citizens. Francophones responded that it was about time les Anglais—also known as *les autres* (the others)—knew what it felt like.

Affected, too, was the food world. By fiat and threat of punishment, hamburgers became *hambourgeois* and hot dog was rechristened *chiens chaud*. And Schwartz's Montréal Hebrew Delicatessen (one of the city's fixtures since 1928)? It became Chez Schwartz Charcuterie Hébraïque de Montréal.

piling up of one culture on another, was the barriers between them. They kept themselves strictly separate, each cleaving to their own language, rituals, and food."

In 1977, Bill 101 passed, all but banning the use of English on public signage. Stop signs now read *ARRÊT,* a word that actually refers to a stop on a bus or train route. (Even in France, the red signs read STOP.) The bill funded the establishment of enforcement units, a virtual language police who let no nit go unpicked. The resulting backlash provoked the flight of an estimated 400,000 Anglophones to other parts of Canada.

In 1987, Prime Minister Brian Mulroney met with the 10 provincial premiers at a retreat at Québec's Meech Lake to cobble together a collection of constitutional reforms. The Meech Lake Accord, as it came to be known, addressed a variety of issues, but most important to the

Québécois was that it recognized Québec as a "distinct society" within the federation. In the end, however, Manitoba and Newfoundland failed to ratify the accord by the June 23, 1990, deadline.

As a result, support for the secessionist cause burgeoned in Québec, fueled by an election that firmly placed the separatist Parti Québécois in control of the provincial government. A referendum held in 1995 was narrowly won in favor of residents who preferred to stay within the Canadian union, but the vote settled nothing. The issue continued to divide families and dominate political discourse.

The year 2007 may have marked the beginning of the end the issue, however. In provincial elections, the Parti Québécois placed third with just 28% of the vote. The election was perceived by many as the first step in closing the door on the campaign for independence. And it's a symbol of what

The Separatist Movement in Brief

- In 1968, Reneé Lévesque and the separatist movement founded the Parti Québécois (PQ) in an earnest attempt to make Québec independent from the rest of Canada.
- In 1976, the PQ came to power in Québec, remaining so until 1985.
- The PQ regained power from the Liberals in 1994 and held it more or less consistently through 2003.
- Forty years after its founding, the PQ suffered an anemic third-place showing in 2007 provincial elections. This was perceived by many as a crushing defeat for both the party and the separatist movement.

many visitors now find in the cities: a meshing and merging of cultures that feels new and exciting.

As *Gourmet*'s Reichl put it in that March 2006 essay, "It was a shock to return last year and discover that the city has completely transformed itself. Montréal is now the most bilingual city in the world, a place where every citizen seems equally at home in French and English. This change is about much more than mere language, however. Today, all the barriers seem to have melted away, allowing the inhabitants to come together and embrace one another's cultures."

Québécois, it's worth noting, are exceedingly gracious hosts. Montréal may be the largest French-speaking city outside Paris, but most Montréalers switch effortlessly from one language to the other as the situation dictates. Telephone operators go from French to English the instant they hear an English word out of the other party, as do most store clerks, waiters, and hotel staff. This is less the case in country villages and in Québec City, but for visitors, there is virtually no problem that can't be solved with a few French words, some expressive gestures, and a little goodwill.

3 MONTREAL & QUEBEC CITY'S ART & ARCHITECTURE

Classic European art and architectural influences meet with an urbane, design-heavy aesthetic in Montréal and Québec City. Here are some art highlights:

FREDERICK LAW OLMSTED & PARC DU MONT-ROYAL

American landscape architect Frederick Law Olmsted, who created New York City's Central Park and California's Stanford University campus, also designed the park that surrounds the "mountain" in the center of Montréal. Parc du Mont-Royal opened in 1876.

Olmsted tried to make the hill seem more mountainous by using exaggerated vegetation—shade trees at the bottom of a path that was to climb the mountain—to create the illusion of being in a valley at the lower elevations—and sparser vegetation higher up, for an exaggerated sense of height.

Unfortunately for Olmsted and future parkgoers, Montréal suffered a depression in the mid-1870s and many of the architect's plans were abandoned. The path was built but not according to the original plan, and vegetation ideas were abandoned. Still, Parc du Mont-Royal is an urban oasis and is used by many in all four seasons. For a walking tour of the park, see p. 145.

BRUCE PRICE & HIS CHATEAU FRONTENAC

It's an American architect, Bruce Price (1845–1903), who is responsible for the most iconic building of the entire Québec province: the Château Frontenac, Québec City's visual center.

"The Château" opened as a hotel in 1893. With its castlelike architecture, soaring turrets, and romantic French-Renaissance mystery, it achieved the goal of becoming the most talked-about accommodation in North America. Today, it's a high-end hotel managed by the Fairmont chain.

The château was one of many similar-styled hotels commissioned by the bigwigs of the Canadian Pacific Railway in the late 19th century, when the company was constructing Canada's first transcontinental railway. The company figured that luxury accommodations would encourage travelers with money to travel by train.

Price also designed Montréal's Windsor Station as part of the same Canadian Pacific Railway project, as well as Dalhousie Station in Montréal, the façade of Royal Victoria College in Montréal, and the Gare du Palais train station in Québec City, whose turrets echo those of the Château Frontenac.

Architecture professor Claude Bergeron of Québec City's Univérsité Laval has noted that as the leading practitioner of the Château style, Price "is sometimes credited with having made it a national Canadian style."

DESIGN MONTREAL

Montréal is one of North America's most stylish cities, and the city has worked in the last few years to capitalize on its design appeal to entice artists' visitors. UNESCO, the United Nations Educational, Scientific, and Cultural Organization designated Montréal a "UNESCO City of Design" in 2006 for "its ability to inspire synergy between public and private players." With the distinction, Montréal joined Buenos Aires and Berlin, other honorees, as a high-style city worth watching.

Design Montréal (www.designmontreal. com) is an organization devoted to celebrating and networking the city's many design communities. Its Design Montréal Open House, launched in 2007, is a 2-day celebration in May that welcomes the public, free of charge, to visit more than 70 Montréal agencies, projects, and sites devoted to design. The 2008 edition featured exhibitions by graduating college design students, and a night dedicated to celebrating emerging design practices.

Making the city a design destination for tourists isn't such a crazy idea. It certainly worked for a much smaller city, Bilbao, Spain. The Institut de Design Montréal (www.idm.qc.ca) has as its mission to "promote design as an economic value and have Montréal become a design centre of international caliber." To that effect, it has. Since 1996, the institute has handed out design awards in categories that now

---

Montréal Impressions

You cannot fancy you are in America; everything about it conveys the idea of a substantial, handsomely built European town, with modern improvements of half-English, half-French architecture.

—English Lt. Col. Burrows Willcocks Arthur Sleigh, writing about his time in Montréal in *Pine Forests and Hacmatack Clearings*, 1853

Geography 101: Telling Mountains from Molehills

Montréal is on an island that's part of the Hochelaga Archipelago. The island is situated in the St. Lawrence River (in French, St-Laurent) near the confluence with the Ottawa River.

At Montréal's center is a 232m (761-ft.) hill which natives like to think of as a mountain. It's called Mont-Royal, and it's the geographic landmark from which the city takes its name.

Real mountains, though, rise nearby: The Laurentides, also called the Laurentians, comprise the world's oldest range and the playground of the Québécois. As well, the Appalachians' northern foothills separate Québec from the U.S.; they add to the beauty of the Cantons-de-l'Est, the bucolic region on the opposite side of the St. Lawrence once known as the Eastern Townships, where many Montréalers have country homes.

include architecture, landscape architecture, and interior design.

Much of what constitutes cutting-edge design in the city is creative reuse of older buildings and materials. Among such venues is the industrial Darling Foundry, which houses in its raw, concrete space a contemporary art center and a small restaurant, the Cluny ArtBar (p. 95). Another is the Canadian Guild of Crafts, which includes a major boutique that sells Amerindian, Inuit, and Canadian crafts (p. 152).

Fashion also simmers throughout the city, with an increasing number of innovative locals setting up shop. It all comes to a boil during early June's Montréal Fashion & Design Festival, which features more than 30 fashion shows on outdoor stages in the heart of downtown. Montréal Fashion Week, another time of heightened fashion happenings, is in mid-October. Information is at www.sensationmode.com or © 514/876-1499.

The city's aesthetic was best summed up by one fashionista quoted in the *Montréal Gazette* a few years ago: "I'm all about the black, the white, and beige. Fall is about comfort—not that American style of sloppy comfort, but casual style."

One designer taking a unique cue from the city's long history with the fur trade is

Mariouche Gagné, who was born on Ile d'Orleans in 1971. Her company, Harricana (www.harricana.qc.ca), recycles old fur into funky patchwork garments. The slogan: "Made from your mother's old coat."

INUIT ART

The region's most compelling artwork is indigenous. In Montréal, the Musée McCord has a First Nations room that displays objects from Canada's native population, including meticulous beadwork, baby carriers, and fishing implements. In Québec City, the Musée des Beaux-Arts du Québec now houses the important Inuit art collection; it was assembled over many years by Québécois Raymond Brousseau.

Also in Québec City, a permanent exhibition at the Musée de la Civilisation, "Nous, les Premières Nations" ("We, the First Nations"), provides a fascinating look at the history and culture of the Abenakis, Algonquins, Atikamekw, Crees, Hurons-Wendat, Inuit, Malecites, Micmacs, Innu, Mohawks, and Naskapis—the 11 First Nation tribes whose combined 70,000 members inhabit Québec today.

The annual First People's Festival, held throughout the city in mid-June, highlights Amerindian and Inuit cultures by way of film, video, visual arts, music, and dance. Visit www.nativelynx.qc.ca or call ℭ **514/572-1799.**

THOSE EXTERNAL STAIRCASES

Stroll through Montréal's Plateau Mont-Royal and Mile End neighborhoods and one of the first things you'll notice are the outside staircases on the two- and three-story houses. Many are made of wrought iron, and most have shapely, sensual curves. One theory has it that they were first designed to accommodate immigrant families, who wanted their own front doors even for second-floor apartments. Another has it that landlords pushed for the outside stairs to cut down on common interior space that wouldn't count toward rental space.

The Catholic church, ever a force in the city, was originally all for the stairs because they allowed neighbors to keep an eye on each other. Then the aesthetic tide turned, and people decided they were ugly. Brick archways called loggia were built to hide them, but the walls created ready-made nooks and crannies for teens to linger in. At that point, the church helped push through legislation that banned the staircases entirely. That ban was lifted in the 1980s so that citywide efforts to maintain and renovate properties could keep the unique features intact.

4 MONTRÉAL & QUEBEC CITY IN POPULAR CULTURE

BOOKS & THEATER The late Jewish Anglophone Mordecai Richler inveighed against the excesses of Québec's separatists and language zealots in a barrage of books and critical essays in newspapers and magazines.

Richler wrote from the perspective of a minority within a minority and set most of his books in the working-class Jewish neighborhood of St. Urbain of the 1940s and 1950s, with protagonists who are poor, streetwise, and intolerant of the prejudices of other Jews, French-Canadians, and WASPs from the city's English-side Westmount neighborhood. His most famous book is *The Apprenticeship of Duddy Kravitz* (Pocket Books, 1959), which in 1974 was made into a movie of the same name starring Richard Dreyfuss.

Montréal journalist Taras Grescoe's *Sacré Blues: An Unsentimental Journey through Québec* (Macfarlane Walter & Ross, 2001) presents an affectionate but balanced assessment of his adopted province.

Legendary singer-songwriter Leonard Cohen wrote two novels set in Montréal: 1963's *The Favorite Game* (Vintage, 2003) and 1966's *Beautiful Losers* (Vintage, 1993).

Playwright Michel Tremblay, an important dramatist, grew up in Montréal's Plateau Mont-Royal neighborhood and uses that setting for much of his work. His *Les Belles-Sœurs (The Sisters-in-Law),* written in 1965, introduced the lives of working-class Francophone Québécois to the world. It was published in English by Talonbooks in 1992.

MUSIC In 2008, the Putumayo World Music record label released a compilation CD called *Québéc* in honor of Québéc City's 400th anniversary. It's a collection of 11 songs that reflect the province's rich musical diversity and provides a great introduction to Québécois music. Highlights include the upbeat, angelic-voiced Chloé Sainte-Marie ("Brûlots"), who was raised in a small village near Drummondville; the pop band DobaCaracol ("Étrange"), which fuses a reggae groove with African rhythms and French-language pop; and the Celtic folk of La Bottine Souriante ("La Brunette Est Là"), who are the preeminent representatives of traditional Québécois music, which has its roots in French, English, Scottish, and Irish folk traditions. Samples of the songs can be heard at the Putumayo website (www.putumayo.com), where there's also a video of DobaCaracol.

Montréal has a strong showing of innovative musicians who hail from its clubs. Singer-songwriter Leonard Cohen is the best known. He grew up in the Westmount neighborhood and attended McGill University. In 2008, he was inducted into the U.S. Rock and Roll Hall of Fame; the same year, he played the Montréal Jazz Festival as part of a long-anticipated and joyously received concert tour after a 15-year hiatus.

Another singer-songwriter, Rufus Wainwright, grew up in Montréal and got his start at city clubs. More recent up-and-comers include the perky pop group Sam Roberts Band, based in Montréal. Alternative rock bands from the city include Arcade Fire and Wolf Parade. (The band called Montreal, however, is from Athens, Georgia.)

FILM & TELEVISION Many U.S. films are made beyond the northern border for financial reasons, even when their American locales are important parts of the stories (*Brokeback Mountain,* for instance, was filmed in Alberta). Québécois films—made in the province, in French, for Québec audiences—can be difficult to track down outside the country. Recent features worth seeking out include Jean-Marc Vallée's box-office hit *C.R.A.Z.Y.,* a gay coming-of-age story, and Louise Archambault's *Familia,* about mothers and daughters.

Documentarian Alanis Obomsawin, a member of the Abenaki Nation who was raised on the Odanak Reserve near Montreal, began making movies for the National Film Board of Canada 40 years ago and has produced more than 30 documentaries about the hard edges of the lives of aboriginal people. As "the first lady of First Nations film"—as Tom Perlmutter, commissioner of the National Film Board, put it— Obomsawin received the Governor General's Performing Arts Award for Lifetime Artistic Achievement in 2008. A major retrospective of her work came to New York's Museum of Modern Art and Boston's Museum of Fine Art in 2008.

Obomsawin has documented police raids of reservation lands, homelessness among natives living in the big cities, and a wrenching incident in 1990 that pitted native peoples against the government over lands that were slated to be turned into a golf course. That last event, covered in the 1993 film *Kanehsatake: 270 Years of Resistance,* took place about an hour west of Montréal and included a months-long armed standoff between Mohawks and authorities.

"The land question and Mohawk sovereignty have been issues since the French and English first settled the area," Obomsawin has said. "A lot of promises were made and never kept. What the confrontation of 1990 showed is that this is a generation that is not going to put up with what happened in the past." Her movies are available through the National Film Board (www.nfb.ca).

In 2006, the television show *Little Mosque on the Prairie* began offering a peek into the religious and cultural issues faced by Québec's large immigrant population (even though the comedy is set in Saskatchewan). In June 2008, 20th Century Fox announced plans to adapt the sitcom into an American version.

5 EATING & DRINKING IN MONTREAL & QUEBEC CITY

A generation ago, most Montréal and Québec City restaurants served only French food. A few temples de cuisine delivered haute standards of gastronomy, while numerous accomplished bistros served up humbler ingredients in less grand settings, and folksy places featured the hearty fare that long employed the ingredients available in New France— game such as caribou, maple syrup, and root vegetables. Everything else was considered "ethnic." The Canadian food crazes of the 1980s focusing on Cajun, Tex-Mex, and fusion didn't make much of a dent at the time: Québec province was French, and that was that.

Over the last 10 years, however, this attitude changed dramatically. The 1990s recession put many restaurateurs out of business and forced others to reexamine their operation. In Montréal, especially, immigrants brought the cooking styles of the world to the city.

Restaurants here are colloquially called "restos," and they range from moderately priced bistros, cafes, and ethnic joints to swank luxury epicurean shrines.

MENU BASICS

One thing to always look for are *table d'hôte* meals. With these fixed-price menus, three- or four-course meals can be had for little more than the price of an a la carte main course. Even the best restaurants offer them, which means that you'll be able to sample some excellent venues without breaking the bank. Table d'hôte meals are often offered at lunch, when they are even less expensive; having your main meal midday instead of in the evening is the most economical way to sample many of the top establishments.

Remember that for the Québécois, *dîner* (dinner) is lunch, and *souper* (supper) is dinner, though the word dinner throughout this book is used in the common American sense. Also note that an *entrée* in Québec is an appetizer, while a *plat principal* is a main course. In fancier places, where a preappetizer nibble is proffered, it's called an *amuse gueule* or *amuse bouche*.

Many higher-end establishments now offer tasting menus, with many smaller dishes over the course of a meal that offer a sampling of the chef's skills. New and gaining popularity are surprise menus, also called "chef's whim"—you don't know what you're getting until it's there in front of you. It's becoming more common to find fine restaurants that offer wine pairings with meals as well, during which the sommelier selects a glass for each course.

LOCAL FOOD HIGHLIGHTS

Be sure to try the inexpensive regional specialties. A Québécois favorite is *poutine:* french fries doused with gravy and cheese curds. It's especially ubiquitous in winter.

Game is popular, including venison, quail, goose, caribou, and wapiti (North American deer). Many menus feature emu and lamb raised north of Québec City in Charlevoix. Mussels and salmon are also standard.

For sandwiches and snacks that only cost a few dollars, try any of the numerous places that go by the generic name *casse-croûte*—literally, "break-crust." You'll find a few stools at a counter and a limited number of menu items that might include soup and *chiens chaud* (hot dogs).

Québec cheeses deserve attention, and many can only be sampled in Canada because they are often unpasteurized— made of *lait cru* (raw milk)—and therefore subject to strict export rules. Better restaurants will offer them as a separate course.

Top Food Links

The best insider website featuring reviews and observations about the Montréal dining scene is www.endlessbanquet.blogspot.com. The delightful essays and reviews of resto critic Lesley Chesterman of the *Montréal Gazette* can be found online at www.montrealgazette.com, while the site www.montrealfood.com also features laudable writing but has had only sporadic updates since early 2008.

Of the estimated 500 varieties available, you might look for Mimolette Jeune (firm, fragrant, orange), Valbert St-Isidor (similar to Swiss in texture), St-Basil de Port Neuf (buttery), Cru des Erables (soft, ripe), Oka (semisoft, made of cow's milk in a monastery), and Le Chèvre Noire (a sharp goat variety covered in black wax).

In 2007, Québec cheeses won 31 prizes in the 23rd annual American Cheese Society competition, North America's largest annual contest of its kind. Québec cheeses won all the prizes in the brie category, and top prizes in the flavored feta and triple crème divisions.

Cheeses with the *fromages de pays* label are made in Québec with whole milk and no modified milk ingredients. The label represents solidarity among artisanal producers and is supported by Solidarité Rurale du Québec, a group devoted to revitalizing rural communities, and Slow Food Québec, which promotes sustainable agriculture and local production. More information is at www.fromageduquebec.qc.ca.

BEER & WINE

In general, alcohol is heavily taxed, and imported varieties even more so than domestic versions, so if you're looking to save a little, buy Canadian. That's not difficult when it comes to beer, for there are many breweries, from Montréal powerhouse Molson to micro, that produce highly palatable products. Among the best local options are Belle Gueule and Boréal. The sign *bieres en fut* means "beers on draft."

Wine is another matter. It is not produced in significant quantities in Canada due to a climate generally inhospitable to the essential grapes. But you might try bottles from the vineyards of the Cantons-de-l'Est region (just east of Montréal). And sample, too, the sweet "ice wines" and "ice ciders" made from fruit after the first frost. Many decent ones come from vineyards and orchards just an hour from Montréal.

One wine you're likely to see on the menu is the Québec L'Orpailleur, Seyval, from the Vignoble de l'Orpailleur (www.orpailleur.ca). *L'orpailleur* refers to someone who mines for gold in the streams—the idea being that trying to make good wine in Québec's cold climate is a similar kind of leap of faith in an ability to defy the odds.

Planning Your Trip to Montréal & Québec City

The province of Québec is immense: It's the largest province in the second-largest country in the world (after Russia), covering an area more than three times as the size of France, and stretching from the northern borders of New York, Vermont, and New Hampshire up to almost the Arctic Circle.

That said, most of the province's population lives in the stretch immediately north of the U.S. border. Its major cities and towns, including Montréal and Québec City, are in this America-neighboring region as well; the greater Montréal metropolitan area is home to nearly half of the province's population. Québec City lies just 263km (163 miles) northeast of Montréal, commanding a stunning location on the rim of a promontory overlooking the St. Lawrence River, which is at its narrowest here. Most of the province's developed resort and scenic areas lie within a 3-hour drive of either city, and Montréal and Québec City themselves are just 3 hours apart by car as well.

It can't be overstated how much the British and French struggle for dominance in the 1700s and 1800s for North America—the New World—continues to shape Québec's character today. A bit of history is in order (and you'll find yourself immersed in even more when you're touring the cities; it's inevitable): Samuel de Champlain arrived in Québec City in 1608, determined to settle the region as a French colony, a year after the Virginia Company founded its fledgling colony of Jamestown, hundreds of miles to the south. French forces ruled the region until 1759, when British troops surprised the French by coming up and over the Cap Diamant cliffs in Québec City. The ensuing battle, fought on the Plains of Abraham just southwest of the city center on September 13, 1759, is one of the most important battles in North American history. Britain won, resulting in a continent that was under British influence for more than a century. That influence carries on today; Queen Elizabeth II's face still graces all Canadian currency.

And yet, while most of Canada is English-speaking, 400 years of French tradition still hold strong in the Québec province. Most residents' first language is French. There are areas of the province, outside of the cities, where the *only* spoken language is French. Much of the music and architecture feels French. And so Québec is a wholly unique blend of French and British influences, coinciding often and sometimes doing battle. So when you're planning a trip to Montréal and Québec City, think of it as planning a trip to a cosmopolitan, European city. Accommodations range from modest inns to luxury hotels, and restaurants run the gamut from bistro-cozy to haute cuisine. Locals are lively and welcoming.

For additional help in planning your trip and for more on-the-ground resources in Québec, see the appendix.

1 VISITOR INFORMATION

Tourism authorities for the Québec province and its major regions and cities produce detailed and highly useful official tourist guides and websites.

Destination Canada: Predeparture Checklist

- If you're flying, you'll need a passport to enter Canada. If you're driving or arriving by bus, train, or boat, bringing a passport is a good idea—and may become required at some point in 2009 (see below).
- If you're driving and are an AAA member, bring your card—it will be honored by CAA, the Canadian Automobile Association (p. 289).
- If you're flying, check with authorities regarding current rules about what you can bring in carry-on bags. The Canadian Air Transport Security Authority is at www.acsta.gc.ca; the American Transportation Security Administration maintains a website at www.tsa.gov.
- Make sure you know the PIN (personal identification number) for your credit card and your bank card. Most Canadian banks only accept four-digit PINs.
- Confirm your daily ATM withdrawal limit.
- To check in at an airport kiosk with an e-ticket, make sure you have the credit card (or frequent-flier card) with which you bought your ticket.
- Bring any cards that could entitle you to discounts, such as AARP cards and student IDs.

Tourisme Québec, which covers the entire province, is online at www.bonjourquebec.com and can also be reached at **info@bonjourquebec.com;** ✆ **877/266-5687** or 514/873-2015; or through the post at C.P. 979, Montréal, Québec H3C 2W3.

Tourisme Montréal, which covers the city and immediate region, is online at www.tourisme-montreal.org and can also be reached at ✆ **877/266-5687** or 514/873-2015; by fax at 514/864-3838; or by mail at Ministère du Tourisme Québec, C.P. 979, Montréal, Québec H3C 2W3.

Québec City Tourism, which covers that city and its immediate region, is online at www.quebecregion.com and can also be reached at ✆ **877/783-1608** or 418/641-6654; by fax at 418/641-6578;

or by mail at 399 Saint-Joseph est, Québec, QC, G1K 8E2.

Montréal's central tourist office is at 1255 rue Peel, just south of rue Ste-Catherine ouest.

Québec City's central tourist office is at 835 av. Wilfrid-Laurier, just outside the wall in Upper Town.

Good city maps are available for free from the tourist offices. The best detailed street guide of Montréal is the pocket-size atlas by JDM Géo. It's published by MapArt (www.mapart.com), which also makes high-quality maps of all the local regions besides Montréal and Québec City that are mentioned in this book. They're for sale online and in shops and gas stations throughout Canada.

2 ENTRY REQUIREMENTS

PASSPORTS

Since January 2007, all air travelers traveling between the U.S. and Canada have

been required to present a valid passport. This was a change from prior travel requirements and was implemented as part of the Intelligence Reform and Terrorism Prevention Act of 2004.

If you're traveling by land or sea between the U.S. and Canada, the rules are a bit fuzzier. A government-issued proof of citizenship, such as a birth certificate, along with a government-issued photo ID, such as a driver's license, is required. A passport or other document may soon be required; implementation of this second requirement was originally scheduled to take place in January 2008, but concerns about the rules' impact on tourism, plus subsequent legislative changes, have caused delays. While a passport is not currently required for U.S. or Canadian citizens entering by land or sea, you're highly encouraged to carry yours.

Alien permanent residents of the U.S. must have their alien registration cards (green cards) with them to enter Canada and reenter the U.S.

If you are driving into Canada, be sure to have your car's registration with you. U.S. citizens do not need an international driver's license; a state-issued license is fine.

Frequent travelers may want to look into getting a **NEXUS membership,** which gets you preapproved by U.S. Customs and Border Protection; it can speed the trip across the border. Details are at www.cbp.gov or © **866-NEXUS26** (639-8726).

Note on DWIs: If you have ever been convicted for driving while intoxicated, you may be denied entrance. A waiver of exclusion may be obtained for a fee from a Canadian consulate in the U.S.

Note for young travelers: Anyone 17 and younger and traveling without a parent must have proof of citizenship and a letter from both parents detailing the length of stay, providing the parents' telephone number, and authorizing the person waiting for them to take care of them while they are in Canada.

Note for parents traveling with children: Because of international concerns about child abduction, if you are divorced, separated, or traveling without your spouse and are bringing your children to Canada, you will need proof of custody or a notarized letter from the other parent giving permission for foreign travel. The letter should include addresses and phone numbers of where the parents or guardians can be reached and identify a person who can confirm that the children are not being abducted or taken against their will. Passport requirements apply to children of all ages.

For information on how to obtain a passport, read "Passports" on p. 293 in the "Fast Facts" appendix.

VISAS

Citizens of the U.S., U.K., Australia, Ireland, and New Zealand do not need visas to enter Canada. Citizens of many other countries must have visas, which they'll need to apply for well in advance at their nearest Canadian embassy or consulate. Information is available at the **Citizenship and Immigration Canada** website: www.cic.gc.ca.

MEDICAL REQUIREMENTS

Inoculations or vaccinations are not required for entry into Canada.

CUSTOMS
What You Can Bring into Canada

Visitors can expect at least a probing question or two at the border or airport. Normal baggage and personal possessions should be no problem, but plants, animals, and other products may be prohibited or require additional documents before they're allowed in.

For specific information about Canadian rules, check with the **Canada Border**

Services Agency (© 506/636-5064 from outside the country or 800/461-9999 within Canada; www.cbsa-asfc.gc.ca). Search for "RC 4161" to get a full list of visitor information.

Tobacco and alcoholic beverages face strict import restrictions: Individuals 18 years or older are allowed to bring in 200 cigarettes, 50 cigars, or 200 grams of tobacco; as far as alcohol goes, only 1.14 liters of liquor, 1.5 liters of wine, or 24 cans or bottles of beer are permitted. Additional amounts face hefty duties and taxes.

Possession of a radar detector is prohibited, whether or not it is connected. Police officers can confiscate it and fine the owner C$500 to C$1,000.

A car driven into Canada can stay for up to a year, but it must leave with the owner or a duty will be levied.

If you do not declare goods or falsely declare them, they can be seized *along with the vehicle with which you brought them in.*

What You Can Take Home from Canada

For information about what U.S. citizens can bring back from Canada, download the invaluable free pamphlet *Know Before You Go* from **U.S. Customs and Border Protection;** it's available as a 68-page PDF at **www.customs.gov,** or obtainable in the paper version by writing to the agency at 1300 Pennsylvania Ave. NW, Washington, DC 20229 (© 877/227–5511).

Consider registering expensive items you're traveling with (laptops, musical equipment) before you leave the country to avoid challenges at the border on your return.

Returning U.S. citizens are allowed to bring back $800 duty-free as "accompanied baggage," so be sure to have receipts handy. There are strict rules about the number of cigarettes and volume of alcoholic beverages you can count toward your exemption: 200 cigarettes, 100 cigars, and

1 liter (33.8 fluid oz.) of alcohol. You'll be charged a flat rate of 3% on the next $1,000 worth of purchases.

If you try to bring back large amounts of alcohol, you may be suspected of importing them for resale and be required to obtain a permit.

On mailed gifts, the duty-free limit is $200. With some exceptions, you cannot bring fresh fruits and vegetables into the U.S. Large quantities of unpasteurized cheeses (*cru lait* in French) are likely to be confiscated, while small amounts for personal use are usually permitted.

U.K. citizens should check with **HM Customs & Excise** at © 0845/010-9000 or 44/2920-501-261 from outside the U.K., or www.hmce.gov.uk (which isn't too easy to navigate since the merger of the Revenue and Customs departments in April 2005). Citizens returning from a non-E.U. country have a Customs allowance of 200 cigarettes or 50 cigars or 250 grams of smoking tobacco; 2 liters of still table wine; 1 liter of spirits or strong liqueurs (22% alcohol or greater) or 2 liters of fortified wine, sparkling wine, or other liqueurs; 60cc (ml) of perfume; 250cc (ml) of eau de toilette; and £145 worth of all other goods, including gifts and souvenirs. Travelers age 16 and younger cannot transport any tobacco or alcohol.

Australian citizens should get the helpful *Know Before You Go* brochure. It's available online as a PDF from the **Australian Customs Service** at **www.customs.gov.au,** or by calling © **1300/363-263** or 61/2-6275-6666 from outside Australia. The duty-free allowance in Australia is A$900 (for those 17 and younger, A$450). Citizens 18 and older can bring in 250 cigarettes or 250 grams of cigars or tobacco products, and 2.25 liters of alcohol. If you're planning to take home valuables such as computers or cameras, register them first by using the "Goods Exported in Passenger Baggage" form in the brochure.

New Zealand citizens can get most questions answered at the **New Zealand Customs Service** at **www.customs.govt. nz** (*C* **0800/428-786,** or 64/9-300-5399 from outside the country). The duty-free allowance is NZ$700. Citizens 17 and older can bring in 200 cigarettes, 50 cigars, or 250 grams of tobacco (or a mixture of all three if their combined weight doesn't exceed 250 grams), plus 4.5 liters of wine or beer and three bottles up to 1.125 liters in size of liquor (the allowance used to be one bottle). If you're planning to take home valuables such as computers or cameras, register them by presenting them at a Customs office before leaving the country and filling out a Certificate of Export.

3 WHEN TO GO

High season in the cities is late May through early September, and, in Québec City, February weekends during the big winter Carnaval. The period from Christmas to New Year's is also busy. Hotels are most likely to be full and charge their highest rates in these periods. **Low season** is during March and April, when few events are scheduled and winter sports start to be iffy. The late-fall months of October and November are also slow, due to their all-but-empty social calendars.

WEATHER

Temperatures are usually a few degrees lower in Québec City than in Montréal. Spring, short but sweet, arrives around the middle of May. Summer (mid-June through mid-Sept) tends to be humid in Montréal, Québec City, and other communities along the St. Lawrence River, and drier at the inland resorts of the Laurentides and the Cantons-de-l'Est. Intense, but usually brief, heat waves mark July and early August, but temperatures rarely remain oppressive in the evenings.

Autumn (Sept–Oct) is as short and changeable as spring, with warm days and cool or chilly nights; it's during this season that Canadian maples blaze with color for weeks.

Winter brings dependable snows for skiing in the Laurentides, the Cantons-de-l'Est, and Charlevoix. After a sleigh ride or a ski run in Parc du Mont-Royal, Montréal's underground city is a climate-controlled blessing. Outside, snow and slush are present from November to March.

For the current Montréal weather forecast, call *C* **514/283-3010** or check www. weather.com.

Montréal's Average Monthly Temperatures (°F/°C)

		Jan	Feb	Mar	Apr	May	June	July	Aug	Sept	Oct	Nov	Dec
High	(°F)	21	24	35	51	65	73	79	76	66	54	41	27
	(°C)	–6	–4	2	11	18	23	26	24	19	12	5	–3
Low	(°F)	7	10	21	35	47	56	61	59	50	39	29	13
	(°C)	–14	–12	–6	2	8	13	16	15	10	4	–2	–11

Québec City's Average Monthly Temperatures (°F/°C)

		Jan	Feb	Mar	Apr	May	June	July	Aug	Sept	Oct	Nov	Dec
High	(°F)	18	21	32	46	62	71	76	74	63	50	37	23
	(°C)	–8	–6	0	8	17	22	24	23	17	10	3	–5
Low	(°F)	2	5	16	31	43	53	58	56	46	36	25	9
	(°C)	–17	–15	–9	–1	6	12	14	13	8	2	–4	–13

Note: To convert Celsius to Fahrenheit, multiply the Celsius reading by 1.8 and then add 32. For example, 17°C × 1.8 is 30.6 + 32 is 62.6°F.

MONTREAL & QUEBEC CITY CALENDAR OF EVENTS

Year-round, it's nearly impossible to miss a celebration of some sort in Montréal and Québec City. For an exhaustive list of events beyond those listed here, check **http://events.frommers.com**, where you'll find a searchable, up-to-the-minute roster of what's happening in cities not only in Canada, but all over the world.

JANUARY

La Fête des Neiges (the Snow Festival), Montréal. Montréal's answer to Québec City's February winter Carnaval (see below) usually features dog-sled runs, a mock survival camp, street hockey, and tobogganing. We say "usually" because the festival was canceled in 2008 for the first time in its 25-year history because of a labor dispute. Go to **www.fetedesneiges.com** or call © 514/872-6120 to see if the show will go on in 2009 (at press time, the dates were yet to be announced).

FEBRUARY

Carnaval de Québec, Québec City. Never mind that temperatures in Québec regularly plummet in winter to well below freezing. Canadians, however, are extraordinarily good-natured about the cold and happily pack the family up to come out and play. A snowman called Bonhomme (Good Fellow) shuffles into town to preside over the merriment, and revelers descend upon the city to eddy around a monumental ice palace erected in front of the Parliament Building, to watch a dog-sledding race on the old town's narrow streets, to play foosball on a human-size scale, to fly over crowds on a zipline, to ride down snowy hills in rubber tubes, and, not least of all, to dance at outdoor concerts. There are even outdoor movies for the truly masochistic.

The party is family-friendly at every turn, even considering the wide availability of plastic trumpets and canes filled with a concoction called caribou, the principal ingredients of which are cheap liquor and sweet red wine. Try not to miss the canoe race that has teams rowing, dragging, and stumbling with canoes across the St. Lawrence's treacherous ice floes. It's an homage to how the city used to break up the ice to keep a path open to Lévis, the town across the river.

A C$10 (£5) pass provides access to most activities over the 17 days. Hotel reservations must be made far in advance. Visit **www.carnaval.qc.ca** or call © 866/422-7628 for details. January 30 to February 15, 2009.

Festival Montréal en Lumière (Montréal High Lights Festival). The centerpiece of this winter celebration is its culinary competitions and wine tastings. There are also multimedia light shows, classical and pop concerts, and a Montréal All-Nighter that ends with a free breakfast at dawn. Visit **www.montrealhighlights.com** or call © 888/477-9955 for details. February 19 to March 1, 2009.

MAY

Montréal Museums Day. Open house for most of the city's museums, with free admission and free shuttle buses. Visit **www.museesmontreal.org** or call the tourism office (© 877/266-5687) for details. Last Sunday in May.

Montréal Bike Fest. Tens of thousands of enthusiasts converge on Montréal to participate in cycling competitions that include a nocturnal bike ride (Un Tour la Nuit) and the grueling Tour de l'Ile, a 50km (31-mile) race around the island's rim; it draws 26,000 cyclists, shuts down roads, and attracts more than 100,000 spectators. The nonprofit biking organization Vélo Québec lists details at **www.velo.qc.ca**. Late May into early June.

Festival Transamériques, Montréal. Formerly the Festival de Théâtre des Amériques, this avant-garde program was renamed and refocused in 2007, when it presented 20 contemporary theater works by companies from Canada and around the world. Visit **www.fta.qc.ca** or call ✆ **514/842-0704.** Late May into early June.

Mondial de la Bière, Montréal. Yes, beer fans, this is a 5-day festival devoted to your favorite beverage. Admission is free and tasting coupons are C$1 (50p) each, with most tastings costing one to five coupons for 3 to 4 ounces. Showcased are world brands and boutique microbreweries, and "courses" lead to a "Diploma in Beer Tasting." Details at **www.festivalmondialbiere.qc.ca** and ✆ **514/722-9640.** June 3 to 7, 2009.

Grand Prix du Canada, Montréal. Montréal's biggest tourism event of the year, bar none. For 3 days, Canada's only Formula 1 auto race roars around a track on Ile Notre-Dame, the small island that's spitting distance from downtown Montréal. Hotel rates typically double during Grand Prix days, and 3-night minimums get emplaced. Streets are shut down, gleaming race cars sit on display, and the city parties around the clock, with much of the action around downtown's rue Crescent. Details at **www.grandprix.ca.** First weekend in June.

Saint-Ambroise Montréal Fringe Festival. This event's website features a hand raising its middle finger, which gives you an idea of the attitude behind this Plateau Mont-Royal fest: It's 11 days of out-there theater with acts such as a one-man *Star Wars* stand-up, clowns gone bad, and drunken drag queens. The festival proclaims that there's "No Artistic Direction. Artists are selected by lottery," and that there's "No Censorship. Artists

have complete freedom to present ANYTHING." *Vive le fringe!* Check **www.montrealfringe.ca** or call ✆ **514/849-3378.** It was held June 12 to 22 in 2008; at press time, 2009 dates were not yet announced.

Jean-Baptiste Day. Honoring St. John the Baptist, the patron saint of French-Canadians, this day is marked by far more festivities and enthusiasm throughout Québec province than is Canada Day on July 1 (listed below). It's Québec's own *fête nationale* and is celebrated with fireworks, bonfires, music in parks, and parades. June 24.

L'International des Feux Loto-Québec (International Fireworks Competition), Montréal. Pitting the shows of different countries against each other, this annual fireworks competition is a spectacular event. Buy tickets to watch from the open-air theater in La Ronde amusement park on Ile Ste-Hélène, or enjoy the pyrotechnics for free from almost anywhere overlooking the river (tickets do, however, have the added benefit of including admission to the amusement park). Kids, needless to say, love the whole explosive business. Go to **www.internationaldesfeuxloto-quebec.com/en** or call ✆ **514/397-2000** for details. Ten Wednesdays and Saturdays in June and July; at press time, the exact 2009 dates were not yet announced.

Canada Day. On July 1, 1867, three British colonies joined together to form the federation of Canada, with further independence from Britain coming in stages in the 1880s. Celebrations of Canada's birthday are biggest in Ottawa, though there are concerts, flag raisings, and family festivities in Montréal and Québec City. **www.celafete.ca.** July 1.

Festival International de Jazz de Montréal. Since Montréal has a long tradition in jazz, this is one of the monster events on the city's calendar and has been enormously successful at celebrating America's art form since 1979. The 2008 edition featured a performance by native son **Leonard Cohen** as well as Steely Dan, Aretha Franklin, Al Green, and Dave Brubeck. It costs serious money to hear stars of such magnitude, and tickets sell out months in advance. Fortunately, 450 free outdoor performances also take place during the late-June/early July party, many right on downtown's streets and plazas. Visit **www.montrealjazzfest.com** or call © **888/515-0515.** July 1 to 12, 2009.

Festival Juste pour Rire (Just for Laughs Festival), Montréal. Well-known comics including Eddie Izzard, Joan Rivers, the Kids in the Hall, and Jeremy Piven have been featured, while smaller-name Francophone and Anglophone groups and stand-ups come from around the world to perform at this festival, which takes place both indoors and on the street. It's held mostly along rue St-Denis and elsewhere in the Latin Quarter. Check **www. hahaha.com** or call © **888/244-3155** for details. All of July.

Festival d'Eté (Summer Festival), Québec City. The world's largest Francophone music festival happens in the heart of Vieux-Québec and, since 2007, in the St-Roch neighborhood. It gathers 200 groups from Africa, Asia, Europe, and North America to showcase theater, music, and dance. Check **www.info festival.com** or call © **888/992-5200.** July 9 to 19, 2009 and July 8 to 18, 2010.

Festival International Nuits d'Afrique, Montréal. A lively 13-day world-beat music showcase featuring musicians from the Caribbean, Africa, and the Americas. The festival also presents concerts year-round. Visit **www.festival nuitsdafrique.com** or call © **514/499-9239.** Mid-July; at press time, exact

2009 dates had not yet been announced.

Les Grands Feux Loto-Québec, Québec City. Overlapping with Montréal's fireworks competition (see p. 29), Québec's event uses the highly scenic Montmorency Falls 15 minutes north of the city center as its setting. Pyrotechnical teams are invited from countries around the world. Tickets get you admission to the base of the falls: there are 6,000 reserved bleacher seats and 22,500 general-admission tickets. Go to **www.quebecfireworks. com** or call © **888/934-3473** for details. Wednesdays and Saturdays from mid-July to early August.

Divers/Cité Festival, Montréal. In partnership with government agencies and sponsored by major corporations, Divers/Cité is one of North America's largest parties for gay, lesbian, bisexual, and transgendered people. It's 6 days of dance, drag, art, and music concerts, and nearly everything is outdoors and free. Details at **www.diverscite.org** or © **514/285-4011.** July 26 to August 2, 2009.

Les FrancoFolies de Montréal. Since 1988, this music fest has featured French-language pop, hip-hop, electronic, world beat, and *chanson*. There are 50 indoor shows and nearly three times as many that are outdoors and free. Check **www.francofolies.com**. Late July into early August.

Festival International de Courses de Bateaux-Dragons de Montréal. The annual dragon boat festival welcomes some 200 teams who pour into the Olympic Basin on Ile Notre-Dame. In addition to races, there are drawing contests for children and opportunities to try paddling on the ancient Chinese boats. Details are at **www.montreal dragonboat.com**. Two days in late July; at press time, exact 2009 dates had not yet been announced.

Festival des Films du Monde (World Film Festival), Montréal. This festival has been an international film event since 1977. A strong panel of actors, directors, and writers from around the world make up the jury each year, giving the event a weight that many festivals lack. Various movie theaters play host. Check **www.ffm-montreal.org** or call ✆ **514/848-3883** for details. Late August to early September; at press time, 2009 dates were not yet announced.

250-Year Anniversary of the Battle of the Plains of Abraham, Québec City. More than 2,000 historical re-enactors will set up encampments in the manner of 1759 to 1760 British and French soldiers on the huge, grassy park at the city's edge. They'll re-create the battles that resulted in France's territory loss and British rule over Canada. **www.quebec09.com**. August 6 to 9, 2009. See p. 239 for more information.

SEPTEMBER

Fall Foliage. Starting mid-month, the maple trees blaze with color and a walk in the parks of Montréal and Québec City is a refreshing tonic. It's also a perfect time to drive to the Laurentians or Cantons-de-L'Est (both near Montréal)

or Ile d'Orléans or Charlevoix (both easy drives from Québec City).

OCTOBER

Black & Blue Festival, Montréal. One of the biggest gay events on the planet, this party was, a few years ago, named the best international fest by France's Pink TV Awards, beating out even Carnival in Rio. And when we say big, we mean *big:* The main event is an all-night party at Olympic Stadium. There's also a Jock Ball, a Leather Ball, and a Military Ball. Visit **www.bbcm.org** or call ✆ **514/875-7026.** Seven days in mid-October.

Festival du Nouveau Cinéma, Montréal. Screenings of new and experimental-edging-to-avant-garde films ignite controversy, and forums discuss the latest trends in cinema and video. Events take place at halls and cinemas throughout the city. Check **www.nouveaucinema.ca** or call ✆ **514/844-2172.** Twelve days in mid-October; at press time, 2009 dates had not yet been announced.

DECEMBER

Christmas through New Year's, Québec City. Celebrating the holidays *a la française* is a particular treat in Québec City, where the streets are almost certainly banked with snow and nearly every ancient building sports wreaths, decorated fir trees, and glittery white lights.

4 GETTING THERE & GETTING AROUND

Served by highways, transcontinental trains and buses, and several airports, Montréal and Québec City are easily accessible from any part of the U.S. and Europe.

GETTING TO MONTREAL & QUEBEC CITY
By Plane

Most of the world's major airlines fly into the **Aéroport International Pierre-Elliot-Trudeau de Montréal** (airport code YUL;

✆ **800/465-1213** and 514/394-7377; www.admtl.com). It's known more commonly as just Montréal-Trudeau Airport. (Note that it used to be called Montréal-Dorval, and that some holdouts still use that name.)

In Québec City, the teeny **Jean Lesage International Airport** (airport code: YQB; ✆ **418/640-2700;** www.aeroportde quebec.com) is served by a number of major airlines. Most air traffic comes by way of Montréal, although there are an increasing number of direct flights from U.S. cities, including Chicago (on United Airlines), Newark and Cleveland (on Continental Airlines), and Detroit (on Northwest Airlines).

For airline toll-free phone numbers, see p. 294 in the "Fast Facts" appendix.

Getting from the Airports to the Cities

Montréal-Trudeau is served by the shuttle bus **L'Aérobus** (© **514/216-8591**), which travels between the airport and downtown, stopping at Berri Terminal (the city's main bus terminal, also known as the Station Centrale d'Autobus). Buses run every 30 minutes daily from 4:30am to 1:30am. One-way fares are C$14 (£7) for adults, C$13 (£6.50) for seniors, and C$11 (£5.50) for children. The ride takes about 30 minutes.

A taxi trip to downtown Montréal costs a flat fare of C$35 (£18) plus tip.

A taxi to downtown Québec City is a fixed-rate C$30 (£15). Bus service is no longer available between the airport and Québec City.

By Car

U.S. citizens do not need an international driver's license to drive in Canada. A U.S. license is sufficient as long as you are a visitor and actually are a U.S. resident.

Driving north to Montréal from the U.S., the entire journey is on expressways. From New York City, all but the last 40 or so miles of the 603km (375-mile) journey are within New York state on Interstate 87. I-87 links up with Canada's Autoroute 15 at the border, which goes straight to Montréal. From Boston, I-93 goes up through New Hampshire (and the beautiful Franconia Notch in the White Mountains) and merges into I-91 to cross the tip of Vermont. At the border, I-91 becomes Autoroute 55. Signs lead to Autoroute 10 west, which goes into Montréal. From Boston to Montréal is about 518km (322 miles).

Québec City is 867km (520 miles) from New York City and 644km (400 miles) from Boston. From New York, follow the directions to Montréal and then pick up Autoroute 20 to Québec City. From Boston, follow the directions to Montréal, but at Autoroute 10, go east instead of west to stay on Autoroute 55. Get on Autoroute 20 to Québec City and follow signs for the Pont Pierre-Laporte (a bridge). To get to the Old City, turn right onto Boulevard Wilfrid-Laurier (Rte. 175) shortly after crossing the bridge. It changes names first to Boulevard Laurier and then to Grande-Allée, the grand boulevard that leads directly into the central Parliament Hill area and the Old City. Once the street passes through the ancient walls that ring the Old City, it becomes rue St-Louis, which leads straight to the famed Château Frontenac on the cliff above the St. Lawrence River.

Another appealing option when you're approaching Québec City from the south is to follow Route 132 along the river's southern side to the town of Lévis. A car ferry there, **Traverse Québec-Lévis** (© **888/787-7483;** www.traversiers.gouv. qc.ca), provides a 10-minute ride across the river and a dramatic way to see the city, especially for the first time. Though the schedule varies substantially through the year, the ferry leaves at least every hour from 6am to 2am. One-way, it costs C$6 (£3) for the car and driver, C$2.70 (£1.35) for each additional adult, and C$11 (£5.30) for a car with up to six passengers. Only cash is accepted, so if you arrive from the U.S. without Canadian money, know that there's an ATM in the small transport terminal next door.

When driving between Québec City from Montréal, there are two main options: Autoroute 40, which runs along the St. Lawrence's north shore, and Autoroute 20, on the south side (although not hugging the water at all). The trip takes a little less than 3 hours without stops.

In Canada, highway distances and speed limits are given in kilometers (km). The speed limit on the autoroutes is 100kmph (62 mph). There's a stiff penalty for neglecting to wear your seatbelt, and all passengers must be buckled up.

For listings of the major car-rental agencies in Canada, see the appendix.

Note on radar detectors: Radar detectors are prohibited in Québec province. They can be confiscated, even if they're not being used.

Also, it is illegal to turn right on a red light on the island of Montréal. It is permitted in the rest of Québec and Canada.

Members of the American Automobile Association (AAA) are covered by the Canadian Automobile Association (CAA) while traveling in Canada. See p. 289 in the appendix for more information.

By Train

Montréal is a major terminus on Canada's **VIA Rail** network (© **888/842-7245;** www.viarail.ca). Its station, **Gare Centrale,** at 895 rue de la Gauchetière ouest (© **514/989-2626**), is centrally located downtown.

Québec City's train station, **Gare du Palais,** is in Lower Town at 450 rue de la Gare-du-Palais. Many of the hotels listed in this book are up an incline from the station, so a short cab ride might be necessary.

VIA Rail trains are comfortable—all have Wi-Fi, and some are equipped with dining cars and sleeping cars.

Amtrak (© **800/USA-RAIL** [872-7245]; www.amtrak.com) has one train per day into Montréal from New York that makes intermediate stops. Called the *Adirondack,* it's very slow, but its scenic route passes along the Hudson River's eastern shore and west of Lake Champlain. The *Adirondack* takes just less than 11 hours from New York if all goes well, but delays aren't unusual.

The train ride between Montréal and Québec City takes about 3 hours.

GETTING AROUND MONTREAL

In 2007, city police began cracking down on jaywalkers in an attempt to cut down on the number of accidents involving pedestrians. So when traveling by foot, be sure to cross only at the corner and only when you have a green light or a walk sign. The fine is C$37 (£19).

Montréal by Métro

For speed and economy, nothing beats Montréal's **Métro system.** The stations are marked on the street by blue-and-white signs that show a circle enclosing a downpointing arrow. Although starting to show its age (the system has run at a financial deficit in recent years), the Métro is relatively clean, and quiet trains whisk passengers through an expanding network of underground tunnels. Information is online at **www.stm.info**.

Fares are by the ride, not by distance. Single rides cost C$2.75 (£1.40), a strip of six tickets goes for C$12 (£6), and a weekly pass, good for unlimited rides, sets you back C$19 (£9.65). Reduced fares are available to children and, with special Métro ID cards, seniors and students. Sales are cash only; buy tickets from the booth attendant in any station or from a convenience store.

Tourist Cards can be a good deal if you plan to use the Métro more than three times in 1 day. You get unlimited access to the bus and Métro network for 1 day for C\$9 (£4.50) or 3 consecutive days for C\$17 (£8.50). The front of the card has scratch-off sections like a lottery card—you scratch out the month and day (or 3 consecutive days) on which you wish to use the card.

To enter the system, slip your ticket into the slot in the turnstile or show your pass to the booth attendant. If you plan to transfer to a bus, take a transfer ticket *(correspondence)* from the machine just inside the turnstile; every Métro station has one, and it allows you a free transfer to a bus wherever you exit the subway. Remember to take the transfer ticket at the station where you *first* enter the system. If you start a trip by bus and intend to continue on the Métro, ask the driver for a transfer.

The Métro runs from about 5:30am to 1am. If you plan to be out late, check the website at www.stm.info or call ℂ **514/ 786-4636** for the exact times of each line's last train.

The system is not immune to transit strikes, and convenient as it is, there can be substantial distances between stations. Accessibility is sometimes difficult for people with mobility restrictions or parents with strollers.

Montréal by Bus

Bus fares cost the same as those for Métro trains, and Métro tickets are good on buses, too. Exact change is required to pay bus fares in cash. Although they run throughout the city (and give tourists the decided advantage of traveling aboveground), buses don't run as frequently or as swiftly as the Métro. If you start a trip on the bus and want to transfer to the Métro, ask the bus driver for a transfer ticket.

Montréal by Taxi

There are plenty of taxis run by several different companies. Cabs come in a variety of colors and styles, so their principal distinguishing feature is the plastic sign on the roof. At night, the sign is illuminated when the cab is available. The initial charge is C\$3.15 (£1.60). Each additional kilometer ($^2/_3$ mile) adds C\$1.45 (75p), and each minute of waiting adds C55¢ (30p). A short ride from one point to another downtown usually costs about C\$6 (£3). Tip about 10% to 15%. Members of hotel and restaurant staffs can call cabs, many of which are dispatched by radio. They line up outside most large hotels or can be hailed on the street.

Montréal taxi drivers range in temperament from sullen cranks to the unstoppably loquacious. Some know their city well, others have sketchy knowledge and poor language skills, so it's a good idea to have your destination written down—with the cross street—to show your driver.

Montréal by Car

Montréal is an easy city to navigate by car. Visitors arriving by plane or train, though, will probably want to rely on public transportation and cabs. A **rental car** can come in handy for trips outside of town or if you plan to drive to Québec City.

Terms, cars, and prices for rentals are similar to those in the U.S., and all the larger American companies operate in Canada. Basic rates are about the same from company to company, although a little comparison shopping can unearth modest savings. A charge is usually levied when you return a car in a location other than the one in which it was rented.

Names and contact information for rental companies are listed on p. 295.

If you'll be doing much driving in the city, you may want to pick up the pocket-size atlas by JDM Géo. It's published by MapArt (www.mapart.com) and sold at gas stations throughout Canada. The map

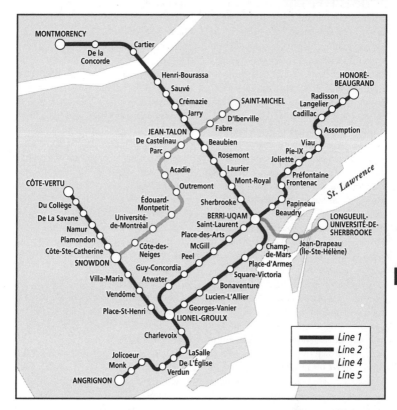

offers more detail than most, especially in the areas outside the primary tourist orbit. The company also sells good maps for the Laurentians and Cantons-de-l'Est regions discussed in chapter 12.

It can be difficult to park for free on downtown Montréal's heavily trafficked streets, but there are plenty of metered spaces. Look around before walking off without paying. Traditional meters are set well back from the curb so they won't be buried by plowed snow in winter. Parking costs C$3 (£1.50) per hour, and meters are in effect weekdays until 9pm and weekends until 6pm.

If there are no parking meters in sight, you're not off the hook. New computerized

Pay 'N Go stations are quickly replacing meters. Look for the black metal kiosks: They're columns about 6 feet tall with a white "P" in a blue circle. Press the "English" button, enter the letter from the space where you are parked, then pay with cash or a credit card, following the on-screen instructions.

In addition, check for signs noting restrictions, usually showing a red circle with a diagonal slash. The words LIVRAISON SEULEMENT, for example, mean "delivery only." Most downtown shopping complexes have underground parking lots, as do the big downtown hotels. Some hotels don't charge extra if you want to take your car in and out during the day—which is useful if you plan to do some sightseeing by car.

The limited-access expressways in Québec are called *autoroutes,* distances are given in kilometers (km), and speed limits are given in kilometers per hour (kmph). Because French is the province's official language, some highway signs are only in French, though Montréal's autoroutes and bridges often bear dual-language signs.

One traffic signal function often confuses newcomers: Should you wish to make a turn and you know that the street runs in the correct direction, you may be surprised to initially see just a green arrow pointing straight ahead instead of a green light permitting the turn. The arrow is just to give pedestrians time to cross the intersection. After a few moments, the light will turn from an arrow to a regular green light and you can proceed with your turn.

A blinking green light means that oncoming traffic still has a red light, making it safe to make a left turn.

Turning right on a red light is prohibited on the island of Montréal, except where specifically allowed by an additional green arrow. Off the island, it is now legal to turn right after stopping at red lights, except where there's a sign specifically prohibiting that move.

Montréal by Bike

The city has a great system of bike paths, and bicycling is common not just for recreation but for transportation as well.

Most Métro stations have large bike racks, and in some neighborhoods, sections of the road where cars would normally park are fenced off for bike parking.

Passengers can take bicycles on the Métro from 10am to 3pm and after 7pm on weekdays and all day on Saturday, Sunday, and holidays. This rule is suspended, however, on special-event days when the trains are too crowded. Bikers should board the first car of the train, which can hold a maximum of four bikes (if there are already that many bikes on that car, you have to wait for the next train).

The nonprofit biking organization **Vélo Québec** (© **800/567-8356** or 514/521-8356 in Montréal; www.velo.qc.ca) has the most up-to-date information on the state of bike paths and offers guided tours throughout the province (*vélo* means bicycle in French).

Several taxi companies participate in the "**Taxi+Vélo**" program. To partake, call one of them, specify that you have a bike to transport, and a cab with a specially designed rack arrives. Up to three bikes can be carried for an extra fee of C$3 (£1.50) each. The companies are listed on a PDF at www.velo.qc.ca (search the French-language pages for "taxi") and include **Taxi Diamond Montréal** (© **514/271-6331**) and **Taxi Union Longueuil** (© **450/679-6262**).

Bicycle rentals are available from **ÇaRoule/Montréal on Wheels** (© **514/866-0633;** www.caroulemontreal.com) at 27 rue de la Commune est, the waterfront road bordering Vieux-Port.

In June 2008, the city announced that it will soon start testing a self-service bicycle rental program. This is similar to programs in Paris, Barcelona, Munich, and Berlin, where users pick up bikes from one station and then drop them off at another for a small fee. Projections call for 2,400 bikes to be in operation by spring 2009 with some 300 stations in Montréal's central boroughs. Find out more at **www. statdemtl.qc.ca/en/bike**.

GETTING AROUND QUEBEC CITY

Once you're within or near the walls of Old Town (Haute-Ville), virtually no place of interest, hotel, or restaurant is beyond walking distance. In bad weather, or when you're traversing between opposite ends of Lower and Upper Towns, a taxi might be necessary, but in general, walking is the best way to explore the city.

Québec City by Bus

Local buses run often and charge C$2.50 (£1.25) in exact change. One-day passes cost C$6.15 (£3.20), and discounts are available for seniors and students with proper ID. The Québec City museum card (p. 234) includes 2 days of unlimited public transport in addition to free entrance to 20 museums for 3 days.

Bus routes are listed online at **www. rtcquebec.ca**. Buses in the most touristy areas include no. 7, which travels up and down rue St-Jean, and nos. 10 and 11, which shuttle along Grande-Allée/rue St-Louis. Bus stops sport easy-to-follow signs that state the bus numbers and direction of travel for each route. Flag down the bus as it approaches so the driver knows to stop.

Québec City by Funicular

To get between Upper and Lower Town, you can take streets, staircases, and a cliffside elevator, known as the funicular, which has long operated along an inclined 64m (210-ft.) track. The upper station is near the front of Château Frontenac and Place d'Armes, while the lower station is at rue du Petit-Champlain's northern end. The device offers excellent aerial views of the historic Lower Town on the short trip, and runs daily from 7:30am until 11pm all year, and until midnight in high season. Wheelchairs and strollers are accommodated. The one-way fare is C$1.75 (90p). Read more about its history at **www. funiculaire-quebec.com**.

Québec City by Taxi

Taxis are everywhere: cruising, parked in front of the big hotels, and in some of Upper Town's larger squares. In theory, they can be hailed, but they are best obtained by locating one of their stands, as in the Place d'Armes or in front of the Hôtel-de-Ville (City Hall). Restaurant managers and hotel bell captains will also summon them upon request. The starting rate is C$3.15 (£1.60), and each kilometer costs C$1.45 (75p).

Tip 10% to 15%. A taxi from the train station to one of the big hotels costs about C$8 (£4) plus tip. To get a cab, call **Taxi Coop** (*☎* **418/525-5191**) or **Taxi Québec** (*☎* **418/525-8123**).

Québec City by Car

Unlike in Montréal, drivers in Québec City are permitted to turn right at red traffic lights, but only after coming to a full stop and yielding to pedestrians in the crosswalk.

Names and contact information for rental companies doing business in Québec City are listed on p. 295. Budget and Hertz both have offices in Upper Town on Côte du Palais at rue St-Jean.

The basic map you get from the rental agency should suffice for Québec City, which is compact. Driving is a little tricky because there are so few roads between Upper and Lower Town and because many streets are one-way.

On-street parking is very difficult in old Québec City's cramped quarters. When you find a rare space on the street, be sure to check the signs for hours when parking is permissible. Meters cost C50¢ (25p) per 15 minutes, and some meters accept payment for up to 5 hours. Meters are generally in effect Monday through Saturday from 9am to 9pm and Sunday 10am to 9pm. But be sure to double-check: Spots along Parc des Champs-de-Bataille (Battlefields Park) have to be paid for 24 hours a day.

Many of the smaller hotels and B&Bs that don't have their own parking lots maintain special arrangements with local garages, with discounts for guests of C$3 or C$4 (£1.50 or £2) off the usual C$18 (£9) or more per day. Check with your hotel before parking in any lot or garage.

If a particular hotel or auberge doesn't have access to a garage or lot, plenty of public ones are available and clearly marked on the foldout city map available at tourist offices. They include, in Upper Town, the one behind Hôtel-de-Ville

(City Hall), with an entrance on rue Ste-Anne, and, in Lower Town, across the street from the Musée de la Civilisation, on rue Dalhousie.

Québec City by Bike

Given Vieux-Québec's hilly topography and tight quarters, cycling isn't a particularly attractive option within the walls or in Lower Town. But beyond the walls is another story. Québec has a good network of cycling paths called the **Route Verte (Green Route),** with both local lanes and access to longer-distance rides. The website, **www.routeverte.com/ang**, lists information for day trips and longer tours.

You can be rent bicycles in Lower Town at **Cyclo Services,** 289 rue St-Paul (© **418/ 692-4052;** www.cycloservices.net), for C$25 (£13) for 4 hours, with other increments available.

5 MONEY & COSTS

It's always advisable to bring money in a variety of forms on a vacation: a mix of cash, credit cards, and traveler's checks. Before you leave home, you should also exchange enough petty cash to cover airport incidentals, tipping, and transportation to your hotel—or be sure to withdraw money upon arrival at an airport ATM.

Avoid exchanging money at commercial exchange bureaus and hotels, which often have the highest transaction fees.

CURRENCY

Canadian money comes in graduated denominations of dollars and cents. Aside from the $2 coin, Canadian coins are similar to their U.S. counterparts: 1¢, 5¢, 10¢, 25¢. Bills—$5, $10, $20, $50, $100—are all the same size but are different colors, depending on the denomination. The gold-colored $1 coin (called a "loonie" by Canadians because of the depiction of a loon on one side) has replaced the $1 bill. French speakers sometimes refer to a dollar as a *piastre*. A $2 coin, with a bronze center surrounded by a nickel disk, has replaced the $2 bill. The $2 coin is sometimes called a "twonie," a reference to the next-smaller coin.

Prices in this book, unless otherwise indicated, are given in Canadian dollars and British pounds.

The Canadian dollar has gathered significant strength in recent years and at the time of this writing was **on par with U.S. currency,** give or take a couple of points' daily variation.

This book uses an exchange rate of one Canadian dollar to 50p in British currency.

CURRENCY EXCHANGE

Main branch banks and *caisses populaires* (credit unions) will exchange most foreign

What Things Cost in Québec Province	C$	US$	UK£
Moderate hotel room, summer	180	180	90
Montréal Métro ticket	2.75	2.75	1.40
Table d'hôte 3-course dinner	25	25	12.50
Double espresso	3.50	3.50	1.75
Museum pass for 3 days	50	50	25
Gasoline: per liter	1.40	1.40	0.70
per gallon equivalent	5.30	5.30	2.65

The Canadian Dollar, the U.S. Dollar & the British Pound

The prices quoted in this guide are in Canadian dollars, with U.K. equivalents in parentheses. The exchange rate we've used is **$1 Canadian to $1 U.S. to 50p U.K.** For the most up-to-date exchange rates, visit **www.xe.com/ucc.**

Although the math is pretty easy, here's a quick table of equivalents:

C$	US$	UK£
1	1	0.50
5	5	2.50
10	10	5
20	20	10
50	50	25
100	100	50

currencies. Tourism offices can often exchange money or point you to a place that will.

ATMS

The easiest way to get cash away from home is from an ATM (automated teller machine), sometimes referred to as a "cash machine" or "cashpoint." As ubiquitous in the Québec province and the rest of Canada as they are in the U.S. or the U.K., ATMs in French are called GABs, or *guichet automatique bancaire.* They are found in most of the same places, too—especially outside or inside bank branches. Look for signs reading GUICHET AUTOMATIQUE or SERVICES AUTOMATISES. Be sure you know your daily withdrawal limit before arriving in Canada.

Note about PINs: PINs (personal identification numbers) can only be four digits at many Canadian ATMs. If your PIN has more numbers, change it before departing; your card may not work otherwise.

Note about bank fees: Many banks impose a fee each time you use a card at another bank's ATM, and that fee can be higher for international transactions (up to $5 or more). In addition, the bank from

which you withdraw cash may charge its own fee. Ask your bank about its international withdrawal fees.

CREDIT CARDS

Credit cards are another safe way to travel. They provide a convenient record of all your expenses and generally offer relatively decent exchange rates. You can withdraw cash advances from your credit cards at banks or ATMs, though high fees make credit card cash advances a pricey way to get cash. Keep in mind that you'll pay interest from the moment of your withdrawal, even if you pay your monthly bill on time. Also, note that many credit card companies now assess a "transaction fee" of 1% to 3% on *all* charges you incur abroad (whether you're using the local currency or your native currency).

MasterCard and Visa are most commonly accepted at hotels, restaurants, and shops in the province. American Express, Diners Club, and Discover are taken less often.

TRAVELER'S CHECKS

Traveler's checks are accepted throughout the Québec province.

6 HEALTH

GENERAL AVAILABILITY OF HEALTHCARE

Canada has a state-run health system, and Québec hospitals are modern and decently equipped, and staffs are well-trained.

The U.S. **Centers for Disease Control and Prevention** (℡ 800/311-3435; www.cdc.gov) provides up-to-date information on health hazards by region or country and offers food-safety tips (though you're unlikely to get sick from Canada's food or water). You can find listings of reliable medical clinics at the **International Society of Travel Medicine** (℡ 770/736-7060; www.istm.org).

WHAT TO DO IF YOU GET SICK AWAY FROM HOME

Familiar over-the-counter medicines are widely available in Canada.

Hospitals are listed on p. 290.

If there is a possibility that you will run out of prescribed medicines during your visit, take along a prescription from your doctor. Carry the generic name of prescription medicines in case a local pharmacist is unfamiliar with the brand name. Prescription drugs are usually less expensive in Canada than in the U.S.

Remember to pack your medications in your carry-on luggage and have them in their original containers with pharmacy labels—otherwise, they may not make it through airport security. If you're entering Canada with syringes used for medical reasons, bring a medical certificate that shows they are for medical use and be sure to declare them to Canadian Customs officials.

If you suffer from a chronic illness, consult your doctor before departure. **Additional emergency numbers** are listed in the "Fast Facts" appendix.

7 SAFETY

STAYING SAFE

Montréal and Québec City are far safer cities than their U.S. or European counterparts of similar size, but common sense insists that visitors stay alert and observe the usual urban precautions. It's best to stay out of parks at night, for example, and to take a taxi when returning from a late dinner or a club in a dicey area.

There have been recent reports of escalating road-rage incidents, so think twice before expressing impatience or anger with the actions of other drivers.

Québec is one of Canada's more liberal provinces; its residents often strongly disagree with U.S. policies, but mass demonstrations are rare and political violence is unusual.

Tolerance of others is a Canadian characteristic, and it's highly unlikely that visitors of ethnic, religious, and racial minorities will encounter even mild forms of discrimination. That applies to sexual orientation as well, especially in Montréal, which has one of North America's largest gay communities.

8 SPECIALIZED TRAVEL RESOURCES

TRAVELERS WITH DISABILITIES

Advice for travelers with physical limitations is provided in the French-language

brochure *Le Québec Accessible* (2005), which lists more than 1,000 hotels, restaurants, theaters, and museums. It costs C$20 (£10) from **Kéroul** (℡ 514/252-3104;

www.keroul.qc.ca). Kéroul also publishes an English-language brochure in downloadable PDF format called *The Accessible Road* (available at www.keroul.qc.ca), which provides information about everything from how to get a handicapped parking sticker to which top attractions are most accessible.

Québec regulations regarding wheelchair accessibility are similar to those in the U.S., including curb cuts, entrance ramps, designated parking spaces, and specially equipped bathrooms. However, access to the restaurants and inns housed in 18th- and 19th-century buildings, especially in Québec City, is often difficult or impossible.

When you're out and about, look for the **Tourist and Leisure Companion Sticker (T.L.C.S.)** at tourist sites; it designates that companions of travelers with disabilities can enter for free. A printable list of participating enterprises (in PDF format) is online at www.vatl-tlcs.org.

For more on organizations that offer resources to travelers with disabilities, go to www.frommers.com/planning.

GAY & LESBIAN TRAVELERS

The Québec province has come far: Gay life here is generally open and accepted (gay marriage is legal here), and gay travelers are heavily marketed to in its two major cities. The official **Tourisme Montréal** website, www.tourisme-montreal.org, has a "Gay and Lesbian" minisite which lists gay-friendly accommodations (more than 200 of them), gay-specific events, and more. Travelers will find the rainbow flag prominently displayed on the doors and websites of many hotel and restaurants in all the city's neighborhoods.

In Montréal, many gay and lesbian travelers head straight to the **Gay Village** (or, simply, "the Village"), a neighborhood located primarily along rue Ste-Catherine est between rue St-Hubert and rue Papineau where there are antiques shops, bars,

B&Bs, and clubs, clubs, clubs. The Beaudry Métro station is at the heart of the neighborhood and marked by the rainbow flag.

The Village is action central on any night, but especially during the weeklong celebration of sexual diversity known as **Divers/Cité** (www.diverscite.org) in late July and early August and the **Black & Blue Festival** (www.bbcm.org), probably the world's largest circuit party with a week of entertainment and club dancing; it's held in October. They're both listed in the calendar earlier in this chapter. (In 2006, Montréal added another pink feather to its cap by hosting the first World Outgames, attracting more than 16,000 athletes.)

The **Village Tourism Information Centre** at 576 rue Ste-Catherine est, Suite 200 (© **888/595-8110** or 514/522-1885), is open daily in the summer and weekdays the rest of the year, and provides information about everything from wine bars to yoga classes. You can call **Gay Line** (© **888/505-1010** or 514/866-5090; www.gayline.qc.ca) to get your questions answered by phone daily from 7 to 11pm; their website has an events-listing page. The **Québec Gay Chamber of Commerce** maintains a website at www.ccgq.ca.

Of several local publications, the most useful is *Fugues*, a magazine which describes current and future events as well as listing gay-friendly lodgings, clubs, saunas, and other resources. Get a copy at the tourist office mentioned above or from the free racks around the city, or check www.fugues.com.

Gay.com (© **800/929-2268** or 415/644-8044; www.gay.com/travel) has a special section about Montréal.

In Québec City, the gay community is smaller and centered in Upper Town just outside the city walls, on rue St-Jean and the parallel rue d'Aiguillon, starting from where they cross rue St-Augustin and heading west. **Le Drague Cabaret Club** (© **418/649-7212;** www.ledrague.com), or "the Drag," is a central gathering place with a cabaret and two dance rooms.

At the end of August, Québec City hosts a 3-day gay-pride fest, **Fête Arc-en-Ciel** (www.glbtquebec.org), which attracts thousands of people to Place d'Youville.

For more gay and lesbian travel resources, visit www.frommers.com/planning.

SENIOR TRAVEL

Mention the fact that you're a senior citizen when you make your travel reservations. Although the major U.S. airlines have canceled their senior discount programs, many Québec hotels still offer discounts for older travelers.

Throughout the Québec province, many theaters, museums, and other attractions also offer reduced admission to people as young as 60.

Show your **AAA** card if you have one. Members of the American Automobile Association get the same discounts as members of the CAA. That means reduced rates at a variety of museums, hotels, and restaurants.

Many reliable agencies and organizations target the 50-plus market. **Elderhostel** (© **800/454-5768;** www.elderhostel. org) arranges worldwide study programs for those aged 55 and older and offers a variety of trips to Québec City and Montréal.

The best-selling paperback *Unbelievably Good Deals and Great Adventures That You Absolutely Can't Get Unless You're Over 50* (McGraw-Hill) by Joann Rattner Heilman, includes information about Canadian travel.

For even more information and resources about travel for seniors, check www.frommers.com/planning.

FAMILY TRAVEL

Montréal and Québec City offer an abundance of family-oriented activities, many of them outdoors, even in winter. Watersports, river cruises, fort climbing, and fireworks displays are among summer's many attractions, with dog sledding and skiing being the top choices in snowy months. Québec City's walls and fortifications are fodder for imagining the days of knights and princesses. In both cities, many museums make special efforts to address children's interests and enthusiasms.

For family-friendly accommodations, restaurants, and attractions that are particularly kid-friendly, look for the "Kids" icon throughout this guide.

The family-travel website **Family Travel Forum** (www.familytravelforum.com) offers customized trip planning and includes information about Canada.

For a list of more family-friendly travel resources, visit www.frommers.com/planning.

VEGETARIAN TRAVEL

Le Commensal is a popular vegetarian restaurant in both Montréal and Québec City (p. 90 for the Montréal information; in Québec City, it's a few blocks outside the walls of Upper Town at 860 rue St-Jean). **Aux Vivres** (p. 104) is a popular vegan spot in Montréal's Mile End.

Two websites in particular, **Happy-Cow's Vegetarian Guide** (www.happycow. net) and **VegDining.com,** list other vegetarian options in Montréal and Québec City.

For more vegetarian-friendly travel resources, go to www.frommers.com/planning.

TRAVELING WITH PETS

Pets with proper rabies vaccination records may be admitted to Canada, but review the necessary procedures with the **Canada Border Services Agency** (CBSA; © **506/ 636-5064;** www.cbsa-asfc.gc.ca).

To ensure a smooth border crossing into the U.S. on your return, check with **U.S. Customs and Border Protection** before departing. The useful brochure "Pets and Wildlife" is available as a PDF from the U.S. Customs website at www.customs.gov.

From the famed Château Frontenac to the high-end boutique hotels of the Groupe Germain to the Hilton and Loews chains, many hotels now accept pets, and some even offer walking services and little beds for dogs. There are often restrictions regarding the animal's size, and most animals are not permitted to be left alone in the hotel room. Most hotels charge an extra fee of C$20 (£10) or more per day or per stay.

For more resources about traveling with pets, go to www.frommers.com/planning.

9 SUSTAINABLE TOURISM

Sustainable tourism is conscientious travel. It means being careful with the environments you explore and respecting the communities you visit. Two overlapping components of sustainable travel are ecotourism and ethical tourism.

The **International Ecotourism Society (TIES)** defines ecotourism as responsible travel that conserves the environment and improves the well-being of local people. TIES suggests that ecotourists follow these principles:

- Minimize environmental impact.
- Build environmental and cultural awareness and respect.
- Provide positive experiences for visitors and hosts.
- Provide direct financial benefits for conservation and local people.
- Raise sensitivity to host countries' political, environmental, and social climates.
- Support international human rights and labor agreements.

Frommers.com: The Complete Travel Resource

Planning a trip or just returned? Head to **Frommers.com,** voted Best Travel Site by *PC Magazine*. We think you'll find our site indispensable before, during, and after your travels—with expert advice and tips; independent reviews of hotels, restaurants, attractions, and shopping and nightlife venues; vacation giveaways; and an online booking tool. We publish the complete contents of more than 135 travel guides in our **Destinations** section, covering more than 4,000 places worldwide. Each weekday, we publish original articles that report on travel deals and news via our free **Frommers.com newsletter.** What's more, Arthur Frommer himself blogs 5 days a week, with cutting opinions about the state of travel in the modern world. We're betting you'll find our **Events** listings an invaluable resource, too; it's an up-to-the-minute roster of what's happening in cities everywhere—including concerts, festivals, lectures, and more. We've also added weekly podcasts, interactive maps, and hundreds of new images across the site. Finally, don't forget to visit our **message boards,** where you can join in conversation with thousands of fellow Frommer's travelers and post your trip report once you return.

Tips **It's Easy Being Green**

Here are a few simple ways to conserve fuel and energy when you travel:

- Each time you take a flight or drive a car, greenhouse gases release into the atmosphere. You can help neutralize this danger to the planet through "carbon offsetting"—paying someone to invest your money in programs that reduce your emissions by the same amount you've added. Before buying carbon-offset credits, make sure that you're using a reputable company, one with a proven program that invests in renewable energy, such as **Carbonfund** (www.carbonfund.org), **TerraPass** (www.terrapass. org), and **Carbon Neutral** (www.carbonneutral.org).

- Whenever possible, choose nonstop flights; they generally require less fuel than indirect flights that stop and take off again. Try to fly during the day—some scientists estimate that nighttime flights are twice as harmful to the environment. And pack light. Each 15 pounds on a 5,000-mile flight adds up to 50 pounds of carbon dioxide emitted.

- Where you stay during your travels can have a major environmental impact. To determine a property's green credentials, ask about trash-disposal and recycling practices, water conservation, and energy use; also question whether sustainable materials were used in constructing the property. The Green Hotels Association's website, **www.greenhotels.com**, recommends green-rated member hotels around the world that fulfill the company's stringent environmental requirements. Also consult **www.environmentally friendlyhotels.com** for more green accommodation ratings.

- At hotels, request that your sheets and towels not be changed daily. (Many hotels already have programs like this in place.) Turn off the lights and air-conditioner (or heater) when you leave your room.

- Use public transit where possible—trains, buses, and even taxis are more energy-efficient forms of transport than driving. Even better is to walk or cycle; you'll produce zero emissions and stay fit and healthy.

- If renting a car is necessary, ask for a hybrid or rent the most fuel-efficient car available. You'll use less gas and save money when filling up.

- Eat at locally owned restaurants that use produce grown in the area. This contributes to the local economy and cuts down on emissions by supporting restaurants that don't fly or truck food in from far away. Visit **www. eatwellguide.org** for tips on eating sustainably in Canada.

You can find some eco-friendly travel tips and statistics, as well as participating touring companies and associations—listed by destination under "Travel Choice"—at the TIES website, www.eco tourism.org.

Also check out **Ecotravel.com,** which lets you search for sustainable touring companies in several categories (water-based, land-based, spiritually oriented, and so on).

While much of the focus of ecotourism is about reducing impacts on the natural environment, ethical tourism concentrates on ways to preserve and enhance local economies and communities, regardless of location. You can embrace ethical tourism by staying at a locally owned hotel or by shopping at stores that employ local workers and sell locally produced goods.

Responsible Travel (www.responsible travel.com) is a great source of sustainable travel ideas. **Sustainable Travel International** (www.sustainabletravelinternational. org) also promotes ethical tourism practices; it also maintains an extensive directory of sustainable properties and tour operators around the world.

10 SPECIAL-INTEREST TRIPS

ADVENTURE & WELLNESS TRIPS

Bike touring is wildly popular and well accommodated in Québec. In summer 2007, the province inaugurated the new **Route Verte (Green Route),** a 4,000km (2,485-mile) bike network. Many hotels and restaurants along the route emphasize the nutritional, safety, and equipment needs of cyclists. See "Biker's Paradise: The New 4,000km Route Verte" on p. 179 for details and contact information.

Vélo Québec (© 800/567-8356 or 514/521-8356 in Montréal; www.velo.qc. ca) was behind the development of the Route Verte and offers excellent biking information at its website. The organization also offers guided bike tours throughout the province and coordinates meals, accommodations, and baggage transport.

The gorgeous Charlevoix region, an hour north of Québec City, is the perfect place in which to take an ecotour. Charlevoix was designated a protected UNESCO World Biosphere Reserve in 1988 and is subject to balanced development and cross-disciplinary research into conservation.

Aventure Ecotourisme Québec (www. aventure-ecotourisme.qc.ca) is an association of tour operators that provides outdoor adventure programs with a focus on environmental care and preservation. It has stringent operational standards and is partner to the **Leave No Trace Center for Outdoor Ethics** (www.lnt.org), which educates operators and tourists about how to minimize the environmental impact of recreation. Aventure Ecotourisme also offers vacation planning.

One association member is **Mer et Monde Ecotours** (© 866/637-6663 or 418/232-6779; www.mer-et-monde.qc. ca), which offers kayak trips that take clients close to the whales that converge in the region each summer. For more information, see p. 287 at the end of chapter 20.

FOOD & WINE TRIPS

Foodies have a number of options to cook with some of the province's top chefs. In Québec City, the famed restaurant **Laurie Raphaël** (p. 228; © 418/692-4555; www.laurieraphael.com) underwent major renovation a few years ago that not only spiffed up its space but added a fancy public kitchen. Chef/owner Daniel Vézina gives 3- to 4-hour cooking classes here on Wednesday evenings and Saturday afternoons for C$185 (£93) per person.

Also in Québec City, **Les Artistes de la Table** (© 418/694-1056; www.lesartistes delatable.com) offers 4-hour custom cooking classes in the first floor of a gorgeous neoclassical building from 1850. Serious cooks will want to walk by just to peek at the kitchen through the vast windows. Cost is about C$100 (£50) per person.

If you're traveling by car, the **Route des Vins (Wine Route),** 103km (64 miles) southeast of Montréal, is a pleasant vineyard tour; see p. 195.

11 STAYING CONNECTED

TELEPHONES

The Canadian telephone system, operated by Bell Canada, closely resembles the U.S. model. All operators speak English and French, and respond in the appropriate language as soon as callers speak to them. In Canada, dial ℂ **00** to reach an **operator.**

A local call at a pay phone in the Québec province costs C50¢ (25p). **Directory information** calls (dial ℂ **411**) are free of charge.

When making a local call within Québec province, you must dial the area code before the seven-digit number.

Toll-free numbers: Phone numbers that begin with 800, 888, 877, and 866 are toll-free. That means they're free to call within Canada and from the U.S. You need to dial 1 first.

Remember that both local as well as long-distance calls usually cost more from hotels—sometimes a lot more, so check before dialing. Some hotels charge you for all phone calls you make, including toll-free ones.

To call Québec province from the U.S.: Calls between Canada and the U.S. do not require the use of country codes. Simply dial the 3-digit area code, then the seven-digit number. *Example:* To call the Infotouriste Centre in Montréal, dial 514/873-2015.

To call the Québec province from the U.K./Ireland/Australia/New Zealand: Dial the international access code 00 (from Australia, 0011), then the Canadian country code 1, then the area code, and then the seven-digit number. *Example:* To call the Infotouriste Centre in Montréal, dial 00-1-514/873-2015.

To call the U.S. from Québec province: Simply dial the three-digit area code and seven-digit number. *Example:* To call the U.S. Passport Agency from Québec province, dial 202/647-0518.

To call the U.K./Ireland/Australia/New Zealand from the Québec province: Dial 011, then the country code (U.K. 44, Ireland 353, Australia 61, New Zealand 64), then the number.

CELLPHONES

Visitors from the U.S. should be able to get roaming service that allows them to use their cellphones in Canada.

Some wireless companies let you adjust your plan to get cheaper rates while traveling. Sprint, for instance, has a "Canadian roaming" option for US$3 per month that reduces the per-minute rate. Ask your provider for options and pricing schedules.

Europeans and most Australians are on the **GSM** (Global System for Mobile Communications) network with removable plastic SIM cards in their phones. Call your wireless provider for information about traveling. You may be able to purchase pay-as-you-go SIM cards in Canada with local providers.

If you end up traveling without a cellphone, **online phone services** or **telephone cards** are your best option (cellphone rental is not a common practice in Canada). With **OneSuite.com** (ℂ 866/417-8483; www.onesuite.com), for instance, you prepay an online account for as little as US$10. You then dial a toll-free or local access number, enter your PIN, then dial the number you're calling. Calls from Canada to mainland U.S. cost just US2.5¢ to US3.5¢ per minute. Calls to a U.K. landline cost 2p per minute; calls to a U.K. mobile cost 10p per minute.

VOICE-OVER INTERNET PROTOCOL (VOIP)

If you have Web access while traveling, consider a broadband-based telephone service (in technical terms, Voice-over Internet

Protocol, or VoIP) such as **Skype** (www. skype.com) or **Vonage** (www.vonage.com), which allow you to make free international calls from your laptop or in a cyber-cafe.

Neither service requires the people you're calling to also have that service, though fees apply if they don't. Check the websites for details.

INTERNET & E-MAIL
With Your Own Computer

Nearly all hotels and many smaller auberges and cafes now offer **Wi-Fi** (wireless fidelity). Many hotels also still offer high-speed Internet access through cable connections and some even still have data-ports for dial-up modems.

If your laptop has wireless capability (most newer models have it built in), check **www.jiwire.com**; its Hotspot Finder holds the world's largest directory of public wireless hotspots.

American travelers need not worry about plugging in to recharge; the electric current in Canada is the same as in the U.S.

Without Your Own Computer

Most hotels maintain business centers with computers for use by guests or outsiders, and most of the smaller boutique hotels now have at least one computer available for guests.

Cybercafes seem to be fading from the Canadian scene with the rise of Wi-Fi hot spots, and new ones do not seem to be opening.

However, a few still stand out: In Vieux-Montréal, **Café-Bistro Van Houtte,** 165 rue St-Paul ouest, is open 7am to 6pm (longer in the summer) and charges C$3 (£1.50) per half-hour. In Québec City, **Centre Internet,** 52 Cote du Palais (© **418/692-3359**), still does good business in Old Québec's Upper Town, just a block off of rue St-Jean.

For more information, refer to the "Internet Access" section of the "Fast Facts" appendix.

12 TIPS REGARDING ACCOMMODATIONS

Both Montréal and Québec City have familiar international hotel chains as well as small B&Bs hosted by locals. In between are the boutique hotels, which combine high-end service with plush room accommodations and decor that ranges from Asian minimalist to country luxury. A good room in one of these smaller hotels could provide the best memories of your trip.

Most Québec hotels offer online specials and package deals that bundle rooms with meals or sightseeing activities. In many cases, this can result in rates significantly below what's quoted in this book.

Tip: Always check hotel websites before calling to make a reservation.

Carefully consider the options for hotel meal plans, which are offered at many properties in the Laurentians and Charlevoix. The European Plan (EP) is for the room alone, with no meals. The Continental Plan (CP) includes breakfast. The Modified American Plan (MAP) includes breakfast and one dinner. The American Plan (AP) is a room plus all three meals each day.

Because the region is so intensely cold so many months of the year, tourism here is cyclical. That means that prices drop—often steeply—for much of the October-through-April period. Rooms get less expensive, though some of the essential vibrancy and *joie de vivre* goes into hibernation.

Tips What's in a Name? Understanding Affiliations

Many tourist businesses in the province are members of groups that offer seals of approval. Here's a quick primer of what some memberships signify:

- **Aventure Ecotourisme Québec** is an association of tour operators who provide outdoor-adventure programs with a focus on environmental care and preservation. It requires stringent operational standards and is a partner of the Leave No Trace Center for Outdoor Ethics (www.lnt.org), which educates operators and tourists about how to minimize the environmental impact of recreation. It also offers vacation planning. Sample member: The kayaking company Mer et Monde Ecotours (p. 287). **www.aventure-eco tourisme.qc.ca**.

- **Hôtellerie Champêtre** is a membership group of 26 Québec inns and resorts that are big on personality and often (but not always) midrange in price. They have to have at least three (out of five possible) stars from the Québec tourist authorities. Many are housed in historic buildings or have access to a dramatic outdoors spot. Sample member: Auberge La Camarine (p. 278), whose structure dates from 1750. **www.hotelleriechampetre. com**.

- **Relais and Châteaux** is a collection of high-end gourmet restaurants and luxury hotels around the world. The group is exclusive, with fewer than 500 properties in 55 countries. Members receive secret visits by reviewers and can be expelled if standards aren't met. Sample member: La Pinsonnière (p. 284) was one of Canada's first hostelries to be invited into the prestigious organization. **www.relaischateaux.com**.

Suggested Montréal & Québec City Itineraries

Public transportation in Montréal and Québec City is excellent, so there is little need for a personal vehicle. The suggested itineraries below focus on each city individually.

---

1 THE BEST OF MONTREAL IN 1 DAY

This carefully paced exploration of cosmopolitan Montréal allows ample time for random exploring, shopping, or lingering in sidewalk cafes. While many suggestions are for warm weather, there are periodic suggestions for inside stops during the winter months. If you're staying only 1 night, do book a room in one of Vieux-Montréal's new boutique hotels. Visitors find themselves drawn to the plazas and narrow cobblestone streets of this 18th- and 19th-century neighborhood, so you might as well be based there. *Start: Vieux-Montréal.*

❶ Place d'Armes ★★★

Begin your day in the heart of **Vieux-Montréal ★★★**, at the site where French settlers fought a bloody and decisive battle with the Iroquois in 1653. At the plaza's southeast corner is the city's oldest building, the **Vieux Séminaire de St-Sulpice** (p. 132), erected by Sulpician priests who arrived in 1657. Next to it is the **Basilique Notre-Dame ★★★** (p. 112), an 1824 church with a stunning interior of intricately gilded rare woods. Its acoustics are so perfect that the late, famed opera star Luciano Pavarotti performed here several times. From here, take Walking Tour 1 in chapter 9, which takes you past every historic structure in Vieux-Montréal.

❷ Pointe-à-Callière ★★★

Otherwise, head down the slope from the basilica to the district's riverside edge and **Pointe-à-Callière (Museum of Archaeology and History).** After viewing the multimedia show above the ruins, descend below the streets to discover remnants of Amerindian camps and early French settlements. See p. 113.

☕ OLIVE ET GOURMANDO

A couple of cobblestone blocks away is Olive et Gourmando, which started as a bakery and evolved into a full-service, French-feeling cafe. Eat in, or put together an appetizing picnic lunch to carry to the nearby park. 351 rue St-Paul ouest (✆ 514/350-1083). See p. 97.

❹ Musée McCord ★

Take the Métro downtown to Peel Station and walk to the **Musée McCord,** which sits across the street from McGill University. The permanent exhibition "Simply Montréal: Glimpses of a Unique History" justifies a trip here; it steeps visitors in city life throughout the centuries. See p. 109.

❺ Musée des Beaux-Arts ★★★

West on rue Sherbrooke from Musée McCord is the city's most important

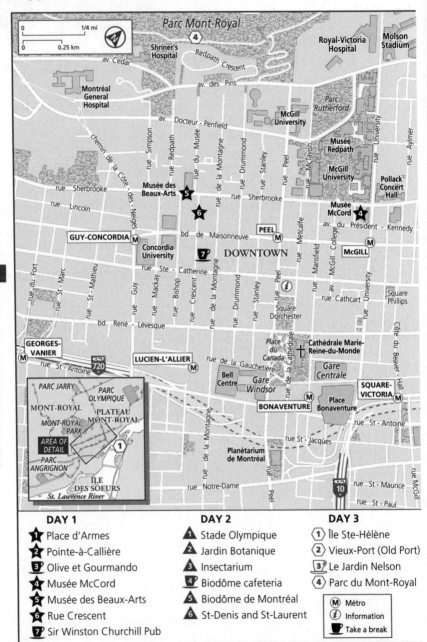

DAY 1

⭐ Place d'Armes
⭐ Pointe-à-Callière
3⃣ Olive et Gourmando
⭐ Musée McCord
⭐ Musée des Beaux-Arts
⭐ Rue Crescent
7⃣ Sir Winston Churchill Pub

DAY 2

1⃣ Stade Olympique
2⃣ Jardin Botanique
3⃣ Insectarium
4⃣ Biodôme cafeteria
5⃣ Biodôme de Montréal
6⃣ St-Denis and St-Laurent

DAY 3

1⃣ Île Ste-Hélène
2⃣ Vieux-Port (Old Port)
3⃣ Le Jardin Nelson
4⃣ Parc du Mont-Royal

Ⓜ Métro
ⓘ Information
☕ Take a break

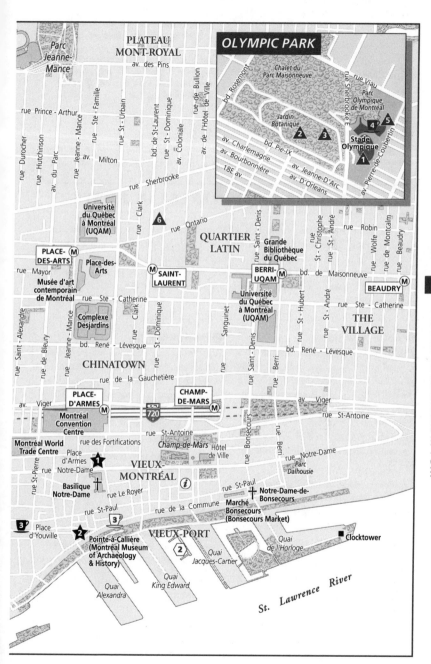

OLYMPIC PARK

Chalet du Parc Maisonneuve

rue Viau

Parc Olympique de Montréal

bd. Rosemont

rue Sherbrooke E

Jardin Botanique

2

3

Stade Olympique

4 **5**

1

av. Charlemagne

bd. Pie-IX

av. Bourbonnière

18E av.

av. Jeanne-D'Arc

av. D'Orleans

av. Pierre-de-Coubertin

Parc Jeanne-Mance

PLATEAU MONT-ROYAL

av. des Pins

rue Prince - Arthur

rue Durocher

rue Hutchinson

av. du Parc

rue Jeanne-Mance

av. Milton

rue Ste - Famille

rue St - Urbain

bd. de St-Laurent

rue St - Dominique

av. Coloniale

rue de Bullion

av. de l'Hôtel de Ville

rue Sherbrooke

Université du Québec à Montréal (UQAM)

rue Clark

6

rue Ontario

QUARTIER LATIN

rue Saint - Denis

Grande Bibliothèque du Québec

rue St - Christophe

rue St - André

rue Robin

rue Wolfe

rue de Montcalm

rue Beaudry

PLACE-DES-ARTS Ⓜ

rue Mayor

Musée d'art contemporain de Montréal

Place-des-Arts

Ⓜ SAINT-LAURENT

rue Ste - Catherine

BERRI-UQAM Ⓜ

bd. de Maisonneuve

BEAUDRY Ⓜ

Complexe Desjardins

rue Clark

rue Ste - Catherine

rue St - Dominique

Université du Québec à Montréal (UQAM)

Sanguinet

rue St - Hubert

rue St - André

rue Ste - Catherine

THE VILLAGE

rue Saint - Alexandre

rue de Bleury

rue Jeanne-Mance

bd. René - Lévesque

rue St - Dominique

rue

rue Saint - Denis

Berri

bd. René - Lévesque

CHINATOWN

rue de la Gauchetière

PLACE-D'ARMES Ⓜ

av. Viger

Montréal Convention Centre

720

CHAMP-DE-MARS Ⓜ

av. Viger

rue St-Antoine

Montréal World Trade Centre

rue St-Pierre

rue Notre-Dame

Place d'Armes ☆

rue des Fortifications

rue St-Antoine

Champ-de-Mars

Hôtel de Ville

Bonsecours

rue Berri

rue Notre-Dame

Parc Dalhousie

Basilique Notre-Dame ✝

rue Le Royer

VIEUX-MONTRÉAL

ⓘ

rue St-Paul

Notre-Dame-de-Bonsecours ✝

3 Place d'Youville

rue St-Paul

2 Pointe-à-Callière (Montréal Museum of Archaeology & History)

3

rue de la Commune

VIEUX-PORT

2

Marché Bonsecours (Bonsecours Market)

Quai de l'Horloge

■ Clocktower

Quai Jacques-Cartier

Quai King Edward

Quai Alexandra

St. Lawrence River

fine-arts museum. Permanent exhibits are free, and temporary shows have recently included a full-career retrospective of Yves Saint Laurent, as well as an exploration of Cuban art history. See p. 108.

❻ Rue Crescent ★★

By now, you're likely craving a stroll and a sit-down, interspersed with shopping and people-watching. Walk south on rue Crescent to get to downtown's primary nightlife district. If it's warm, take a seat on a terrace.

▨ SIR WINSTON CHURCHILL PUB

This pub has been an epicenter of the rue Crescent scene for ages, filled with chatty 20- to 40-somethings. It's a good spot to nurse a pint or two of cold beer while taking in the passing parade. 1459 rue Crescent near rue Ste-Catherine (✆ 514/288-3814). See p. 168.

To decide where to go for dinner, peruse the listings—in chapter 7—of the worthy restaurants on this and adjacent streets.

---

2 THE BEST OF MONTRÉAL IN 2 DAYS

With the absolute essentials of historic Old Montréal and downtown Anglophone cultural institutions under your belt, prepare to take a journey deep into French Montréal. Just before Montréal hosted the 1976 Olympics, municipal authorities erected some principal venues in the city's eastern, overwhelmingly Francophone precincts, which is where we start. *Start: Viau Station (take the Métro there, since a taxi would be expensive due to the distance).*

---

❶ Stade Olympique

The controversial Olympic Stadium was scorned as the "Big Owe" and then "Big Woe" due to cost overruns that provoked elevated taxes. It now houses five public pools and sports an inclined tower that's more than 175m (574 ft.) high. There's also a funicular that scoots to the observation level at the top in seconds. See p. 115.

A shuttle van carries you from the Stade Olympique to the Jardin Botanique.

❷ Jardin Botanique ★★★

This botanical garden encompasses 75 hectares (185 acres) of plants and flowers in dozens of specialized sections, including ones sponsored by China and Japan. Ten large greenhouses assure that there are sights to see all year, though May through September comprise the highlight months. Plan to spend at least an hour or two. See p. 115.

❸ Insectarium ★

Kids love the collection of live bugs, beetles, spiders, and other creepy critters here. Adults are more likely to enjoy the summer displays of gorgeous specimens in the adjacent Butterfly House. The Insectarium is on the grounds of the Jardin Botanique (see above).

Take the shuttle back to the Stade Olympique and walk to the adjacent Biodôme.

▨ LA BRISE

You might want to eat before you take on the Biodôme (see below), which can easily occupy another hour or so, especially if you have youngsters in tow. The in-house, self-serve cafeteria won't soon win any gastronomic awards, but it's serviceable.

❺ Biodôme de Montréal ★★

Originally a velodrome (cycling track) built for the 1976 Olympics, this unique facility's four sections replicate four ecosystems, complete with tropical trees and golden lion tamarins that swing on branches just an arm's length away. See p. 114.

Take the Métro to Square Victoria or Place d'Armes.

❻ St-Denis & St-Laurent ★★

After all this, it might well be time to get back to your hotel for a recuperative rest. But if you're ready to continue on, walk due north on boulevard St-Laurent (French for Saint Lawrence), which passes through the **Quartier Chinois (Chinatown),** past the western edge of **the Village,** the gay neighborhood, through the student-heavy **Quartier Latin (Latin Quarter),** and into the lower precincts of Plateau Mont-Royal. Turn right on the pedestrian rue Prince Arthur to reach rue St-Denis. Then turn north (left). There are no must-see monuments or sights along this route, so surrender to the heart of French Montréal's color and vitality.

Walking Tour 3 in chapter 9 provides guidance to some shops and restaurants along the way.

The Main, as boulevard St-Laurent is locally known, is lined with amiable places at which to bend an elbow and listen to music. The best stretch is from avenue du Mont-Royal on the north to rue Sherbrooke on the south.

---

3 THE BEST OF MONTREAL IN 3 DAYS

If you've followed the above itineraries, you've already visited Montéal's primary must-see sights. On this third day, then, you can slack off a bit, combining a morning of re-created history with idylls in the park and a ride on the St. Lawrence—tranquil or thrilling, your choice. *Start: Take the Métro to the Parc Jean-Drapeau stop. Follow the signs to the Vieux Fort and Musée David M. Stewart, about a 15-minute walk.*

❶ Ile Ste-Hélène ★

The island in the middle of the St. Lawrence River was doubled in size with landfill for Expo 67, the world's fair, to allow national pavilions to be constructed. A facility that dated from long before that event was the moated fortress ordered built by the Duke of Wellington and completed in 1824. It's now the **Musée David M. Stewart ★;** the original low stone barracks of the fort now house a museum of military history and host parades and simulated military ceremonies from late June to late August. While the island is pleasant for strolling due to its views of the downtown skyline, there's no compelling reason to stay for more than an hour or two. See p. 119.

Take the Métro to Place d'Armes and walk down to the Vieux-Port.

❷ Vieux-Port ★★

Though it was a gray, ragged industrial harbor less than 20 years ago, the Old Port at the edge of Vieux-Montréal has been transformed into a broad, linear park with several attractions of note. Principal among these is the **Centre des Sciences de Montréal** (p. 113), on King Edward Pier, which contains a popular IMAX theater in addition to room after room of interactive computer-driven displays sure to enthrall your inner geek.

At the park's east end, near the old clock tower, is the departure point for **Les Sautes-Moutons** (✆ **514/284-9607**). The company entices adventurous spirits with special flat-bottomed boats that travel upriver in wet and wild challenges on the roiling Lachine Rapids. Other companies provide more sedate river cruises.

It's also easy to rent bicycles and in-line skates by the hour or day. See p. 125.

> **☕ LE JARDIN NELSON**
>
> As you've probably noticed, Vieux-Montréal is home to a considerable number of restaurants catering to most tastes and wallets. One of the most popular is **Le Jardin Nelson** on the main square, Place Jacques-Cartier. If the weather's right, head for the garden in back, where musicians perform throughout the day. The menu offers something for everyone, from soups, sandwiches, and pizzas to a delectable roster of main-course and dessert crepes. 407 Place Jacques-Cartier (**✆ 514/861-5731**).

❹ Parc du Mont-Royal

Still have some stamina? Montréalers think of the hill that rises behind downtown as the "mountain" that gave the city its name.

The hill's rounded crest became a public park according to plans by architect **Frederick Law Olmsted** (p. 145). It draws throngs to its woods, rolling lawns, and meadows—regardless of season. You can join them with a stroll up from Peel station (if you're in reasonably good shape) or take a taxi up to Lac des Castors (Beaver Lake). See p. 146 for a walking tour.

Make your way to the mountain's southern edge as dusk approaches. A building called **Chalet du Mont-Royal** provides a sweeping view of the city from its terrace—an unforgettable panorama.

4 THE BEST OF QUÉBEC CITY IN 1 DAY

The capital of this singular province bears scant resemblance to Montréal. The oldest walled city north of Mexico's Campeche sustains the look of a provincial European city that keeps watch over the powerful St. Lawrence River. Entrancing in all seasons, it lays out a yearlong banquet of festivals and celebrations. To take greatest advantage of all the city has to offer, book a hotel or B&B within the walls of the Haute-Ville (Upper Town) or in the revitalized Basse-Ville (Lower Town). *Start: Château Frontenac.*

❶ Terrasse Dufferin ★★★

First thing after unpacking, get to **Château Frontenac** ★ (p. 210)—its peaked copper roofs are visible from everywhere in the city. In front of the hotel is a long promenade, the Terrasse Dufferin, which affords panoramic views of the Old City's **Basse-Ville (Lower Town)** ★★★ (see chapter. 13) and the wide, wide river. In good weather, street performers entertain passersby; in winter, an old-fashioned toboggan runs on the steep staircase at the south end.

❷ Funicular ★

Take the funicular down from the Terrasse Dufferin's north end. Traveling at a steep angle, it's enclosed in glass to take advantage of the views.

An alternative descent is via **L'Escalier du Casse-Cou,** which translates as "Breakneck Stairs" for reasons that are immediately apparent.

Both the funicular and the stairs wind up at rue du Petit-Champlain, a pedestrian street of shops and cafes populated largely by tourists. Save a visit to the street for later.

Continue straight ahead down rue Sous-le-Fort, and make the first left turn.

❸ Place-Royale ★★★

This small but picturesque square was the site of the first European colony in Canada and is surrounded by restored 17th- and 18th-century houses. The church on one side is **Eglise Notre-Dame-des-Victoires,** built in 1688. Walk straight ahead and you'll pass the Centre d'Interprétation de

Place-Royale on the left. At the end of the block, turn around to view a *trompe l'oeil* mural depicting citizens of the early city. See p. 235.

Continue in the same direction, making the first right turn (rue de la Barricade) down toward the river. Turn left on rue Dalhousie and follow it for a couple of blocks until you get to:

❹ Musée de la Civilisation ★★★

This ambitious museum, filled with fascinating exhibits, can easily fill 2 or 3 hours. Take in the permanent exhibit, "*People of Québec . . . Then and Now,*" which explores the province's roots as a fur-trading colony and gives visitors a rich sense of Québec's daily life over the generations. See p. 234.

After leaving, turn left, then left again, and right on rue du Sainte-au-Matelot.

🍴 A BOUNTY OF BISTROS

Within a block of the corner of rues St-Paul and du Sault-au-Matelot is a continuous strand of bistros and casual eating places. Almost any of them will do for a snack or a meal, but our top choices are **L'Echaudé ★★**, 73 rue du Sault-au-Matelot (𝄐 **418/692-1299**), and **L'Ardoise,** 71 rue St-Paul (𝄐 **418/694-0213**). Both offer excellent value for classic French dishes, and both put out sidewalk tables in summer. The former has an edge in quality and wine list; the latter is more casual and probably preferable for families. See p. 228 and 230.

After eating, continue west along St-Paul.

❻ Rue St-Paul ★ & Marché du Vieux-Port

Rue St-Paul has become a good street on which to browse and buy antiques and collectibles. At the end of the strip, turn right at rue St-Thomas and cross busy rue St-André. Over to the left is the Marché du Vieux-Port (Old Port Market). Produce and other agricultural products of the farming island of Ile d'Orléans, seen downriver beyond the market, are sold here. See p. 264.

❼ Espace 400ᵉ

To the right (south) of the market is **Espace 400ᵉ** (p. 241) a new waterfront pavilion where the Centre d'Interprétation du Vieux-Port used to be. Québec City spruced itself up for the blowout celebrations in 2008 to commemorate its 400th anniversary, and the pavilion was the celebration's hub. It now is a Parks Canada discovery center, though what exactly is going to be housed at the center was still up in the air at press time.

Retrace your steps along rue Dalhousie. Soon you'll see the dock for the ferry to Lévis, a town on the opposite shore. While the boat is intended for commuters, it makes for an inexpensive, scenic trip if you're on foot. A round-trip takes less than an hour.

From the dock, the funicular back to Upper Town is a short walk away.

---

5 THE BEST OF QUEBEC CITY IN 2 DAYS

During the repeated conflicts with the British in the 18th century, the residents of New France moved to the top of the cliffs of Cap Diamant that rise behind the river-level Basse-Ville. Over the years, they threw up fortifications with battlements and artillery emplacements that eventually encircled the city as it existed at that time. Most of them remain, albeit restored repeatedly. Along with the narrow streets, leafy plazas, and leaning houses that compose the old town, these fortifications are the reason to spend the day within the walls. ***Start:*** *Terrasse Dufferin.*

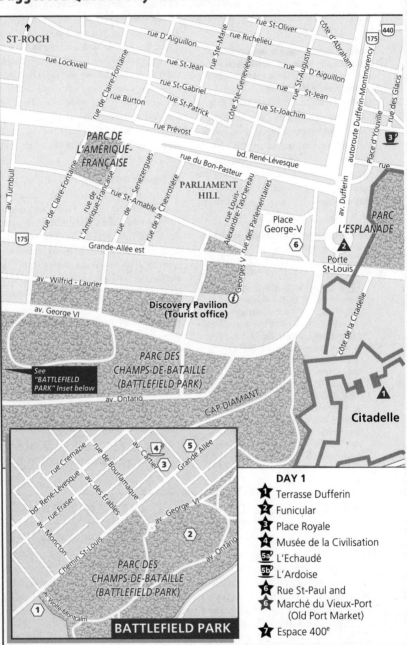

DAY 1

⭐1 Terrasse Dufferin

⭐2 Funicular

⭐3 Place Royale

⭐4 Musée de la Civilisation

⭐5a L'Echaudé

⭐5b L'Ardoise

⭐6 Rue St-Paul and

⭐6 Marché du Vieux-Port
    (Old Port Market)

⭐7 Espace 400e

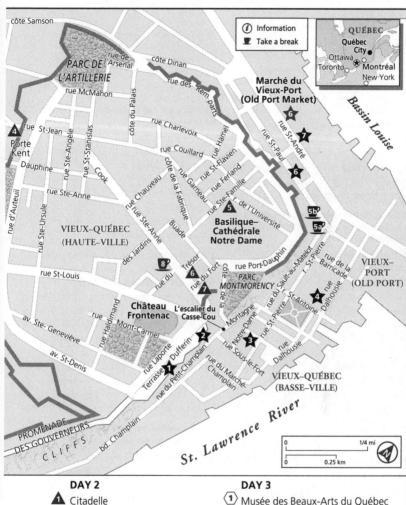

DAY 2

1 Citadelle

2 Porte St-Louis to
     Parc de l'Artillerie

3 Il Teatro

4 Rue St-Jean

5 Basilique Notre-Dame

6 Rue du Trésor

7 Musée du Fort

8 Restaurant Le Relais

DAY 3

1 Musée des Beaux-Arts du Québec

2 Parc des Champs-de-Bataille

3 Avenue Cartier

4 Café Krieghoff

5 Grande-Allée

6 Hôtel du Parlement

① La Citadelle ★★

Today, start by walking south on the Terrasse. At the end, go up the staircase to the **Promenade des Gouverneurs.** Spread below is an extension of the views seen from the Terrasse, and to the right is La Citadelle, a partially star-shaped fortress built in anticipation of an American invasion that never happened. When you reach the top, walk around the rim. The fortress has a low profile, dug into the land rather than rising above it. At the far end is a courtyard where a ceremonial changing of the guard occurs at 10am every day in summer. It can be viewed from above, saving the admission fee. See p. 235.

Walk down the hill to avenue St-Denis, continuing as it drops down to the corner of rue St-Louis, the main road into the old town.

② Porte St-Louis to Parc de l'Artillerie

The main gate in the city walls is over to the left. Near it is a gathering place for some of the city's horse-drawn carriages. If you're in the mood and are willing to shell out C$80 (£40) for fare, take a ride.

Otherwise, cross over to the long greenway known as the **Parc l'Esplanade** and continue along the walls to rue Ste-Ursule and down a steep hill to the other main gate in the wall, **Porte St-Jean** (a 20th-c. re-creation). Next to it is the entrance to Parc de l'Artillerie, recently reconstituted as a national park. On view are an officer's mess and their quarters, and an old iron foundry, shown by costumed guides.

Walk west on rue St-Jean through the gate and out of the walled city. This is **Place d'Youville,** a plaza with hotels, a concert hall, vending stalls, and an open-air venue for the concerts of the city's many festivals.

Bear right around the plaza.

☕ RISTORANTE IL TEATRO

A good bet for lunch, especially if you can snare a table out under the umbrellas on the sidewalk, is Ristorante il Teatro. It's part of Le Capitole, a hotel-theater complex. Pasta is a specialty. 972 rue St-Jean (② **418/694-9996**).

After lunch, walk back to the gate and down bustling rue St-Jean.

④ Rue St-Jean

One of the liveliest of Vieux-Québec's Haute-Ville streets, rue St-Jean is lined with an interesting variety of shops, cafes, pubs, and restaurants. A stroll down its length can easily occupy an hour or two. Read about some of the shopping possibilities here in chapter 18.

At the end of the street, bear right up Côte de la Fabrique. At the end is the:

⑤ Basilique Notre-Dame ★

What with bombardments, fires, and repeated rebuilding, this representative of the oldest Christian parish north of Mexico is nothing if not perseverant. Parts of it, including the bell tower, survive from the original 1647 building, but most of what remains is from a 1771 reconstruction. Step inside to see the blindingly bright gold leaf. See p. 239.

When leaving the church, walk left along rue Baude until you reach, on your right:

⑥ Rue du Trésor

This narrow pedestrian alley cuts up to the Place d'Armes. It's lined with the etchings, drawings, and watercolors of artists seeking tourist dollars. Nearly all the renderings are of Québec City scenes, and while they won't soon join the collections of major museums, they are competently done and make worthwhile souvenirs. See p. 252.

Turn left at the top of the alley.

❼ Musée du Fort

This daylong walk through history may have whetted your curiosity about the facts and figures of the city's past. If so, see the Musée du Fort's 25-minute multimedia show that outlines Québec City's battles and evolutions. A 36-sq.-m (400-sq.-ft.) scale model of the city with film, light, and rousing music tells the tale. See p. 241.

See p. 241.

> ### ❽ RESTAURANT LE RELAIS
> Snag an outdoor table at this restaurant in the Auberge du Trésor, a red-roofed building with a mock-Tudor façade at 16 rue Ste-Anne, half a block from the Musée du Fort. You might want to stick to coffee or a pint and save the food-related calories for one of the superior restos described in chapter 15.

6 THE BEST OF QUEBEC CITY IN 3 DAYS

While the romance of the capital is largely contained within Vieux-Québec's Lower and Upper Towns, there's much to experience outside the Old City. And though the suggested itineraries for the first 2 days can easily be extended over 3 days, especially if children and those with limited mobility are involved, do try to make time for at least one or two of the following attractions. **Start:** *Musée des Beaux-Arts.*

❶ Musée des Beaux-Arts du Québec ★★★

At the southwestern end of the Parc des Champs-de-Bataille (Battlefields Park, also known as the Plains of Abraham), the capital's most important art museum focuses on Inuit art and the works of Québec-born painters and sculptors. Jean-Paul Riopelle, one of the best-known abstract expressionists, has his own permanent exhibition. Other galleries feature works of provincial artists from the earliest days of the colony to the present. The original 1933 museum is now connected to a newer structure by a glass-roofed pavilion that houses the reception area, museum shop, and cafe. Note the presence of the latter, for you might wish to return for lunch as it is one of the area's better eateries. See p. 238.

Walk outside and around back to:

❷ Parc des Champs-de-Bataille ★★

Get some fresh air with a stroll through the 108 hectares (267 acres) that comprise Canada's first national urban park and the city's playground. Within the park are two Martello towers, cylindrical stone defensive structures built between 1808 and 1812, as well as cycling and rollerblading paths, picnic grounds, and a bandstand called **Kiosque Edwin-Bélanger** where free concerts are held in summer. See p. 239.

Go to the main street, Grand-Allée, near the Musée, and cross over to the perpendicular street av. Cartier.

❸ Avenue Cartier

Nearly opposite the museum, avenue Cartier is a street of intriguing shops and restaurants. Foodies will want to check out **Le Petit-Cartier,** 1191 av. Cartier, 1 block off Grand-Allée. The indoor mall houses shops that sell fish, meats, cheeses, produce, pâtés, and deli treats. It's open 7 days a week. Down the street is one of the city's largest **SAQ** outlets, selling a wide selection of wines and spirits. See p. 231 and 265.

☕ CAFÉ KRIEGHOFF

This cheerful cafe features an outdoor terrace a few steps up from the sidewalk. On weekend mornings it's packed with artsy locals of all ages, whose tables get piled high with bowls of café au lait and huge plates of egg dishes, sweet pastries, or classics like steak frites. 1091 av. Cartier (© **418/522-3711**). See p. 231.

➎ Grande-Allée

Walk back to Grande-Allée and turn left to head back to the Old City. It's a lot easier this way, as it's mostly downhill. After about 3 blocks, the shoulder-to-shoulder rows of cafes and clubs begin, with one of the largest on the right, **Maurice** (p. 268). Keep it in mind for this evening; it's a one-stop dining and entertainment emporium with terrace bars, a good restaurant, **Voo Doo Grill ★** (p. 231), and a disco.

Continue on Grand-Allée to the commanding Second Empire château on your left:

➏ Hôtel du Parlement

This august structure houses the provincial legislative body that Québécois proudly proclaim their National Assembly. You can tour the building on your own, but guided tours are available weekdays year-round from 9am to 4:30pm, and weekends in summer from 10am to 4:30pm. Go to door no. 3 to enter. Among the best sights are the Assembly Chamber and the Room of the Old Legislative Council. See p. 242.

As you exit, the walls of the Old City will be directly in front of you.

Getting to Know Montréal

Getting oriented in Montréal is remarkably easy. The airport is only 23km (14 miles) away at most, and once you're in town, the Métro (subway) is fast and efficient.

Walking, of course, is the best way to enjoy and appreciate this vigorous, multidimensional city. Take it in, neighborhood by neighborhood.

---

1 ORIENTATION

ARRIVING

BY PLANE   The **Aéroport International Pierre-Elliot-Trudeau de Montréal** (① **800/ 465-1213** or 514/394-7377; www.admtl.com; airport code YUL), known less cumbersomely as Montréal-Trudeau Airport, is 23km (14 miles) southwest of downtown. A C$716-million (£358-million) expansion was completed in 2006, and the terminal is now twice its old size and features a new Customs Hall. Note that Montréal-Trudeau used to be called Montréal-Dorval, and some older maps and guides still use that name. Also, Aéroport Mirabel, 55km (34 miles) northwest of the city, is an all-cargo facility.

Montréal-Trudeau is served by **L'Aérobus** (① **514/216-8591**), a shuttle bus which travels between the airport and downtown, stopping at **Berri Terminal** (also known as the **Station Centrale d'Autobus,** the city's main bus terminal). Buses run every 30 minutes daily from 4:30am to 1:30am. One-way fares are C$14 (£7) for adults, C$13 (£6.50) for seniors, and C$11 (£5.50) for children. The ride takes about 30 minutes.

A taxi trip to downtown Montréal costs a flat fare of C$35 (£18) plus tip. Other destinations are charged by meter.

BY TRAIN   Montréal has one intercity rail terminus, **Gare Centrale (Central Station),** 895 rue de la Gauchetière ouest (① **514/989-2626**), below Fairmont The Queen Elizabeth hotel. The station is connected to the Métro subway system at **Bonaventure Station.** (Gare Windsor, which you might see on some maps, is the city's former train station. It's a beautiful castlelike building now used for offices.)

BY BUS   The central bus station, called **Station Centrale d'Autobus** (① **514/842-2281**), is at 505 bd. de Maisonneuve est. It has a bar, a cafeteria, and an information booth. Beneath the terminal is **Berri-UQAM Station,** the junction of several important Métro lines and a good starting point for trips to most quarters of the city. (UQAM—pronounced "*Oo*-kahm"—stands for Université de Québec à Montréal.) Alternatively, **taxis** usually line up outside the terminal building.

BY CAR   For driving directions to Montréal, see "Getting There & Getting Around," in chapter 3. If you come over Pont Champlain, the main bridge, you'll likely be greeted by one of its charming LED messages, such as "Someone loves you, drive with care" and "Carpooling is an interesting energy saver."

Tips Montréal: Where the Sun Rises in the South

For the duration of your visit to Montréal, you'll need to accept local directional conventions, strange as they may seem. The city borders the St. Lawrence River, and as far as locals are concerned, that's south, looking toward the U.S. Never mind that the river, in fact, runs almost north and south at that point. For this reason, it has been observed that Montréal is the only city in the world where the sun rises in the south. Don't fight it: Face the river. That's south. Turn around. That's north. *Tout est clair?*

To ease the confusion, the directions given throughout the Montréal chapters conform to this local directional tradition. However, the maps in this book also have the true compass on them.

When examining a map of the city, note that prominent thoroughfares such as rue Ste-Catherine and boulevard René-Lévesque are said to run either "east" or "west," with the dividing line being boulevard St-Laurent, which runs "north" and "south." For streets that run east and west, the numbers start at St-Laurent and then *go in both directions*. They're labeled either *est,* for east, or *ouest,* for west. That means, for instance, that an address at 500 *est* is actually blocks and blocks from 501 *ouest*—and not directly across the street.

VISITOR INFORMATION

The main tourist center for visitors in downtown Montréal is the large **Infotouriste Centre,** at 1255 rue Peel (© **877/266-5687** or 514/873-2015; Métro: Peel). It's open daily and the bilingual staff can provide suggestions for accommodations, dining, car rentals, and attractions.

In Vieux-Montréal, there's a small **Tourist Information Office** at 174 rue Notre-Dame est, at the corner of Place Jacques-Cartier (Métro: Champ-de-Mars). It's open daily in warmer months, Wednesday through Sunday in winter, and proffers brochures, maps, and a helpful staff.

The city of Montréal maintains a terrific website at **www.tourisme-montreal.org**.

CITY LAYOUT

For a map of greater Montréal, see the color insert at the front of this guide.

MAIN ARTERIES & STREETS   In downtown Montréal, the principal east-west streets include boulevard René-Lévesque, rue Ste-Catherine (*rue* is the French word for "street"), boulevard de Maisonneuve, and rue Sherbrooke. The north-south arteries include rue Crescent, rue McGill, rue St-Denis, and boulevard St-Laurent, which serves as the line of demarcation between east and west Montréal. Most of the downtown areas featured in this book lie west of boulevard St-Laurent.

In Plateau Mont-Royal, northeast of the downtown area, major streets are avenue du Mont-Royal and avenue Laurier.

In Vieux-Montréal, rue St-Jacques, rue Notre-Dame, and rue St-Paul are the main thoroughfares, along with rue de la Commune, the waterfront road that hugs the promenade bordering the St. Lawrence River.

FINDING AN ADDRESS   As outlined above, boulevard St-Laurent is the dividing point between east and west (*est* and *ouest*) in Montréal. There's no equivalent division for north and south (*nord* and *sud*)—the numbers start at the river and climb from there, just as the topography does. The odd numbers are to the east and the even numbers are to the west. Make sure you know your east from your west, and confirm the cross street for all addresses.

In earlier days, Montréal was split geographically along cultural lines. Those who spoke English lived predominantly west of boulevard St-Laurent, while French speakers were concentrated to the east. Things still do sound more French as you walk east: Street names and Métro station names change from Peel and Atwater to Papineau and Beaudry.

THE NEIGHBORHOODS IN BRIEF

Centre Ville/Downtown This area contains the Montréal skyline's most dramatic elements and includes most of the city's large luxury and first-class hotels, principal museums, corporate headquarters, main transportation hubs, and department stores.

The district is loosely bounded by rue Sherbrooke to the north, boulevard René-Lévesque to the south, boulevard St-Laurent to the east, and rue Drummond to the west.

Within this neighborhood is the area often called "the Golden Square Mile," an Anglophone district once characterized by dozens of mansions erected by the wealthy Scottish and English merchants and industrialists who dominated the city's political and social life well into the 20th century. Many of those stately homes were torn down when skyscrapers began to rise here after World War II, but some remain. At downtown's northern edge is the urban campus of prestigious McGill University, which retains its Anglophone identity.

Vieux-Montréal The city was born here in 1642, down by the river at Pointe-à-Callière. Today, especially in summer, most people converge around Place Jacques-Cartier, where cafe tables line narrow terraces. This is where street performers, strolling locals, and tourists congregate.

The area is larger than it might seem at first. It's bounded on the north by rue St-Antoine, once the "Wall Street" of Montréal and still home to some banks. Its southern boundary is the Vieux-Port (Old Port), a waterfront promenade bordering rue de la Commune that provides welcome breathing room for cyclists, in-line skaters, and picnickers. To the east, Vieux-Montréal is bordered by rue Berri and to the west, by rue McGill.

Several small but intriguing museums are housed in historic buildings, and the district's architectural heritage has been substantially preserved. Restored 18th- and 19th-century structures have been adapted for use as shops, boutique hotels, studios, galleries, cafes, bars, offices, and apartments. In the evening, many of the finer buildings are beautifully illuminated. In the summer, sections of rue St-Paul and rue Notre Dame turn into pedestrian-only walkways. The neighborhood's official website is **www.vieux.montreal.qc.ca**; at press time, it included a live webcam of Place Jacques-Cartier.

Plateau Mont-Royal This is where Montréalers feel most at home—away from downtown's chattering pace and the more touristed Vieux-Montréal. It's where they come to shop, dine, and play.

Bounded roughly by boulevard St-Joseph to the north, rue Sherbrooke to the south, avenue Papineau to the east, and rue St-Urbain to the west, the Plateau has a vibrant ethnic atmosphere that fluctuates with each new immigration surge.

Rue St-Denis runs the length of the district and is to Montréal what boulevard St-Germain is to Paris, while boulevard St-Laurent, running parallel, has a more polyglot flavor.

Known as "the Main," St-Laurent was the boulevard first encountered by foreigners tumbling off ships at the waterfront. They simply shouldered their belongings and walked north, peeling off into adjoining streets when they heard familiar tongues or smelled the drifting aromas of food reminiscent of the old country. New arrivals still come here to start their lives in Canada.

Without its gumbo of languages and cultures, St-Laurent would be an urban eyesore. But its ground-floor windows are filled with glistening golden chickens, collages of shoes and pastries and aluminum cookware, curtains of sausages, and the daringly far-fetched garments of those designers on the forward edge of Montréal's active fashion industry.

Many warehouses and former tenements have been converted to house this panoply of shops, bars, and high- and low-cost eateries, their often-garish signs drawing eyes away from the still-dilapidated upper stories. See p. 141 for a walking tour of this fascinating neighborhood.

Parc du Mont-Royal Not many cities have a mountain at their core. True, reality insists that Montréal doesn't either, as what it calls a "mountain" most other people would call a large hill. Still, Montréal is named for this outcrop—the "Royal Mountain."

It's a soothing urban pleasure to drive, walk, or take a horse-drawn *calèche* to the top for a view of the city and its river.

The famous American landscape architect Frederick Law Olmsted designed Parc du Mont-Royal, which opened in 1876.

On its far slope are two cemeteries, one that used to be Anglophone and Protestant, the other Francophone and Catholic—reminders of the linguistic and religious division that persists in the city.

With its trails for strolling, hiking, and cross-country skiing, the park is well used by Montréalers, who refer to it simply and affectionately as "the Mountain."

Rue Crescent One of Montréal's major dining and nightlife districts lies in the western shadow of the massed phalanxes of downtown skyscrapers. While a few streets on its northern end house luxury boutiques in Victorian brownstones, its southern end holds dozens of restaurants, bars, and clubs of all styles between Sherbrooke and René-Lévesque, and spilling over onto neighboring streets.

The quarter's Anglophone origins are evident in the street names: Stanley, Drummond, Crescent, Bishop, and MacKay.

The party atmosphere that pervades after dark never quite fades, and builds to crescendos as weekends approach, especially in warm weather, when the area's largely 20- and 30-something denizens spill out into sidewalk cafes and onto balcony terraces.

The Village Also known as the Gay Village, the city's gay and lesbian enclave is one of North America's largest. This compact but vibrant district is filled with clothing stores, antiques shops, dance clubs, and cafes.

It runs east along rue Ste-Catherine from rue St-Hubert to rue Papineau and onto side streets.

In 2008, for the first time, the city made the entire length of rue Ste-Catherine in the neighborhood pedestrian-only for the entire summer, and bars and restaurants built ad-hoc terraces into the street.

A rainbow, the symbol of the gay community, marks the **Beaudry Station,** which is on rue Ste-Catherine in the heart of the neighborhood.

St-Denis Rue St-Denis, which runs from the Latin Quarter downtown near rue Ste-Catherine est and continues north into the Plateau Mont-Royal district, is the thumping central artery of Francophone Montréal, thick with cafes, bistros, offbeat shops, and lively nightspots.

At its southern end, near the concrete campus of the Université du Québec à Montréal (UQAM), the avenue is decidedly student oriented, with indie rock cranked up in the inexpensive bars and clubs, and kids in jeans and leather swapping philosophical insights and telephone numbers. It is rife with the visual messiness that characterizes student and bohemian quarters.

Farther north, above Sherbrooke, a raffish quality persists along the rows of three- and four-story Victorian houses, but the average age of residents and visitors nudges past 30. Prices are higher, too, and some of the city's better restaurants are here.

This is a district in which to take in the pulse of Francophone life, not for absorbing art and culture of the refined sort, for there are no museums or important galleries on St-Denis, nor is the architecture notable. But, then, that relieves visitors of the chore of obligatory

sightseeing and allows them to take in the passing scene—just as the locals do—over bowls of café au lait at any of the numerous terraces that line the avenue.

Mile End Adjoining Plateau Mont-Royal at its upper west corner, this blossoming neighborhood is contained by rue St-Laurent on the east, avenue Du Parc on the west, rue Bernard in the north, and boulevard St-Joseph on the south. Though it's outside of the usual tourist orbit, it has a growing number of retail attractions, including designer clothing stores and places at which to buy household goods.

Mile End has pockets of many ethnic mini-neighborhoods, including Italian, Portuguese, Armenian, Hassidic, and Greek. An area some still call Greektown is along avenue du Parc, largely in the form of restaurants and taverns.

Mile End has seen a surge of worthwhile restaurants in recent years, several of which are reviewed in chapter 7.

Ile Ste-Hélène & Ile Notre-Dame St. Helen's Island in the St. Lawrence River was altered extensively to become the site of Expo 67, Montréal's very successful world's fair. In the 4 years before the Expo, construction crews doubled its surface area with landfill and then went on to create beside it an island that hadn't existed before, Ile Notre-Dame. Much of the earth for this was dredged up from the bottom of the St. Lawrence River, and 15 million tons of rock from the excavations for the Métro and the Décarie Expressway were carried in by truck.

When the world's fair was over, the city preserved the site and a few of its exhibition buildings. Parts were used for the 1976 Olympics, and today, Ile Ste-Hélène is home to an amusement park, La Ronde (p. 121), as well as the popular Casino de Montréal (p. 170).

Every June, the Grand Prix of Canada is held on the racing track on Ile Notre-Dame.

Connected by two bridges, the islands now comprise the recently designated **Parc Jean-Drapeau,** which is almost entirely car-free and accessible by Métro.

Quartier International When Route 720 was constructed some years ago, it left behind a desolate swath of derelict buildings, parking lots, and empty spaces smack-dab between downtown and Vieux- Montréal.

Bounded, more or less, by rue St-Antoine on the south, avenue Viger on the north, rue St-Urbain on the east, and rue University on the west, this no-man's land is slowly being spruced up with new parks, office buildings, and a recently expanded **Palais des Congrès (Convention Center).**

A small plaza, opposite the convention center's west end, is named for Jean-Paul-Piopelle, a prominent Québec artist, since one of his sculptures stands there.

The Quartier incorporates the World Trade Center Montréal, a complex of brokerage houses, law firms, and import-export companies.

Chinatown Tucked just north of Vieux-Montréal, centered on the intersection of rue Clark and the pedestrianized section of rue de la Gauchetière, Chinatown is mostly comprised of restaurants and a tiny park. The fancy gates to the area on boulevard St-Laurent are guarded by white stone lions.

Community spirit is strong and inhabitants remain faithful to their traditions despite the encroaching modernism all around them.

The Underground City During Montréal's long winters, life slows on the streets of downtown as people escape into *la ville souterraine,* a parallel subterranean universe. Down there, in a controlled climate that recalls an eternal spring, it's possible to arrive at the railroad station, check into a hotel, shop, go out for dinner, see a movie, attend a concert—all without donning an overcoat or putting on snow boots.

This underground city evolved when major downtown developments—such as Place Ville-Marie (the city's first skyscraper), Place Bonaventure, Complexe Desjardins, Palais des Congrès, and Place des Arts—put their below-street-level areas to profitable use, leasing space for shops and other enterprises. Over time, in fits and starts and with no master plan, these spaces became connected with Métro stations and then with each other. It became possible to ride long distances and walk the shorter ones, through mazes of corridors, tunnels, and plazas. Today, there are 938 retailers, 362 eateries, and 13 cinemas in or connected to the network.

Admittedly, the term "underground city" is not entirely accurate because of how some complexes funnel people through their own spaces. In Place Bonaventure, for instance, passengers may leave the Métro and wander on the same level only to find themselves peering out a window several floors above the street.

The city beneath the city has obvious advantages, including no traffic accidents and avoidance of winter slush (or summer rain). Natural light is let in wherever possible, which drastically reduces the feeling of claustrophobia that some malls evoke. However, the underground city covers a vast area, without the convenience of a logical street grid, and can be confusing. There are plenty of signs, but it's wise to make careful note of landmarks at key corners along your route. Expect to get lost anyway—but, being that you're in an underground maze, consider it part of the fun.

(Fun Facts) July 1: Citywide Moving Day

Montréal is an island of renters, and close to 100,000 of them move from old apartments to new ones every July 1—on that date, and only that date. It coincides with Canada's National Day, ensuring that separatist-minded Francophone Québécois won't have time to celebrate a holiday they have no intention of observing anyway.

All but certain to be miserably hot and humid, July 1 is a trial that can, nevertheless, be hilarious to observe. You'll see families struggling to get bedroom sets and large appliances down narrow outdoor staircases, and watch as sidewalks become obstacle courses of baby cribs, bicycles, and overflowing cardboard boxes. A cacophony of horns arises as streets become clogged with every serviceable van, truck, and SUV.

Later in the day, hundreds of people arrive at their new digs and discover gifts of junk no longer desired by their predecessors—busted furniture, pantries of old food, pitiful plants.

No one can explain why reason didn't prevail long ago in the form of a mandated staggered schedule. Unless you're interested in simply observing the mayhem, you'll want to either be someplace else on that day, or put on a strong backpack to wear while walking around for some good trash picking.

2 GETTING AROUND

See "Getting Around Montréal" on p. 33.

Where to Stay in Montréal

Accommodations in Montréal range from grand boulevard skyscrapers to converted row houses to stylish inns and boutique luxury hotels—the latter of which are appearing in ever-increasing numbers, especially in Vieux-Montréal.

B&Bs boast cozier settings than many hotels, often (but not always) at lower prices than comparable hotels. They also give visitors the opportunity to get to know a Montréaler or two, since their owners are among the most outgoing and knowledgeable guides one might want. Information is available from the **Bed & Breakfast Downtown Network,** 3458 av. Laval (at rue Sherbrooke), Montréal, PQ H2X 3C8 (© **800/267-5180** or 514/289-9749; www.bbmontreal.qc.ca).

The rules at B&Bs can vary significantly, so ask pertinent questions upfront, such as whether children are welcome or if bathrooms are shared (rooms with private bathrooms are generally more expensive than those with shared facilities).

Except in B&Bs, visitors can almost always find discounts and package deals. That's especially the case on weekends, when business clients have already left.

See "Tips Regarding Accommodations," in chapter 3 for more lodging suggestions.

STAR SYSTEM The tourist authorities in Québec province have a six-level rating system (zero to five stars) for all establishments offering six or more rooms to travelers. An ocher-and-brown shield bearing the assigned rating is posted near the entrance to most hotels and inns. The Québec system is based on quantitative measures such as the range of services and amenities. No star is assigned to properties that meet only the basic minimum standards, while five stars are reserved for establishments deemed exceptional. Most of the recommendations below have gotten at least three stars from the state system.

The stars you see in the reviews in this chapter are based on Frommer's own rating system, which assigns between zero and three stars. The Frommer's ratings are more subjective than the state's, taking into account such considerations as price-to-value ratios, quality of service, ambience, location, helpfulness of staff, and the presence of such facilities as spas and exercise rooms.

RATES The rates quoted in the listings in this chapter are "rack rates"—the standard rates charged for double-occupancy rooms. These rates are used to divide the hotels into four price categories, ranging from "Very Expensive" to "Inexpensive," for easy reference. Remember that rack rates are only guidelines, and that you can often find better deals.

Hotel rates are highest during the region's busiest times, from May to October, reaching a peak in July and August. Rates also inflate during the frequent summer festivals, annual holidays (Canadian *and* American), Grand Prix days in Montréal in June, and winter carnivals in January and February. (Festivals and dates are listed in "Montréal and Québec City Calendar of Events" in chapter 3.) For those periods, reserve well in advance, especially if you're looking for special rates or packages.

The hotels listed below are near most attractions in downtown and Vieux-Montréal. The listings are categorized first by neighborhood, then by price.

All rooms have private bathrooms unless otherwise noted. Many of the more luxurious hotels have stopped providing in-room coffeemakers, so ask in advance if this feature is important to you. Most hotels provide Wi-Fi in either part of or all of their facilities, although this continues to be a work in progress for many properties; if you need it, ask whether your hotel provides it before reserving a room.

Most Montréal hotels are entirely non-smoking. Those that aren't have a limited number of smoking rooms available; check with the hotel before booking.

TAXES Most goods and services in Canada are taxed 5% by the federal government (the GST, or Goods and Services Tax). On top of that, the province of Québec adds an additional 7.5% tax (the TVQ). A 3% accommodations tax (which goes toward promoting tourism) is in effect in Montréal. Prices listed in this book do not include taxes.

1 BEST HOTEL BETS

- **Best Boutique Hotel (Downtown): Hôtel Le Germain,** 2050 rue Mansfield (② 877/333-2050 or 514/849-2050), brought a needed jolt of panache to the downtown business-hotel scene when it opened in 1999 and has added to its allure with its 2007 opening of the restaurant **Laurie Raphaël Montréal.** See p. 70.
- **Best Boutique Hotels (Vieux-Montréal):** The **Hôtel Le St-James,** 355 rue St-Jacques ouest, Vieux-Montréal (② 866/841-3111 or 514/841-3111), raises the bar to an almost impossibly high level and has a superbly sybaritic spa and gorgeous grand hall. See p. 76. The **Hôtel Nelligan,** 106 rue St-Paul ouest, Vieux-Montréal (② 877/788-2040 or 514/788-2040), which expanded from 63 to 105 units in 2007, counters with a popular rooftop terrace. See p. 79.
- **Best Historic Hotel: Fairmont The Queen Elizabeth,** 900 bd. René-Lévesque ouest (② 866/540-4483 or 514/861-3511), marked its 50th anniversary in 2008 and was one of North America's first hotels with escalators, central air-conditioning, and direct-dial phones in each room. Its reception lobby still impresses. (The venerable **Ritz-Carlton Montréal,** at 1228 rue Sherbrooke ouest, is getting a 15-month renovation that has shut it down until October 2009.) See p. 71 and 75.
- **Best Hotel for Business Travelers (Expensive): Sofitel Montréal Golden Mile,** 1155 rue Sherbrooke ouest (② 514/285-9000), the first Canadian branch of the pervasive French luxury hotel chain, has floor-to-ceiling windows, easy-to-use thrust-desks, a well-appointed exercise room open 24 hours, and a good restaurant with a pretty bar and outdoor terrace. See p. 70.
- **Best Hotel for Business Travelers (Discount): Hôtel Le Dauphin,** 1025 rue de Bleury (② 888/784-3888 or 514/788-3888), adjacent to the convention center and a few blocks from Vieux-Montréal's northern end, offers big-hotel touches at a small-budget price. See p. 75.
- **Best Hotels for a Romantic Getaway:** So many options. **Hostellerie Pierre du Calvet,** 405 rue Bonsecours (② 866/544-1725 or 514/282-1725), has ancient cut-stone walls, swags of velvet and brocade, and tilting floors that Benjamin Franklin once trod upon; the entire effect is reminiscent of lovers' hotels by the Seine. Meanwhile,

Auberge du Vieux-Port, 97 rue de la Commune est (✆ **888/660-7678** or 514/876-0081), offers a different kind of retreat: hideaway bedrooms, many with unobstructed views of the waterfront. See p. 77.

- **Best Design Hotels: St. Paul Hotel,** 355 rue McGill (✆ **866/380-2202** or 514/380-2222), softens its austere lines with pale-cream walls, while the **Hotel Gault,** at 449 rue Ste-Hélène (✆ **866/904-1616** or 514/904-1616), leaves its raw concrete walls uncovered and incorporates candy-colored furniture. See p. 79 and 80.

- **Best B&B:** In a 1723 structure in Vieux-Montréal, **Auberge Les Passants du Sans Soucy,** 171 rue St-Paul ouest (✆ **514/842-2634**), is more upscale and stylish than most of its peers, and it's near the Old City's top restaurants and clubs. See p. 80.

- **Best Hotel Breakfast:** At **Auberge Bonaparte,** 447 rue St-François-Xavier (✆ **514/844-1448**), breakfasts are large and, better yet, served in the elegant Bonaparte restaurant. See p. 80.

- **Best Service at a Hotel:** It's tough to choose among the troops at the **Hôtel Le St-James,** 355 rue St-Jacques ouest, Vieux-Montréal (✆ **866/841-3111** or 514/841-3111), and the **Hotel InterContinental Montréal,** 360 rue St-Antoine ouest (✆ **514/987-9900**). Both teams display an almost equal amount of grace and care when it comes to tending to their guests. See p. 76 and 78.

2 CENTRE VILLE/DOWNTOWN

VERY EXPENSIVE

Hôtel Le Germain ★★★　This undertaking by the owner of Québec City's equally desirable boutique hotel, **Dominion 1912** (p. 216), brought a big shot of panache to the downtown lodging scene when it opened in 1999, and it added to its allure with the 2007 opening of **Laurie Raphaël Montréal** inside the hotel. The restaurant is an offshoot of hotshot chef Daniel Vézina's much-esteemed restaurant of the same name in Québec City. The vibe in the hotel is one of a stylish loft, achieved through that magical mix of Asian minimalism and Western comforts: plush bedding, ergonomic work areas, wicker chairs with fat cushions, self-serve breakfasts of perfect croissants and café au lait, and a lobby fireplace.

2050 rue Mansfield (at av. du President-Kennedy), Montréal, PQ H3A 1Y9. ✆ **877/333-2050** or 514/849-2050. Fax 514/849-1437. www.hotelgermain.com. 101 units. C$210–C$475 (£105–£238) double. Packages available. Rates include breakfast. AE, DC, MC, V. Valet parking C$23 (£12). Métro: Peel. Pets accepted, C$30 (£15) a night. **Amenities:** Restaurant; bar; exercise room; concierge; room service; babysitting. *In room:* A/C, TV, CD player, free Wi-Fi, minibar, hair dryer.

Sofitel Montréal Golden Mile ★★　The French luxury hotel chain transformed a bland 1970s downtown office tower into a coveted destination for visiting celebrities and the power elite. It wows from the moment of arrival, from the light-filled stone-and-wood lobby to the universally warm welcome visitors get from the staff. The 100 standard rooms (called "Superior") have floor-to-ceiling windows, furnishings made from Québec-grown cherrywood, down duvets, and a soothing oatmeal-cream decor featuring black-and-white photos of Montréal by local photographers. Though chairs with right-angled backs are a bit too overdesigned for comfort, the thrust-desks attached to the wall are easy to use from either side. Bathrooms have an Asian touch. The ambitious **Renoir** restaurant (p. 88) features a bar and outdoor terrace. Catering to the international and

Tips **Keep Up Your Workout Schedule**

Don't want to slack off on your fitness routine just because you're on vacation? If you're staying at a hotel that doesn't have a fitness center or whose exercise room is modest, keep upscale **Club Sportiff MAA** in mind. Located downtown at rue Peel between rue Sherbrooke and boulevard De Maisonneuve, this 743-sq.-m (8,000-sq.-ft), state-of-the-art gym provides cardio and strength-training equipment, a lap pool, and a full schedule of back-to-back classes in everything from spinning to Pilates to ashtanga yoga. A few hotels, like Loews Hôtel Vogue, provide free passes to their overnight guests. For everyone else, day passes are available for C$20 (£10) for adults and C$10 (£5) for children 17 and younger. Information is at ℂ **514/845-2233** and www.clubsportifmaa.com.

business guests whose bodies are still operating on different time zones, the exercise room is open 24 hours per day.

1155 rue Sherbrooke ouest (at Peel), Montréal, PQ H3A 2N3. ℂ **514/285-9000.** Fax 514/289-1155. www. sofitel.com. 258 units. C$185–C$400 (£93–£200) double; suites from C$295 (£148). Packages available. AE, DC, MC, V. Valet parking C$26 (£13). Métro: Peel. Pets accepted. **Amenities:** Restaurant; bar; 24-hr. exercise room w/sauna; concierge; Wi-Fi in lobby and restaurant; room service; babysitting. *In room:* A/C, TV, CD player, high-speed Internet, minibar, hair dryer.

EXPENSIVE

Fairmont The Queen Elizabeth (Le Reine Elizabeth) ★★   Montréal's largest hotel—it has more than 1,000 rooms—stacks its 21 floors atop VIA Rail's Gare Centrale, the main train station, with the Métro and popular shopping areas such as Place Ville-Marie and Place Bonaventure accessible through underground arcades. This desirable location makes "the Queenie" a frequent choice for heads of state and touring celebrities, even though other hotels in town offer more luxurious pampering. The Fairmont Gold 18th and 19th floors, on which anyone can stay—for a price—are the best choice, offering a private concierge lounge with complimentary breakfasts and cocktail-hour canapés. Less exalted rooms on floors 4 through 17 are satisfactory, furnished traditionally and feature easy chairs, ottomans, and bright reading lamps. A full on-site spa was renovated in 2006. February 2009 marks the 40th anniversary of John Lennon and Yoko Ono's weeklong "Bed-in for Peace" in suite no. 1742.

900 bd. René-Lévesque ouest (at rue Mansfield), Montréal, PQ H3B 4A5. ℂ **866/540-4483** or 514/861-3511. Fax 514/954-2296. www.fairmont.com/queenelizabeth. 1,039 units. C$229–C$349 (£115–£175) double; C$329 (£180) and up suite. Children 18 and younger stay free in parent's room. Packages available. AE, DC, MC, V. Valet parking C$26 (£13). Métro: Bonaventure. Pets accepted. **Amenities:** 3 restaurants; 2 bars; heated indoor pool; exceptional health club and spa w/Jacuzzi, steam room, and instructors; concierge; room service; babysitting; executive level. *In room:* A/C, TV, high-speed Internet, hair dryer.

Hôtel de la Montagne ★   Two white lion sculptures stand sentinel at the front door, and a crowded lobby incorporates a pair of gold-colored crocodile sculptures and a nude female figure with stained-glass butterfly wings sitting atop a splashing fountain. Welcome to Montréal, Vegas-style! The hotel offers a bit of old-fashioned pizzazz that others

WHERE TO STAY IN MONTRÉAL

6

CENTRE VILLE/DOWNTOWN

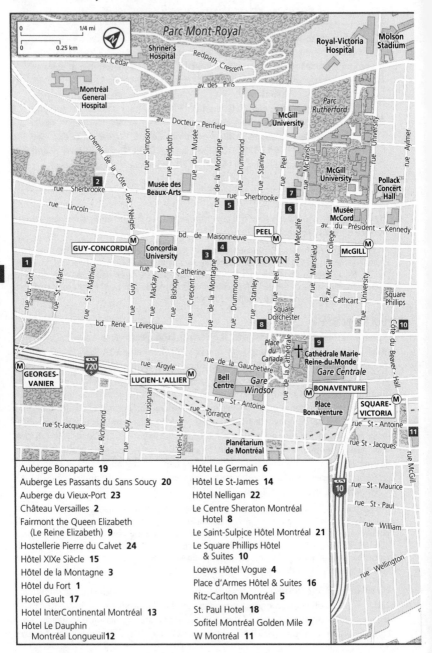

Auberge Bonaparte **19**
Auberge Les Passants du Sans Soucy **20**
Auberge du Vieux-Port **23**
Château Versailles **2**
Fairmont the Queen Elizabeth
  (Le Reine Elizabeth) **9**
Hostellerie Pierre du Calvet **24**
Hôtel XIXe Siècle **15**
Hôtel de la Montagne **3**
Hôtel du Fort **1**
Hotel Gault **17**
Hotel InterContinental Montréal **13**
Hôtel Le Dauphin
  Montréal Longueuil**12**

Hôtel Le Germain **6**
Hôtel Le St-James **14**
Hôtel Nelligan **22**
Le Centre Sheraton Montréal
  Hotel **8**
Le Saint-Sulpice Hôtel Montréal **21**
Le Square Phillips Hôtel
  & Suites **10**
Loews Hôtel Vogue **4**
Place d'Armes Hôtel & Suites **16**
Ritz-Carlton Montréal **5**
St. Paul Hotel **18**
Sofitel Montréal Golden Mile **7**
W Montréal **11**

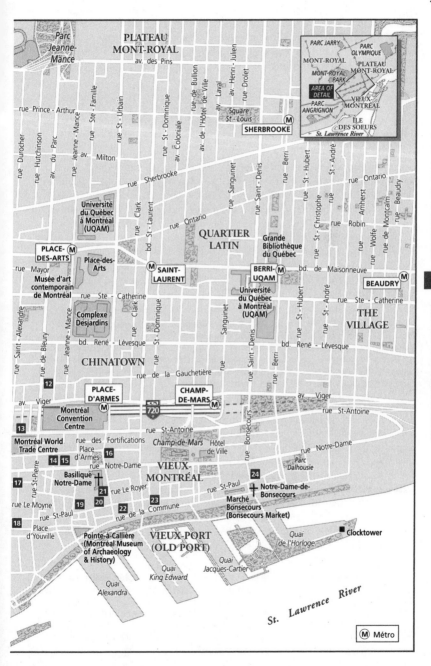

don't, including lunches at the rooftop pool and a cabaret lounge enhanced by a piano player and jazz duos on weekends. It's also home to **Thursday's** (p. 168), a singles bar and restaurant with a spangly disco and a terrace opening onto lively rue Crescent. After all that, the relatively serene bedrooms seem downright bland, but they're clean and include good-size bathrooms and high-end bedding. Rooms were being renovated in 2008, so some have benefited from a sleek update (these cost more), while others have the older decor.

1430 rue de la Montagne (north of rue Ste-Catherine), Montréal, PQ H3G 1Z5. © **800/361-6262** or 514/288-5656. Fax 514/288-9658. www.hoteldelamontagne.com. 143 units. C$185–C$269 (£93–£135) double. Packages available. AE, DC, DISC, MC, V. Valet parking C$15, for SUV C$30 (£7.50 or £15). Métro: Peel. **Amenities:** 2 restaurants; 3 bars; heated outdoor pool; concierge; room service. *In room:* A/C, TV, free Wi-Fi, minibar, hair dryer.

Le Centre Sheraton Montreal Hotel ★

Ever bustling, this branch of the familiar brand goes about its business with efficiency and surety of purpose. That figures, since earnest people in suits make up most of the clientele. They gravitate toward the Club Rooms, which include a free breakfast and a private lounge with expansive views and evening hors d'oeuvres. Regular guest rooms are decorated in modest corporate style but are clean and have good beds. The health club includes an indoor pool, a sauna, a fully equipped fitness center with skylights, a massage studio, and a landscaped summer terrace. True to its name, this hotel has a central downtown location that's near Dorchester Square, Gare Centrale (the main train station), and the high-stepping rue Crescent dining and nightlife district.

1201 bd. René-Lévesque ouest (between rue Drummond and rue Stanley), Montréal, PQ H3B 2L7. © **800/325-3535** or 514/878-2000. Fax 514/878-3958. www.sheraton.com/lecentre. 825 units. C$199–C$329 (£100–£165) double; C$349 (£175) and up suite. Children 16 and younger stay free in parent's room. Packages available. AE, DC, DISC, MC, V. Valet parking C$26 (£13), self-parking C$20 (£10). Métro: Bonaventure. If you're driving, note that the entrance is on rue Drummond. Pets accepted. **Amenities:** 2 restaurants; bar; indoor pool; health club and spa; concierge; room service; babysitting; executive-level floors. *In room:* A/C, TV, high-speed Internet, minibar, hair dryer.

Loews Hôtel Vogue ★★

When the Vogue opened in 1990, it instantly joined the Ritz-Carlton at the top tier of the local luxury-hotel pantheon. Nearly 20 years on, confidence and capability continues to resonate from every member of its staff, and luxury permeates the hotel from the lobby to the well-appointed guest rooms. Feather pillows and duvets dress oversize beds, and huge marble bathrooms are fitted with Jacuzzis—double-size in suites—and separate shower stalls. Rooms all have consistent decor, so what you see on the website is what you'll get when you arrive. The hotel's **L'Opéra Bar** is a two-story room with floor-to-ceiling windows and is open until 2am. For families, Loews offers special kids' menus, free in-room movies, and child-size bathrobes. The only sour note is something common to many Montréal properties in busy neighborhoods: The street noise—including shrieks from late-night partiers—sometimes travels to rooms, even on top floors.

1425 rue de la Montagne (near rue Ste-Catherine), Montréal, PQ H3G 1Z3. © **888/465-6654** or 514/285-5555. Fax 514/849-8903. www.loewshotels.com. 142 units. High season C$249–C$269 (£125–£135) double, C$369 (£185) suite; from C$179 (£90) low season. Children 17 or younger stay free in parent's room. Packages available. AE, DC, DISC, MC, V. Valet parking C$30 (£15). Métro: Peel. Pets accepted, free. **Amenities:** Restaurant; 2 bars; 24-hr. exercise room; free access to the Club Sportif MAA gym and pool; children's services; concierge; room service; babysitting. *In room:* A/C, TV/DVD/VCR, CD player, iPod/MP3 docking station, high-speed Internet, minibar, hair dryer, iron.

Ritz-Carlton Montréal ★★   This Ritz-Carlton and its restaurants will be closed for most of 2009. Since it first opened its doors in 1912, the luxe hotel has been a favorite for both accommodations and dining, with its **Café de Paris** favored for high tea and **Le Jardin du Ritz** for its duck pond and ducklings. A 15-month, C$100-million (£50 million) renovation project started in June 2008 and is expected to run through October 2009. Check the hotel's website for updates about the reopening.

1228 rue Sherbrooke ouest (at rue Drummond), Montréal, PQ H3G 1H6. ☏ **800/363-0366** or 514/842-4212. www.ritzmontreal.com.

MODERATE

Château Versailles ★   The official lodging of the **Musée des Beaux-Arts** (p. 108), the Versailles's location near the museum and high-end shopping make it popular (note, though, that it's outside most of the tourist orbit). The château began as a European-style pension in 1958, expanding into adjacent pre-WWI town houses. The most spacious rooms have enjoyed the full decorator treatment, with modern furnishings that have faint Deco tinges and Second Empire touches. Some have fireplaces. A buffet breakfast is served in the main living room, where you can sit at a small table or in an easy chair in front of a fireplace. One deficiency: the lack of an elevator by which to deal with the three floors. The modern tower across the street is sister hotel **Le Meridien Versailles,** 1808 rue Sherbrooke ouest (☏ **888/933-8111** or 514/933-8111). It is home to the well-regarded restaurant **Brontë.**

1659 rue Sherbrooke ouest (at rue St-Mathieu), Montréal, PQ H3A 1E3. ☏ **888/933-8111** or 514/933-3611. Fax 514/933-6967. www.versailleshotels.com. 65 units. C$165–C$300 (£85–£150) double; suites from C$380 (£190). Rates include breakfast. Packages available. AE, DC, DISC, MC, V. Valet parking C$23 (£12). Métro: Guy-Concordia. **Amenities:** 24-hr. exercise room w/sauna; room service; babysitting. *In room:* A/C, TV, CD player, high-speed Internet, minibar, hair dryer.

Hôtel du Fort (Kids)   While hardly grand, this reliable hotel takes as its primary duty providing lodging to longer-term business travelers. That includes providing a fitness room (newly renovated) sufficient enough for a thorough morning workout, basic kitchenettes with fridges and microwave ovens in every room (the concierge can have groceries delivered), and an underground parking garage. Since all rooms are a good size and many have sofas with hide-a-beds, small families would do well to stay here, too. A buffet breakfast is served in the lounge; other meals can be taken at the **Café Suprême** in the adjoining Complexe du Fort mall.

1390 rue du Fort (at rue Ste-Catherine), Montréal, PQ H3H 2R7. ☏ **800/565-6333** or 514/938-8333. www.hoteldufort.com. 124 units. C$135–C$175 (£68–£88) double; suites from C$165 (£83). Children 11 and younger stay free in parent's room. AE, DC, MC, V. Métro: Guy-Concordia. **Amenities:** Exercise room; concierge; room service; babysitting. *In room:* A/C, TV, Wi-Fi (fee), kitchenette, hair dryer.

Hôtel Le Dauphin (Value)   This member of the small Dauphin hotel chain opened in February 2007 and presents a terrific new option for travelers on a budget. Its nine floors are decorated in tans and putty, and room furnishings are simple and clean (if reminiscent of dorm-room functional). Bathrooms are sleek with black counters, slate floors, and glass-walled shower stalls, beds are comfy, and—get this—all units are equipped with a computer terminal and free Internet access. Rooms also have bigger-hotel touches: flatscreen TVs, in-room safes big enough for a laptop, large refrigerators (unstocked), and morning newspaper delivery. A key is required to access the elevator, for an added bit of safety. There are four extra-large rooms. The location, next to the convention center and a few blocks from Vieux-Montréal's northern end, is central, though the immediate surroundings are nondescript.

1025 rue de Bleury (near av. Viger), Montréal, PQ H2Z 1M7. ℭ **888/784-3888** or 514/788-3888. Fax 514/788-3889. www.hoteldauphin.ca. 72 units. C$150–C$170 (£75–£85) double. Rates include breakfast. AE, MC, V. Métro: Place d'Armes. **Amenities:** Exercise room; washers and dryers. *In room:* A/C, TV/DVD, free Wi-Fi, in-room computer w/free high-speed Internet, fridge, hair dryer.

Le Square Phillips Hôtel & Suites   The advantage here is space. Originally designed as a warehouse by the noted Québec architect Ernest Cormier, the building was converted to its present function in 2003. The vaguely cathedral-like spaces were largely retained, making for capacious studio bedrooms and suites fully equipped for long stays. Full kitchens in every unit come with all essential appliances—toasters, fridges, stoves, dishwashers, crockery, and pots and pans. There's a rooftop pool and exercise room; a laundry room is also available for guest use. The location, at the edge of the downtown shopping district, is ideal and an easy walk to Vieux-Montréal and the rue Crescent nightlife district.

1193 Square Phillips (south of rue Ste-Catherine), Montréal, PQ H3B 3C9. ℭ **866/393-1193** or 514/393-1193. Fax 514/393-1192. www.squarephillips.com. 160 units. C$159 (£80) double; C$174–C$325 (£87–£163) suite; discounts for stays of 7 or more days. Rates include breakfast. AE, DC, DISC, MC, V. Parking C$20 (£10). Métro: McGill. Pets accepted. **Amenities:** Heated indoor rooftop pool; exercise room; concierge; babysitting. *In room:* A/C, TV, free high-speed Internet, kitchen, hair dryer.

3 VIEUX-MONTREAL (OLD MONTREAL)

VERY EXPENSIVE

Hôtel Le St-James ★★★   This hotel represents a triumph of design and preservation for visiting royalty, or those who want to be treated like it. Montréal's surge of designer hotels spans the spectrum from superminimalist to gentlemen's club, and Le St-James sits squarely at the gentlemen's end of the range. It began life as a merchant's bank in 1870, and the opulence of that station has been retained: A richly paneled entry leads to a grand hall with Corinthian columns, carved urns, and balconies with gilded metal balustrades. Meals and afternoon tea are served right in this "Banker's Hall," often accompanied by harp music. Rooms are furnished with entrancing antiques and impeccable reproductions. All have video screens that control lights, room temperature, and even the DO NOT DISTURB sign. The stone-walled, candlelit **Le Spa** specializes in full-body water therapy.

355 rue St-Jacques ouest, Montréal, PQ H2Y 1N9. ℭ **866/841-3111** or 514/841-3111. Fax 514/841-1232. www.hotellestjames.com. 61 units. C$400–C$475 (£200–£238) double; C$575 (£288) and way up. Packages available. AE, DC, DISC, MC, V. Valet parking C$30 (£15). Métro: Square Victoria. Pets accepted. **Amenities:** Restaurant; bar; exercise room w/steam and sauna; concierge; room service; babysitting. *In room:* A/C, TV, Wi-Fi, high-speed Internet, wire to connect iPod, minibar, hair dryer.

Le Saint-Sulpice Hôtel ★★ (Kids)   Open since 2002 and part of the wave of high-style boutique hotels that has washed across Vieux-Montréal, Le Saint-Sulpice impresses with an all-suites configuration, an ambitious eatery called **S le Restaurant,** and courtly service. The hotel is a member of the Concorde chain, and easily meets that brand's demanding, sophisticated standards. Three levels of suites come with myriad conveniences and gadgets, including minikitchens with microwave ovens, stoves, and fridges.

Some have fireplaces. The largest suites, at the executive level, sleep six and are often taken by film crews in town for movie productions. There's an outdoor terrace where lunch, dinner, and drinks are served facing the gardens of the Sulpician Seminary. Children's services include gaming consoles in every room, board games, kid-friendly TV programming, a children's menu, and day care.

414 rue St-Sulpice (next to the Basilique Notre-Dame), Montréal, PQ H2Y 2V5. ℂ **877/785-7423** or 514/288-1000. Fax 514/288-0077. www.lesaintsulpice.com. 108 units. Summer C$509–C$539 (£255–£270) for superior and deluxe suites; winter C$255 (£130) and up. Rates include full breakfast. Children 11 and younger stay free in parent's room. Packages available. AE, DC, DISC, MC, V. Valet parking C$25 or C$32 for SUV (£13 or £16). Métro: Place d'Armes. Pets accepted, C$40 (£20). **Amenities:** Restaurant; compact health club and spa; sauna; concierge; room service; babysitting. *In room:* A/C, TV, free Wi-Fi, kitchenette.

W Montréal ★★★ If it weren't for the reception and concierge desks at each end of the lobby, you might think you'd stepped into an exclusive dance club, what with the thumping music, the fire-engine-red glow of the wall panels, and the 3.6m (12-ft.) waterfall. That tone pervades: Employees, male and female, are young and distractingly attractive, and the hotel's restaurant, **Otto,** attracts a sleek crowd of models, people who date models, and people who pretend they're one or the other. The intimate **W Café/Bartini** concocts specialty martinis and is open until 3am, while **Wunderbar** picks up the pace with beat-spinning DJs, also until 3am. Bedrooms follow through, with pillow-top mattresses, goose-down comforters, and 350-count Egyptian cotton sheets. That flatscreen TVs and DVD players are standard in even the basic (called "Cozy") rooms is only to be expected. The W is located where Vieux-Montréal meets downtown.

901 rue Square-Victoria, Montréal, PQ H2Z 1R1. ℂ **877-W-HOTELS** (946-8357) or 514/395-3100. Fax 514/395-3150. www.whotels.com/montreal. 152 units. From C$299 (£150) double. Packages available. AE, DC, DISC, MC, V. Valet parking C$35 (£18). Métro: Square Victoria. Pets accepted. **Amenities:** Restaurant; 3 bars; exercise room and spa; concierge; room service; babysitting. *In room:* A/C, TV/DVD, high-speed Internet, hair dryer.

EXPENSIVE

Auberge du Vieux-Port ★★ Terrifically romantic, this tidy luxury inn is housed in an 1882 building facing the waterfront, and many of the rooms as well as a rooftop terrace offer unobstructed views of Vieux-Port—a particular treat during those summer nights when there are fireworks on the river or in winter when it's snowing. Exposed brick and stone walls, massive beams, polished hardwood floors, and windows that open define the hideaway bedrooms; number 403, for instance, allows expansive views, space to stretch out, and a king bed. In the late afternoon, guests get a complimentary glass of wine with cheese in **Narcisse,** the small, sophisticated wine bar off the lobby; live jazz adds to the mood Thursday through Sunday starting at 6pm. The auberge also runs the **Lofts du Vieux-Port** (www.loftsduvieuxport.com), with suites that have kitchenettes and other amenities for longer stays.

97 rue de la Commune est (near rue St-Gabriel), Montréal, PQ H2Y 1J1. ℂ **888/660-7678** or 514/876-0081. Fax 514/876-8923. www.aubergeduvieuxport.com. 27 units. Summer C$230–C$285 (£115–£145) double; winter C$159–C$189 (£80–£95) double. Rates include full breakfast and afternoon wine and cheese. Children 11 and younger stay free in parent's room. AE, DC, DISC, MC, V. Valet parking C$19 (£9.50). Métro: Champs-de-Mars. **Amenities:** Wine bar; exercise room; concierge; room service; babysitting. *In room:* A/C, TV, CD player, free Wi-Fi, minibar, hair dryer.

Hostellerie Pierre du Calvet ★ Step from cobblestone streets into an opulent 18th-century home boasting beamed ceilings, plush velvet curtains, gold-leafed writing desks, and four-poster beds of teak mahogany. The wildly atmospheric public spaces are furnished with original antiques—not reproductions. Likewise, the voluptuous dining room, **Les Filles du Roy,** suggests a 19th-century hunting lodge. (If you've ever watched *Masterpiece Theatre* and thought, "What I wouldn't give to live there," this hotel is for you.) Some bedrooms sport fireplaces, and room no. 6 even has a shower with stone walls. Two unfortunate notes: The new flatscreen TVs appear as discordant here as Victoria Beckham does at Versailles (although they will be removed upon request), and door locks are awfully rickety (it's best to try to imagine them as romantic period pieces). In 2006, a walled-in outdoor courtyard with a small fountain was converted into a dining terrace; it makes for a wonderful little hideaway.

405 rue Bonsecours (at rue St-Paul), Montréal, PQ H27 3C3. ℭ **866/544-1725** or 514/282-1725. Fax 514/282-0456. www.pierreducalvet.ca. 9 units. C$265–C$295 (£133–£148). Rates include breakfast. Packages available. AE, MC, V. Métro: Champ-de-Mars. **Amenities:** Restaurant. *In room:* A/C, TV, free Wi-Fi, hair dryer.

Hotel Gault ★★　This hotel explores the far reaches of minimalism, and design aficionados will likely love it. With raw, monumental concrete walls and brushed-steel work surfaces, Gault's structural austerity is stark, but tempered by lollipop-colored reproductions of mod furniture from the 1950s and blonde woods which keep things more playful than chilly. The large bedrooms on its five floors are all loft-style and large (the smallest are 29 sq. m/310 sq. ft.), and employ curtains instead of walls to define spaces. Bedding comes from the high-end Italian company FLOU, and hypoallergenic pillows are available. The first floor's "Existential" rooms feature the highest ceilings. Tubs aren't available in all rooms, but plush robes are. The sleek lobby, with its massive arched windows, also functions as a bar/cafe/breakfast area. Nonguests may want to set aside one morning for the generous C$20 (£10) brunch.

449 rue Ste-Hélène, Montréal, PQ H2Y 2K9. ℭ **866/904-1616** or 514/904-1616. Fax 866/904-1717. www.hotelgault.com. 30 units. C$220–C$235 (£110–£118) double; C$749 (£375) suite. Rates include full breakfast. Children 12 and younger stay free in parent's room. Packages available. AE, MC, V. Valet parking C$22 (£11). Métro: Square Victoria. Pets accepted, C$20 (£10). **Amenities:** Restaurant; bar; 24-hr. exercise room; concierge; room service; babysitting. *In room:* A/C, TV/DVD, CD player, high-speed Internet, Wi-Fi (fee), minibar.

Hotel InterContinental Montréal ★★　Across the street from the convention center and a few minutes' walk from the Basilique Notre-Dame and Vieux-Montréal's restaurants and nightspots, this striking luxury hotel opened in 1991, and in 2008 started a 5-year renovation of its rooms, lobby, health club, and reception area, all to better compete with a new Westin hotel (Le Westin Montréal) opening directly across the street in 2009. But one can only wonder how the hotel could significantly improve the guest rooms: They're already spacious, quiet, spotless, well lit, and, in many cases, romantic. They're also decorated with photographs and lithographs by local artists. The turret rooms are fun, with their wraparound windows, and guests of the club rooms get access to an exclusive lounge serving complimentary continental breakfast and afternoon hors d'oeuvres, beer, and wine. The restored 1888 Nordheimer building adjacent to the lobby contains a bar-bistro, and the hotel has direct access to the underground city.

360 rue St-Antoine ouest (near rue de Bleury), Montréal, PQ H2Y 3X4. ℭ **514/987-9900.** Fax 514/987-9904. www.montreal.intercontinental.com. 357 units. Summer C$300 (£150) and up double; C$700 (£350) and up suite. Up to 4 people in room for same price. Packages available. AE, DC, DISC, MC, V. Valet parking C$26 (£13), self-parking C$18 (£9). Métro: Square Victoria. **Amenities:** 2 restaurants; bar; small enclosed rooftop lap pool; health club w/sauna and steam rooms; concierge; room service; babysitting; executive-level rooms. *In room:* A/C, TV, Internet, Wi-Fi (fee), minibar, hair dryer.

Hôtel Nelligan ★★★ Occupying adjoining 1850 buildings, the Nelligan opened in 2002 and spent C$8 million to expand in 2007, going from 63 to 105 units; more than half of the overnight accommodations are now suites. Bedrooms are dark-wooded, masculine retreats, with puffy duvets, heaps of pillows, and quality mattresses. The staff performs its duties admirably, and the building maintains beautiful public spaces, from the **Verses** restaurant (p. 94) on the ground floor to the rooftop terrace, where drinks and light meals are served until 11pm. The hotel is named for the 19th-century Québécois poet Emile Nelligan, whose lines are excerpted on the bedroom walls. The one distraction is that the hotel's center atrium can sometimes pull noise from the downstairs bar up to rooms. Still, claiming an enveloping lobby chair facing the open front to the street, with a book and a cold drink at hand, is one definition of utter contentment.

106 rue St-Paul ouest (at rue St-Sulpice), Montréal, PQ H2Y 1Z3. ✆ **877/788-2040** or 514/788-2040. Fax 514/788-2041. www.hotelnelligan.com. 105 units. C$235–C$260 (£118–£130) double; suites from C$365 (£183). Rates include breakfast and afternoon wine and cheese. Packages available. AE, DC, DISC, MC, V. Valet parking C$24 (£12). Métro: Place d'Armes. **Amenities:** 2 restaurants; bar; exercise room; concierge; room service; babysitting. In room: A/C, TV, CD player, free high-speed Internet, Wi-Fi (fee), hair dryer.

Place d'Armes Hôtel & Suites ★★ This highly desirable property is housed in three cunningly converted adjoining buildings dating from the late 19th and early 20th centuries. The elaborate architectural details of that era are in abundant evidence inside, with high ceilings and richly carved capitals and moldings. Many rooms have original brick walls and all are decorated in simple, contemporary fashion; slate floors in the bathrooms, deluxe bedding, and spotlight lighting. Many bathrooms feature disc-shaped rain-shower nozzles in the showers. The elaborate **Rainspa** incorporates a *hammam*—a traditional Middle-Eastern steam bath—in addition to offering massage, microdermabrasion, and body wraps. The hotel houses an acclaimed restaurant, **Aix Cuisine du Terroir** (p. 90), and the **Suite 701** bar (p. 169), where a complimentary afternoon wine-and-cheese party is held for guests and the *cinq-à-sept* (5-to-7) after-work crowd gathers in the evenings.

55 rue St-Jacques ouest, Montréal, PQ H2Y 3X2. ✆ **888/450-1887** or 514/842-1887. Fax 514/842-6469. www.hotelplacedarmes.com. 135 units. C$230–C$285 (£115–£143) double; C$340 (£170) and up suite. Rates include breakfast and afternoon wine and cheese. Packages available. AE, DC, DISC, MC, V. Valet parking C$24 (£12). Métro: Place d'Armes. **Amenities:** Restaurant; bar; 24-hr. exercise room; large spa; concierge; room service; babysitting. In room: A/C, TV, Wi-Fi (fee), free high-speed Internet, minibar, hair dryer.

St. Paul Hotel ★★ The St. Paul has been a star to design and architecture aficionados since its 2001 opening; it ranks among the most worthwhile of old buildings converted to hotels. Minimalism pervades, with simple lines and muted tones, and most of the guests appear as trim as the surroundings. Hallways are hushed and dark (truth be told, they border on pitch black) and open into bright rooms with furnishings in various cream shades. This being Canada, pops of texture come from pelt rugs. In the bathroom, the high design continues: Marble sinks are square, and clear plastic cubes cover the toiletries. Many rooms face Vieux-Montréal's less touristed far western edge, with its mixture of stone and brick buildings midconversion into modern condos and office spaces. The hotel's splashy restaurant was renovated in 2007 and reopened as **Vauvert**, with main courses ranging from C$19 to C$42 (£9.50–£21).

355 rue McGill (at rue St-Paul), Montréal, PQ H2Y 2E8. ✆ **866/380-2202** or 514/380-2222. Fax 514/380-2200. www.hotelstpaul.com. 120 units. C$259 (£130) double. Rates include breakfast. Children 11 and younger stay free in parent's room. Packages available. AE, MC, V. Valet parking C$20 (£10). Pets accepted.

Métro: Square Victoria. **Amenities:** Restaurant; bar; 24-hr. exercise room; concierge; free Wi-Fi in lobby and breakfast room; room service; babysitting. *In room:* A/C, TV, CD player, free high-speed Internet, minibar, hair dryer.

MODERATE

Auberge Bonaparte ★   Even the smallest rooms in this fashionable urban inn are gracefully presented—they're sizeable, with comfortable, firm beds. About half of them feature whirlpool tubs with separate showers. Guests can spend time on the rooftop terrace, which overlooks the Basilique Notre-Dame; one suite, on the top floor, offers superb views of the basilica's cloistered gardens. **Bonaparte** restaurant (p. 92) on the ground floor—romantic and faded in a Left Bank of Paris sort of way—has long been one of Vieux-Montréal's favorites. Generous breakfasts, included in the cost of the room, are served here, and sitting at one of the elegant window tables with a newspaper, croissant, coffee, and an omelet feels like an especially civilized way to start the day.

447 rue St-François-Xavier (north of rue St-Paul), Montréal, PQ H2Y 2T1. ⓒ **514/844-1448.** Fax 514/844-0272. www.bonaparte.com. 31 units. C$170–C$215 (£85–£108) double; C$355 (£178) suite. Rates include full breakfast. AE, DC, MC, V. Parking C$15 (£7.50) per calendar day. Métro: Place d'Armes. **Amenities:** Restaurant; access to nearby health club; concierge; laptop w/Wi-Fi for borrowing (free); room service; babysitting; bike storage in basement. *In room:* A/C, TV, free Wi-Fi, hair dryer.

Hôtel XIXe Siècle ★   In English, the name translates to "Hotel 19th Century," which is apt, as the building began life in 1870 as a bank (three vaults remain and one is now a small guest room) in the Second Empire style; its interior reflects these stately origins, starting with a lobby that looks like a Victorian library. This tidy little hotel is worth seeking out for its central location and quiet demeanor. Rooms are spacious, with 4.5m (15-ft.) ceilings and spacious working areas. Rooms facing the nondescript inner courtyard may not be scenic, but they're nearly silent and a dream for light sleepers. Twenty rooms on the first and second floors were renovated in 2008. Despite its faintly aristocratic air, the hotel gives nods to green living, with energy-saving light bulbs and recycling buckets in each room.

262 rue St-Jacques ouest (at rue St-Jean), Montréal, PQ H2Y 1N1. ⓒ **877/553-0019** or 514/985-0019. Fax 514/985-0059. www.hotelxixsiecle.com. 59 units. C$185–C$295 (£93–£148) double. Children 11 and younger stay free in parent's room. AE, DC, DISC, MC, V. Valet parking C$20 (£10). Pets accepted, C$50 (£25) additional per day. Métro: Place d'Armes. **Amenities:** Bar; concierge; room service. *In room:* A/C, TV, Wi-Fi (fee), hair dryer.

INEXPENSIVE

Auberge Les Passants du Sans Soucy ★ Ⓥⓐⓛⓤⓔ   This cheery B&B in the heart of Vieux-Montréal is a former 1723 fur warehouse gracefully converted into a tip-top inn. Its romantic rooms feature mortared stone walls, beamed ceilings, wrought-iron or brass beds, and buffed wood floors (photos of each room are posted online). All units now have jet tubs, flatscreen TVs, and electric fireplaces, and 2008 renovations knocked out some walls and brought in sleeker furnishings to make four smaller rooms larger. Breakfast is a special selling point: A sky-lit dining nook features communal tables on either side of a fireplace imported from Bordeaux. The substantial morning meals include chocolate croissants and made-to-order omelets. The marble-floored front entry doubles as a gallery space—unusual for a B&B—immediately setting a relaxed, urbane tone.

171 rue St-Paul ouest (at rue St-François-Xavier), Montréal, PQ H2Y 1Z5. ⓒ **514/842-2634.** Fax 514/842-2912. www.lesanssoucy.com. 9 units. May to early Jan C$160–C$195 (£80–£98) double, C$225 (£113) suite; early Jan to Apr from C$120 (£60). Rates include full breakfast. AE, MC, V. Parking C$15 (£7.50). Métro: Place d'Armes. *In room:* A/C, TV, free Wi-Fi, hair dryer.

Where to Dine in Montréal

There was a time not so long ago when eating out in Québec meant eating French food, and that was that.

Over the last 10 years, however, this has changed dramatically. That is, in large part, because of immigration: Montréalers now routinely indulge in Portuguese, Indian, Moroccan, Thai, Turkish, Mexican, and Japanese cuisines. An intermingling of styles, ingredients, and techniques was inevitable, and Montréal is now as cosmopolitan in its offerings as any city on the continent. Indeed, in some eyes, it has taken Canada's lead role in gastronomy; a meal here can equal the best offered anywhere in the world.

THE DINING SCENE Deciding where to dine among the many tempting choices can be bewildering. Keeping that in mind, we've highlighted the restaurants that are most honored, most special, or that offer the best value.

Restaurants—colloquially called "restos"— are often clustered together in certain neighborhoods. Many moderately priced bistros and cafes offer outstanding food, congenial surroundings, and amiable service at reasonable prices. Nearly all have menus posted outside, making it easy to do a little comparison shopping.

It's wise to make a reservation if you wish to dine at one of the city's top restaurants, especially on a weekend evening. Unlike in larger American and European cities, however, a day or two in advance is sufficient for most places on most days. A hotel concierge can make the reservation, though nearly all restaurant hosts will switch immediately into English when they sense that a caller doesn't speak French.

Except in a handful of luxury restaurants, dress codes are all but nonexistent. But Montréalers are a fashionable lot and manage to look smart even in casual clothes. Save the T-shirts and sneakers for another city.

Always look for *table d'hôte* meals. Less common in the U.S. but ubiquitous here, they are fixed-price menus with three or four courses, and usually cost just a little more than the price of a single à la carte main course. Restaurants at all price ranges offer them, and they represent the best value around. If you want to try many of the top restaurants, schedule some for noon-time meals if they offer *table d'hôte* menus at lunch, when the deal becomes even better.

Remember that for the Québécois, *dîner* (dinner) is lunch, and *souper* (supper) is dinner. An *entrée* is an appetizer, and a *plat principal* is a main course.

Insider websites featuring reviews and observations about the Montréal dining scene include **www.midnightpoutine.ca/food** and **www.endlessbanquet.blogspot.com**. Restaurant critic Lesley Chesterman's really solid reviews are online at **www.montrealgazette.com**.

For other tips about Québéc eating, see chapter 2, "Montréal and Québec City in Depth."

PRICES The restaurants recommended here are categorized by neighborhood and then by the cost of the main courses. Prices listed are for dinner unless otherwise indicated (lunch prices are usually lower) and do not include the cost of wine, tip, or the 5% federal tax and 7.5% provincial tax that are tacked on the restaurant bill. In all, count on taxes and tip to add another 30% to the bill.

PARKING Because parking space is at a premium in most restaurant districts, it's easiest to take the Métro or a taxi. If you're driving, find out whether valet parking is available.

SMOKING Québec has long had a smoking culture, but smoking in bars and restaurants has been banned since 2006.

TIPPING Montréalers consider 15% of the check (before taxes) to be a fair tip, increased only for exceptional food and service.

1 BEST DINING BETS

- **Best Classic French Bistro:** Plateau Mont-Royal's most Parisian spot, **L'Express,** 3927 rue St-Denis (at rue Roy; ✆ **514/845-5333**), is where you come to see what the Francophone part of this city is all about. From the black-and-white-checkered floor to the grand, high ceilings, this is where Old France meets New France. See p. 100.
- **Best Room for a Celebration: Nuances,** 1 av. du Casino (✆ **514/392-2708**), got a dazzling face-lift in 2007 and now looks as contemporary as the food on its plates. It's a gracious, multistarred *temple de cuisine* atop the Montréal casino on Ile Ste-Hélène. See p. 105.
- **Best Exotic Downtown Restaurant:** In a city where French food and its derivations rule, the lush orange and blue Mediterranean decor at Portuguese **Ferreira Café,** 1446 rue Peel (✆ **514/848-0988**), as well as its big, fleshy mounds of grilled squid and black cod feel downright sexy. See p. 85.
- **Best Restaurant at Which to Eat So Much You Can't Move:** As the name—"The Pig's Foot"—suggests, **Au Pied de Cochon,** 536 rue Duluth est (✆ **514/281-1114**), is mostly about slabs of meat, especially pork. The "PDC's Cut," weighing in at more than a pound, is emblematic. See p. 98.
- **Best Vegan Restaurant:** A standard-bearer since 1997, Plateau Mont-Royal's **Aux Vivres** moved to new digs at 4631 bd. St-Laurent, near avenue du Mont-Royal (✆ **514/842-3479**), in 2006 and has been packing in vegans, vegetarians—and the meat eaters who love them—ever since. See p. 104.
- **Best Guilty Treat:** *Poutine* is a plate of french fries (frites) drenched with gravy afloat with cheese curds. It's a bedrock Québec comfort food that tastes better than it sounds. **La Banquise,** 994 rue Rachel est (✆ **514/525-2415**), near Parc La Fontaine's northwest corner, offers upwards of 25 variations and is open 24 hours a day, 7 days a week. See p. 102.
- **Best Old-Fashioned French Meal:** Right on Place Jacques-Cartier in Vieux-Montréal, **Chez Queux,** 158 rue St-Paul est (✆ **514/866-5194**), is a throwback to a time when the only cuisine was French and the only proper romantic meal was chateaubriand for two, alongside showy tableside preparations and flaming desserts. The food is decidedly retro, but the execution is superb. And the waiters wear tuxedos. See p. 92.
- **Best Out-of-the-Way Place for a Date:** Little **La Montée de Lait,** tucked on a nondescript side street in Plateau Mont-Royal at 371 rue Villeneuve est, at the corner of rue Drolet (✆ **514/289-9921**), keeps you close to your honey and elbow-to-elbow with neighbors. The room can get loud, though, so consider that in your planning. See p. 99.
- **Best Breakfast:** The city has seven outposts of **Eggspectation,** and they all do brisk business serving funky, creative breakfasts with loads of egg options. The menu is extensive, prices are fair, and portions are huge. See p. 95.

- **Best Smoked Meat:** There are other contenders, but **Chez Schwartz Charcuterie Hébraïque de Montréal,** known simply as Schwartz's, at 3895 bd. St-Laurent, north of rue Prince-Arthur in Plateau Mont-Royal (© **514/842-4813**), serves up the definitive version of regional brisket. See p. 101.
- **Best Burgers:** Local wisdom holds that the biggest, juiciest burgers are assembled at the Latin Quarter's **La Paryse,** 302 rue Ontario est (© **514/842-2040**). See p. 105. Nipping at its heels (although in entirely different neighborhoods) are **MeatMarket,** 4415 bd. St-Laurent (© **514/223-2292**), a gourmet burger joint in Mile End, and the new **m brgr,** at 2015 rue Drummond (© **514/ 906-2747**) in downtown. The latter was launched by steakhouse stalwart Moishes in early 2008. See p. 104 and 98.
- **Best Bagel:** Even native New Yorkers have to give it up for Montréal's bagels, which are sweeter and chewier than those produced south of the border. Both **St-Viateur Bagel & Café,** at 1127 av. Mont-Royal est in Plateau Mont-Royal (© **514/528-6361**), and **Fairmont Bagel,** at 74 av. Fairmont ouest in Mile End (© **514/272-0667**), are the places to assess that claim. See p. 102 and 104.
- **Best Restaurant at Which to Share Food:** The tapas phenomenon gave rise to **Pintxo,** in Plateau Mont-Royal at 256 rue Roy est (© **514/844-0222**), which does its own variations on the Spanish-Basque originals. See p. 100.
- **Best Restaurant, Period:** Ever-questing Normand Laprise and partner Christine Lamarche keep Vieux-Montréal's **Toqué!,** 900 Place Jean-Paul Riopelle, near rue St-Antoine (© **514/499-2084**), in a league of its own. This dazzlingly postmodern venue is now a deserving member of the gold-standard organization Relais & Châteaux. See p. 90.

2 RESTAURANTS BY CUISINE

Breakfast

Café Cherrier (Plateau Mont-Royal, $, p. 101)
Cluny ArtBar (Vieux-Montréal, $, p. 95)
Eggspectation (Vieux-Montréal, $, p. 95)
Fairmont Bagel (Mile End, $, p. 104)

Deli

Chez Schwartz Charcuterie Hébraïque de Montréal ★ (Plateau Mont-Royal, $, p. 101)

French Bistro

Boris Bistro ★ (Vieux-Montréal, $$, p. 94)

La Montée de Lait ★ (Plateau Mont-Royal, $$$, p. 99)
Le Bourlingueur (Vieux-Montréal, $, p. 95)
Leméac ★ (Mile End, $$, p. 103)
L'Express ★ (Plateau Mont-Royal, $$, p. 100)

French Contemporary

Aix Cuisine du Terroir ★ (Vieux-Montréal, $$$, p. 90)
Café Méliès (Plateau Mont-Royal, $$, p. 100)
Europea ★★ (Downtown, $$$, p. 85)
Julien (Downtown, $$$, p. 88)
Nuances ★★★ (Outer Districts, $$$$, p. 105)

Key to Abbreviations: $$$$ = Very Expensive $$$ = Expensive $$ = Moderate $ = Inexpensive
The prices within each review refer to the cost in Canadian dollars of individual main courses, using the following categories: Very Expensive ($$$$), main courses at dinner average more than C$35; Expensive ($$$), C$25 to C$35; Moderate ($$), C$12 to C$25; and Inexpensive ($), C$12 and less. Restaurants are listed alphabetically at the end of the index in the back of this book.

Restaurant de l'Institut ★ (Plateau Mont-Royal, $$, p. 101)

Rosalie ★ (Downtown, $$$, p. 88)

Toqué! ★★★ (Vieux-Montréal, $$$$, p. 90)

Verses Restaurant ★ (Vieux-Montréal, $$$, p. 94)

French Traditional

Bonaparte ★ (Vieux-Montréal, $$$, p. 92)

Chez Queux ★ (Vieux-Montréal, $$$, p. 92)

Marché de la Villete ★ (Vieux-Montréal, $, p. 96)

Fusion

Chez l'Epicier ★ (Vieux-Montréal, $$$, p. 92)

Jun-I ★ (Mile End, $$$, p. 102)

La Chronique ★★ (Mile End, $$$$, p. 102)

Le Blanc ★ (Plateau Mont-Royal, $$$, p. 99)

Le Club Chasse et Pêche ★ (Vieux-Montréal, $$$, p. 93)

Renoir (Downtown, $$$, p. 88)

Ice Cream

Bilboquet ★ (Mile End, $, p. 104)

Indian

Gandhi ★ (Vieux-Montréal, $$, p. 95)

Le Taj (Downtown, $$, p. 88)

Italian

BU (Mile End, $$, p. 103)

Buonanotte ★ (Plateau Mont-Royal, $$$, p. 98)

Cavalli ★★ (Downtown, $$$, p. 85)

Globe ★ (Plateau Mont-Royal, $$$, p. 99)

Lebanese

Boustan (Downtown, $, p. 89)

Light Fare

Café Cherrier (Plateau Mont-Royal, $, p. 101)

Claude Postel (Vieux-Montréal, $, p. 95)

Cluny ArtBar (Vieux-Montréal, $, p. 95)

Eggspectation (Vieux-Montréal, $, p. 95)

Fairmont Bagel (Mile End, $, p. 104)

La Banquise (Plateau Mont-Royal, $, p. 102)

MeatMarket Restaurant Café (Mile End, $$, p. 104)

Nocochi (Downtown, $, p. 90)

Olive et Gourmando ★ (Vieux-Montréal, $, p. 97)

St-Viateur Bagel & Café ★ (Plateau Mont-Royal, $, p. 102)

Titanic (Vieux-Montréal, $, p. 97)

Wilensky Light Lunch (Mile End, $, p. 105)

Mediterranean

Modavie ★ (Vieux-Montréal, $$$, p. 93)

Version Laurent Godbout ★★ (Vieux-Montréal, $$$, p. 94)

Pizza

Pizzédélic (Vieux-Montréal, $, p. 97)

Polish

Stash Café (Vieux-Montréal, $, p. 97)

Quebecois

Au Pied de Cochon ★★ (Plateau Mont-Royal, $$$, p. 98)

Sandwiches

La Paryse (Latin Quarter, $, p. 105)

Seafood

Ferreira Café ★ (Downtown, $$$, p. 85)

Joe Beef ★ (Outer Districts, $$$, p. 107)

Le Garde Manger (Vieux-Montréal, $$$, p. 93)

Maestro S.V.P. (Plateau Mont-Royal, $$$, p. 99)

Spanish

Pintxo ★★ (Plateau Mont-Royal, $$, p. 100)

Steakhouse

Joe Beef ★ (Outer Districts, $$$, p. 107)

Moishes ★ (Plateau Mont-Royal, $$$$, p. 98)

Thai

Chao Phraya (Mile End, $$, p. 103)

Vegetarian/Vegan

Aux Vivres (Mile End, $, p. 104)

Le Commensal (Downtown, $, p. 90)

---

3 CENTRE VILLE/DOWNTOWN

EXPENSIVE

Cavalli ★★ ITALIAN   Employing a formula more common in the restaurants over on boulevard St-Laurent than here in the middle of the business district, the owners filled a glamorous space with striking young women in snug black dresses and hunky young men with requisite 4-day-old beards. It's like joining the after-party of a Hollywood premiere with 300 of the beautiful people. Being seen is top priority, but the food is noteworthy, too. Tempting as it is to simply make a meal of any of the dozen antipasti, that would mean ignoring such eminently worthwhile main events as the pine nut–crusted filet mignon or rack of lamb with oregano crust and olive *jus*. Prices are high, assuring a more prosperous crowd than usually found at similar emporia. The glowing pink bar turns into a heavy scene later in the evening.

2040 rue Peel (at bd. de Maisonneuve). ℭ **514/843-5100.** www.ristorantecavalli.com. Reservations recommended. Main courses C$26–C$43 (£13–£22); *table d'hôte* C$28–C$32 (£14–£16). AE, MC, V. Mon-Fri noon–3pm and 6–10:30pm; Sat 6–10:30pm (bar open later). Métro: Peel.

Europea ★★ FRENCH CONTEMPORARY   When viewed from the outside, Europea doesn't particularly impress; it looks like any of the city's multitude of low-brow cellar eateries. Even once inside, the low ceiling, bare wood floors, and brick walls are more simple than stunning. But then comes the food, and you come to see why the title of "Chef of the Year" was bestowed on chef Jérôme Ferrer by the Société des Chefs, Cuisiniers et Pâtissiers du Québec, in 2007, and why gourmands put Europea in the "bistro deluxe" category. The *amuse* arrives in a three-segment dish with different tasty nibbles in each. It's followed by an unannounced "teaser," a demitasse of lobster bisque with a shot of truffle oil. Gaps in the procession are short, leading to the main event—perhaps the *roasted Alaska crab legs and warm lobster salad or the beef filet*. For the full treatment, order the nine-course *menu dégustation* for C$80 (£40). Europea doesn't draw families, and the average age of diners tends to be older than 40. Service is watchful and efficient. For a bargain, come at lunch, when the *table d'hôte* starts at C$17 (£8.50).

1227 rue de la Montagne (at rue Ste-Catherine). ℭ **514/398-9229.** www.europea.ca. Reservations strongly recommended. Main courses C$27–C$41 (£14–£21); *table d'hôte* lunch C$17–C$28 (£8.50–£14), dinner C$50 (£25); 9-course *menu dégustation* C$80 (£40). AE, DC, MC, V. Mon-Fri noon–2pm; daily 6–10pm. Métro: Peel.

Ferreira Café ★ SEAFOOD   *Cataplana* is the name of both a venerated Portuguese recipe and the hinged copper clamshell-style pot in which it is cooked. Ingredients vary depending on the chef, but at this extremely popular downtown spot, the recipe results in a fragrant stew of mussels, clams, potatoes, shrimp, *chouriço* sausage, and chunks of

Where to Dine in Downtown Montréal

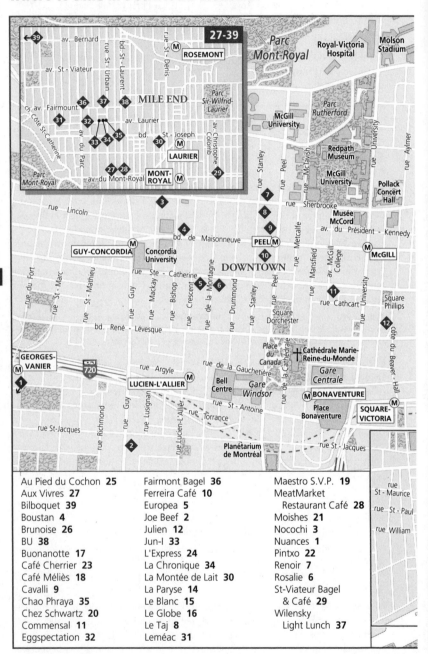

Au Pied du Cochon **25**	Fairmont Bagel **36**	Maestro S.V.P. **19**
Aux Vivres **27**	Ferreira Café **10**	MeatMarket
Bilboquet **39**	Europea **5**	Restaurant Café **28**
Boustan **4**	Joe Beef **2**	Moishes **21**
Brunoise **26**	Julien **12**	Nocochi **3**
BU **38**	Jun-I **33**	Nuances **1**
Buonanotte **17**	L'Express **24**	Pintxo **22**
Café Cherrier **23**	La Chronique **34**	Renoir **7**
Café Méliès **18**	La Montée de Lait **30**	Rosalie **6**
Cavalli **9**	La Paryse **14**	St-Viateur Bagel
Chao Phraya **35**	Le Blanc **15**	& Café **29**
Chez Schwartz **20**	Le Globe **16**	Wilensky
Commensal **11**	Le Taj **8**	Light Lunch **37**
Eggspectation **32**	Leméac **31**	

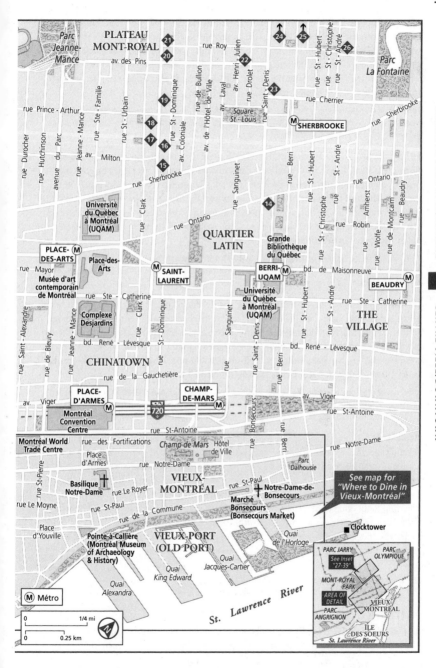

cod and salmon. You'll feel transported to Portugal as you sit in the romantic lighting facing a cleverly decorated wall embedded with a mosaic of broken white and cobalt ceramic plates. At lunchtime, customers are mostly middle-aged and dressed in business suits; at night, the restaurant's festive side comes out to play. Be sure to finish your meal with a selection from the ample dessert-wine offerings. A smaller late-night menu is available after 10pm Thursday through Saturday for those looking to satisfy their hunger while out on the town. Keep in mind that some dishes are priced according to the daily market, so they can be higher than what's listed below.

1446 rue Peel (near bd. de Maisonneuve). ✆ 514/848-0988. www.ferreiracafe.com. Reservations recommended. Main courses C$28–C$42 (£14–£21). AE, DC, MC, V. Mon–Fri noon–3pm; Mon–Thurs 6–11pm; Fri–Sat 6–11:30pm. Métro: Peel.

Julien FRENCH CONTEMPORARY   A quiet downtown block in the financial district has been home to this relaxed Parisian-style bistro for years, hosting business-people at lunch and after-work cocktails and mostly tourists from nearby hotels in the evening. Much of the year, diners have the option of sitting at tables on the heated terrace. The menu, which offers solid food without the pyrotechnics, features selections such as breast of duck hamburger, or scallops with fennel in pine nut butter. There's always a vegetarian pasta option, too.

1191 av. Union (at bd. René-Lévesque). ✆ 514/871-1581. www.restaurantjulien.com. Reservations recommended. Main courses C$18–C$38 (£9–£19); *table d'hôte* dinner C$23–C$32 (£12–£16). AE, DC, MC, V. Mon–Fri 11:30am–3pm; Mon–Sat 5:30–10pm. Métro: McGill.

Renoir FUSION   Lodged in the popular **Sofitel** hotel (p. 70), this ambitious restaurant calls its food "inspired." Make that "cautiously creative"—not ostentatious enough to halt conversation in midsentence, but worth an approving comment *en passant*. Plates are beautifully presented, with main events including lamb rack and Chilean sea bass. Lunch is the busiest time, while dinner is quieter and populated mostly by well-dressed hotel guests. A large terrace thrusts out toward busy Sherbrooke.

1155 rue Sherbrooke ouest (in the Sofitel Hotel, at rue Stanley). ✆ **514/285-9000.** www.restaurant-renoir.com. Reservations recommended. Main courses C$22–C$34 (£11–£17); table d'hôte lunch C$32 (£16), dinner C$49 (£25). AE, DC, MC, V. Daily 6am–10:30pm, with bar menu 3–5pm. Métro: Peel.

Rosalie ★ FRENCH CONTEMPORARY   Big, boisterous, congenial—this eating-and-meeting spot in the midst of the rue Crescent hubbub is all of that. There's still a bottomless source of great-looking young men and women on the staff who are very friendly, and good enough at their tasks, attending to throngs of people who look like they spend most of their evenings in places like this. Out front is an active terrace; inside, patrons draw leather sling chairs up to the ranks of bare tables or perch along the long marble bar. Food is of the updated bistro style, including a goat cheese tart with roasted beets and pine nuts, and grilled hanger steak with fries and *maître d'hôtel* butter. None of the food is too complicated, and most of it tasty. After 8pm, the lights go down and the decibel level shoots up.

1232 rue de la Montagne (south of rue Ste-Catherine). ✆ **514/392-1970.** www.rosalierestaurant. com. Reservations recommended. Main courses C$18–C$38 (£9–£19). AE, DC, MC, V. Mon–Fri noon–3pm; Sun–Wed 5:30–11pm; Thurs–Sat 5:30pm–midnight. Métro: Peel.

MODERATE

Le Taj Ⓥalue INDIAN   This remains one of downtown's tastiest bargains. The price of the lunch buffet (C$12/£6) has barely changed since the restaurant opened in 1985, and

Fun Facts **Poutine, Smoked Meat &
the World's Best Bagels**

While you're in Montréal, indulge in at least a couple of Québec staples. Though you'll find them dolled up on some menus, these are generally thought of as the region's basic comfort foods:

- *Poutine:* French fries doused with gravy and cheese curds.
- *Smoked meat:* A maddeningly tasty sandwich component particular to Montréal whose taste hovers in the neighborhood of pastrami and corned beef.
- *Cretons:* A pâté of minced pork, allspice, and parsley.
- *Tourtière:* A meat pie of beans and pork baked in maple syrup.
- *Queues de Castor:* A deep-fried pastry the size of a man's footprint served with melted chocolate or cinnamon. The name means "beaver tails."
- *Tarte au sucre:* Maple-sugar pie.
- **Bagel:** A doughnut-shaped bread roll that in Montréal is smaller, chewier, and—it must be said—tastier than its New York brethren.

the five-course dinner costs C$28 (£14). The kitchen specializes in the Mughlai cuisine of the Indian subcontinent, and seasonings tend more toward the tangy than the incendiary, but say you want your food spicy and you'll get it (watch out for the innocent-looking green coriander sauce). Dishes are perfumed with turmeric, saffron, ginger, cumin, mango powder, and *garam masala* (a spice combination that usually includes cloves, cardamom, and cinnamon). The marinated boneless lamb chops roasted in the tandoor arrive at the table sizzling and nested on braised vegetables. Vegetarians have ample choices, with the chickpea-based *channa masala* among the most complex. Main courses are huge, arriving with the expected array of sauces and condiments in bowls, saucers, cups, and dishes, all accompanied by *naan* (a pillowy flat bread) and basmati rice. Evenings are quiet, and lunchtimes are busy but not hectic. On one large wall, a bas-relief mud wall depicts a village scene; that wall was part of the Indian Pavilion at Expo 67.

2077 rue Stanley (near rue Sherbrooke). (C) **514/845-9015.** www.restaurantletaj.com. Main courses C$9–C$26 (£4.50–£13); lunch buffet C$12 (£6); *table d'hôte* dinner C$28 (£14). AE, DC, MC, V. Mon–Fri 11:30am–2:30pm and 5–10:30pm; Sat 5–11pm; Sun noon–2:30 and 5–10:30pm. Métro: Peel.

INEXPENSIVE

Boustan (Finds) LEBANESE   In the middle of the hubbub among the bars and clubs on rue Crescent, this Lebanese pizza parlor–style eatery, completely nondescript and consistently popular, has a line out the door at 2pm (office workers) and again at 2am (late-night partiers), all jonesing for its famed falafel, shish taouk, or shawarma sandwiches. Yes, that's former Prime Minister Pierre Trudeau in the photo at the cash register; he was a regular.

2020A rue Crescent (at bd. de Maisonneuve). (C) **514/843-3576.** www.boustan.ca. Most items cost less than C$10 (£5). AE, MC, V. Daily 11am–4am. Métro: Peel.

Le Commensal (Value) VEGETARIAN   This vegetarian fare is presented buffet-style, and patrons help themselves from dozens of options before paying the cashier by weight—about C$10 (£5) for an ample portion. Dishes include quinoa, garbanzo curry, several types of salads, a large variety of hot dishes, tofu with ginger sauce, and so on. Even avowed meat eaters are likely to not feel deprived. The only potential complaint is that the food that's supposed to be hot is sometimes lukewarm. Beer and wine are available, too. With white tablecloths and a second-floor location tucked off rue Ste-Catherine, this is a relaxing, satisfying spot to keep in mind when you're downtown. There's another branch at 1720 rue St-Denis (℃ **514/845-2627**).

1204 av. McGill College (at rue Ste-Catherine). ℃ **514/871-1480.** www.commensal.com. Pay by weight; most meals cost less than C$12 (£6). A, MC, V. Daily 11:30am–10pm. Métro: McGill.

Nocochi LIGHT FARE   At a posh spot on the corner of rue Sherbrooke ouest a block west of the Musée des Beaux-Arts is this cute little cafe and patisserie—just the place for panini, sandwiches, or scones with afternoon tea. After a few hours of museum-browsing or power-shopping, this all-white room, decorated with large close-up photos of decadent pastries, is a relief.

2156 rue Mackay (at rue Sherbrooke). ℃ **514/989-7514.** Most meals cost less than C$8 (£4). MC, V. Daily 8am–7pm. Métro: Guy-Concordia.

4 VIEUX-MONTREAL (OLD MONTREAL)

VERY EXPENSIVE

Toqué! ★★★ FRENCH CONTEMPORARY   Toqué! is the gem that single-handedly raised the entire city's gastronomic expectations. A meal here is obligatory for anyone who admires superb, dazzlingly presented food. "Post-nouvelle" might be an apt description for chef Normand Laprise's creations; his presentations are eye-opening, his portions quite sufficient, and his singular combinations of fixings are intensely flavorful. A short menu and top-of-the-bin ingredients, some of them rarely seen together—for example, cauliflower soup with foie gras shavings and milk foam, or smoked suckling pig cheek with maple-water sponge toffee, or olive oil sorbet with blood orange—ensure a unique tasting experience. If you choose one of the two seven-course tasting menus—and on weekends, as much as 80% of the crowd does—opt for wine pairings. The decor is 1960s loungey, with bulbous lamps hanging from the ceiling and low-back chairs. Most diners are prosperous-looking, so while the stated dress code is casual, you'll want to wear sharp attire. Service, headed by co-owner Christine Lamarche, is efficient, helpful, and not a bit self-important. Fifteen years on the scene, and Toqué! is still at the top of its game.

900 Place Jean-Paul-Riopelle (near rue St-Antoine). ℃ **514/499-2084.** www.restaurant-toque.com. Reservations required. Main courses C$32–C$45 (£16–£23); tasting menus C$92 (£46) or C$104 (£52). AE, DC, MC, V. Tues–Sat 5:30–10:30pm. Métro: Square-Victoria.

EXPENSIVE

Aix Cuisine du Terroir ★ FRENCH CONTEMPORARY   Lodged in the high-end **Place d'Armes Hôtel** (p. 79), this resto (just say "X") has been pulling in critical plaudits since its 2004 opening and is one of the highlights of Vieux-Montréal dining. *Terroir* refers to soil, and a gastronomical allegiance to products grown in the immediate region

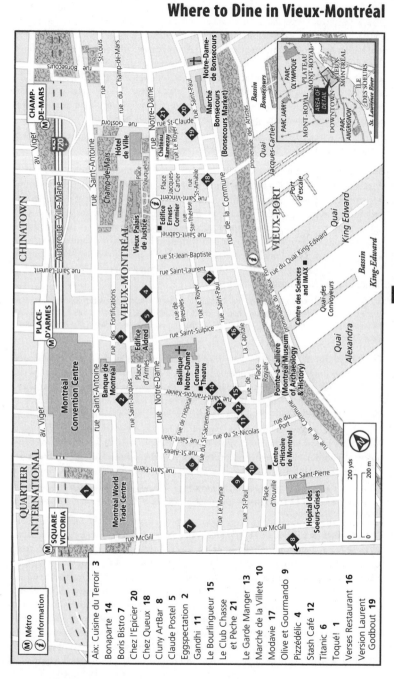

Aix: Cuisine du Terroir **3**
Bonaparte **14**
Boris Bistro **7**
Chez l'Epicier **20**
Chez Queux **18**
Cluny ArtBar **8**
Claude Postel **5**
Eggspectation **2**
Gandhi **11**
Le Bourlingueur **15**
Le Club Chasse
et Pêche **21**
Le Garde Manger **13**
Marché de la Villette **10**
Modavie **17**
Olive et Gourmando **9**
Pizzédélic **4**
Stash Café **12**
Titanic **6**
Toqué! **1**
Verses Restaurant **16**
Version Laurent
Godbout **19**

dominates, evidenced in dishes like the caramelized-leek-and-onion tart to the game fricassee with root vegetables. An *amuse* of caviar with eggplant and aioli might set the course, and portions are generous enough that you could graze on a few appetizers alone (the lobster bisque with shrimp quenelle and Abitibi caviar, for example, is quite filling). Restful earth tones, tan banquettes, and flickering gas lamps reiterate the focus on the food of the earth, especially in the evening. Those with lighter appetites or looking for a more buzzing atmosphere should head to the snazzy **Suite 701** bar, also in the hotel, where young professionals convene after work and into the evening. Food here—like the Kobe burger and fish and chips—comes from the same kitchen.

711 côte de la Place d'Armes (near rue St-Antoine). ✆ **514/904-1201.** www.aixcuisine.com. Main courses C$23–C$41 (£12–£21). AE, DC, MC, V. Daily 11am–3pm and 5:30–11pm. Métro: Place d'Armes.

Bonaparte ★ FRENCH TRADITIONAL   In a city brimming with accomplished French restaurants, this is a personal favorite. The dining rooms run through the ground floors of two old row houses, and with rich decorative details suggestive of the namesake's era. Adroit service is provided by schooled pros who manage to be knowledgeable without being stuffy. Highlights have included salmon in a phyllo-dough crust stuffed with leeks and a dash of vanilla, Dover sole filet with fresh herbs, and mushroom ravioli seasoned with fresh sage. Lunches cater to an upscale business crowd, and the restaurant offers an early evening menu for theatergoers. The clean and bright 31-room **Auberge Bonaparte** (p. 80) is upstairs.

447 rue St-François-Xavier (north of rue St-Paul). ✆ **514/844-4368.** www.bonaparte.com. Main courses C$21–C$37 (£10–£18); *table d'hôte* lunch C$16–C$23 (£8–£11), dinner C$28–C$39 (£14–£20); 6-course tasting menu C$62 (£31). AE, DC, MC, V. Mon–Fri noon–2:30pm; daily 5:30–10:30pm. Métro: Place d'Armes.

Chez l'Epicier ★ FUSION   This crisp little eatery opposite the Marché Bonsecours does double duty: It's simultaneously a high-end restaurant and a gourmet delicatessen with an abundance of tempting prepared foods, so remember it when you're planning a picnic down the hill in Vieux-Port. The kitchen here is wont to fashionable, extravagant preparations, with creative flourishes equaled by only a few other local establishments. Asian ingredients and techniques are part of the mix, as are witty surprises: Witness as your waiter injects tomato confit into a humble turnip . . . using a syringe! Success has nurtured ambition, and the chef-proprietor now runs the **Version Laurent Godbout** (see below) restaurant a few doors away as well.

331 rue St-Paul est (at rue St-Claude). ✆ **514/878-2232.** www.chezlepicier.com. Main courses C$26–C$39 (£13–£20); 7-course tasting menu C$80 (£40). AE, DC, MC, V. Mon–Fri 11:30am–2pm; daily 5:30–10pm. Métro: Champ-de-Mars.

Chez Queux ★ FRENCH TRADITIONAL   No fancy foams or colorful nasturtiums on these plates. Chez Queux is a throwback to a time when the only cuisine was French and the only proper romantic meal consisted of chateaubriand for two, showy tableside preparations, and flaming desserts—all the usual suspects that may be remembered from big nights out in the 1960s. A menu like this could result in tired renditions from chefs bored to tears, but not here. The food is decidedly retro but the execution is superb. Shellfish bisque, Dover sole meunière, sweetbreads with morels, and even crêpes suzette are better than those of a certain age will recall and will be a revelation to those too young to remember. The mood is nurtured by the baronial setting of a mansion built for the mayor in 1862; deep paneling contrasts with exposed brick walls, fringed lampshades, wrought-iron chandeliers, weighty velvet drapes, a baby grand, and a two-sided gas fire-place that casts shadows over all. The waiters even wear tuxedos. A summer dining terrace adds views of Vieux-Port to the experience. In short, this is a place at which to fire up a new relationship or cement an old one.

158 rue St-Paul est (at Place Jacques Cartier). ✆ 514/866-5194. www.chezqueux.com. Reservations recommended. Main courses C$28–C$42 (£14–£21); *table d'hôte* lunch C$14–C$28 (£7–£14). AE, DC, DISC, MC, V. Tues–Fri 11:30am–2:30pm; Tues–Thurs 5–10pm; Fri–Sat 5–10:30pm. Métro: Place d'Armes.

Le Club Chasse et Pêche ★ FUSION   The name "Hunting and Fishing Club" doesn't suggest fine dining, but here *chasse et pêche* more accurately means "new-school surf and turf." This restaurant received enthusiastic reviews upon its 2005 opening and works hard to keep bringing the crowds in. The restaurant's website includes a quirky blog of reviews, YouTube films, and other stuff the staff likes, and hints at the hip following the restaurant has. Recent items have included Kobe beef and short rib with artichoke and fava beans; wild mushroom risotto; and yellowfin tuna with mushrooms, truffles, and eggplant.

423 rue St-Claude (between rue St-Paul and rue Notre-Dame). ✆ 514/861-1112. www.leclubchasseet peche.com. Reservations recommended. Main courses C$28–C$32 (£14–£16). AE, DC, MC, V. Tues–Fri 11:30am–2pm; Tues–Sat 6–10:30pm. Métro: Champ-de-Mars.

Le Garde Manger SEAFOOD   There's nothing delicate about this newcomer. From the dark roadhouse decor to the rowdy slip of a bar to the moderately attentive baseball-capped servers, this giddy, buzzing resto delivers a smackdown to its gentrified Vieux-Montréal neighbors. On the plus side, the food is pretty good and generously portioned. The menu changes nightly, but options might include Chilean sea bass, beef cheeks with bok choy, or the terrifically hot-and-heavy General Tao's lobster. The *assiette de fruits de mer* comes in a small, wooden barrel perched sideways. You'll need a lead stomach to survive a whole portion of the signature dessert, a fried Mars bar, unless deafening rock music helps you digest. There's no sign outside, just a blank, white cube that glows pink when there's action inside.

408 rue St-François-Xavier (north of rue St-Paul). ✆ 514/678-5044. Reservations recommended. Main courses C$18–C$34 (£9–£17). AE, MC. Tues–Sun 6–11pm; bar open until 3am. Métro: Place d'Armes.

Modavie ★ MEDITERRANEAN   A highly visible location directly on the main pedestrian street no doubt helps keep this restaurant and wine bar full, but the management leaves little to chance. Live jazz is presented nightly from 7 until about 10pm, making this a comfortable place for singles as well as couples and groups (and a special treat on snowy Sunday nights, when many other restaurants are closed). Food is put together well and generously portioned. Lamb is the house specialty and comes in six iterations, including a rack of lamb with Dijon mustard, rosemary, and thyme. Other options include bison medallion, tiger shrimp in Grand Marnier sauce, and goat-cheese ravioli. On summer nights, candle flames flicker in river breezes that flow in through the tall front and side windows flung wide. A handsome horseshoe-shaped bar with a dozen stools boasts walls stacked with bottles of wine and single-malt scotches; ceiling fans twirl gently overhead.

1 rue St-Paul ouest (corner of rue St-Laurent). ✆ 514/287-9582. www.modavie.com. Reservations recommended. Main courses C$17–C$37 (£8.50–£19); *table d'hôte* dinner C$27–C$32 (£14–£16). AE, MC, V. Sun–Wed 11:30am–10:30pm; Thurs 11:30am–11pm; Fri–Sat 11:30am–midnight. Métro: Place d'Armes.

Verses Restaurant ★ FRENCH CONTEMPORARY The flowering of boutique hotels has given multiple jolts of glamour to Old Montréal, joining daring design with the preservation of historic buildings. With this movement have come hotel restaurants that destroy the image of bland, threadbare dining rooms. Among them is this snazzy space in the top-notch **Hôtel Nelligan** (p. 72). With ancient stone-and-brick walls, high ceilings, and a horseshoe bar, it's welcoming and clubby. The ambience contributes to an active social scene with the *cinq-à-sept* (5-to-7) crowd toward week's end, especially when the weather is warm enough to open the front doors. Service is adroit and thankfully short on pretension, and the pace of a meal is sedate. Lunch might be grilled beef with Pont-Neuf potatoes or seafood risotto, while dinner choices include lamb *osso buco,* duck breast with juniper berry demi-glace, and a 20-ounce angus rib steak. Not everything works; we had a near-flavorless duo of mackerel and sturgeon in white-bean *velouté*—but a recent seared tuna with grilled fennel was fabulous. The dessert menu features expected classics such as crème brûlée, as well as some playful options, like a sticky, gooey pineapple upside-down cake.

100 rue St-Paul ouest (at St-Sulpice). ✆ 514/788-4000. www.versesrestaurant.com. Reservations recommended. Main courses C$28–C$40 (£14–£20), *table d'hôte* lunch C$25 (£13). AE, DC, MC, V. Daily 6:30am–10:30pm (until 11pm Fri–Sat); bar until midnight Sun–Wed, 1am Thurs–Sat. Métro: Place d'Armes.

Version Laurent Godbout ★★ MEDITERRANEAN Epicures will want to put this on their top-five list. Flush with the ongoing success of his **Chez L'Epicier** just down the block (p. 92), the chef-proprietor (Laurent Godbout, of course) took on this space on the ground floor of the 19th-century Hotel Rasco. There's nothing Victorian about his interior, though; it's furnished with thoroughly modern tables and sensibilities. Options include crispy black cod with shellfish foam, smoked chipotle beef rib, and ricotta-and-sesame tortellini with creamed spinach. There are about 30 seats inside and a terrace out back, so it's an intimate venue. If you love the aesthetic, an on-site boutique sells the glassware, plates, and wooden wine buckets so you can re-create the look at home.

295 rue St-Paul est (at rue St-Claude). ✆ 514/871-9135. www.version-restaurant.com. Reservations recommended. Main courses C$26–C$34 (£13–£17). AE, DC, MC, V. Tues–Fri 11:30am–2pm; Tues–Sat 5:30–10pm. Métro: Place d'Armes or Champ-d-Mars.

MODERATE

Boris Bistro ★ FRENCH BISTRO In a city full of restaurants with outdoor terraces and gardens, this bistro's outdoor space stands out as being especially pretty. In warm months, the restaurant opens its side doors to what feels like an adjacent vacant lot (the façade of the building that once was here remains at one end), but there are leafy trees, large umbrellas, and, at night, subtle lighting and candles. It's filled with business folk and journalists by day—the *Montréal Mirror* newsweekly is in the same building—and all sorts at night: couples, families, and groups of young adults. It's special and, for some, a place to see and be seen, but it's not a *scene.* Cod can be a bland fish but it's buttery and melty here, roasted and served over a sublime basil-citrus risotto. The french fries cooked in duck fat are a signature dish, and there's a choice of about a half-dozen *fromages du terroir,* local cheeses, along with sweet treats, to close a meal. The restaurant does big volume, but even on a Saturday night in June, service is fast and efficient.

465 rue McGill (1 block south of rue Notre-Dame). ✆ 514/848-9575. www.borisbistro.com. Main courses C$14–C$20 (£7–£10). AE, MC, V. Mon–Fri 11:30am–11pm; Sat–Sun noon–11pm. Métro: Square-Victoria.

Gandhi ★ (**Value**) INDIAN   Classy but inexpensive enough to accommodate student and retiree budgets, Gandhi got so busy that the owners expanded into the adjacent building in 2007, doubling their seating space. Painted creamy yellow in one room and relaxing lavender in the other, the rooms are bright, and service is polite but brisk. The cooking is mostly to order and arrives fresh from the pot, pan, or oven. Flavors are delicate and subtle, but ask that they be ramped up to spicier levels and the kitchen will oblige. (Request "Madras hot" for medium heat.) Tandoori duck and lamb, and chicken tikka are popular, and vegetarian dishes fill a large section of the card.

230 rue St-Paul ouest (near rue St-François-Xavier). (✆) **514/845-5866.** www.restaurantgandhi.com. Main courses C$13–C$19 (£7–£10); *table d'hôte* lunch C$15–C$19 (£8–£10). AE, MC, V. Mon–Fri noon–2pm; daily 5:30–10:30pm. Métro: Place d'Armes.

INEXPENSIVE

Claude Postel LIGHT FARE   This sandwich shop started out as a patisserie and chocolatier, then added some tables and a short menu of daily hot specials. Most customers seem to go for pâtés, paninis, and pastries. Sandwiches are made to order from an intriguing range of ingredients, and breads are chewy and crusty in proper proportion. It's a logical place for a snack or a treat in the midst of a stroll through Vieux-Montréal.

75 rue Notre-Dame ouest (near rue St-Sulpice). (✆) **514/844-8750.** www.claudepostel.com. Most items cost less than C$7 (£3.50). AE, MC, V. Mon–Fri 7am–7pm; Sat–Sun 9am–5pm. Métro: Place d'Armes.

Cluny ArtBar (**Finds**) LIGHT FARE   Artists and high-tech businesses are moving into the loft-and-factory district west of avenue McGill, at the edge of Vieux-Montréal, though the streets are still very quiet here. Among the pioneers is the Darling Foundry, an avant-garde exhibition space in a vast, raw, former foundry. Room is provided for Cluny, which serves coffee, croissants, and lunch, with such fare as vegetarian antipasto, cream of parsnip soup, and smoked salmon panini. Though it's called a bar, its main hours are during the daylight, when the sun streams in through mammoth industrial windows; it's open past 5pm only on Thursday. Tables are topped with recycled bowling alley floors, just so you know. Free Wi-Fi is available.

257 rue Prince (near rue William). (✆) **514/866-1213.** www.cluny.info. Main courses C$4–C$19 (£2–£9.50). MC, V. Mon–Fri 8:30am–5pm (Thurs until 8pm). Métro: Square Victoria.

Eggspectation BREAKFAST/LIGHT FARE   Let the punny-funny name deter you and you'll miss a meal that may constitute one of your fondest food memories of Montréal, especially if you're in the breakfast-is-best school of gastronomy. The atmosphere and food here are far funkier and more creative than the name might imply, and prices are fair for the huge portions. What's more, the kitchen knows how to deal with volume and turns out good meals in nearly lightning speed, even on packed weekend mornings. There are eight variations of eggs Benedict alone, as well as sandwiches, burgers, and pasta options. Dishes are tagged with names like "Eggiliration" and "Oy Vegg." This is a chain ("constantly egg-spanding," as they put it), with another half-dozen locations in the city.

201 rue St-Jacques ouest (at rue St-François-Xavier). (✆) **514/282-0119.** www.eggspectation.ca. Most items cost less than C$12 (£6). AE, DC, MC, V. Mon–Fri 6am–3pm; Sat–Sun 7am–4pm. Métro: Place d'Armes.

Le Bourlingueur (**Value**) FRENCH BISTRO   Although it doesn't look especially promising at first, Le Bourlingueur is a keeper. The restaurant charges unbelievably low

> ⓜ Moments **Finding a Warm Corner After a Snowstorm**
>
> Lots of people save their vacation time for summer to come to Montréal when it's flush with outdoor music festivals, sidewalk cafes, sunny-day street fairs, and easy biking and strolling.
>
> But winter offers its own pleasures, especially if you're ensconced in the city after a big snowfall hits. In the early morning after such weather, Vieux-Montréal transforms into a wonderland blanketed in pure, white snow, still and quiet. Against the blank palette, the grey and black architecture of the 18th-century buildings stands out in high relief.
>
> Compared to when the city is offering up all sorts of sensory experiences, it becomes easier with sound and color stripped away to try to imagine what life might have been like in the settlement's earliest days.
>
> **Cluny ArtBar** (p. 95), on the far western end of Vieux-Montréal, is an excellent destination for a day like this. Classical music soars through the raw foundry space, and hot, frothy cappuccinos comfort you under a massive 1.2m (4-ft.) candelabra festooned with teeny Hindu gods and tea candles. Everything becomes new and old at the same time, cocooned by the awesome powers of Mother Nature.

prices for several four-course meals daily. The blackboard menu changes depending on what's available at the market that day, making it possible to dine here twice a day for a week without repeating anything, except the uninteresting salad. Roast pork with applesauce, glazed duck leg, and *choucroute garnie* (sauerkraut with meat) are likely to show up, but the house specialty is seafood—look for the shrimp in Pernod sauce. Well short of chic, the interior doesn't make the most of its stone walls and old beams, but the decor hardly matters at these prices.

363 rue St-François-Xavier (at rue St-Paul). ⓒ **514/845-3646.** Reservations recommended on weekends. Main courses and *table d'hôte* lunch and dinner C$11–C$22 (£5.50–£11). MC, V. Daily 11:30am–9pm. Métro: Place d'Armes.

Marché de la Villete ★ ⓥ Value FRENCH TRADITIONAL   If you close your eyes, you might convince yourself that there's a quiet French village outside of this charmingly simple restaurant. While it started life as an atmospheric *boucherie* and *charcuterie* specializing in cheeses, meats, and breads, the couple of tables in front multiplied quickly due to demand. Serving breakfast, snacks, and meals throughout the day, Marché de la Villete packs in neighbors and office workers much of the day, especially between noon and 2pm. The staff is flirty, boisterous, and extremely welcoming (even to guests who speak very little French). The several available platters of merguez and Toulouse sausages, various cheeses, and smoked meats are beguiling. Quiches, pâtés, and sandwiches are other possibilities. The *cassoulet de maison* is a must-try: it's full of duck confit, pork belly, homemade sausage, and silky smooth cassoulet beans, all topped with crunchy, seasoned bread crumbs. Wine is available.

324 rue St-Paul ouest (at rue St-Pierre). ✆ **514/807-8084.** Reservations not accepte
less than C$13 (£6.50). AE, MC, V. Mon–Sat 9am–6pm; Sun 9am–5pm. Métro: Square V

Olive et Gourmando ★ LIGHT FARE   This local favorite launched
Toqué! (p. 90) started out as an earthy bakery painted in reds, pinks, and
Then it added table service and transformed itself into a full-fledged ca.... ıt still sells
near-perfect baguettes, as well as many croissants, pastries, and specialty breads—a lot of
which is out the door by midmorning. Have a sandwich put together from the cheeses
and sausages in the cold case, or choose from the menu's interesting compositions,
including a grilled portobello mushroom with a purée of olives and goat cheese, served
on funky pottery or a wooden cutting board. The delightful sweets of local purveyor **Les
Chocolats de Chloé** (p. 156) have been added to the menu. The only pity is that this
eminently appealing spot is not open Sunday, Monday, or evenings.

351 rue St-Paul ouest (at rue St-Pierre). ✆ **514/350-1083.** www.oliveetgourmando.com. Most items cost
less than C$10 (£5). No credit cards. Tues–Sat 8am–6pm. Métro: Square-Victoria.

Pizzédélic Kids PIZZA   Pizza here runs the gamut from the traditional to the wildly
imaginative, with toppings such as your basic tomato sauce and mozzarella to more
startling concoctions involving black tiger shrimp and pickled ginger, or seafood in cream
sauce. The base crusts are thin and not quite crispy, and the selling point over ordinary
pizzerias is the use of fresh, not canned, ingredients. Pastas and burgers are also available,
and a breakfast menu is presented until 3pm daily. There's also a location at 3467 bd.
St-Laurent (✆ **514/845-0404**), about a block north of rue Sherbrooke.

39 rue Notre-Dame ouest (near bd. St-Laurent). ✆ **514/286-1200.** www.pizzedelic-montreal.com. Pizzas
and pastas C$8.50–C$17 (£4–£8.50). MC, V. Mon–Thurs 11am–10pm; Fri 11am–11pm; Sat 9:30am–11pm;
Sun 9:30am–10pm. Métro: Place d'Armes.

Stash Café Value POLISH   At this site for more than 30 years, this *restauracja polska*
continues to draw throngs of enthusiastic returnees for its abundant offerings and low
prices. The interior is composed of brick-and-stone walls, hanging lamps, wood refractory
tables, and pews salvaged from an old convent. Roast wild boar has long been featured,
along with *bigos* (a cabbage-and-meat stew) and *pirogis* (dumplings stuffed with meat and
cheese)—as to be expected in a Polish restaurant. Filling options and sides include potato
pancakes and borscht with sour cream. A jolly tone prevails, with animated patrons and
such menu admonitions as "anything tastes better with wodka, even wodka."

200 rue St-Paul oust (at rue St-François-Xavier). ✆ **514/845-6611.** www.stashcafe.com. Main courses
C$10–C$16 (£5–£8); *table d'hôte* dinner C$26–C$36 (£13–£18). AE, MC, V. Mon–Fri 11:30am–10:30pm;
Sat–Sun noon–10:30pm. Métro: Place d'Armes.

Titanic Finds LIGHT FARE   Really good sandwiches aren't easy to locate, but they
come to luscious life in these ramshackle rooms with overhead pipes. Freshly baked
baguettes are split and filled with such savory combos as coarse country pâté with green
peppercorns, or smoked ham and brie, or roast pork with chutney. There's a short cafeteria line of cold dishes and hot daily specials. You can also stop in for a breakfast omelet,
a meal-sized antipasto plate, or an afternoon snack. No alcoholic beverages, but with
good ol' Dad's Root Beer, who needs chablis? Note that the restaurant closes at 4pm.
There's free Wi-Fi on-site.

445 rue St-Pierre (near rue Le Moyne). ✆ **514/849-0894.** www.titanic-mtl.ca. Most items cost less than
C$10 (£5). Cash only. Mon–Fri 7:30am–4pm. Métro: Place d'Armes.

VERY EXPENSIVE

Moishes ★ STEAKHOUSE Those who care to spend serious money for a slab of beef should bring their credit scores here. The oldest steak-and-seafood house in town is also arguably the finest, with fewer tourists than popular Gibby's in Vieux-Montréal. It has traded in its dark, musty decor for a lighter, brighter look, and now positions itself as a home for delicious classics. Patrons include the trim new breed of up-and-coming executives as well as those members of the older generation who didn't know about triglycerides until it was too late. The former are more likely to go for the chicken teriyaki or arctic char, while the latter stick with steak. The wine list is substantial, and the restaurant offers tasting evenings.

In early 2008, Moishes opened a hipper, (relatively) less expensive burger joint in the heart of downtown, called **m brgr,** at 2015 rue Drummond (𝒞 **514/ 906-2747**). It features salads, sandwiches, and a variety of hamburgers, with options for what it candidly terms "crazy expensive toppings" such as black truffle carpaccio. The "deal" is still pricey: C$13 (£6.50) for a burger, fries, and soda, but the burger is *very good.*

3961 bd. St-Laurent (north of rue Prince Arthur). 𝒞 **514/845-3509.** www.moishes.ca. Reservations recommended. Main courses C$28–C$52 (£14–£26). AE, DC, MC, V. Mon–Fri 5:30–11pm; Sat–Sun 5–11pm. Métro: Sherbrooke.

EXPENSIVE

Au Pied de Cochon ★★ QUEBECOIS Packed to the walls 6 nights per week, this Plateau restaurant has become something of a cult favorite, and we've drunk the Kool-Aid, too. Though it looks like another of the amiable but mediocre storefront restos that line most streets in the neighborhood, famed chef Normand Laprise of **Toqué!** (p. 90) and American chef Anthony Bourdain both love the place. As the name—which means "the pig's foot"—suggests, the menu here is mostly about slabs of meat, especially pork. The PDC's Cut, weighing in at more than a pound, is emblematic. Meats are roasted to the point of falling off the bone in the brick oven, which survives from a previous pizza joint that occupied this space. There's a grand selection of seafood, from oysters to lobster to softshell crab, and chef Martin Picard gets particularly clever with one pervasive product: foie gras. It comes in 10 combinations, including as a tart, with *poutine,* and in a goofy creation called Duck in a Can which does, indeed, come to the table with a can opener. When you feel like another bite will send you into a cholesterol-induced coma, sugar pie is the only fitting finish.

536 rue Duluth est (near rue St-Hubert). 𝒞 **514/281-1114.** www.restaurantaupieddecochon.ca. Reservations strongly recommended. Main courses C$19–C$45 (£9.50–£23). MC, V. Tues–Sun 5pm–midnight. Métro: Sherbrooke.

Buonanotte ★ ITALIAN The decor of this high-ceilinged room was recently freshened up, but Buonanotte still resembles something out of New York's SoHo. Bass-heavy dance music, waitresses who look ready to depart to their next fashion shoot, everyone clad head to toe in black—it's all fabulous and dizzying. Though the food takes second place to the preening, the contemporary Italian dishes are good. The noise level cranks up after 7pm and the venue's real personality kicks in as a bar and nightclub with pretty people and DJs adjusting music to the crowd's mood.

3518 bd. St-Laurent (near rue Sherbrooke). ℂ **514/848-0644.** www.buonanotte.com. Reservations recommended. Main courses C$16–C$48 (£8–£24). AE, DC, MC, V. Mon–Sat 11:30am–midnight (until 1am Thurs–Sat); Sun 4pm–midnight; bar until 3am daily. Métro: St-Laurent.

Globe ★ ITALIAN   Owned by the same folks behind **Buonanotte** (see above) and **Rosalie** (p. 88), Globe is a similarly erotically charged, high-end undertaking that starts with a hostess at the podium who looks like she's stopped by between runway gigs, continuing with waitresses who bring food that's better than it has to be, and ends with dancing at midnight and lots of hooking up. There's a bar, where the activity intensifies after 9pm, and DJs. Still, the website claims that "a 4-letter F word is at the centre of this hot spot: FOOD!" Meals, if that's why you're here, can begin with selections from an oyster bar, minicheeseburgers, or wild salmon tartar with roasted yellow peppers and gazpacho. After that, options include bison, lamb, and strip steak. A fun splurge is a *fruits de mer* platter; it starts at C$55 (£28) for two. A late-night menu is offered from midnight to 2am Thursday through Saturday.

3455 bd. St-Laurent (north of rue Sherbrooke). ℂ **514/284-3823.** www.restaurantglobe.com. Reservations recommended. Main courses C$26–C$49 (£13–£25). AE, DC, MC, V. Sun–Wed 6–11pm; Thurs–Sat 6–midnight, with a smaller menu available until 2am. Métro: St-Laurent.

La Montée de Lait ★ ⦿**Finds**   FRENCH BISTRO   This compact bistro began life as a purveyor of dairy products (the "cheese and milk" of its name). When that proved too confining, the staff opened up the menu—quite successfully. Now the cramped corner space is filled nightly with neighborhood regulars, post-grads, and moneyed gourmands from upscale *quartiers*. They squeeze in around tipsy wood tables to partake in starters like red deer tartare (forget "venison"; Québécois don't need euphemisms for their food) or a seared scallop with green beans and a hard-boiled quail egg, and main dishes like buttery tuna over pencil asparagus and mushrooms, and rabbit terrine with a foie gras mousse and arugula salad. To take into account the initial enthusiasm that inspired the resto, order cheese for one of your courses; the selection is impeccable. *One warning:* When it's at capacity, the room's noise level can get super high.

371 rue Villeneuve est (corner rue Drolet). ℂ **514/289-9921.** Reservations recommended. *Table d'hôte* dinner C$40 (£20) for 4 courses, C$60 (£30) for 7 courses. MC, V. Tues–Sun 6–10pm; Wed–Fri noon–2pm. Métro: Mont-Royal.

Le Blanc ★ FUSION   Once a jinxed location that had seen three other attempts at restaurants crash in no time, this latest manifestation has lasted a decade, and 24m (80-ft.) stretch limos regularly pull up to the door. Le Blanc shifted its formula in early 2007 to more of a club-and-lounge atmosphere for a 20- and 30-something crowd. The pleasingly Art Deco space has a few romantically secluded booths to one side; the front opens to the street in good weather.

3435 bd. St-Laurent (north of rue Sherbrooke). ℂ **514/288-9909.** www.restaurantleblanc.com. Main courses C$38–C$45 (£19–£23); *table d'hôte* C$19–C$35 (£9.50–£18). AE, DC, MC, V. Mon–Sat 4–11pm; bar until 3am daily. Métro: Sherbrooke.

Maestro S.V.P. SEAFOOD   Smaller and more relaxed than many of the other restaurants packed in the 2 blocks of the Main north of Sherbrooke, the highlight of this storefront bistro is its oysters. A typical night features 14 varieties from the Atlantic (New Brunswick, Prince Edward Island, Nova Scotia) and Pacific (British Columbia, Japan). The staff, which claims that Maestro offers the biggest oyster selection in town regardless of season, is happy to help you pick a few to taste. The PEI Raspberry Point (who knew?)

is particularly salty when contrasted with the smooth and creamy BC Kusshi. A wall of fame of signed oyster shells includes signatures by the mayor of Montréal and scary guy Marilyn Manson. Main-course options include grilled shrimp in a foie gras velouté with a fennel-and-spinach purée, and the Maestro Platter, an extravagant medley of clams, mussels, calamari, a half lobster, *and* king crab. A 30-item tapas menu tantalizes Tuesday through Friday until 5pm, as well as all night on Tuesday and Wednesday, with nothing costing more than C$10 (£5). An all-you-can-eat mussel special is available on Sunday and Monday nights for C$12 (£6).

3615 bd. St-Laurent (at rue Prince Arthur). ⓒ **514/842-6447.** www.maestrosvp.com. Reservations recommended. Main courses C$16–C$56 (£8–£28). AE, DC, MC, V. Mon 5–10pm; Tues–Wed 11am–10pm; Thurs–Fri 11am–11pm; Sat 4pm–midnight; Sun 4–10pm. Métro: Sherbrooke.

MODERATE

Café Méliès FRENCH CONTEMPORARY   In a section of the Main that bristles with hipness, this well-appointed but much lower-key cafe-lounge sports decor that can best be described as "space-age submarine" (there are portholes throughout). Located inside the Ex-Centris film center, this electric-red spot has grown into a neighborhood favorite independent of its original function as an appendage to the movie theater. Certainly it can be good for a quick dinner before catching a film, but people also drop in for light or bountiful breakfasts on the weekends, a midday meal such as risotto with truffle oil and four kinds of mushrooms, or simply espresso or a glass of wine. Steel, chrome, and glass define the generous space, updating the traditional bistro concept, and it's open nearly 24 hours a day on the weekends.

3540 bd. St-Laurent (near av. des Pins). ⓒ **514/847-9218.** www.cafemelies.com. Main courses C$20–C$28 (£10–£14); *table d'hôte* C$35 (£18). AE, MC, V. Mon–Wed 11am–1am; Thurs–Fri 11am–3am; Sat–Sun 8:30am–3am. Métro: Sherbrooke.

L'Express ★ FRENCH BISTRO   No obvious sign announces this restaurant, with its name only spelled out discreetly in white tiles in the sidewalk. There's no need to call attention to itself, since *tout* Montréal knows exactly where this most classic of Parisian-style bistros is. The food is fairly priced for such an eternally busy place, costing the same at noon as it does at midnight. The atmosphere hits all the notes, from checkered floor to high ceiling to mirrored walls. After a substantial starter like ham-and-cheese quiche, opt for one of the lighter main courses, such as the ravioli *maison,* which are round pasta pockets filled with a flavorful mixture of beef, pork, and veal. Or just stop by for a bowl of *soupe de poisson* or a simple croque-monsieur. L'Express serves satisfying, unpretentious food, and is open until 3am. Though reservations are usually necessary for tables, single diners can often find a seat at the zinc-topped bar, where full meals are also served. Service is usually spot-on, although unpleasantly long waits for food during brunch hours are not unheard of.

3927 rue St-Denis (just north of rue Roy). ⓒ **514/845-5333.** Reservations recommended. Main courses C$13–C$22 (£6.50–£11). AE, DC, MC, V. Mon–Fri 8am–3am; Sat–Sun 10am–3am. Métro: Sherbrooke.

Pintxo ★★ (Value SPANISH   Pronounced "Peent-choo," the Basque word for tapas, this tucked-away resto draws from the Spanish Basque tradition, going in for exquisitely composed dishes at fair prices in pleasant surroundings. Cooking happens in an open kitchen in the middle of a two-part room with antique wood floors and brick walls. Each *pintxo* is true tapa size, only three or four bites, so order recklessly. Some of our favorites include the braised beef cheek, the seared foie gras on a bed of lentils, and the white

asparagus with Serrano ham and fried onion cut so fine it looks like tinsel. Dinners aren't
confined to meals composed solely of tapas presented on 4-inch tiles or slates, although
that isn't a bad way to go. For C$30 (£15), the *menu dégustation* provides four chef's-
choice *pintxos* and a main dish of your choice, in considerably larger proportion.

256 rue Roy est (2 blocks west of St-Denis). ℂ **514/844-0222.** www.pintxo.ca. Main courses C$19–C$21
(£9.50–£11); tapas C$6 (£3) or less; *menu dégustation* C$30 (£15). MC, V. Wed–Fri noon–2pm; Mon–Sat
6–11pm; Sun 6–10pm. Métro: Sherbrooke.

Restaurant de l'Institut ★ FRENCH CONTEMPORARY   The Institut de Tourisme et d'Hôtellerie du Québec is a premiere training ground for city tour guides, hotel
managers, front-of-the-room staff—and chefs. It runs two operations of particular interest to visitors: a **42-room training hotel** at this prime Plateau location, where rooms can
be let for C$99 to C$290 (£50–£145), and a training restaurant where students practice
innovative twists on classic dishes under the close eye of their teachers. The express menu
at lunch is popular, and recently included gazpacho garnished with quinoa and *crème de
bocconcini,* maple-and-chipotle-glazed pork chop with sautéed yams, and a delightful
blueberry foam "cake." The dining room is elegant and proper, and service, not surprisingly, is attentive and friendly.

3535 rue St-Denis (1 block north of rue Sherbrooke). ℂ **514/282-5161.** www.ithq.qc.ca. Main courses
C$28–C$38 (£14–£19); discovery menu C$45 (£23); *table d'hôte* dinner C$28–C$38 (£14–19), lunch C$19
(£9.50). MC, V. Mon–Fri 7–9:30am, noon–1:30pm, and 6–8:30pm (closed Mon night); Sat 7:30–10:30am
and 6–8:30pm; Sun 7:30–10:30am. Métro: Sherbrooke.

INEXPENSIVE

Café Cherrier BREAKFAST/LIGHT FARE   The tables on the terrace that wraps
around this corner building are filled whenever there's even a slim possibility that a heavy
sweater and a bowl of café au lait will fend off frostbite. In summer, loyalists stay out until
way past midnight, after the kitchen has closed. Brunch is popular even if the food is
unexceptional, but do consider this place any time a snack is in order: Croques-monsieur,
quiche, black pudding, and Toulouse sausage are all staples. Portions are ample and
inexpensive, and an easygoing atmosphere prevails. It's popular with musicians, actors,
and artists, so contrive to look mysterious or celebrated.

3635 rue St-Denis (2 blocks north of Sherbrooke). ℂ **514/843-4308.** Main courses C$10–C$21 (£5–£11).
AE, DC, MC, V. Mon–Fri 7:30am–10pm; Sat–Sun 8:30am–10pm. Métro: Sherbrooke.

Chez Schwartz Charcuterie Hébraïque de Montréal ★ DELI   French-first language
laws turned this old-time delicatessen into a linguistic mouthful, but it's still known simply
as Schwartz's to its ardent fans. Many are convinced it's the only place to indulge in the
guilty treat of *viande fumée*—a kind of brisket that's called, simply, smoked meat. Housed
in a long, narrow storefront, with a lunch counter and simple tables and chairs crammed
impossibly close to each other, this is as nondescript a culinary landmark as you'll find. If
there's not a line out the door, any empty seat is up for grabs. Sandwiches or plates are
described either as small (meaning large) or large (meaning humongous) and come heaped
with smoked meat and piles of rye bread. Most people also order sides of fries and mammoth garlicky pickles. There are a handful of alternative edibles, but leafy green vegetables
aren't among them. Expect a wait. Schwartz's has no liquor license, but it's open late.

3895 bd. St-Laurent (just north of rue Roy). ℂ **514/842-4813.** www.schwartzsdeli.com. Sandwiches
and meat plates C$4–C$17 (£2–£8.50). No credit cards. Sun–Thurs 8am–12:30am; Fri 8am–1:30am; Sat
8am–2:30am. Métro: Sherbrooke.

La Banquise LIGHT FARE   Open 24 hours a day in the heart of the Plateau (on Parc La Fontaine's north end), this colorful, friendly, funky, chatty, hippy-meets-hipster diner is a city landmark for its *poutine:* La Banquise offers some two dozen variations on the standard french fries with gravy and cheese curds, with add-ons ranging from smoked sausage to hot peppers to smoked meat to bacon. "Regular" size is huge and enough for two. Also on the menu are steamed hot dogs ("steamies") served with hot cabbage cole-slaw, burgers, omelets, and club sandwiches. Everything is best washed down with a local brew like Belle Gueule or Boréale. The restaurant expanded in 2006 and now has an outside terrace.

994 rue Rachel est (at rue Boyer). ✆ 514/525-2415. www.restolabanquise.com. *Poutine* plates C$5–C$7 (£2.50–£3.50); most other items cost less than C$10 (£5). No credit cards. Daily 24 hr. Métro: Mont-Royal.

St-Viateur Bagel & Café ★ LIGHT FARE   The bagel wars flare as hotly as Mon-tréal's eternal smoked-meat battles, but this, an offshoot of the original bakery still on rue St-Viateur in the Mile End neighborhood, is among the top contenders (we're also partial to **Fairmont Bagel,** p. 104). Here, you can get bagels to go or to eat in, with sandwiches, soup, or salad. The company notes on its website that it uses "the same old-fashioned baking techniques that founder Meyer Lewkowicz brought with him from eastern Europe." Those methods include hand-rolling the bagels and baking them in a wood-burning oven. To keep with tradition, "the factory only produces sesame and poppy seed bagels, the only two varieties that existed over 40 years ago." Expect a short wait, espe-cially on weekends. Montréal, by the way, has one of the world's largest Hasidic Jewish communities, 12,000 people, and many live in this neighborhood.

1127 Mont-Royal est (at av. Christophe-Colomb). ✆ 514/528-6361. www.stviateurbagel.com. Most items cost less than C$12 (£6). No credit cards. Daily 5:30am–midnight. Métro: Mont-Royal.

6 MILE END/AVENUE LAURIER

VERY EXPENSIVE

La Chronique ★★ FUSION   Montréal's top chefs have been recommending this modest-looking restaurant near Outremont for several years. It was feared that the result-ing buzz might spoil the place, but it has only improved, unless you count the hefty increase in prices. You'll discover how remarkable traditional recipes can be in the hands of a master. Presentations are so impeccable that you hate to disturb them, and flavors are so eye-rolling that you want to scrape up every last smear of food. Even diners leery of organ meats will find the veal sweetbreads a silky revelation. The menu features Mediterranean and Southwestern touches, as well as expensive ingredients like foie gras and caviar. A small but judicious selection of cheeses can precede or replace the tantaliz-ing desserts, which look as if they might take flight.

99 av. Laurier ouest (at rue St-Urbain). ✆ 514/271-3095. www.lachronique.qc.ca. Reservations recom-mended. Main courses C$32–C$38 (£16–£19); tasting menu C$100 (£50). AE, DC, MC, V. Tues–Fri 11:30am–2pm; daily 6–10pm. Métro: Laurier.

EXPENSIVE

Jun-I ★ FUSION   Many give this the nod for best sushi in town. At first glance, it looks like a standard sushi bar—effusive greetings from the chefs behind the counter,

traditional-looking maki, and other bits of fish and rice. But the eponymous chef, Junichi
Ikematsu, has ideas that go far beyond what you probably consider typical. You won't
soon forget the unagi roll—the thick rounds of sticky rice encasing grilled eel and avo-
cado stand on end, sprinkled with flying fish roe and supporting a tiny grove of colorful
micro-greens. Stick with the sushi and you won't go wrong, although there are options
of more conventional, but precisely grilled, meats and fish.

156 av. Laurier ouest (near rue St-Urbain). ⓒ **514/276-5864.** Reservations recommended on weekends.
Main courses C$26–C$35 (£13–£18); *table d'hôte* lunch C$23–C$29 (£12–£15). AE, DC, MC, V. Tues–Fri
11:30am–2pm; Mon–Thurs 6–10pm; Fri–Sat 6–11pm. Métro: Laurier.

MODERATE

BU ITALIAN   Not only has BU won awards for its sleek decor since its 2003 opening,
but it strikes just the right balance between wine and food. Focus on the antipasti: The
Assiette BU is a satisfying assortment of meats, cheese, and grilled vegetables, and some
come to this Mile End locale just for its silky rendition of *vitello tonnato*—veal and cream
of tuna. A handful of hot dishes are offered nightly, but the purpose of all the food is to
complement, not do battle with, the wines. The long card of 500 selections eschews the
same old bottlings, and even those who regard themselves as connoisseurs make delightful discoveries, guided by the knowledgeable staff. There are about 25 wines by the glass.
The crowd gets younger as the night rolls on, and because the bar stays open late, off-
duty chefs are often in the mix.

5245 bd. St-Laurent (at av. Fairmount). ⓒ **514/276-0249.** www.bu-mtl.com. Reservations
recommended. Antipasti and main courses C$4–C$25 (£2–£13). AE, MC, V. Daily 5pm–1am.
Métro: Laurier.

Chao Phraya (Finds) THAI   Open since 1988 and still a contender for the title of best
Thai in town, Chao Phraya has a panache that sets it a few notches above most of its
rivals, which means that every table is filled on the weekends. Named for a river in Thai-
land, Chao Phraya brightens its corner of the increasingly fashionable Laurier Avenue
with white table linens and sprays of orchids on each table. The host provides suggestions
about the menu's most popular items: dumplings in peanut sauce as an appetizer, and a
mixed seafood dish composed of squid, scallops, shrimp, crab claws, mussels, or red snap-
per as a main course. The food is tangy; menu items are given one to three hot-pepper
symbols grading hotness (two peppers are about right for most people). A cooling
cucumber salad helps, and you'll want a side of sticky rice, too. There is a good selection
of vegetarian options, as well. Everything comes in attractive bowls and platters, and the
atmosphere is warm and cozy. All 12 pages of the menu are posted online.

50 av. Laurier ouest (1 block west of bd. St-Laurent). ⓒ **514/272-5339.** www.chao-phraya.com. Reservations recommended. Main courses C$10–C$20 (£5–£10). AE, DC, MC, V. Thurs–Sat 5–11pm; Sun–Wed
5–10pm. Métro: Laurier.

Leméac ★ FRENCH BISTRO   This sprightly restaurant on the far western end of
the avenue Laurier scene has a long, tin-topped bar along one side; well-spaced tables;
and a crew of cheerful waitstaff. While the bistro dishes sound conventional on the page,
they are put together in freshly conceived ways. Two examples: A curried mussel soup is
capped by a nicely browned pillow of puff pastry, and the salmon *pot-au-feu* is a perfectly
cooked filet laid over a healthful selection of small potatoes, carrots, tender Brussels
sprouts, and their collective broth. Food is different but not startlingly so, and served in
an atmosphere that invites lingering. Weekend brunch is popular, as is the C$22 (£11)

appetizer-plus-main menu that kicks in at 10pm. The name comes from the publishing firm that used to occupy the building.

1045 av. Laurier ouest (corner of av. Durocher). ✆ **514/270-0999.** www.restaurantlemeac.com. Reservations recommended. Main courses C$18–C$38 (£9–£19); late-night menu C$22 (£11); weekend brunch C$13–C$16 (£7–£8). AE, DC, MC, V. Mon–Fri noon–midnight; Sat–Sun 10:30am–midnight. Métro: Laurier.

MeatMarket Restaurant Café (Finds) LIGHT FARE   Neither a butcher shop nor a pickup joint, MeatMarket is actually a stylish, gourmet sandwich-and-burger cafe. It's on a nondescript block of boulevard St-Laurent well north of the fancier restaurant action. There are vegetarian and salad options, but meats are the main attraction, including one of five burgers or the Cuba Libre sandwich with grilled pork, plantain, Cuban marinade, and mint-and-mango ketchup. The Swiss Miss burger, with bacon, Swiss cheese, caramelized onion, and pesto mayo, is short of sublime, but only just. Led Zeppelin on the stereo adds exactly the right kick.

4415 bd. St-Laurent (just south of av. du Mont-Royal). ✆ **514/223-2292.** www.meatmarketfood.com. Main courses C$6.50–C$29 (£3–£15); most items cost less than C$13 (£6.50). AE, MC, V. Mon 11am–3pm; Tues–Sat 11am–11pm. Métro: Mont-Royal.

INEXPENSIVE

Aux Vivres VEGAN   In business since 1997, this bright restaurant with white Formica tables, raw blonde walls, and pink Chinese lanterns has been humming and busy since moving into its current location in 2006. A large menu includes bowls of chili with guacamole, and bok choi with grilled tofu and peanut sauce. Other options include salads, sandwiches, desserts, and a daily chef's special. All foods are vegan, all vegetables are organic, and all tofu and tempeh are local and organic. In addition to inside tables, there is a juice bar off to one side and a back terrace.

4631 bd. St-Laurent (at av. du Mont-Royal). ✆ **514/842-3479.** Most items cost less than C$12 (£6). No credit cards. Tues–Sun 11am–11pm. Métro: Mont-Royal.

Bilboquet ★ (Kids) ICE CREAM   You can get a good croque-monsieur here, but the reasons to seek out this humble spot in Mile End's ritzy Outremont section are the splendid ice creams and sorbets. This *artisan glacier* makes its own sweet stuff, rich with caramel, nuts, fruit . . . whatever is fresh and available and strikes the chef's fancy. Flavors include maple taffy, passion fruit, chocolate-orange, and vanilla-raspberry. In warm weather, there's always a line. With just a few tables inside and benches outside, prepare to stroll with your cone. If you don't want to make the trek all the way north, you can also find Bilboquet ice cream at a push cart in the heart of Vieux-Port and downtown at the cheery **Java U Café,** 626 rue Sherbrooke.

1311 rue Bernard ouest (at av. Outremont). ✆ **514/276-0414.** Most items cost less than C$8 (£4). No credit cards. Daily 11am–midnight. Closed Jan–Mar. Métro: Outremont.

Fairmont Bagel BREAKFAST/LIGHT FARE   Bagels in these parts of North America are thinner, smaller, and crustier than the cottony monsters posing as the real thing south of the border. They're hand-rolled, twist-flipped into circles, and baked in big wood-fired ovens right on the premises. Fairmont was founded in 1919 and now offers 20 types, including unfortunate options like muesli and (shudder) blueberry, but why opt for oddball tastes when you can get a perfect sesame bagel? A 24-hour hole in the wall, Fairmont sells its bagels and accouterments such as lox and cream cheese to-go

week—even on Jewish holidays.

74 av. Fairmont ouest (near rue St-Urbain). $\mathcal{C}$ **514/272-0667.** www.fairmountbagel.com. Less than C$1 (50p) per bagel. No credit cards. Daily 24 hr. Métro: Laurier.

Wilensky Light Lunch LIGHT FARE Wilensky's has been a Montréal tradition since 1932, and has its share of regular pilgrims nostalgic for its grilled-meat sandwiches, low prices, curt service, and utter lack of decor. This is Duddy Kravitz/Mordecai Richler territory, and the ambience can best be described as Early Jewish Immigrant. There are nine counter stools, no tables. The house special is grilled salami and bologna, with mustard, thrown on a bun and squashed on a grill, and never, for whatever reason, cut in two. You can wash it down with an egg cream or Cherry Coke jerked from the rank of syrups—this place has drinks typical of the old-time soda fountain that it still is. Enter Wilensky's to take a step back in time; we're talking tradition here, not cuisine.

34 rue Fairmount ouest (1 block west of bd. St-Laurent). $\mathcal{C}$ **514/271-0247.** Most items cost less than C$4 (£2). No credit cards. Mon–Fri 9am–4pm. Métro: Laurier.

7 QUARTIER LATIN

INEXPENSIVE

La Paryse Value SANDWICHES Only slightly larger than your basic hole in the wall, this Latin Quarter standby packs in students, profs, young execs, and middleagers. They come for the burgers, as much the consensus choice for "best in town" as Schwartz's (p. 101) is for smoked meat. Unless you possess a really large appetite and a capacious mouth, you certainly won't need the double burger or the *frites grosse* (big fries). Wines are available by the glass. If you can, get a seat in the teeny venue, a sunny, funky place with handmade mosaic walls and yummy cakes displayed under glass domes. For vegetarians, there is either a tofu burger or a nut burger that can be topped with blue cheese, apple slices, lettuce, and grilled mushrooms. The inevitable line moves quickly.

302 rue Ontario est (at rue Sanguinet). $\mathcal{C}$ **514/842-2040.** All items cost less than C$10 (£5). MC, V. Tues–Fri 11am–11pm; Sat noon–10:30pm; Sun noon–10pm. Métro: Berri-UQAM.

8 OUTER DISTRICTS

VERY EXPENSIVE

Nuances ★★★ FRENCH CONTEMPORARY Nuances serves haute cuisine in a casino, as unlikely as that seems. Ensconced atop four floors of blinking lights and the crash of cascading jackpots, this dazzling entry into Montréal's gastronomic landscape got a face-lift in early 2007 that made the decor as contemporary and elegant as the food. A dramatic crystal chandelier may evoke the ghost of Liberace, but gone is the dark presidential decor and in are creamy walls, white linen, pale leather banquettes, and Granny Smith–green candles. Every staff member is a sommelier and qualified to advise about wines from the extensive cellar. Recent triumphs have included loin of caribou (killed by an Inuit arrow, purportedly) with parsley gnocchi and caramelized squash, and

Tips   Late-Night Bites

Most Montréal restaurants serve until 10 or 11pm, but sometimes you need something else—a meal or just a snack—a little later. Here are some places to keep in mind:

- **Boustan** (p. 89): In the middle of the late-night hubbub on downtown's rue Crescent, Boustan has lines out the door at 2am of night birds jonesing for a falafel or shawarma sandwich. Open until 4am daily.
- **Café Cherrier** (p. 101): This Plateau restaurant's kitchen typically closes at 10pm, but on warm summer nights, the terrace stays open to midnight or 1am.
- **Chez Schwartz** (p. 101): Also on the Plateau, Schwartz's meets all your smoked-meat needs until 12:30am every night, until 1:30am on Friday, and until 2:30am on Saturday.
- **Globe** (p. 99): Like its sister restaurant **Buonanotte** across the street (they share owners), this erotically charged restaurant at boulevard St-Laurent near rue Sherbrooke changes personality after about 10pm to something more akin to a nightclub. Thursday through Saturday, the regular menu is available until midnight, and a smaller menu kicks in from midnight until 2am.
- **La Banquise** (p. 102): Not only is Banquise known citywide for its *poutine,* but it's open 24 hours a day, 7 days a week—that is, whenever the urge strikes to indulge in any of 25 variations of french fries with gravy and cheese curds.
- **Leméac** (p. 103): This Mile End spot offers a special C$22 (£11) appetizer-plus–main menu from 10pm to midnight daily.
- **L'Express** (p. 100): This classic Paris-style bistro stays open until 3am nightly.
- **m brgr** (p. 98): Launched in the heart of downtown by the owners of its parent restaurant, Moishes, in early 2008, this chic little burger joint (whose name looks like a typo) serves salads and sandwiches, but the noise is about the hamburgers. They're on the pricey side but worth it. It's open Friday and Saturday to midnight, other evenings until 11pm.

Chilean sea bass with wine-butter emulsion. *Le fromage du sommelier* is a selection of cheeses including admirable Québec options. Save room for the spiced Genoa cake, which is served with mascarpone-cream fig chips, and espresso, which comes with rock-candy sugar on a stick. Dress code is businesslike, but women will feel equally comfortable in a little red dress. This is a room with real star power, but note that those younger than 18 are not admitted.

1 av. du Casino (in the Casino de Montréal, Ile Ste-Hélène). © **514/392-2708.** www.casino-de-montreal. com. Reservations recommended. Main courses C$40–C$45 (£20–£23); discovery menus C$95 and C$115 (£48 and £58). AE, DC, MC, V. Sun–Thurs 5:30–11pm; Fri–Sat 5:30–11:30pm. Métro: Parc Jean-Drapeau.

Joe Beef ★ SEAFOOD/STEAKHOUSE   This little beef-and-fish house opened in 2005 far from the brightest lights of downtown by folks who used to run those glamorous resto-clubs. Here, where the warehouses haven't all turned into high-end lofts yet, two other restaurants were added in 2007 and 2008 directly adjacent: **Liverpool House** (at no. 2501), an Italian gastropub, and **McKiernan** (no. 2485), a luncheonette and wine bar. Chef and restaurateur David McMillan spends his nights floating between the three venues; he's the big guy in the shorts and arm-sleeve tattoos (he's a wine connoisseur, too, so seek his advice regarding a claret to go with the beef). Atmosphere is moneyed roadhouse; Joe Beef is in a narrow storefront that keeps diners elbow to elbow, with the restaurant's menu and wine list written on a big blackboard occupying one wall. Customary starters are oysters, including many rarely seen, such as Caraquets, Cortez Islands, and Marina Gems. The menu might include *salade Joe Beef*, a tangy tangle of green beans, boiled potatoes, pickled beets, jicama, duck breast, and a poached egg. Main courses can include trout, suckling pig, cabbage stuffed with veal cheeks, and, of course, steak au poivre. With the Atwater Market just steps away, food is fresh and seasonal.

2491 rue Notre-Dame ouest (near av. Atwater). ℭ **514/935-6504.** www.joebeef.com. Reservations necessary. Main courses C$24–C$36 (£12–£18). MC, V. Tues–Sat with seatings at 7 and 9:30pm. Métro: Lionel-Groulx.

---

9 PICNIC FARE

If you're planning a picnic, bike ride, or simply an evening in, pick up supplies in Vieux-Montréal at any of three shops along rue St-Paul. On the street's west end is **Olive et Gourmando** (p. 97) at no. 351 and, just across the street, **Marché de la Villete** (p. 96) at no. 324. Both sell fresh breads, fine cheeses, sandwiches, salads, and pâtés. On rue St-Paul's east end, a block and a half from Place Jacques-Cartier, is **Chez l'Epicier** (p. 92), at no. 331. It's an ambitious restaurant with a gourmet delicatessen's worth of takeout goodies.

Better still, make a short excursion by bicycle or Métro (the Lionel-Groulx stop) to **Marché Atwater (Atwater Market),** the farmer's market at 138 av. Atwater which is open daily. The long interior shed is bordered by stalls stocked with gleaming produce and flowers. The two-story center section is devoted to vintners, butchers, bakeries, and cheese stores. In the *marché,* **Boulangerie Première Moisson** (ℭ **514/932-0328**) is filled with the tantalizing aromas of breads and pastries—oh, the pastries!—and has a seating area at which to nibble baguettes or sip a bowl of café au lait. Nearby, **Fromagerie du Marché Atwater** (ℭ **514/932-4653**) lays out more than 500 kinds of cheeses—scores of them from Québec—and also sells pâtés and charcuterie. Marché Atwater is on the Lachine Canal, where you can stroll and find a picnic table.

Exploring Montréal

Montréal is a feast of choices, able to satisfy the desires of physically active and culturally curious visitors. Hike up the city's mountain, Mont-Royal, in the middle of the city, cycle for miles beside 19th-century warehouses and locks on the Lachine Canal, take in artworks and ephemera at some 30 museums and as many historic buildings, attend a Canadiens hockey match, party until dawn on rue Crescent and the Main, or soak up the history of some 400 years of conquest and immigration: It's all here for the taking.

Getting from hotel to museum to attraction is fairly easy. Montréal has an efficient Métro system, a logical street grid; wide boulevards, and a vehicle-free underground city that all aid in the swift, largely uncomplicated movement of people from place to place.

If you're planning to check out several museums, consider buying the Montréal

Museums Pass (see the "Money Savers" box on p. 109).

For families with children, few cities assure kids of as good a time as this one. There are riverboat rides, the fascinating Biodôme—which replicates four distinct ecosystems—the creepy-crawlies of the Insectarium, a sprawling amusement park, the Centre des Sciences de Montréal down by the water, and magical circus performances by the many troupes that come through this circus-centric city.

In this book, attractions that are recommended for children are flagged with the **Kids** icon, and an "Especially for Kids" section is on p. 120.

Tip: Note which museums have restaurants or cafes so that you can plan a meal there. Remember, too, that most museums, though not all, are closed on Monday.

1 TOP ATTRACTIONS

DOWNTOWN

If this is your first trip to Montréal, consider starting with any of the walking tours in ch. 9.

Musée des Beaux-Arts ★★★ Montréal's Museum of Fine Arts is the city's most prominent museum, opened in 1912 in Canada's first building designed specifically for the visual arts. The original neoclassical pavilion is on the north side of Sherbrooke, with a striking annex built in 1991 directly across the street. The annex tripled exhibition space, adding sub-street-level floors and underground galleries that connect to the old building. Art on display is dramatically mounted, carefully lit, and diligently explained in both French and English.

Our recommendation is to enter the annex, take the elevator to the top, and work your way down. The permanent collection is largely devoted to Canadian and international contemporary art created after 1960, and to European painting, sculpture, and decorative art from the Middle Ages to the 19th century. The upper floors house many of the collection's gems—paintings by 12th- to 19th-century artists Hogarth, Tintoretto, Bruegel, El Greco, Ribera, and portraitist George Romney—and illustrative, if not world-class, works by more recent artists including Renoir, Monet, Picasso, Cézanne, and

Tips **Money Savers**

- **Buy the Montréal Museums Pass.** Good for 3 consecutive days, this pass grants entry to 31 museums and attractions, including most of those mentioned in this chapter. The full price, C$50 (£25), includes unlimited access to public transportation; pay C$45 (£22) for just the museums. There are no separate rates for seniors or children. The pass is available at all participating museums, many hotels, and the tourist offices at 174 rue Notre-Dame (in Vieux-Montréal) and 1255 rue Peel (downtown). To find out more, go to www.montrealmuseums.org.

- **Visit Vitrine Culturelle de Montréal for last-minute ticket deals.** The discount ticket office for Montréal cultural events opened in summer 2007 at 145 rue Sainte-Catherine ouest in Place des Arts. More at ℂ **866/924-5538** or www.vitrineculturelle.com.

- **Flash your AAA card.** Members of the American Automobile Association get the same discounts as do members of its Canadian sister organization, the CAA. That includes reduced rates at many museums, hotels, and restaurants.

- **Time your trip to coincide with Montréal Museums Day.** On the last Sunday in May, more than two dozen museums welcome visitors for free in a citywide open house. Free shuttle buses run between the venues as well.

EXPLORING MONTRÉAL

8

TOP ATTRACTIONS

Rodin. French-Canadian landscape watercolorist Marc-Aurèle Fortin (1888–1970) has been well represented ever since a separate museum that had been devoted just to him donated its entire collection to Beaux-Arts in 2007.

Temporary exhibitions can be dazzling: A show a few years ago brought the treasures of Catherine the Great, including her spectacular coronation coach, from the Hermitage Museum of Saint Petersburg. An exhibition of early-20th-century modernist Van Dongen's works is scheduled for 2009.

The museum's street-level store on the annex (south) side of rue Sherbrooke sells an impressive selection of quality books, games, and folk art. A good restaurant, **Café des Beaux-Arts,** is adjacent.

1379–80 rue Sherbrooke ouest (at rue Crescent). ℂ **514/285-2000.** www.mmfa.qc.ca. Free admission to the permanent collection (donations accepted). Admission to temporary exhibitions: C$15 (£7.50) adults, C$7.50 (£3) seniors and students, free for children 12 and younger, C$30 (£15) family (1 adult and 3 children 16 and younger, or 2 adults and 2 children 16 and younger); half price for adults Wed 5–8:30pm. AE, MC, V. Tues 11am–5pm; Wed–Fri 11am–9pm; Sat–Sun 10am–5pm. Métro: Guy-Corcordia. Bus: 24.

Musée McCord ★ The permanent exhibition "Simply Montréal: Glimpses of a Unique History" justifies a trip here all on its own; the show steeps visitors in what city life was like over the centuries. It even includes a substantial section about how the city handles the massive amounts of snow and ice it receives each year. Associated with McGill University, McCord showcases the eclectic—and, not infrequently, the eccentric—collections of scores of benefactors from the 19th century through today. More than 16,600 costumes, 65,000 paintings, and 1,250,000 historical photographs documenting Canada's history are rotated in and out of storage to be displayed. A First

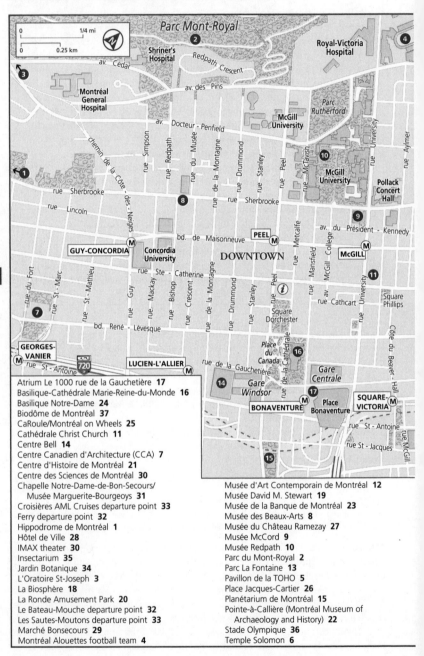

Atrium Le 1000 rue de la Gauchetière **17**
Basilique-Cathédrale Marie-Reine-du-Monde **16**
Basilique Notre-Dame **24**
Biodôme de Montréal **37**
CaRoule/Montréal on Wheels **25**
Cathédrale Christ Church **11**
Centre Bell **14**
Centre Canadien d'Architecture (CCA) **7**
Centre d'Histoire de Montréal **21**
Centre des Sciences de Montréal **30**
Chapelle Notre-Dame-de-Bon-Secours/
   Musée Marguerite-Bourgeoys **31**
Croisières AML Cruises departure point **33**
Ferry departure point **32**
Hippodrome de Montréal **1**
Hôtel de Ville **28**
IMAX theater **30**
Insectarium **35**
Jardin Botanique **34**
L'Oratoire St-Joseph **3**
La Biosphère **18**
La Ronde Amusement Park **20**
Le Bateau-Mouche departure point **32**
Les Sautes-Moutons departure point **33**
Marché Bonsecours **29**
Montréal Alouettes football team **4**

Musée d'Art Contemporain de Montréal **12**
Musée David M. Stewart **19**
Musée de la Banque de Montréal **23**
Musée des Beaux-Arts **8**
Musée du Château Ramezay **27**
Musée McCord **9**
Musée Redpath **10**
Parc du Mont-Royal **2**
Parc La Fontaine **13**
Pavillon de la TOHO **5**
Place Jacques-Cartier **26**
Planétarium de Montréal **15**
Pointe-à-Callière (Montréal Museum of
   Archaeology and History) **22**
Stade Olympique **36**
Temple Solomon **6**

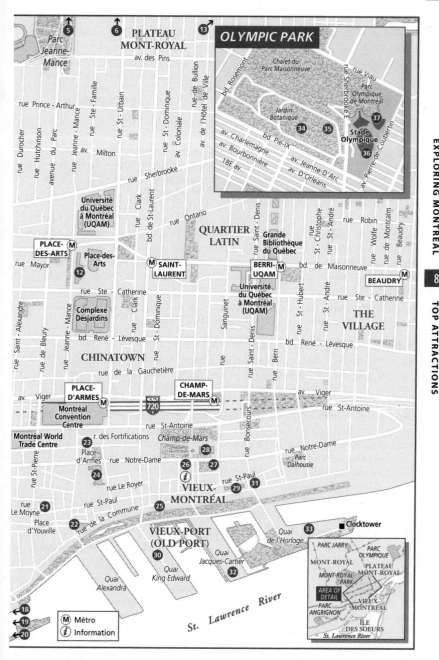

EXPLORING MONTRÉAL

TOP ATTRACTIONS

8

Nations room is where to see portions of the museum's extensive collection of objects from Canada's native population, including meticulous beadwork, baby carriers, and fishing implements. Exhibits are intelligently mounted, with texts in English and French. There's a small cafe near the front entrance, and a shop that sells Canadian arts and crafts, pottery, and more.

690 rue Sherbrooke ouest (at rue Victoria). ℂ **514/398-7100.** www.mccord-museum.qc.ca. Admission C$13 (£6.50) adults, C$10 (£5) seniors, C$7 (£3.50) students, C$5 (£2.50) ages 6–12, free for children 5 and younger; free admission on the first Sat of the month 10am–noon. MC, V. Tues–Fri 10am–6pm; Sat–Sun 10am–5pm. June 24 to Sept 1 and holiday weekends also Mon 10am–5pm. Métro: McGill. Bus: 24.

Parc du Mont-Royal   Montréal is named for this 232m (761-ft.) hill that rises at its heart—the "Royal Mountain." Walkers, joggers, cyclists, dog owners, and skaters all use this largest of the city's green spaces throughout the year. In summer, **Lac des Castors (Beaver Lake)** is surrounded by sunbathers and picnickers (no swimming allowed, however). In winter, cross-country skiers and snowshoers follow miles of paths and trails laid out for their use. The large, refurbished **Chalet du Mont-Royal** near the crest of the hill is a popular destination, providing a sweeping view of the city from its terrace and an opportunity for a snack. Up the hill behind the chalet is the spot where, legend says, Paul de Chomedey, Sieur de Maisonneuve (1612–76), erected a wooden cross after the colony sidestepped the threat of a flood in 1643. The present incarnation of the steel **Croix du Mont-Royal** was installed in 1924 and is lit at night. It usually glows white, though it was red in the 1980s during a march against AIDS and purple in 2005 in recognition of Pope John Paul II's death.

Downtown. ℂ **514/843-8240** for the Maison Smith information center in the park's center. www.lemont royal.qc.ca. Métro: Mont-Royal. Bus: 11; get off at Lac des Castors (Beaver Lake).

VIEUX-MONTREAL (OLD MONTREAL)

Vieux-Montréal's central plaza is **Place Jacques-Cartier,** the focus of much activity in the warm months. The plaza consists of two repaved streets bracketing a center promenade that slopes down from rue Notre-Dame to Old Port, with venerable stone buildings from the 1700s along both sides. Horse-drawn carriages gather at the plaza's base, and outdoor cafes, street performers, and flower sellers recall a Montréal of a century ago. Locals insist they would never go to a place so overrun by tourists—which makes one wonder why so many of them do, in fact, congregate here. They take the sun and sip sangria on the bordering terraces just as much as visitors do, enjoying the unfolding pageant.

If this is your first trip to Montréal, consider starting with the Vieux-Montréal walking tour in chapter 9 for an overview of the neighborhood and its attractions. The walk leads past most of the sites listed here and can help you get your bearings. For further information about this quarter, go to its official website: **www.vieux.montreal.qc.ca**.

Basilique Notre-Dame ★★★   Breathtaking in the richness of its interior furnishings and big enough to hold 4,000 worshipers, this magnificent structure was designed in 1824 by James O'Donnell, an Irish-American Protestant architect from New York—who was so profoundly moved by the experience of creating this basilica that he converted to Catholicism after its completion. The impact is understandable. Of Montréal's hundreds of churches, Notre-Dame's interior is the most stunning, with a wealth of exquisite details, most of them carved from rare woods that have been delicately gilded and painted. O'Donnell, clearly a proponent of the Gothic Revival style, is the only person honored by burial in the crypt.

The main altar was carved from linden wood, the work of Québécois architect Victor Bourgeau. Behind it is the **Chapelle Sacré-Coeur (Sacred Heart Chapel),** much of which was destroyed by an arsonist in 1978; it was rebuilt and rededicated in 1982. The altar displays 32 bronze panels representing birth, life, and death, cast by a Montréal artist named Charles Daudelin. A 10-bell carillon resides in the east tower, while the west tower contains a single massive bell, nicknamed **"Le Gros Bourdon,"** which weighs more than 12 tons and emanates a low, resonant rumble that vibrates right up through your feet.

A sound-and-light show called **"Et la lumière fut"** ("And then there was light")—advertised on garish banners in front of the church—is presented nightly Tuesday through Saturday.

110 rue Notre-Dame ouest (on Place d'Armes). (*C*) **514/842-2925.** www.basiliquendm.org. Basilica C$5 (£2.50) adults, C$4 (£2) ages 7–17, free ages 6 and younger. Light show C$10 (£5) adults, C$9 (£4.50) seniors, C$5 (£2.50) ages 17 and younger. MC, V. Mon–Fri 8am–4:30pm, Sat 8am–4pm, Sun 12:30–4pm; light shows Tues–Thurs 6:30pm, Fri 6:30 and 8:30pm, Sat 7 and 8:30pm. Métro: Place d'Armes.

Centre des Sciences de Montréal ★ (Kids) Running the length of a central pier in Vieux-Port (Old Port), this ambitious complex (called the Montréal Science Centre in English) got a big overhaul in 2007. Focusing on science and technology, its attractions include interactive displays, multimedia challenges, and a popular **IMAX theater** (p. 120). Designed to bring to life the concepts of energy conservation, 21st-century communications, and the life sciences, the center's extensive use of computers and electronic visual displays are particularly appealing to youngsters; indeed, the whole place is designed for ages 9 to 14. Admission fees vary according to the combination of exhibits and movie showings you choose. To avoid long lines, preorder tickets for special exhibits. Several outdoor and indoor cafes sell sandwiches, salads, and sweets.

Vieux-Port, Quai King Edward. (*C*) **514/496-4724.** www.montrealsciencecentre.com. Admission for exhibitions C$12 (£6) adults, C$11 (£5.50) seniors and ages 13–17, C$9 (£4.50) ages 4–12, free for children 3 and younger. Movie tickets from C$12 (£6) adults, C$11 (£5.50) seniors and ages 13–17, C$9 (£4.50) ages 4–12, free for children 3 and younger. MC, V. Daily 10am–5pm. Métro: Place d'Armes or Champ-de-Mars.

Pointe-à-Callière (Montréal Museum of Archaeology and History) ★★★ A first visit to Montréal might best begin here. Built on the very site where the original colony was established in 1642 (called Pointe-à-Callière), this modern museum engages visitors in rare, beguiling ways. The triangular new building echoes the Royal Insurance building (1861) that stood here for many years.

Go first to the 16-minute multimedia show in an auditorium that actually stands above exposed ruins of the earlier city. Music and a playful bilingual narration keeps the history slick and painless if a little chamber-of-commerce upbeat (children 11 and younger may find it a snooze).

Evidence of the area's many inhabitants—from Amerindians to French trappers to Scottish merchants—was unearthed during archaeological digs that took more than a decade. Artifacts are on view in display cases set among the ancient building foundations and burial grounds below street level. Wind your way on the self-guided tour through the subterranean complex until you find yourself in the former Custom House, where there are more exhibits and a well-stocked gift shop.

L'Arrivage Café is open daily for lunch and presents a fine view of Vieux-Montréal and Vieux-Port. Allow 1½ hours to visit this museum, which is wheelchair accessible.

350 Place Royale (at rue de la Commune). ⓒ **514/872-9150.** www.pacmuseum.qc.ca. Admission C$13 (£6.50) adults, C$9 (£4.50) seniors, C$7.50 (£4) students, C$5 (£2.50) children 6–12, free for children 5 and younger. July–Aug Mon–Fri 10am–6pm, Sat–Sun 11am–6pm; Sept–June Tues–Fri 10am–5pm, Sat–Sun 11am–5pm. L'Arrivage Café Mon 11:30am–2pm, Tues–Sun 11:30am–3pm. Métro: Place d'Armes.

Vieux-Port ★★ Kids Montréal's Old Port was transformed in 1992 from a dreary commercial wharf area into a 2km-long (1¼-mile), 53-hectare (131-acre) promenade and public park with bicycle paths, exhibition halls, and a variety of family activities, including the **Centre des Sciences de Montréal** (see above).

The area is most active from mid-May through October, when harbor cruises take to the waters and bicycles, in-line skates, and family-friendly Quadricycle carts are available to rent. Warm months also bring information booths staffed by bilingual attendants and 50-minute guided tours in the open-sided **La Balade,** a small, motorized tram. In winter, things are quieter, but an outdoor ice-skating rink is a big attraction.

At the port's far eastern end, in the last of the old warehouses, is a 1922 clock tower, **La Tour de l'Horloge,** with 192 steps leading past the exposed clockworks to observation decks overlooking the St. Lawrence River (admission is free).

Vieux-Port stretches along the waterfront parallel to rue de la Commune from rue McGill to rue Berri.

Information booth for the Vieux-Port expanse is at the Centre des Sciences de Montréal on Quai King Edward (King Edward Pier). ⓒ **800/971-PORT** (971-7678). www.quaysoftheoldport.com. La Balade tram C$5 (£2.50) adults, C$3.50 (£2) seniors (60 and older) and teens (13–17), C$3 (£1.50) children 12 and younger. Métro: Champ-de-Mars, Place d'Armes, or Square Victoria.

ELSEWHERE IN THE CITY

A 20-minute drive east on rue Sherbrooke or an easy Métro ride from downtown is **Olympic Park** (in a neighborhood called Hochelaga-Maisonneuve). It has four attractions: Stade Olympique (Olympic Stadium), Biodôme de Montréal, Jardin Botanique (Botanical Garden), and Insectarium de Montréal. The first three are described below, and the Insectarium on p. 120. All are walking distance from each other, and there's a free shuttle in summer. You could spend a day touring all four sites, and kids will especially love the Biodôme and Insectarium. Combination ticket packages are available, and the Biodôme, Jardin, and Insectarium are all included in the **Montréal Museum Pass** (see the "Money Savers" box on p. 109). Underground parking at the Olympic Stadium is C$12 (£6) per day, with additional parking at the Jardin Botanique and Insectarium.

Biodôme de Montréal ★★ Kids A terrifically engaging attraction for children of nearly any age, the delightful Biodôme houses replications of four ecosystems: a tropical rainforest, a Laurentian forest, the St. Lawrence marine system, and a polar environment. Visitors walk through each and hear the animals, smell the flora, and, except in the polar region, which is behind glass, feel the changes in temperature. The rainforest area is the most engrossing (the subsequent rooms increasingly less so), so take your time here. It's a kind of "Where's Waldo" challenge to find all the critters, from the huge groundhog called a capybara to the golden lion tamarin monkeys that swing on branches only an arm's length away. Only the bats, fish, penguins, and puffins are behind glass. A giant tank in the St. Lawrence area holds Atlantic sturgeon nearly 1.5m (5 ft.) long, while the open-air space features hundreds of shore birds whose shrieks can transport you to the beach. A continual parade of temporary exhibits and new programs keeps things fresh. The building was originally the velodrome for cycling during the 1976 Olympics. The facility also has a game room called Naturalia, a shop, a bistro, and a cafeteria.

4777 av. Pierre-de-Coubertin (next to Stade Olympique). $\textcircled{C}$ **514/868-3000.** www.biodome.qc.ca. Admission C$16 (£8) adults, C$12 (£6) seniors and students, C$8 (£4) children 5–17, C$2.50 (£1.25) children 2–4. Audio guide C$4 (£2). AE, MC, V. Daily 9am–5pm (until 6pm late June through Aug). Closed most Mon Sept–Dec. Métro: Viau.

Jardin Botanique ★★★   Spread across 75 hectares (185 acres), Montréal's Botanical Garden is a fragrant oasis 12 months a year. Ten large conservatory greenhouses each have a theme: one houses orchids, another has begonias and African violets, and yet another features rainforest flora.

Outdoors, spring is when things really kick in: lilacs in May, lilies in June, and roses from mid-June until the first frost. The **Chinese Garden**, a joint project of Montréal and Shanghai, evokes the 14th- to 17th-century era of the Ming Dynasty and was built according to the Chinese landscape principles of yin and yang. It incorporates pavilions, inner courtyards, ponds, and myriad plants indigenous to China. The serene **Japanese Garden** fills 6 hectares (15 acres) and includes a cultural pavilion with an art gallery, a tearoom where ancient ceremonies are performed, a stunning bonsai collection, and a Zen garden.

A small train runs through the gardens from mid-May to October and is worth the small fee charged to ride it.

The grounds are also home to the **Insectarium** (p. 120), which displays some of the world's most beautiful and sinister insects. Birders should bring binoculars with which to spot some of the more than 190 species here. An extensive website (listed below) provides great details on everything.

4101 rue Sherbrooke est (opposite Olympic Stadium). $\textcircled{C}$ **514/872-1400.** www.ville.montreal.qc.ca/jardin. Admission includes access to the Insectarium. May 15–Oct 31 C$16 (£8) adults, C$12 (£6) seniors and students, C$8 (£4) children 5–17, C$2.50 (£1) children 2–4. Rates drop about 10% the rest of the year. MC, V. Daily 9am–5pm (until 6pm May 15 to Sept 4, until 9pm Sept–Oct). Closed Mon Nov to mid-May. No bicycles or dogs. Métro: Pie-IX, then walk up the hill; or take free shuttle bus from Olympic Park (Métro: Viau).

Stade Olympique   Montréal's space-age and controversial Olympic Stadium, the centerpiece of the 1976 Olympic Games and looking kind of like a giant stapler, is likely to induce only moderate interest for most visitors. The main event is the 175m (574-ft.) inclined tower, which leans at a 45-degree angle and does duty as an observation deck, with a funicular that whisks passengers to the top in 95 seconds. On a clear day, the deck bestows an expansive view over Montréal and into the neighboring Laurentian mountains, but at C$14 (£7), the admission price is as steep as the tower.

The complex includes a stadium that seats up to 56,000 for sporting events and music concerts (it was home to the Montréal Expos before that baseball team relocated to Washington, D.C., in 2005). The Sports Centre houses five swimming pools open for public swimming and classes, including one deep enough for scuba diving. Thirty-minute guided tours that describe the 1976 Olympic Games and current center are available daily for C$8 (£4).

The roof doesn't retract anymore—it never retracted well anyway. That's one reason that what was first known as "the Big O" was scorned as "the Big Woe," then "the Big Owe" after cost overruns led to heavy tax increases.

4141 av. Pierre-de-Coubertin. $\textcircled{C}$ **514/252-4141.** www.rio.gouv.qc.ca. Tower admission C$14 (£7) adults, C$11 (£5) seniors and students, C$7 (£3.50) ages 5–17. Public swimming scheduled daily, admission C$4 (£2) adults, C$3 (£1.50) children 17 and younger. Tower daily 9am–7pm in summer; until 5pm in winter. Closed mid-Jan to mid-Feb. Métro: Viau.

2 MORE ATTRACTIONS

DOWNTOWN

Basilique-Cathédrale Marie-Reine-du-Monde   No one who has seen both will confuse Montréal's "Mary Queen of the World" cathedral with St. Peter's Basilica in Rome, but a scaled-down homage was the intention of Bishop Ignace Bourget, who oversaw its construction after the first Catholic cathedral here burned to the ground in 1852. Construction lasted from 1875 to 1894, its start delayed by the bishop's desire to place it not in Francophone east Montréal but in the heart of the Protestant Anglophone west. The resulting structure covers less than a quarter of the area of its Roman inspiration. Most impressive is the 76m-high (249-ft.) dome, about a third of the size of the original. The statues standing on the roofline represent patron saints of the region, providing a local touch. The interior is less rewarding visually than the exterior, but the high altar is worth a look. Masses are held daily.

1085 rue de la Cathédrale (at rue Mansfield). ℂ **514/866-1661.** www.cathedralecatholiquedemontreal. org. Free admission; donations accepted. Daily 7:30am–6pm. Métro: Bonaventure.

Cathédrale Christ Church   This Anglican cathedral, which is reflected in the shiny exterior of the pink-glassed postmodern Tour KPMG office tower, stands in glorious Gothic contrast to the city's downtown skyscrapers. The building was completed in 1859. The original steeple was too heavy for the structure, so a lighter aluminum version replaced it in 1940. It's sometimes called the "floating cathedral" because of the many tiers of malls and corridors in the underground city beneath it and the way it was elevated during their construction. The choirs offer music each Sunday at 10am and at 4pm with Choral Evensong, both live and broadcast at www.radiovm.com. The church also hosts concerts throughout the year.

635 rue Ste-Catherine (at rue University). ℂ **514/843-6577,** ext. 371 (recorded information about services and concerts). www.montreal.anglican.org/cathedral. Free admission; donations accepted. Daily 10am–6pm; services Sun 8am, 10am, and 4pm; weekdays noon and 5:15pm. Métro: McGill.

Musée d'Art Contemporain de Montréal ★   Montréal's Museum of Contemporary Art is Canada's only museum devoted exclusively to contemporary art. Focusing on works created since 1939, much of the permanent collection (some 7,000 pieces) is composed of the work of Québécois artists such as Jean-Paul Riopelle and Betty Goodwin, but also includes examples of such international artists as Richard Serra, Bruce Nauman, Sam Taylor-Wood, and Nan Goldin. No single style prevails, so expect to see installations, video displays, and examples of pop, op, and abstract expressionism. That the works often arouse strong opinions signifies a museum that is doing something right. On "Friday Nocturnes"—the first Friday of the month—the museum stays open until 9pm with live music, bar service, and tours of the exhibition galleries. The museum's glass-walled restaurant, **La Rotonde,** serves such dishes as breast of duck in lavender honey, and has a summer dining terrace.

185 rue Ste-Catherine ouest. ℂ **514/847-6226.** www.macm.org. Admission C$8 (£4) adults, C$6 (£3) seniors, C$4 (£2) students, free for children 11 and younger, free to all Wed 6–9pm. Tues–Sun 11am–6pm (until 9pm Wed). Métro: Place des Arts.

VIEUX-MONTRÉAL (OLD MONTREAL)

Chapelle Notre-Dame-de-Bon-Secours/Musée Marguerite-Bourgeoys   Just to the east of Marché Bonsecours, Notre Dame de Bon-Secours Chapel is called the

Sailors' Church because of the special attachment that fishermen and other mariners have to it; their devotion is manifest in the several ship models hanging from the ceiling inside. Also, there's an excellent view of the harbor from the church's tower.

The first building, which no longer stands, was the project of an energetic teacher named Marguerite Bourgeoys, and built in 1675. Bourgeoys had come from France to undertake the education of the children of Montréal; later, she and other teachers founded the Congregation of Notre-Dame, Canada's first nuns' order. The pioneering Bourgeoys was canonized in 1982 as the Canadian church's first female saint and in 2005, for the chapel's 350th birthday, her remains were brought to the church and interred in the left-side altar.

A restored 18th-century crypt under the chapel houses the museum. Part of it is devoted to relating Bourgeoys' life and work, while another section displays artifacts from an archaeological site here, including ruins and materials from the colony's earliest days. An Amerindian fire pit on display dates to 400 B.C.

400 rue St-Paul est (at the foot of rue Bonsecours). ℰ **514/282-8670.** www.marguerite-bourgeoys.com. Free admission to chapel. Museum C\$8 (£4) adults, C\$5 (£2.50) seniors and students, C\$4 (£2) children ages 6–12, free for children 5 and younger; archaeological site with guide and access to museum C\$18 (£9) for family. May–Oct Tues–Sun 10am–5pm; Nov to mid-Jan and Mar–Apr Tues–Sun 11am–3:30pm. Métro: Champ-de-Mars.

Hôtel de Ville City Hall, finished in 1878, is relatively young by Vieux-Montréal standards. It's still in use, with the mayor's office on the main floor. The French Second Empire design makes it look as though it was imported stone by stone from the mother country; balconies, turrets, and mansard roofs decorate the exterior. The details are particularly visible when the exterior is illuminated at night. The Hall of Honour is made of green marble from Campagna, Italy, and houses Art Deco lamps from Paris and a bronze-and-glass chandelier, also from France, that weighs a metric ton. It was from the balcony above the awning that, in 1967, an ill-mannered Charles de Gaulle, then president of France, proclaimed, "Vive le Québec Libre!"—a gesture that pleased his immediate audience but strained relations with the Canadian government for years.

275 rue Notre-Dame est (at the corner of rue Gosford). ℰ **514/872-3355.** Free admission. Mon–Fri 9am–4:30pm. Guided tours on weekdays May–Oct. Métro: Champ-de-Mars.

Marché Bonsecours Bonsecours Market, an imposing neoclassical building with a long facade, a colonnaded portico, and a silvery dome, was built in the mid-1800s—the Doric columns of the portico were cast of iron in England—and first used as the Parliament of United Canada and then as Montréal's City Hall until 1878. The architecture alone makes a brief visit worthwhile. For many years after 1878, it served as the city's central market. Essentially abandoned for much of the 20th century, it was restored in 1964 to house city government offices and in 1992, became the information and exhibition center for the celebration of the city's 350th birthday. It continues to be used as an exhibition space and also houses three restaurants, a dozen art galleries, and high-end but affordable boutiques featuring Québécois products.

350 rue St-Paul est (at the foot of rue St-Claude). ℰ **514/872-7730.** www.marchebonsecours.qc.ca. Free admission. Daily 10am–6pm (until 9pm during summer). Métro: Champ-de-Mars.

Musée du Château Ramezay ★ (Kids) Benjamin Franklin was here. So, too, was Claude de Ramezay, the colony's 11th governor, who built his residence here in 1705. The château became home to the city's royal French governors for almost 4 decades, until Ramezay's heirs sold it to a trading company in 1745. Fifteen years later, British conquerors

EXPLORING MONTRÉAL

8

MORE ATTRACTIONS

took it over, and in 1775, an army of American revolutionaries invaded and held Montréal, using the château as their headquarters. For 6 weeks in 1776, Benjamin Franklin spent his days here, trying to persuade the Québécois to rise with the American colonists against British rule (he failed).

After the American interlude, the house was used as a courthouse, a government office building, and headquarters for Laval University before being converted into a museum in 1895.

Old coins and prints, portraits, furnishings, tools, a loom, Amerindian artifacts, and other memorabilia related to the economic and social activities of the 18th and 19th centuries fill the main floor. In the cellar are the original house's vaults.

Between October and May, the château invites families to join in on the last Sunday of the month for an old-timey bread-making session using its 18th-century hearth. In the summer, there are workshops in the garden that teach, for example, how to make soap and beeswax candles. Dates and details are listed on the website.

Sculpted, formal gardens *(jardins)* ringed by a low stone wall evoke 18th-century Parisian scenes and provide a soothing respite from the bustle of Place Jacques-Cartier, a few steps away. A cafe, open in summer, overlooks the gardens.

In 2008, the Québec tourism office awarded the museum the grand prize in its category (attractions with fewer than 100,000 yearly visitors).

280 rue Notre-Dame est. ✆ **514/861-3708.** www.chateauramezay.qc.ca. Admission C$9 (£4.50) adults, C$7 (£3.50) seniors, C$6 (£3) students, C$4.50 (£2) ages 5–17, free for children 4 and younger, C$18 (£9) families. MC, V. June to late Nov daily 10am–6pm; late Nov to May Tues–Sun 10am–4:30pm. Métro: Champ-de-Mars.

MONT-ROYAL & PLATEAU MONT-ROYAL

To explore these areas, take the walking tours in chapter 9.

L'Oratoire St-Joseph ★ This huge Catholic church—dominating Mont-Royal's north slope—is seen by some as inspiring, by others as forbidding. It's Montréal's highest point, with an enormous dome 97m (318 ft) high. Consecrated as a basilica in 2004, it came into being through the efforts of Brother André, a lay brother in the Holy Cross order who earned a reputation as a healer. By the time he had built a small wooden chapel in 1904 on the mountain, he was said to have performed hundreds of cures. His powers attracted supplicants from great distances, and he performed his work until his death in 1937. In 1982, he was beatified by the pope—a status one step below sainthood—and Brother André's dream of building a shrine to honor St. Joseph, patron saint of Canada, became a completed reality in 1967.

The church is largely Italian Renaissance in style, its giant copper dome recalling the shape of the Duomo in Florence, but of greater size and lesser grace. Inside is a sanctuary and museum where a central exhibit displays a formalin-filled urn that holds Brother André's actual heart. His original wooden chapel, with its tiny bedroom, is on the grounds and open to the public. Two million pilgrims visit annually, many of whom seek intercession from St. Joseph and Brother André by climbing the middle set of 99 steps on their knees. Guided tours are offered in French, English, and nine other languages. The 56-bell carillon plays Thursday and Friday at noon and on Saturday and Sunday at noon and 2:30pm.

A modest 14-room hostel on the grounds is called the **Jean XXIII Pavilion;** rooms start at C$45 (£23).

3800 chemin Queen Mary (on the north slope of Mont-Royal). ℂ **514/733-8211.** www.saint-joseph.org. Free admission, donations requested. Crypt and votive chapel daily 6am–10:30pm; basilica and exhibition on Brother André daily 7am–5:30pm. Métro: Côtes-des-Neiges. Bus: 166 or 51.

Parc La Fontaine   The European-style park in Plateau Mont-Royal is one of the city's oldest and most popular. Illustrating the traditional dual identities of the city's populace, half the park is landscaped in the formal French manner, the other in the more casual English style. A central lake is used for ice-skating in winter, when snowshoe and cross-country trails wind through trees. In summer, these become bike paths, and there are tennis courts on the premises. An open amphitheater, the **Théâtre de Verdure,** features free outdoor theater, movies, and tango dancing in summer. The northern end is more pleasant than the southern end (along rue Sherbrooke), which seems to attract a seedier crowd.

Bounded by rue Sherbrooke, rue Rachel, av. Parc LaFontaine, and av. Papineau. ℂ **514/872-2644.** Free admission; fee for use of tennis courts. Park daily 24 hr.; tennis courts 9am–10pm weekdays, 9am–9pm weekends (ℂ 514/872-3626 reservations). Métro: Sherbrooke.

ILE STE-HELENE ★

The small Ile Ste-Hélène and adjacent Ile Notre-Dame sit in the St. Lawrence River near Vieux-Port's waterfront. Connected by two bridges, they now comprise the recently designated **Parc Jean-Drapeau,** which is almost entirely car-free and accessible by Métro, bicycle, or foot.

La Biosphère (**Kids**)   Not to be confused with the **Biodôme** at Olympic Park (p. 114), this interactive science facility is housed under a geodesic dome designed by Buckminster Fuller to serve as the American Pavilion for Expo 67. A fire destroyed the sphere's acrylic skin in 1976, and until 1995, it served no purpose other than as a harbor landmark. Then, Environment Canada (www.ec.gc.ca) joined with the city of Montréal to convert the space. The motivation behind the Biosphère, then, is unabashedly environmentalist, with exhibition areas, a theater, and an amphitheater, all devoted to promoting awareness of the St. Lawrence–Great Lakes ecosystem. Multimedia shows and hands-on displays invite visitors' active participation, and "Planète Bucky," a permanent exhibit, highlights Fuller's forward-thinking inventions for sustainable development. Though the center has a preaching-to-the-choir quality that sometimes slips over the edge into zealous philosophizing, the displays and exhibits are put together thoughtfully and engage and enlighten most visitors, at least for a while. Don't make a special trip, but if you're on the island, stop by.

160 chemin Tour-de-l'Isle (Ile Ste-Hélène). ℂ **514/283-5000.** www.biosphere.ec.gc.ca. Admission C$10 (£5) adults, C$8 (£4) seniors and students 18 and older, free for children 17 and younger. June–Oct daily 10am–6pm; Nov–May Tues–Sun 10am–6pm. Métro: Parc Jean-Drapeau.

Musée David M. Stewart ★ (**Kids**)   If you're in downtown Montréal and hear what sounds like a gun salute, check your watch: If it's just before noon, the sound is coming from this museum.

After the War of 1812, the British prepared for a possible future American invasion of Montréal by building a moated fortress, which now houses the David M. Stewart Museum. The Duke of Wellington ordered the fort's construction as another link in the chain of defenses along the St. Lawrence River. Completed in 1824, it was never involved in armed conflict. The British garrison left in 1870, after the former Canadian colonies confederated.

Today, the low stone barracks and blockhouses house the museum and staff in period costume performing firing drills, tending campfires, attempting to recruit visitors into the king's army, and generally doing all they can to bring this piece of history alive.

The museum displays maps and scientific instruments that helped Europeans explore the New World, military and naval artifacts, and related paraphernalia from the time of French voyager Jacques Cartier (1535) through the end of the colonial period (1763); useful labels appear in French and English.

From late June to late August, the fort really comes to life with daily reenactments of military parades and retreats by troupes known as La Compagnie Franche de la Marine and the Olde 78th Fraser Highlanders. (The presence of the French unit is an unhistorical bow to Francophone sensibilities; New France had become English Canada almost 65 years before the fort was erected.) If you absolutely must be photographed in stocks, they are on the parade grounds.

Vieux-Fort, Ile Ste-Hélène. ✆ **514/861-6701.** www.stewart-museum.org. Admission C$10 (£5) adults, C$7 (£3.50) seniors and students, free for children 6 and younger. May 21–Oct 8 daily 10am–5pm; rest of year Wed–Mon 10am–5pm. Métro: Parc Jean-Drapeau, and then a 10-min. walk. By car: Take the Jacques-Cartier Bridge to the Parc Jean-Drapeau exit, then follow the signs.

3 ESPECIALLY FOR KIDS

In addition to the three Bs—the **Biodôme** (p. 114), **La Biosphère** (p. 119), and **boat tours** (p. 124)—and the other attractions flagged in this chapter as especially appealing to children, here are some spots that cater primarily to the under-18 crowd.

Atrium Le 1000 (Kids) This indoor ice-skating rink in the heart of downtown is open year-round. Skate rentals are available on-site, and restaurants ring the rink. A "Tiny Tot" hour for children 12 and younger and their parents takes place from 10:30 to 11:30am on Saturday and Sunday. Saturday, DJs entertain after 7pm.

1000 rue de la Gauchetière ouest, downtown. ✆ **514/395-0555.** www.le1000.com. Admission C$6 (£3) adults, C$4 (£2) children 12 and younger. Skate rental C$5 (£2.50). MC, V. Daily 11:30am–6pm or later. Métro: Bonaventure.

IMAX Theater (Kids) Images and special effects are larger than life, visually dazzling, and often vertiginous on this five-story screen in the **Centre des Sciences de Montréal** (p. 113). Recent films have highlighted the Grand Canyon, as well as the band U2, in 3D. Running time is usually less than an hour, and about a quarter of the screenings are in English. Tickets can be ordered online, and the movie schedule is available on the website as well.

Quai King Edward, Vieux-Port. ✆ **877/496-4724** or 514/496-4724. www.montrealsciencecentre.com. Movie tickets from C$12 (£6) adults, C$11 (£5.50) seniors and ages 13–17, C$9 (£4.50) ages 4–12, free for children 3 and younger. MC, V. Shows daily 10am–9:45pm. Métro: Place d'Armes or Champ-de-Mars.

Insectarium de Montréal ★ (Kids) Live exhibits featuring scorpions, tarantulas, hissing cockroaches, assassin bugs, praying mantises, and other "misunderstood creatures, which are so often wrongly feared and despised," as the Insectarium puts it, are displayed in this two-level structure near the rue Sherbrooke gate of the **Jardin Botanique** (**Botanical Garden;** p. 115). Needless to say, kids are delighted by the creepy critters. During summer, the Butterfly House is full of beautiful live specimens fluttering among the nectar-bearing plants, and in September, visitors can watch monarch butterflies being tagged and released for their annual migration to Mexico. More than 3,000 mounted butterflies, beetles, scarabs, maggots, locusts, and giraffe weevils also are featured. The annual award-winning insect-tasting *(croque-insectes)* dinner seems to no longer be on the schedule, but last time we checked, you could still buy lollipops with scorpions inside at the gift shop.

4581 rue Sherbrooke est. (✆ **514/872-1400.** www.ville.montreal.qc.ca/insectarium. Admission includes access to the Botanical Garden next door. May 15–Oct C$16 (£8) adults, C$12 (£6) seniors and students, C$8 (£4) children 5–17, C$2.50 (£1) children 2–4, free for children 1 and younger. Rates drop about 15% rest of the year. See p. 109 for information about combination tickets with the Stade Olympique and Biodôme. MC, V. May 15–Sept 6 daily 9am–6pm; Sept 7–Oct 31 daily 9am–9pm; Nov 1–May 14 Tues–Sun 9am–5pm. Métro: Pie-IX or Viau.

La Ronde Amusement Park (Kids) Montréal's amusement park, opened as part of Expo 67, the World's Fair, was run for its first 34 years by the city. It was sold to the American-owned Six Flags theme-park empire in 2001 and at first seemed pretty much to be the same old park, minus the threat of insolvency. But new rides have since been delivered. Like hot sauces, they're categorized by "thrill rating": moderate, mild, or max. There are 11 rides in the "max thrill" category, including Le Vampire, a suspended coaster which has riders experiencing five head-over-heels loops at more than 80kmph (50 mph). Other attractions include Ferris wheels, carnival booths, and plenty of places to eat and drink. An antique carousel, Le Galopant, was built by Belgian artisans in 1885 and was part of the Belgian Pavilion at the 1964 to 1965 New York World's Fair. The Minirail is an elevated train that circles the park. Young children also have ample selection, including the Tchou Tchou Train and *tasses magiques,* in which they sit in one of 12 giant rotating tea cups.

On 10 Wednesdays and Saturdays in June and July, La Ronde hosts a huge fireworks competition, **L'International Des Feux Loto-Québec.** Although the pyrotechnics can be enjoyed for free from almost anywhere in the city overlooking the river, tickets can be purchased to watch from the open-air theater at the amusement park and include entrance to the park. Call (✆ **514/397-2000** or go to www.internationaldesfeuxloto-quebec.com/en for details.

Parc Jean-Drapeau Ile Ste-Hélène. (✆ **514/397-2000.** www.laronde.com. Admission prices by height: C$38 (£19) for patrons 1.37m (54 in.) or taller, C$26 (£13) for patrons shorter than 1.37m (54 in.), free for children 2 and younger. Parking C$15 (£7.50). Late June to Aug daily 11am–9pm (to 11:30pm Sat); spring and fall Sat–Sun 11am–7pm. Closed winter. Métro: Papineau, and then bus no. 169, or Parc Jean-Drapeau, and then bus no. 167.

Planétarium de Montréal (Kids) A window on the night sky with mythical monsters and magical heroes, Montréal's planetarium is in the heart of the city. Shows under the 20m (66-ft.) dome dazzle and inform kids at the same time. Multimedia presentations change with the season, exploring time and space travel and collisions of celestial bodies; up to five different shows are screened daily. The special Christmas production, "Season of Light," plays from November through early January. Shows in English alternate with those in French.

1000 rue St-Jacques ouest (at Peel). (✆ **514/872-4530.** www.planetarium.montreal.qc.ca. Admission C$8 (£4) adults, C$6 (£3) seniors and students, C$4 (£2) children 5–17, free for children 4 and younger. MC, V. Hours vary according to show schedule; call or go online for details. Métro: Bonaventure (exit toward rue de la Cathédrale).

4 SPECIAL-INTEREST SIGHTSEEING

Centre Canadien d'Architecture (CCA) The understated but handsome Canadian Centre for Architecture occupies a city block, joining a contemporary structure with an older building, the 1875 Shaughnessy House. Opened in 1989, this museum has received rave reviews from scholars, critics, and serious architecture buffs.

CCA functions as both a study center and a museum, with changing exhibits devoted to the art and history of architecture; they include architects' sketchbooks, elevation drawings, and photography. The collection is international in scope and encompasses architecture, urban planning, and landscape design. Texts are in French and English. The bookstore has a special section about Canadian architecture with an emphasis on Montréal and Québec City. Podcasts of lectures and conferences that have taken place here are available for free on iTunes via the CCA's website.

A **sculpture garden** that faces the CCA from boulevard René-Lévesque's south side is part of the museum. Designed by Montréal artist/architect Melvin Charney, it's a quiet retreat in the center of downtown.

1920 rue Baile (at rue du Fort). (*C*) **514/939-7026.** www.cca.qc.ca. Admission C$10 (£5) adults, C$7 (£3.50) seniors, C$5 (£2.50) students, C$3 (£1.50) children 6–12, free for ages 5 and younger. Free Thurs after 5:30pm. Wed–Sun 10am–5pm (until 9pm Thurs). Métro: Atwater or Guy-Concordia.

Centre d'Histoire de Montréal Built in 1903 as Montréal's central fire station, this redbrick-and-sandstone building on the edge of Vieux-Montréal is now the CHM, which traces the city's development from when it had its first residents, the Amerindians, to the European settlers who arrived in 1642, to the present day. A recent exhibit, for example, displayed the ghostly winners of a competition to submit photos themed around "Industrial Montréal." On the second floor, reached by a spiral staircase, is memorabilia from the early 20th century.

335 Place d'Youville (at rue St-Pierre). (*C*) **514/872-3207.** www.ville.montreal.qc.ca/chm. Admission C$6 (£3) adults, C$5 (£2.50) seniors, C$4 (£2) children 6–17 and students, free for children 5 and younger. Jan–Nov Tues–Sun 10am–5pm. Métro: Square Victoria.

Musée de la Banque de Montréal Facing the **Basilique Notre-Dame** (p. 112) and Place d'Armes is Montréal's oldest bank building, with its classic facade beneath a graceful dome, a carved pediment, and six Corinthian columns. The outside dimensions and appearance remain largely unchanged since the building's completion in 1847. Pop in for 5 minutes to see the small museum just off the front hall. It features a replica of the bank's first office, a display showing how to spot a forged bill, and a collection of 100-year-old mechanical banks. Take a look at the building's sumptuous interior: It was renovated from 1901 through 1905 by the famed U.S. firm McKim, Mead, and White, and features Ionic and Corinthian columns of Vermont granite and walls of pink marble from Tennessee.

119 rue St-Jacques ouest (at Place d'Armes). (*C*) **514/877-6810.** Free admission. Mon–Fri 10am–4pm. Métro: Place d'Armes.

Musée Redpath This quirky natural history museum, housed in an 1882 building with a grandly proportioned and richly appointed interior, is on the McGill University campus. The main draws—worth a half-hour visit—are the mummies and coffin that are part of Canada's second-largest collection of Egyptian antiquities, and skeletons of whales

(Moments) Cirque du Soleil: Montréal's Hometown Circus

The whimsical, talented band of artists that became Cirque du Soleil began as street performers in **Baie-St-Paul** (see p. 281), a river town an hour north of Québec City. These stilt-walkers, fire-breathers, and musicians raised a small ruckus with one pure intention: to entertain. The troupe formally founded as Cirque du Soleil ("Circus of the Sun") in 1984 and celebrates its 25th year in 2009.

In that time, it has matured into a spectacle like no other. Using human-size gyroscopes, trampoline beds, trapezes suspended from massive chandeliers, and the like (but no animals), Cirque creates worlds that are spooky, sensual, otherworldly, and beautifully ambiguous.

More than 1,000 of the company's acrobats, contortionists, jugglers, clowns, and dancers tour the world. Resident shows are established in Las Vegas and Orlando, Florida. But the company's offices are in Montréal in the northern Saint-Michel district, not far beyond the Mile End neighborhood.

And they're not just offices: Cirque has been developing a small campus of buildings in this industrial zone since 1997. All new artists come here to train for a few weeks to a few months and live in residences on-site. The complex has acrobatic training rooms, a dance studio, workshops in which the elaborate costumes and props are made, and a space large enough to erect a circus tent indoors. Some 1,800 are employed at the Montréal facility, including more than 300 who work on costumes alone.

The company doesn't have regular performances in Montréal, alas. For information about where you can find a show, visit **www.cirquedusoleil.com**.

and prehistoric beasts. If the unusual name seems slightly familiar, it could be because you've seen it on the wrappings of sugar cubes in many Canadian restaurants: John Redpath was a 19th-century industrialist who built Canada's first sugar refinery.

859 rue Sherbrooke ouest (rue University). © **514/398-4086.** www.mcgill.ca/redpath. Free admission. Mon–Fri 9am–5pm; Sun 1–5pm. Closed long weekends and public holidays. Métro: McGill.

Pavillon de la TOHO Adjacent to the Cirque du Soleil training complex on reclaimed industrial land, TOHO is many things, most especially a performance facility that brings small circus companies to its intimate in-the-round theater (which doesn't have a name; p. 161). But it's also a model building for green architecture. It's heated by biogas from a landfill next door and uses an "ice bunker" for cooling in the summer. Both processes produce zero greenhouse-effect gases and are explained in free brochures. For one weekend in August, TOHO hosts an outdoor fair promoting green technologies. For the rest of the year, it's worth a special trip only if you're an environmental architecture fan—guided tours are available with advance reservations—but if there's a show playing you may want to build a trip around that.

2345 rue Jarry est (corner of rue d'Iberville, at Autoroute 40). © **888/376-TOHU** (376-8648). www.tohu.ca. Free to view facility and exhibits; tour admission C$6 (£3) adults; C$4 (£2) seniors, students, and children 7–11; free for children 6 and younger (although not recommended for young children). Daily 9am–5pm.

Temple Solomon Author Mordecai Richler set most of his books in the working-class Jewish neighborhood of St. Urbain of the 1940s and 1950s (his most famous book is *The Apprenticeship of Duddy Kravitz*). Temple Solomon is the heart of this neighborhood and one of the last signs of the Plateau's long history as a Jewish enclave. A replica of the old Eastern European synagogues of Poland and Ukraine, its interior features robin's-egg-blue walls and paintings of the 12 zodiac signs, labeled in Hebrew. It's the city's oldest synagogue in continuous use, but it's been plagued by financial troubles and the need for significant repairs. If it's closed, head north a mile to Wilensky Light Lunch (p. 105), where you're bound to get an update.

3919 rue Clark (at rue Bagg). No phone or website. Free admission. Métro: Sherbrooke.

5 ORGANIZED TOURS

An introductory guided tour is often the best—or, at least, most efficient—way to begin exploring a new city, and can certainly give you a good lay of the land and overview of Montréal's history. You'll see many of the attractions listed in this chapter and get a better sense of which you'll want to spend more time exploring on your own.

For a complete listing of tours and tour operators, check under "Guided Tours" in the annually revised *Montréal Official Tourist Guide,* available at the downtown **Infotouriste Centre** at 1255 rue Peel (© **877/266-5687** or 514/873-2015; Métro: Peel).

Most land tours leave from the Square Dorchester, right at the tourist office. Most boat tours depart from Vieux-Port (Old Port), at the waterfront bordering Vieux-Montréal. There's parking at the dock, or take the Métro to the Champ-de-Mars or Square Victoria station and walk toward the river.

BOAT TOURS

Among numerous opportunities for experiencing Montréal and environs by water, here are a few of the most popular:

Le Bateau-Mouche (© **800/361-9952** or 514/849-9952; www.bateau-mouche.com) is an air-conditioned, glass-enclosed vessel reminiscent of those on the Seine in Paris. It plies the St. Lawrence River from mid-May to mid-October. Cruises depart for 60-minute excursions at 1:30, 3, and 4:30pm; for a 90-minute cruise at 11:30am; and for a 3½-hour dinner cruise at 7pm. The shallow-draft boat takes passengers on a route inaccessible by traditional vessels, passing under several bridges and providing sweeping views of the city, Mont-Royal, and the St. Lawrence and its islands. Daytime snacks are available onboard. The 60-minute tours cost C$23 (£12) adults, C$21 (£11) students and seniors 65 and older, and C$11 (£5.50) children 6 to 16, and are free for children 5 and younger. The 90-minute tour costs C$27 (£14) adults, C$25 (£13) students and seniors, and C$11 (£5.50) children 6 to 16. Dinner cruises, with meals prepared by the kitchen of Fairmont the Queen Elizabeth, cost C$87, C$125, or C$149 (£44, £63, or £75) per person, regardless of age, and reservations are essential. The tours depart from the Jacques-Cartier Pier, opposite Place Jacques-Cartier.

Croisières AML Cruises (© **800/563-4643** or 514/842-3871; www.croisieresaml.com) also travels the harbor and the St. Lawrence. Options include a weekend brunch cruise that departs at 11:30am and lasts 1½-hours for C$42 (£21) adults, C$40 (£20) students and seniors, and C$21 (£10.50) children 6 to 16, and free for children 5 and younger. There are also 60- or 90-minute history trips throughout the day, as well as 4-hour "Love Boat" dinner cruises that depart at 7pm, and 3-hour Latin Fiesta dance parties that leave at midnight. Call or check the website for prices and times. Boats depart from the Jacques-Cartier Pier, opposite Place Jacques-Cartier.

Croisière Historique sur le Canal de Lachine (© **514/283-6054**) is a leisurely Parks Canada trip up the Lachine Canal, which was inaugurated in 1824 so that ships could bypass the Lachine Rapids on the way to the Great Lakes. The canal was reopened for recreational use in 1997 after much renovation. It's lined with 19th-century industrial buildings, many of which are being converted into high-end apartments. The 2-hour guided tours are on a glass-topped *bateau-mouche,* which carries up to 49 passengers. From mid-May to mid-June and early September to mid-October, departures are at 1 and 3:30pm on Saturday, Sunday, and holidays; from late June to early September, departures are at 1 and 3:30pm daily. Reservations required. Fares are C$18 (£9) adults, C$15 (£7.50) children 13 to 17, C$11 (£5.50) children 6 to 12, and free for children 5 and younger. There are also 1-hour tours Saturday and Sunday in summer at 10:30am and Thursday and Friday in summer at 7pm that cost C$11 (£5.50) adults, C$9 (£4.50) children 13 to 17, C$7 (£3.50) children 6 to 12, and free for children 5 and younger. The tour departs from a dock near the Marché Atwater farmer's market (Métro: Lionel-Groulx).

Les Sautes-Moutons, also known as **Lachine Rapids Tours** (© **514/284-9607;** www.jetboatingmontreal.com) provides an exciting—and wet—experience. Its wave-jumper powerboats take on the St. Lawrence River's roiling Lachine Rapids. The stream-lined hydrojet makes the 1-hour trip from May to mid-October daily, with departures every 2 hours from 10am to 6pm. It takes a half-hour to get to and from the rapids, which leaves 30 minutes for storming along the waves. Reservations are required. Plan to arrive 45 minutes early to obtain and don rain gear and a life jacket. Bring a change of clothes, as you almost certainly will get splashed or even soaked. Fares are C$60 (£30) adults, C$50 (£25) ages 13 to 18, C$40 (£20) children 6 to 12, and free for children 5 and younger. Boats depart from the Clock Tower Pier (Quai de l'Horloge; Métro: Champ-de-Mars).

Les Descentes sur le St-Laurent (© **514/767-2230;** www.raftingmontreal.com) also provides hydrojet rides on the rapids. This operation is a little farther out than the others, so a bit more of an adventure. Rafting and jet-boat options are available for C$40 and C$49 (£20 and £25) adults, C$34 and C$39 (£17 and £20) ages 13 to 18, and C$23 and C$29 (£12 and £15) for children 12 and younger, though kids must be at least 6 years old to go rafting and at least 8 years old to go jet-boating. Take the Métro to the Angrignon station and take bus no. 110, or pick up a free shuttle at the downtown Info-touriste Centre at 1255 rue Peel (Métro: Peel). Reservations are required.

The **ferry** (© **514/281-8000;** www.navettesmaritimes.com) from Jacques-Cartier Pier in Vieux-Montréal to Ile Ste-Hélène is a much milder water voyage, but still offers great views. It's a one way to begin or end a picnic outing or to visit to the old fort at Musée David M. Stewart. The ferry operates from mid-May to mid-October, with daily departures every hour in the high season, and costs C$6 (£3) per person.

LAND TOURS

Gray Line de Montréal (© **514/934-1222;** www.coachcanada.com) offers commercial guided tours in air-conditioned buses daily year-round. The basic city tour takes 3 hours and costs C$40 (£20) for ages 12 and up, C$36 (£18) for seniors, C$28 (£14) for ages 5 to 11, and free for children 4 and younger. Tours depart from 1255 rue Peel in downtown.

Amphi-Bus (☎ 514/849-5181; www.montreal-amphibus-tour.com) is something a little different: It tours Vieux-Montréal much like any other bus—until it waddles into the waters of the harbor for a dramatic finish. Departures are on the hour from 10am until midnight June through September, and at noon, 2, 4, and 6pm in May and October. Fares are C$32 (£16) adults, C$29 (£15) seniors, C$23 (£12) students, C$18 (£9) children 4 to 12, and C$10 (£5) children 3 and younger. Reservations are required. The bus departs from the intersection of rue de la Commune and bd. St-Laurent.

Montréal's *calèches* (☎ 514/934-6105; www.calechesluckyluc.com) are horse-drawn open carriages whose drivers serve as guides. They operate year-round; in winter, the horse puff steam clouds in the cold air as the passengers bundle up in lap rugs. Carriages depart from Square Dorchester in downtown and, in Vieux-Montréal, at Place Jacques-Cartier and rue de la Commune and Place d'Armes opposite the Notre-Dame Basilica.

WALKING & CYCLING TOURS

Walking tours of Vieux-Montréal, the underground city, and most other interesting areas are available through **Guidatour** (☎ 514/844-4021; www.guidatour.qc.ca), which developed its circuit in collaboration with the Centre d'Histoire de Montréal (p. 122).

ÇaRoule/Montréal on Wheels (☎ 514/866-0633; www.caroulemontreal.com) offers a 3-hour guided bicycle tour that starts at 9am and costs C$44 (£22), a fee that includes a full-day bike rental. Tours are available Thursday and Friday from late June to early September, and Saturday and Sunday mid-May to early October. The bike shop is at 27 rue de la Commune est in Vieux-Port (also see "Bicycling & In-Line Skating" on p. 128).

---

6 SPECTATOR SPORTS

Montréalers are as devoted to ice hockey as other Canadians are, with plenty of enthusiasm left over for soccer, U.S.-style football, and the other distinctive national sport, curling. They liked baseball too, but not enough: In 2005, the Montréal Expos, plagued by poor attendance, left for Washington, D.C., where they became the Nationals. (Fun fact: Pioneering black athlete **Jackie Robinson** played for the Montréal Royals in 1946, and there's a sculpture of him outside of Olympic Stadium.) The biggest single event on the Montréal sports calendar is its version of the Indy 500, the Grand Prix car race that roars into town for 3 days every June (see below).

AUTO RACING

For 3 days—in 2008, it was June 6, 7, and 8—Montréal's entire focus is on the **Grand Prix,** the FIA's only stop in Canada. Each day, more than 100,000 people pour onto Ile Notre-Dame, where a permanent track is installed (the rest of the year the circuit is used by cyclists and walkers). The race cars make 70 laps at up to 318kmph (198 mph). In the rest of city, particularly rue Crescent in downtown, Formula 1 cars are on display, streets are shut down, and revelers party deep into the night. Hotel prices typically double and most require 3-night stays. It's estimated that C$100 million (£50 million) funnels into the city on these days, making it the biggest highlight on the tourism industry's calendar. One-day tickets cost as little as C$25 (£13), with the best 3-day tickets costing C$495 (£248). Details and tickets are at **www.grandprix.ca.**

Meanwhile, since 2007, the **NASCAR Busch Series** (www.circuitgillesvilleneuve.ca) comes to Montréal for 2 days in early August on the same track as the Grand Prix, bringing

> ## Popular Canadian Pastimes: Name That Sport!
>
> "With Ontario leading 6 to 4 in the 10th end, Manitoba skip Jennifer Jones pre-
> pared for her last shot. Manitoba had three rocks in the house, but Ontario had
> shot rock and had two guards sitting near one another, high atop the house,
> toward Jones; another guard sat just outside the rings. Jones was left with one
> option: She hit and rolled off the lone Ontario stone outside the rings to remove
> Ontario's shot rock near the button."
>
> So was the verbatim report in *The Globe and Mail* of the Canadian women's
> championship game in February 2005. Manitoba won, 8 to 6.
>
> The sport? Curling.

more than 40 top drivers and race cars. One-day general-admission tickets cost C$30 to
C$40 (£15–£20), with 2-day tickets between C$55 and C$165 (£28–£83).

FOOTBALL & SOCCER

What Americans call soccer most of the rest of the world calls football, and there's a big
fan base for *that* kind of football in Montréal—not surprising, given the city's wide and
varied immigrant population.

Montréal doesn't have a team in the Major League Soccer network, but it's on the list
of possible expansion cities. The **Montréal Impact** (✆ 514/328-3668; www.montreal
impact.com) is part of the United Soccer League's First Division and plays at Saputo
Stadium, rue 4750 Sherbrooke est, near the Olympic Stadium. Tickets are C$10 to
C$40 (£5–£20).

Meanwhile, there's also U.S.-style professional football in Canada. The website for the
Montréal Alouettes (French for "larks") claims, somewhat dubiously, that "Montréal is
synonymous with football," citing that "the first recorded game ever played in North
America was on the downtown cricket grounds on Oct. 10, 1868." The team does enjoy
considerable success, frequently appearing in the Grey Cup, the Canadian Football
League's version of the U.S. Super Bowl. The "Als," as they're fondly known, play at
McGill University's Percival-Molson Memorial Stadium from June to November. Tickets
start at C$25 (£13). Details are at ✆ **514/871-2255** and www.montrealalouettes.com.

HOCKEY

The beloved **Montréal Canadiens** play downtown at the Centre Bell arena. The team
has won 24 Stanley Cups (the most recent in 1992–93), and the season runs from October to April, with playoffs continuing into June. Tickets are usually priced from C$23
to C$198 (£12–£99). Check www.canadiens.com for schedules and ticketing or call
✆ **514/790-1245.**

TENNIS

The **Rogers Cup** tournament (✆ **514/273-1515;** www.rogerscup.com) comes each July
and August to the Uniprix Stadium, which is near the De Castelnau and the Jarry Métro
stops, with singles and doubles matches. The stadium's Centre Court holds more than
11,000. To make the tournament more green, the stadium provides 175 bike-rack slots
and 24-hour bike surveillance, free public transit tickets to all spectators, and a downtown shuttle service.

7 OUTDOOR ACTIVITIES

After such long winters, locals pour outdoors to get sun and warm air at every possible opportunity (though there's also lots to do when there's snow on the ground). Even if you come to Montréal without your regular outdoor gear, it's easy to join in.

WARM-WEATHER ACTIVITIES
Bicycling & In-Line Skating

Bicycling and rollerblading are hugely popular in Montréal, and the city helps people indulge these passions: It boasts an expanding network of more than 350km (217 miles) of cycling paths and year-round bike lanes. In warm months, car lanes in heavily biked areas are blocked off with concrete barriers, effectively turning them into two-way lanes for bikers.

If you're serious about cycling, get in touch with the nonprofit biking organization **Vélo Québec** (✆ 800/567-8356, or 514/521-8356 in Montréal; www.velo.qc.ca). Vélo (which means bicycle) was behind the development of a 4,000km (2,485-mile) bike network called **Route Verte (Green Route)** that stretches from one end of Québec province to the other. The route was officially inaugurated in summer 2007. The Vélo website has the most up-to-date information on the state of the paths, the Montréal Bike Fest, road races, new bike lanes, and more. It also offers guided tours throughout the province. (*Tip:* Several taxi companies provide bike racks and charge C$3/£1.50 extra for each bike. See p. 36.)

If you're looking to rent a bike or pair of skates for an afternoon, you've got several options, depending on where you're based. In Vieux-Montréal, the shop **ÇaRoule/Montréal on Wheels** (✆ 514/866-0633; www.caroulemontreal.com) at 27 rue de la Commune est, the waterfront road bordering Vieux-Port, rents bikes and skates from April to October (and by appointment in Mar and Nov). Bikes cost C$9 (£4.50) per hour and C$30 (£15) per day on the weekend, rollerblades a little less. Helmets are included and a deposit is required. The staff will set you up with a map (also downloadable from their website) and likely point you toward the peaceful **Lachine Canal,** a nearly flat 11km (6.8-mile) bicycle path, open year-round (but only maintained by Parks Canada from mid-Apr to the end of Oct), that travels alongside locks and over small bridges. The canal starts just a few blocks away.

Other options for short bike tours from Vieux-Port are Ile Notre-Dame, less than 20 minutes away, where the Grand Prix auto-racing track is a biker's dream, or simply out to the 2.5km (1.5-mile) promenade that runs along the piers. See p. 126 for information about ÇaRoule's 3-hour guided bike tours.

Also for rent at Vieux-Port in spring and summer are **Quadricycles,** or "Q-cycles"—4-wheeled roofed bike-buggies that can hold three to six people. You can only ride them along Vieux-Port, and the rental booth is in the heart of the waterfront area, next to the Pavillian Jacques-Cartier. Rentals are by the half-hour and cost C$15 (£7.50) for a three-seater, C$20 (£10) for a three-seater with spots for two small children, and C$30 (£15) for a six-seater.

Hiking

The most popular hike is to the top of **Mont-Royal.** They call it a mountain, but it's more of a large hill. There are a web of options for trekking it, from using the broad and handsome pedestrian-only **chemin Olmsted** (a bridle path named for Frederick Law

Olmsted, the park's landscape architect), to following smaller paths and sets of stairs. The park is well-marked and small enough that you can wander without fear of getting too lost, but our walking tour on p. 141 suggests one place to start and a number of options once you've headed in.

Jogging

There are many possibilities for running. In addition to the areas described above for biking and hiking, consider heading to either of the city's most prominent parks: **Parc La Fontaine** in the Plateau Mont-Royal neighborhood (p. 119), or **Parc Maisonneuve** in the city's east side, adjacent to the **Jardin Botanique** and across the street from **Olympic Park** (p. 114). Both parks are formally landscaped and well used for recreation and relaxation.

Kayaking & Electric Boating

It's fun to rent kayaks, large Rabaska canoes, pedal boats, or small eco-friendly electric boats on the quiet **Lachine Canal,** just to the west of Vieux-Port. **H2O Adventures** (© **514/842-1306;** www.h2oadventures.com) won a 2007 *Grand Prix du tourisme Québécois* award for being a standout operation. Their rentals start at C$10 (£5) per hour. Two-hour introductory kayak lessons go for C$39 (£20) on weekdays, C$45 (£23) on weekends. The shop is open daily. Find it at the **Marché Atwater,** where you can also pick up lunch from the inside *boulangerie* and *fromagerie,* adjacent to the canal. Métro: Lionel-Groulx.

COLD-WEATHER ACTIVITIES

Cross-Country Skiing

Parc Mont-Royal has an extensive cross-country course, as do many of the other city parks, though skiers have to supply their own equipment. Just an hour from the city, north in the Laurentides and east in the Cantons de l'Est, there are numerous options for skiing and rentals.

Ice-Skating

In the winter, outdoor skating rinks are set up in Vieux-Port, Lac des Castors (Beaver Lake), and other spots around the city; check tourist offices for your best options. One of the most agreeable venues for skating any time of the year is **Atrium Le 1000** (p. 120) in the downtown skyscraper at that address. For one thing, it's indoors and warm. For another, it's surrounded by cafes at which to relax after twirling around the big rink. And yes, it's even open in the summer.

Montréal Strolls

Cities best reveal themselves on foot, and Montréal is one of North America's most pedestrian-friendly locales. There's much to see in the concentrated districts—cobblestoned Vieux-Montréal, downtown and its luxurious "Golden Square Mile," bustling Plateau Mont-Royal, and Mont-Royal itself—and in this chapter are strolls that will take you to the best of all of them.

Also listed is a destination walk that gets you to Marché Atwater, a large year-round market that provides some of the best antiquing in the city; it's an area to take the way locals do.

The city's layout is mostly straightforward and simple to navigate, and the extensive Métro system gets you to and from neighborhoods with ease.

These strolls will give you a taste of what's best about old and new Montréal, and send you off to discover highlights of your own.

WALKING TOUR 1 — VIEUX-MONTREAL

START:	Place d' Armes, opposite the Notre-Dame Basilica.
FINISH:	Vieux-Port.
TIME:	2 hours.
BEST TIMES:	Almost any day the weather is decent. Vieux-Montréal is lively and safe day or night. Note, however, that most museums are closed on Monday. On warm weekends and holidays, Montréalers and visitors turn out in full force, enjoying the plazas, the 18th- and 19th-century architecture, and the ambience of the most picturesque part of their city.
WORST TIMES:	Evenings, days that are too cold, and when museums and historic buildings are closed.

Vieux-Montréal is where the city was born. Its architectural heritage has been substantially preserved, and restored 18th- and 19th-century structures now house shops, boutique hotels, galleries, cafes, bars, and apartments. This tour gives you a lay of the land, passing many of the neighborhood's highlights and some of its best and most atmospheric dining spots.

If you're coming from outside Vieux-Montréal, take the Métro to the Place d'Armes station, which lets off next to the expanded Palais des Congrès. Follow the signs up the short hill 2 blocks toward Vieux-Montréal (Old Montréal) and the Place d'Armes. Turn right on rue St-Jacques. On your immediate right, at 119 rue St-Jacques, is the domed, colonnaded:

❶ Banque de Montréal

Montréal's oldest bank building dates from 1847. From 1901 to 1905, American architect Stanford White extended the original building, and in this enlarged space, he created a vast chamber with high, green-marble columns topped with golden capitals. The public is welcome to stop in for a look. Besides being lavishly appointed inside and out, the bank also houses a small **banking museum** (p. 122) which illustrates early operations. It's just off the main lobby and admission is free.

Exiting the bank, cross the street to:

❷ Place d'Armes

The centerpiece of this square is a monument to city founder Paul de Chomedey, Sieur de Maisonneuve (1612–76). These

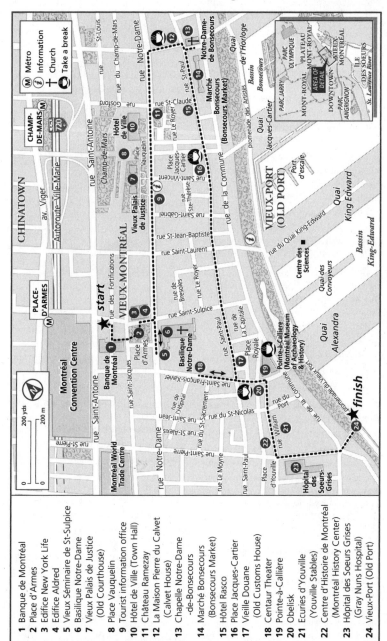

M Métro
i Information
✝ Church
☕ Take a break

CHINATOWN

Montréal Convention Centre

start

VIEUX-MONTRÉAL

Banque de Montréal

Hôtel de Ville

Vieux Palais de Justice

Basilique Notre-Dame

Place Jacques-Cartier

Marché Bonsecours (Bonsecours Market)

Notre-Dame-de-Bonsecours

Pointe-à-Callière (Montréal Museum of Archaeology & History)

VIEUX-PORT (OLD PORT)

Centre des Sciences

finish

Hôpital des Soeurs Grises

Montréal World Trade Centre

1 Banque de Montréal
2 Place d'Armes
3 Edifice New York Life
4 Edifice Aldred
5 Vieux Séminaire de St-Sulpice
6 Basilique Notre-Dame
7 Vieux Palais de Justice (Old Courthouse)
8 Place Vauquelin
9 Tourist information office
10 Hôtel de Ville (Town Hall)
11 Château Ramezay
12 La Maison Pierre du Calvet (Calvet House)
13 Chapelle Notre-Dame-de-Bonsecours
14 Marché Bonsecours (Bonsecours Market)
15 Hôtel Rasco
16 Place Jacques-Cartier
17 Vieille Douane (Old Customs House)
18 Centaur Theater
19 Pointe-à-Callière
20 Obelisk
21 Ecuries d'Youville (Youville Stables)
22 Centre d'Histoire de Montréal (Montréal History Center)
23 Hôpital des Soeurs Grises (Gray Nuns Hospital)
24 Vieux-Port (Old Port)

five statues mark the spot where settlers defeated Iroquois warriors in bloody hand-to-hand fighting, with de Maisonneuve himself locked in combat with the Iroquois chief. De Maisonneuve won and lived here another 23 years. The inscription on the monument reads (in French): YOU ARE THE BUCKWHEAT SEED WHICH WILL GROW AND MULTIPLY AND SPREAD THROUGHOUT THE COUNTRY.

The sculptures at the base of the monument represent other prominent citizens of early Montréal: Charles Lemoyne, a farmer; Jeanne Mance, the woman who founded the city's first hospital; Raphael-Lambert Closse, a soldier and the mayor of Ville-Marie; and an unnamed Iroquois brave. Closse is depicted with his dog, Pilote, whose bark once warned the early settlers of an impending Iroquois attack.

Facing the Notre-Dame Basilica from the square, look over to the left. At the corner of St-Jacques is the:

❸ Edifice New York Life

This red-stone Richardson Romanesque building, with a striking wrought-iron door and clock tower, is at 511 Place d'Armes. At all of eight stories, this became Montréal's first skyscraper in 1888, and it was equipped with a technological marvel—an elevator.

Next to it, on the right, stands the 23-story Art Deco:

❹ Edifice Aldred

If this building looks somehow familiar, there's a reason: Built in 1931, it clearly resembles New York's Empire State Building, also completed that year. The building's original tenant was Aldred and Co. Ltd., a New York–based finance company with other offices in New York, London, and Paris.

From the square, cross rue Notre-Dame, bearing right of the basilica to the:

❺ Vieux Séminaire de St-Sulpice

The city's oldest building is surrounded by equally ancient stone walls. This seminary was erected by Sulpician priests who arrived in Ville-Marie in 1657, 15 years after the colony was founded (the Sulpicians are part of an order founded in Paris by Jean-Jacques Olier in 1641). The clock on the façade dates from 1701; its gears are made almost entirely of wood. The seminary is not open to the public.

After a look through the iron gate, head east on rue Notre-Dame to the magnificent Gothic Revival–style:

❻ Basilique Notre-Dame

This brilliantly crafted church was designed in 1824 by James O'Donnell, an Irish Protestant architect living in New York. Transformed by his experience, he converted to Roman Catholicism and is the only person interred here.

The main altar is made from a hand-carved linden tree. Behind it is the Chapel of the Sacred Heart (1982), a perennially popular choice for weddings. The chapel's altar, 32 bronze panels by Montréal artist Charles Daudelin, represents birth, life, and death. Some 4,000 people can attend at a time, and the bell, one of North America's largest, weighs 12 tons. There's a small museum beside the chapel.

Come back at night for a romantic take on the city, when more than a score of buildings in the area, including this one, are illuminated.

See p. 112 for more about the church.

Exiting the basilica, turn right (east) on rue Notre-Dame, crossing rue St-Sulpice. Walk 4 blocks, passing chintzy souvenir shops, then face left to see the:

❼ Vieux Palais de Justice (Old Courthouse)

Most of this structure was built in 1856. The third floor and dome were added in 1891, and the difference between the original structure and the addition can be easily discerned with a close look.

The city's civil cases were tried here until a new courthouse, the Palais de Justice, was built next door in 1978. Civic departments for the city of Montréal are housed in the old courthouse now.

The statue beside the Old Courthouse, called *Homage to Marguerite Bourgeoys,* depicts a teacher and nun and is the work of sculptor Jules LaSalle.

Also on your left, just past the courthouse, is:

⑧ Place Vauquelin

This small public square, with a splashing fountain and view of the Champ-de-Mars park, was created in 1858. The statue is of Jean Vauquelin, commander of the French fleet in New France; he stares across rue Notre-Dame at his counterpart, the English admiral Horatio Nelson. The two statues are symbols of Montréal's French and British duality.

On the opposite corner is a small but helpful:

⑨ Tourist Information Office

A bilingual staff stands ready to answer questions and hand out useful brochures and maps (daily in warmer months, Wed–Sun in winter). The famed Silver Dollar Saloon, named for the 350 silver dollars that were embedded in its floor, once stood on this site, though it has long since been torn down.

Around the corner, on the right, is the Place Jacques-Cartier, a magnet for citizens and visitors year-round which we will visit later in the tour. Rising on the other side of rue Notre-Dame, opposite the top of the square, is the impressive, green-capped:

⑩ Hôtel de Ville (City Hall)

Built between 1872 and 1878 in the florid French Second Empire style, the edifice is seen to particular advantage when it is illuminated at night. In 1922, it barely survived a disastrous fire. Only the exterior walls remained, and after substantial rebuilding and the addition of another floor, it reopened in 1926. Take a minute to look inside at the generous use of Italian marble, the Art Deco lamps, and the bronze-and-glass chandelier. The sculptures at the entry are *Woman with a Pail* and *The Sower,* both by Québec sculptor Alfred Laliberté. See p. 117 for more details.

Exiting City Hall, you'll see, across rue Notre-Dame, a small, terraced park with orderly ranks of trees. The statue inside the park honors Montréal's controversial longtime mayor, Jean Drapeau. Next to it is:

⑪ Château Ramezay

Built by Claude de Ramezay between 1705 and 1706 in the French Regime style of the period, this was the home of the city's French governors for 4 decades, starting with de Ramezay, before being taken over and used for the same purpose by the British.

In 1775, an army of American rebels invaded and held Montréal, using the house as their headquarters. Benjamin Franklin was sent to persuade Montréalers to join the American revolt against British rule. He stayed in this château but failed to sway Québec's leaders to join his cause.

The house had a number of uses before becoming a museum in 1895. Today, it shows off furnishings, oil paintings, costumes, and other objects related to the economic and social activities of the 18th century and the first half of the 19th century. See p. 117 for more about the museum.

Continue in the same direction (east) along rue Notre-Dame. In the far distance, you'll see the Molson beer factory. At rue Bonsecours, turn right. Near the bottom of the street, on the left, is a house with a low maroon roof and an attached stone building on the corner. This is:

⑫ La Maison Pierre du Calvet (Calvet House)

Built in the 18th century and sumptuously restored between 1964 and 1966, this house was inhabited by a fairly well-to-do family in its first years. Pierre du Calvet, believed to be the original owner, was a French Huguenot who supported the American Revolution. Calvet met with Benjamin Franklin here in 1775 and was imprisoned from 1780 to 1783 for supplying money to the Americans. With a characteristic sloped roof meant to discourage snow buildup and raised end walls that serve as firebreaks, the building is constructed of Montréal graystone. It is now a *hostellerie* and **restaurant** with an entrance at no. 405. Visitors are invited to come in for a look.

TAKE A BREAK
There is a voluptuously appointed dining room inside the **Hostellerie Pierre du Calvet,** 405 rue Bonsecours, but in the warm months, lunches, dinners, and Sunday brunches are served in a lovely outdoor courtyard that opened to the public in 2007 (before then, it was privately used by the owner). Take a peek to see the greenhouse and songbirds that lead to the stone-walled terrace.

The next street, rue St-Paul, is Montréal's oldest thoroughfare, dating from 1672. The church at this intersection is the small:

⑬ Chapelle Notre-Dame-de-Bon-Secours

Called the Sailors' Church because so many seamen made pilgrimages here to give thanks for being saved at sea (look for the ship models hanging from the ceiling inside), this chapel was founded by Marguerite Bourgeoys, a nun and teacher who was canonized in 1982. Though recent excavations have unearthed foundations of her original 1675 church, the building has been much altered, and the present façade was built in the late 18th century. A **museum** (entrance on the left) tells the story of Bourgeoys' life and incorporates the archaeological site, where discoveries dated to 400 B.C. See p. 116 for more museum information.

Climb up to the tower for a view of the port and old town.

Just beyond the Sailor's Church, head west on rue St-Paul to see an imposing building with a colonnaded façade and silvery dome, the limestone:

⑭ Marché Bonsecours (Bonsecours Market)

Completed in 1847, this building was used first as the Parliament of United Canada and then as the City Hall, the central market, a music hall, and then the home of the municipality's housing and planning offices. It was restored in 1992 for the city's 350th birthday celebration to house temporary exhibitions and musical performances. It continues to be used for exhibitions, but it's more of a retail center now, with a terrific selection of art shops, clothing boutiques, and sidewalk cafes (p. 117).

When Bonsecours Market was first built, the dome could be seen from everywhere in the city and served as a landmark for seafarers sailing into the harbor. Today it is lit at night.

Continue down rue St-Paul. At no. 281 is the former:

⑮ Hôtel Rasco

An Italian, Francisco Rasco, came to Canada to manage a hotel for the Molson family (of beer-brewing fame) and later became successful with his own hotel on this spot. The 150-room Rasco was the Ritz-Carlton of its day, hosting Charles Dickens and his wife in 1842, when the author was directing his plays at a theater that used to stand across the street. The hotel lives on in legend if not in fact, as it's devoid of much of its original architectural detail and no longer hosts overnight guests. Between 1960 and 1981, the space stood empty, but the city took it over and restored it in 1982. It has contained a succession of eateries on the ground floor and now is home to a standout Mediterranean restaurant called **Version Laurent Godbout** (p. 94).

Continue heading west on rue St-Paul, turning right when you reach:

⑯ Place Jacques-Cartier

Opened as a marketplace in 1804, this is the most appealing of Vieux-Montréal's squares, even with its obviously touristy aspects. The square's cobbled cross streets, gentle downhill slope, and ancient buildings set the mood, while outdoor cafes, street entertainers, itinerant artists, and fruit and flower vendors invite lingering in warm weather. *Calèches* (horse-drawn carriages) depart from both the lower and the upper ends of the square for tours of Vieux-Montréal.

Walk slowly uphill, taking in the old buildings that bracket the plaza (plaques describe some of them in French and English). All these houses were well suited to the rigors of life in the raw young settlement. Their steeply pitched roofs shed the heavy winter snows rather than collapsing under the burden, and small windows with double casements let in light while keeping out wintry breezes. When shuttered, the windows were almost as effective as the heavy stone walls in deflecting hostile arrows or the antics of trappers fresh from raucous evenings in nearby taverns.

At the plaza's northern end stands a monument to Horatio Nelson, hero of Trafalgar, erected in 1809. This monument preceded London's much larger version by several years. After years of vandalism, presumably by Québec separatists, the statue had to be temporarily removed for restoration; the original Nelson is now back in place at the crown of the column.

TAKE A BREAK
Most of the old buildings in and around the inclined plaza house restaurants and cafes. For a drink or snack during the warm months, try to find a seat in **Le Jardin Nelson** (no. 407), near the bottom of the hill. The courtyard in back often has live jazz, while on the terrace overlooks the square's activity.

Return to rue St-Paul and continue west. Take time to window-shop the many art galleries that have sprung up alongside the loud souvenir shops on the street. The street numbers will get lower as you approach boulevard St-Laurent, the north-south thoroughfare that divides Montréal into its east and west halves. Numbers will start to rise again as you move onto St-Paul ouest (west). At 150 rue St-Paul ouest is the neoclassical:

⑰ Vieille Douane (Old Customs House)

Erected from 1836 to 1838, this building was doubled in size when an extension to the south side was added in 1882; walk

around to the building's other side to see how it's different. That end of the building faces Place Royale, the first public square in the 17th-century settlement of Ville-Marie. It's where Europeans and Amerindians used to come to trade. The building now houses a **boutique** (p. 158) for the **Pointe-à-Callière museum** (p. 113).

Continue on rue St-Paul to rue St-François-Xavier. Turn right for a short detour; up rue St-François-Xavier, on the right, is the stately:

⑱ Centaur Theatre

The home of Montréal's principal English-language theater is a former stock-exchange building. The Beaux-Arts architecture is interesting in that the two entrances are on either side rather than in the center of the façade. American architect George Post, who was also responsible for designing the New York Stock Exchange, designed this building, erected in 1903. It served its original function until 1965, when it was redesigned as a theater with two stages. See p. 163 for theater information.

Return back down rue St-François-Xavier to rue St-Paul.

TAKE A BREAK
One possibility for lunch or a pick-me-up is the moderately priced **Stash Café** (p. 97) at 200 rue St-Paul ouest at the corner of rue St-François-Xavier. It specializes in Polish fare and opens at 11:30am on weekdays and noon on weekends. Another option is the glass-walled, second-floor **L'Arrivage Café** at the Pointe-à-Callière museum, your next stop. Its lunchtime *table d'hôte* menu starts at C$10 (£5).

Continue on rue St-François-Xavier past St-Paul. At the next corner, the gray wedge-shaped building to the left is the:

⑲ Pointe-à-Callière

Housing the **Museum of Archaeology and History,** with artifacts unearthed here during more than a decade of excavation, this is where the settlement of Ville-Marie was founded in 1642. The museum also incorporates, via an underground connection, the **Old Customs House** you just passed. See p. 113 for more about this topnotch museum.

A fort stood here in 1645. Thirty years later, this same spot became the château of Louis-Hector de Callière, the governor of New France, from whom the building and triangular square take their names. At that time, the St. Pierre River separated this piece of land from the mainland. It was made a canal in the 19th century and later filled in.

Proceeding west from Pointe-à-Callière, near rue St-François-Xavier, stands an:

⑳ Obelisk

Commemorating the founding of Ville-Marie on May 18, 1642, the obelisk was erected here in 1893 by the Montréal Historical Society. It bears the names of the city's early pioneers, including French officer Paul Chomedey de Maisonneuve, who landed in Montréal in 1642, and fellow settler Jeanne Mance, who founded North America's first hospital, l'Hôtel-Dieu de Montréal.

Continuing west from the obelisk 2 blocks to 296–316 Place d'Youville, you'll find, on the left, the:

㉑ Ecuries d'Youville (Youville Stables)

Despite the name, the rooms in the iron-gated compound, built in 1825 on land owned by the Gray Nuns, were used mainly as warehouses rather than as horse stables (the actual stables, next door, were made of wood and disappeared long ago). Like much of the waterfront area, the U-shaped Youville building was run-down and forgotten until the 1960s, when a group of enterprising businesspeople bought and renovated it. Today the compound contains offices and a popular steakhouse, **Gibby's.** Go through the passage toward the restaurant door for a look at the inner courtyard if the gates are open (they usually are).

Continue another block west to the front door of the brick building on your right, 335 rue St-Pierre and the:

㉒ Centre d'Histoire de Montréal (Montréal History Center)

Built in 1903 as Montréal's central fire station, this building now houses exhibits, including many audiovisual ones, about the city's past and present. Visitors learn about early exploration routes, the fur trade, architecture, public squares, the railroad, and life in Montréal from 1920 to 1950. See p. 122 for details.

Head down rue St-Pierre toward the water. Midway down the block, on the right at no. 138, is the former:

㉓ Hôpital des Soeurs Grises (Gray Nuns Hospital)

The hospital was in operation from 1693 to 1871 and served as a novitiate for future nuns. The order, founded by Marguerite d'Youville in 1737, is officially known as the Sisters of Charity of Montréal. The present building incorporates several additions and was part of the city's general hospital, run by the Charon Brothers but administered by d'Youville, who died here in 1771. The wing in which she died was restored in 1980. The building is not open to the public.

From here, continue down rue St-Pierre and cross the main street, rue de la Commune, and then the railroad tracks to this tour's final stop:

㉔ Vieux-Port (Old Port)

Montréal's historic commercial wharves have been reborn as a waterfront park, which, in good weather, is frequented by cyclists, in-line skaters, joggers, walkers, strollers, lovers, and picnickers. Across the water is the distinctive modular housing project **Habitat 67,** built by famed architect Moshe Safdie for Expo 67; it's now a high-end apartment complex.

Walk to your right; the little triangular concrete building you see is the entrance to **Parc des Ecluses (Locks Park),** a canalside path where the St. Lawrence River's first locks are located.

From here, you have several options: If the weather's nice, consider entering the Parc des Ecluses to stroll the path along **Lachine Canal.** In an hour or less, you'll arrive at Montréal's colorful **Atwater Market** (p. 156).

If you walk the other direction, you'll take in the busiest section of the waterfront park and end up back at Place Jacques-Cartier.

To get to the subway, walk north along rue McGill to the Square-Victoria Métro station, the staircase to which is marked by an authentic Art Nouveau portal, designed by Hector Guimard for the Paris subway system.

Or, return to the small streets parallel to rue St-Paul; you'll find more boutiques and one of the highest concentrations of art galleries in Canada.

WALKING TOUR 2   **DOWNTOWN**

START:	Bonaventure Métro station.
FINISH:	Musée des Beaux-Arts and rue Crescent.
TIME:	1½ hours.
BEST TIMES:	Weekdays in the morning or after 2pm, when the streets hum with big-city vibrancy but aren't *too* busy.
WORST TIMES:	Weekdays from noon to 2pm, when the streets, stores, and restaurants are crowded with businesspeople on lunch-break errands; Monday, when museums are closed; and Sunday, when many stores are closed and the area is nearly deserted.

After a tour of Vieux-Montréal, a look around the commercial heart of the 21st-century city will highlight the ample contrast between these two areas. To see the city at its contemporary best, take the Métro to the Bonaventure stop to start this tour.

After you've emerged from the Métro station, the dramatic skyscraper immediately to the west is:

❶ 1000 rue de la Gauchetière

This new contribution to downtown Montréal's already memorable skyline is easily identified by its copper-and-blue pyramidal top, which rises to the maximum height permitted by the municipal building code. Inside, past an atrium planted with live trees, is an indoor skating rink bordered by cafes.

Walk west on rue de la Gauchetière. Ahead is Le Marriott Château Champlain, whose distinctive façade of half-moon windows inspired its nickname: "the Cheese Grater." Turn right on rue de la Cathedrale, heading north. At the next corner, you reach:

❷ Boulevard René-Lévesque

Formerly Dorchester Boulevard, this primary street was renamed in 1988 following the death of René-Lévesque, the Parti Québécois leader who led the movement for Québec independence and the use of the French language. Boulevard René-Lévesque is the city's broadest downtown thoroughfare.

Across bd. René-Lévesque is:

❸ Square Dorchester

This is one of downtown's central locations. It's a gathering point for tour buses and horse-drawn *calèches,* and the square's tall, old trees and benches invite lunchtime brown-baggers. This used to be called Dominion Square, but it was renamed for Baron Dorchester, an early English governor, when the adjacent street, once named for Dorchester, was changed to boulevard René-Lévesque. Along the square's east side is the **Sun Life Insurance building,** built in three stages between 1914 and 1931, and the tallest building in Québec from 1931 until the skyscraper boom of the post-World War II era.

At the north end of the square is:

❹ Montréal's Central Tourist Office

The Infotouriste Centre at 1255 rue Peel provides maps and brochures, most of them free for the taking. Visitors can also ask questions of the bilingual attendants, purchase tour tickets, make hotel reservations, or rent a car. Open daily.

On bd. René-Lévesque at the corner of Square Dorchester is the:

❺ Basilique-Cathédrale Marie-Reine-du-Monde

Suddenly get the feeling you're in Rome? This cathedral is a copy of St. Peter's Basilica, albeit roughly one-quarter of the size. It was built between 1875 and 1894 as the headquarters for Montréal's Roman Catholic bishop. The statue in front is of Bishop Ignace Bourget (1799–1885), the force behind the construction. See p. 116 for more details.

Continue on bd. René-Lévesque past the cathedral. In the next block, on the right, is:

❻ Fairmont The Queen Elizabeth (Le Reine Elizabeth)

Montréal's largest hotel (p. 71) stands above **Gare Centrale,** the main railroad station. There are buses to and from Montréal-Trudeau airport from here. Opened in 1958, the Fairmont is where John Lennon and Yoko Ono had their famous weeklong "Bed-in for Peace" in 1969.

On the other side of bd. René-Lévesque, directly across from the hotel, is:

❼ Place Ville-Marie

One thing to keep in mind is that the French word "place," or "plaza," sometimes means an outdoor square, such as Place Jacques-Cartier in Vieux- Montréal. Other times, it refers to an indoor building or complex that includes stores and offices. Place Ville-Marie is in the later category. Known as PVM to Montréalers, it's a glass box of a building that was considered a gem of the 1960s urban redevelopment efforts. Its architect? None other than I. M. Pei, who also designed the glass

pyramid at the Louvre in Paris. Pei gave the skyscraper a cross-shaped footprint, recalling the cross atop Mont-Royal. The complex was completed in 1962.

Continue on bd. René-Lévesque to the end of the block and turn left on rue University. As you walk, look to the top of the skyscraper a few blocks down; this pink, postmodern glass office building is Tour KPMG and was completed in 1987. The two-peaked top is meant to resemble a bishop's mitre, or cap, but many see the ears and mask of a certain DC Comics superhero; see if you can tell which one. In 2 blocks you'll reach:

❽ Rue Ste-Catherine

This is one of the city's prime shopping streets, with name brands, local businesses, and department stores. Among them, to the right, is **La Baie**—or "the Bay"—successor to the famous fur-trapping firm Hudson's Bay Co., founded in the 17th century (see "Department Stores," p. 155).

If you're in the mood to shop, stroll west on this main shopping drag to its center. (Be aware that there are several adult shops, too.) To continue the tour, return to this corner and the:

❾ Cathédrale Christ Church

Built from 1856 to 1859, this neo-Gothic building is the seat of the Anglican bishop of Montréal. The church garden is modeled on a medieval European cloister. In addition to Sunday's 10am Sung Eucharist and 4pm Choral Evensong, the church has services at noon and 5:15pm weekdays. See p. 116.

Walk east on rue Ste-Catherine to avenue Union, to La Baie department store. Turn left on avenue Union and go north 3 blocks, to rue Sherbrooke. You'll be in front of McGill University's Schulich School of Music.

 TAKE A BREAK
At the corner of Union and Sherbrooke is an outpost of the cheery **Java U** (626 rue Sherbrooke), an expanding local coffee chain that got its start in 1996 at Concordia University. In a high-design venue with friendly, laid-back staff, it serves quiches, salads, wraps, and cake. Also featured is ice cream from local master purveyor Bilboquet (p. 104).

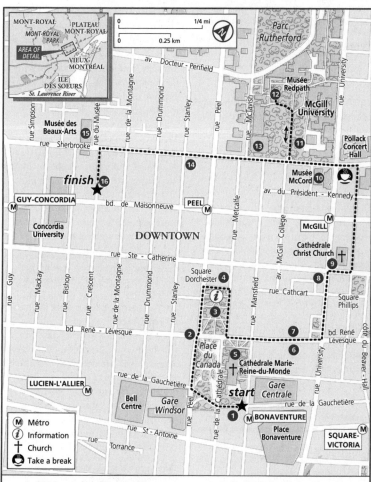

1 1000 rue de la Gauchetière

2 Boulevard Réne-Lévesque

3 Square Dorchester

4 Central tourist office

5 Basilique-Cathédrale
  Marie-Reine-du-Monde

6 Fairmont the Queen Elizabeth
  (Le Reine Elizabeth)

7 Place Ville-Marie

8 Rue Ste-Catherine

9 Cathédrale Christ Church

10 Musée McCord

11 McGill University

12 Musée Redpath

13 Site of the Amerindian
   Horchelaga settlement

14 Maison Alcan

15 Musée des Beaux-Arts

16 Rue Crescent

Head left (west) on rue Sherbrooke. This is the city's grand boulevard, and the rest of the tour will take you past the former mansions, ritzy hotels, high-end boutiques, and special museums that give it its personality today. One block down on the left is:

⑩ Musée McCord

This museum of Canadian history opened in 1921 and was substantially renovated in 1992. Named for its founder, David Ross McCord (1844–1930), the museum maintains an eclectic and often eccentric collection of photographs, paintings, and First Nations folk art. Its special exhibits make it especially worth a visit. Hours and other details are on p. 109.

Continue west. On your right is:

⑪ McGill University

The gate is usually open to Canada's most prestigious university. It was founded after a bequest from a Scottish-born fur trader, James McGill. The central campus mixes modern concrete and glass structures alongside older stone buildings and is the focal point for the school's 33,500 students.

On campus is the:

⑫ Musée Redpath

Housed in a building dating from 1882, this museum's main draws are the mummies in its Egyptian antiquities collection (p. 122).

Continue on rue Sherbrooke. About 9m (30 ft.) past McGill's front gate, note the large stone on the lawn. This marks the:

⑬ Site of the Amerindian Horchelaga Settlement

Near this spot was the village of Hochelaga, a community of Iroquois who lived and farmed here before the first Europeans arrived. When French explorer Jacques Cartier stepped from his ship onto the land and visited Hochelaga in 1535, he noted that the village had 50 large homes, each housing several families. When the French returned in 1603, the village was empty.

Two blocks farther, at no. 1188, just past rue Stanley, is:

⑭ Maison Alcan

Rue Sherbrooke is the heart of what's known as the "Golden Square Mile." This is where the city's most luxurious residences of the 19th and early 20th centuries were, and where the vast majority of the country's wealthiest citizens lived. (For a period of time, 79 families who lived in this neighborhood controlled 80% of Canada's wealth.) Look across the street at Maison Louis-Joseph Forget at no. 1195 and Maison Reid Wilson at no 1201, both designated historic monuments. Maison Alcan is an example of an office building that has nicely incorporated one of those 19th-century mansions into its late-20th-century façade. Step inside the lobby to see the results over to the right.

Continue on rue Sherbrooke, passing on your left the Holt Renfrew department store, identified on the side of its marquee only as HR. At the corner of rue Crescent is the:

⑮ Musée des Beaux-Arts (Museum of Fine Arts)

This is Canada's oldest museum, and Montréal's most prominent. The modern annex on the left side of rue Sherbrooke was added in 1991 and is connected to the original stately Beaux-Arts building (1912) on the right side by an underground tunnel that doubles as a gallery. Both buildings are made of Vermont marble. See p. 108 for additional details.

There are several options at this point. If you have time to explore the museum, take the opportunity—a visit to the Musée des Beaux-Arts should be part of any trip to Montréal. For high-end boutique shopping, continue on rue Sherbrooke. For drinking or eating, turn left onto:

⑯ Rue Crescent

Welcome to party central. Rue Crescent and nearby streets are the locus of the downtown social and dining district. The area is largely yuppie-Anglo in character, if not necessarily in strict demographics. Crescent's first block is stocked with boutiques and jewelers, but the next 2 blocks are a gumbo of terraced bars and dance clubs, inexpensive pizza joints, and upscale restaurants, all drawing enthusiastic consumers looking to party the afternoon and evening away.

It's hard to imagine that this center of gilded youth and glamour was once a run-down slum slated for demolition. Luckily, buyers with good aesthetic sense saw potential in these late-19th-century row houses and brought them back to life.

> **TAKE A BREAK**
> Lively spots for food and drink are abundant along rue Crescent. **Thursday's** (no. 1449, in L'Hôtel de la Montagne) is one, if you can find a seat on the balcony.
>
> For a satisfying snack, head to the unassuming Lebanese joint **Boustan** (no. 2020) for a filling shawarma sandwich. Yes, that's former Prime ·Minster Pierre Trudeau's photo at the register; he was a regular.

WALKING TOUR 3   PLATEAU MONT-ROYAL

START:	The corner of avenue du Mont-Royal and rue St-Denis.
FINISH:	Square St-Louis or Parc LaFontaine.
TIME:	At least 2 hours, but allow more time if you want to linger in shops, restaurants, or the major park of this intriguing neighborhood.
BEST TIMES:	Monday through Saturday during the day, when shops are open. Most of this area is at its liveliest on Saturday. For barhopping, evenings work well.
WORST TIMES:	Early mornings, when stores and restaurants are closed.

This is essentially a browsing and grazing tour, designed to provide a sampling of the sea of ethnicities that make up Plateau Mont-Royal, north of downtown Montréal and east of Mont-Royal Park. The largely Francophone neighborhood has seen an unprecedented flourishing of restaurants, cafes, clubs, and shops in recent years. It's bounded on the south by rue Sherbrooke, on the north by boulevard St-Joseph (where the Mile End neighborhood begins), on the east by avenue Papineau, and on the west by boulevard St-Laurent. The residential side streets are filled with row houses that are home to students, young professionals, and immigrants old and new. This walk provides a glance into the lives of both established and freshly minted Montréalers and the ways in which they spend their leisure time. Stores and bistros open and close with considerable frequency in this neighborhood, so be forewarned that some of the highlights listed below may not exist when you visit.

To begin, take the Métro to the Mont-Royal station. Turn left out of the station and walk west on avenue du Mont-Royal to rue St-Denis. Turn left again onto rue St-Denis; the next 4 blocks are filled with some of the best local boutique shopping and Francophone dining in the city. On the left side of the street, at 4481 rue St-Denis, is:

❶ Quai des Brumes

This popular gathering spot for electronic, rock, jazz, and blues music—and beer— offers live music on most evenings.

Stroll down rue St-Denis, pausing at shops and cafes that fill the two stories of the small buildings. Toward the end of the block, on the other side of the street, is no. 4380 (but don't cross midstreet; police give tickets for jaywalking):

❷ Champigny

A large bookstore with mostly French stock, it also carries travel guides and literature in English, as well as CDs, magazines, and newspapers from around the world. Most of the books are upstairs. It's open daily from 9am until 10pm.

Continue south on rue St-Denis. On the next block, at no. 4306, is:

❸ Départ en Mer

This small shop with "antiquitiés marines" carries model ships, boating clothes, and shoes.

In the same block, at no. 4268, is:

❹ Jacob Outlet

With pop music through the speakers and a steady stream of locals, this clothing store is an outlet to the popular Jacob chain (there's one next door). You'll find inexpensive T-shirts, denim jackets, and other casual clothes for the under-25 set.

A little farther, at no. 4246, is:

❺ Zone

This shop is part of a small Montréal-based chain; there are two other stores in the city and one each in Québec City and Ottawa. Its specialty is contemporary housewares, sleekly monochromatic and brightly hued.

A little farther still, at no. 4228, is:

❻ Bedo

Another Montréal-based chain, this one has higher-end men's and women's designer sportswear, with colorful blouses in the C$50 (£25) range, fun dresses, and well-fit shirts. This outlet is one of 10 in the city.

At the next intersection, rue Rachel, turn left for a short diversion off of rue St-Denis. On your left at no. 485 is:

❼ Kanuk

One of Canada's top manufacturers of high-end winter coats and accessories has its factory store right here. Like EMS or LL Bean in the U.S, Kanuk first sold its heavy parkas primarily to outdoor enthusiasts. Back then, the company wryly notes on its website, customers had a choice of royal blue or royal blue. Today, their jackets come in 30 colors and 35 models. They're an extremely popular practical necessity—and status symbol.

TAKE A BREAK

If you haven't yet tried *poutine,* the national comfort food, by all means hop into **La Banquise,** at 995 rue Rachel est. The restaurant is practically a city landmark, what with its 25 variations on *poutine:* the standard french fries with gravy and cheese curds are offered with add-ons ranging from smoked sausage to hot peppers to smoked meat to bacon. It's open 24 hours a day, every day.

Just beyond the restaurant is the grand:

❽ Parc La Fontaine

Strolling this park, particularly on a warm day, is an enormously satisfying way to see Montréal at play. This northwestern end of La Fontaine is well used by people (and puppies) of all ages.

In summer, the 2,500-seat **Théâtre de Verdure,** near where rue Duluth runs into the park, becomes an open-air venue for dance, music, theater, and film. In winter, the two ponds are linked and turned into a skating rink (skate rentals available).

There's a bike-rental shop at this corner just before you enter the park, at 1000 rue Rachel est (www.cyclepop.ca). If you're keen to explore the park or head off for a bike ride, consider this tour done. The Sherbrooke Métro will be closest if you leave the park on its west side. To continue the stroll, retrace your steps to go back to rue St-Denis. Turn left and continue south. Among the boutiques still to explore, at 4117 rue St-Denis, is:

❾ Artéfact

Québécois designers sell clothing and paintings at this bright little boutique, where a slip of a summer dress runs about C$250 (£125).

After that, find no. 4107:

❿ Kaliyana

More women's clothes from a Canadian designer: This shop's natural-fiber outfits are flowing, angular, and border on being avant-garde—think Asian-influenced Eileen Fisher. It also stocks contemporary footwear including Arche from France and Trippen from Germany.

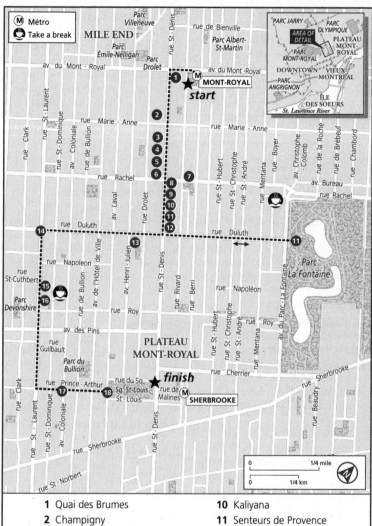

MONTRÉAL STROLLS

9

PLATEAU MONT-ROYAL

1 Quai des Brumes	**10** Kaliyana
2 Champigny	**11** Senteurs de Provence
3 Départ en Mer	**12** Jacob Lush
4 Jacob Outlet	**13** Rue Duluth
5 Zone	**14** Boulevard St-Laurent
6 Bedo	**15** Schwartz's
7 Kanuk	**16** La Vieille Europe
8 Parc la Fonatine	**17** Rue Prince-Arthur
9 Artefact	**18** Square St-Louis

At 4077 rue St-Denis, you'll come upon:

⓫ Senteurs de Provence

One of a small chain, this store displays hand-painted pottery and printed linens, as well as soaps, shower gels, and lotions of high order, all from France.

At no. 4067, take a whiff of:

⓬ Lush

On the ground floor of one of the street's prettiest Queen Anne Victorian row houses, Lush sells soaps presented and wrapped as if they were aromatic, bubble-gum-colored hunks of cheese.

At the next corner is rue Duluth. Turn right here to get a taste of:

⓭ Rue Duluth

This street is dotted with an ever-changing collection of Greek, Portuguese, Italian, North African, Malaysian, and Vietnamese eateries. Many of the restaurants state that you can *apportez votre vin* (bring your own wine). There are also several small antiques shops.

Continue along rue Duluth until boulevard St-Laurent, the north-south thoroughfare that divides Montréal into its east and west sides. Turn left.

⓮ Boulevard St-Laurent

St-Laurent is so prominent in Montréal's cultural history that it's known to Anglophones, Francophones, and Allophones (people whose primary language is neither English nor French) alike simply as "the Main." Traditionally a beachhead for immigrants to the city, St-Laurent has become a street of chic bistros and clubs. The late-night section runs for several miles, roughly from rue Laurier in the north all the way down to rue Sherbrooke in the south. The bistro and club boom was fueled by low rent prices and the large number of industrial lofts in this area, a legacy of St-Laurent's heyday as a garment-manufacturing center. Today, these cavernous spaces are places for the city's hipsters, professionals, artists, and guests to eat and play. Many spots have the life spans of fireflies, but some pound on for years.

At 3895 bd. St-Laurent, you'll find:

⓯ Schwartz's

The language police insisted on the exterior sign with the French mouthful CHEZ SCHWARZ CHARCUTERIE HEBRAIQUE DE MONTREAL, but everyone just calls it Schwartz's (p. 101). This narrow, no-frills Hebrew deli might appear completely unassuming, but it serves smoked meat against which all other smoked meats must be measured. Don't forget a side of fries and a couple of garlicky pickles.

Next, a few steps along at no. 3855, is:

⓰ La Vieille Europe

This old-Europe deli sells aromatic coffee beans from around the world, sausages and meats, cheeses, cooking utensils, and other gourmet fare. Stock up here if you're thinking of having a picnic in the next day or two.

Continue down bd. St-Laurent 2 more blocks and turn left (east) onto:

⓱ Rue Prince-Arthur

Named after Queen Victoria's third son, who was governor-general of Canada from 1911 to 1916, this pedestrian street is filled with bars and restaurants, most of which add more to the street's liveliness than to the city's gastronomic reputation. The older establishments go by such names as La Cabane Grecque, La Caverne Grec, Casa Grecque—no doubt you will discern an emerging theme—but the Greek stalwarts are being challenged by Latino and Asian newcomers. Their owners vie constantly with gimmicks to haul in passersby, including two-for-one drinks and dueling *tables d'hôte* prices. Beer and sangria are the popular drinks at the white tables and chairs set out along the sides of the street, although some of the restaurants are BYOB. In warmer weather, street performers, vendors, and caricaturists also compete for tourist dollars.

Five short blocks later, rue Prince-Arthur ends at:

⑱ Square St-Louis

This public garden plaza is framed by attractive row houses erected for well-to-do Francophones in the late 19th and early 20th centuries. People stretch out on the grass to take in the sun, or sit bundled on benches willing March away (there often are a few harmless derelicts among them). The square ends at rue St-Denis.

To pick up the Métro, cross rue St-Denis and walk east on rue des Malines. The Sherbrooke station is just ahead at the corner of rue Berri.

WALKING TOUR 4   MONT-ROYAL

START:	At the corner of rue Peel and avenue des Pins.
FINISH:	At the cross on top of the mountain (la Croix du Mont-Royal).
TIME:	1 hour to ascend to the Chalet du Mont-Royal and its lookout over the city and come back down by the fastest route; 3 hours to take the more leisurely chemin Olmstead route and see all the sites listed below. It's easy to leave out some sites to truncate the walk.
BEST TIMES:	Spring, summer, and autumn mornings.
WORST TIMES:	Winter, when snow and slush make a sleigh ride to the top of the mountain much more enticing than a hike, or during the high heat of midday in summer.

Join the locals: Assuming a reasonable measure of physical fitness, the best way to explore the jewel that is Parc Mont-Royal is simply to walk up it from downtown. It's called a mountain but it's more like a very large hill. A broad pedestrian-only road and smaller footpaths form a web of options for strollers, joggers, cyclists, and in-line skaters of all ages. Anyone in search of a little greenery and space heads here in warm weather, while in winter, cross-country skiers follow miles of paths and snowshoers tramp along trails laid out especially for them.

The 200-hectare (494-acre) urban park was created in 1876 by American landscape architect Frederick Law Olmsted, who also designed Central Park in New York City and parks in Philadelphia, Boston, and Chicago (although in the end, relatively little of Olmsted's full design for Mont-Royal actually came into being). For more about the park's history, as well as its most current events and happenings, go to **www.lemontroyal.qc.ca**.

Start at the corner of rue Peel and avenue des Pins, at the:

❶ Downtown Park Entrance

A map at the site helps to set bearings. From here, it's possible to reach the top of this small mountain by a variety of routes. Hearty souls can choose the quickest and most strenuous approach—taking the steepest sets of stairs at every opportunity, which go directly to the Chalet du Mont-Royal and its lookout at the top (see no. 7). Those who prefer to take their time and gain altitude slowly can use the switchback bridle path. Or mix and match the options as you go along. Don't be too worried about getting lost; the park is small enough that it's easy to regain your sense of direction no matter which way you head.

Head up either footpath from the entrance (the paths are not particularly well maintained here, but improve the further up you go). You'll soon reach the broad bridle path:

❷ Chemin Olmsted (Olmsted Road)

Frederick Law Olmsted designed this road, which is closed to automobiles, at a gradual grade for horse-drawn carriages. Horses could pull their loads up the hill at a steady pace, and on the way down would not be pushed from behind by the weight of the carriage.

Early on, the road passes some beautiful stone houses off Redpath Circle, to the left. If you want to bypass some of the switchbacks, use any of a number of paths for a shortcut—but stay only on established trails to prevent erosion.

After about the fourth switchback, you'll reach an intersection with the option to go left or right. Turn left. Following this shaded, pleasant road in the woods will get you to Maison Smith (see no. 4) in about 45 minutes.

Another option is to take the:

❸ Stairs

There are numerous sets of stairs through the woods that let you bypass chemin Olmstead's broad switchbacks. These steps get walkers to the Chalet du Mont-Royal and its lookout (see no. 7) more quickly.

Fair warning: The last 100 or so steps go almost straight up. On the plus side, you'll get to share sympathetic smiles with strangers. Taking the steps bypasses sites no. 4, 5, and 6.

If you're taking chemin Olmsted, you eventually arrive at:

❹ Maison Smith

Built in 1858, this structure has been used as a park rangers' station and park police headquarters. Today, it's a year-round information center with a small exhibit about the park and a gift shop. **Café Smith,** a terrace restaurant, offers soups, sandwiches, beverages, and sweets.

From Maison Smith, walk through the field of sculptures, away from the radio tower, until you reach:

❺ Lac des Castors (Beaver Lake)

This lake's name refers to the once-profitable fur industry, not to the actual presence of the long-gone animals. In summer, it's surrounded by sunbathers and picnickers, and you can rent a paddleboat. In the winter, before the snow sets in, it becomes an ice skater's paradise.

There's a small concession stand in the pavilion, along with restrooms and telephones.

Walk across the road behind the pavilion, called chemin de la Remembrance (Remembrance Rd.), to enter:

❻ Notre-Dame-des-Neiges Cemetery

This is the city's predominantly Catholic cemetery, and from here you can visit the adjacent Protestant Mount Royal graveyard. Behind it (to the north), if you're up for a longer walk, is the small adjoining Jewish and Spanish-Portuguese cemetery.

Notre-Dame-des-Neiges Cemetery reveals much about Montréal's ethnic mix: Headstones, some with likenesses in photos or tiles, are engraved with surnames as diverse as Zagorska, Skwyrska, De Ciccio, Sen, Lavoie, O'Neill, Hammerschmid, Fernandez, Müller, Haddad, and Boudreault.

If you've had enough walking, find a no. 11 bus on chemin de la Remembrance that heads east toward the Guy Métro station. To continue the tour, head back to Maison Smith and follow the signs on the main path for:

❼ Chalet du Mont-Royal & Its Lookout

The front terrace here offers the most popular panoramic view of the city and the river. The chalet itself was constructed from 1931 to 1932 at a cost of $230,000 and has been used over the years for receptions, concerts, and various other events. Inside the chalet, take a look at the 17 paintings hanging just below the ceiling, starting to the right of the door that leads into the snack bar. They relate the region's history and the story of the French explorations of North America. In winter, there's a warming room for skiers.

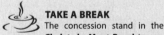

TAKE A BREAK
The concession stand in the **Chalet du Mont-Royal** is usually open from 9am to 5pm daily and sells sandwiches, fruit, ice cream, and beverages. Heed the signs that ask patrons to refrain from feeding the squirrels, no matter how adorably they're begging.

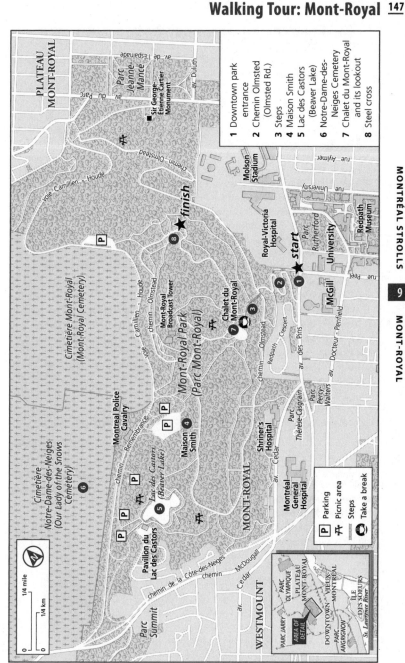

Walking Tour: Mont-Royal

1 Downtown park entrance
2 Chemin Olmsted (Olmsted Rd.)
3 Steps
4 Maison Smith
5 Lac des Castors (Beaver Lake)
6 Notre-Dame-des-Neiges Cemetery
7 Chalet du Mont-Royal and its lookout
8 Steel cross

PLATEAU MONT-ROYAL

Parc Jeanne-Mance
av. de l'Esplanade
av. Duluth
av. du Parc
Sir George-Étienne Cartier Monument
chemin – Olmsted
voie Camillien – Houde

finish

Molson Stadium
Royal-Victoria Hospital
rue Aylmer
rue University

start
Parc Rutherford
Redpath Museum
McGill University
rue Peel

Mont-Royal Broadcast Tower
voie Camillien – Houde
chemin – Olmsted
Chalet du Mont-Royal
chemin Olmsted
Redpath Crescent
av. des Pins
av. Docteur – Penfield

Cimetière Mont-Royal (Mont-Royal Cemetery)

Montreal Police Cavalry
chemin Remembrance
Maison Smith

Shriner's Hospital
av. Cedar
Parc Percy Walters
Parc Thérèse-Casgrain

Cimetière Notre-Dame-des-Neiges (Our Lady of the Snows Cemetery)

Lac des Castors (Beaver Lake)
Montréal General Hospital

Pavillon du Lac des Castors
chemin de la Côte-des-Neiges
chemin Cedar
av. McDougall

Parc Summit

WESTMOUNT
MONT-ROYAL

P Parking
☂ Picnic area
Steps
☕ Take a break

N
0 1/4 mile
0 1/4 km

PARC JARRY
PARC OLYMPIQUE
PLATEAU MONT-ROYAL
VIEUX-MONTRÉAL
DOWNTOWN
ÎLE DES SŒURS
PARC ANGRIGNON
AREA OF DETAIL
St. Lawrence River

Destination: Antique Alley & Marche Atwater

This is a great walk to take if you 1) are in Vieux-Montréal and want to get out-side the tourist orbit into a nearby, interesting neighborhood; 2) like antiques shops; 3) are looking for a stroll that concludes (preferably at lunchtime) at one of the city's two great farmers' markets.

The walk itself is simple: Start in Vieux-Montréal on rue Notre-Dame and head west. About an hour later, if you don't make many stops, you'll reach **Marché Atwater,** a farmer's market that in summer is lined with stalls and stalls of fresh fruit, vegetables, flowers, and snacks, as well as indoors cheese and meat shops, cafes and food stores that stay open year-round. From rue McGill, the street at the western side of Vieux-Montréal, the walk is about 3km (2 miles).

You first come upon a tangle of highways, where the downtown skyline is displayed in a great expanse. After that are some of the city's newer (and then older) condominium complexes.

After about 20 minutes, the gentrified "Antique Alley" begins. The first sign is no. 1510 rue Notre-Dame ouest, the **Thamar** tea room, which serves cakes and chocolates (✆ **514/937-2222;** www.thamar.ca). The next corner is at rue Guy, and here's where the antiquing really begins. Little shops door to door on the next few streets are chock-a-block with every kind of high- and low-end antique under the sun. Business has been tougher of late thanks to eBay, but antiquers will find loads to look at. **Michel Richard Antiquaire,** at no. 1700 (✆ **514/933-0314**), is one of the grandest stores, housed in a former post office with pillars outside and chandeliers, marble tables, and overstuffed divans inside. Pick up the *Antiques Art Galleries* guidebook here for free—it prints ads for many of the shops on this street.

The antiquing stops for a few blocks but picks up again at rue Vinet, on which there are some culinary highlights. At no. 2491 is the seafood-and-meat neigh-borhood joint **Joe Beef** (✆ **514/935-6504**), whose oyster bar is especially

---

Facing the chalet from the terrace, locate the path running off to the right, marked by a sign that says CROIX. Follow it for about 10 minutes to the giant:

❽ Croix du Mont-Royal

Legend has it that Paul de Chomedey, Sieur de Maisonneuve (1612–76), erected a wooden cross here in 1643 after the young colony survived a flood threat. The present incarnation of the Croix du Mont-Royal, installed in 1924, is lit at night and visible from all over the city.

Beside the cross is a plaque marking where a time capsule was interred in August 1992, during Montréal's 350th-birthday

acclaimed (p. 107), and two new adjacent operations run by the same folks: **Liverpool House** (no. 2501), an Italian gastropub, and the **McKiernan** luncheonette and wine bar (no. 2485). Graphic-design fans will appreciate the old-fashioned type used by all three properties with the oversight of typographer Glenn Goluska, who also designs for the Canadian Centre for Architecture.

In the next block, **itsi bitsi,** at no. 2621 (© **514/509-3926;** www.itsi-bitsi.com) sells designer cupcakes and gelato; the latter comes in flavors like mojito and chocolate-wasabi.

Barcelona has its Boqueria market, Venice has the Rialto fish market, New York City has the Union Square Greenmarket, and Montréal has **Marché Atwater,** at 138 av. Atwater, www.marchespublics-mtl.com (and, further north, near Little Italy, the **Marché Jean-Talon**). The market has been in business since 1933 and is housed in an Art Deco–style brick tower building.

One of the must-sees is **Première-Moisson** (© **514/932-0328;** www.premieremoisson.com). It's the first bakery to use wheat flour made from wheat grown in Québec, but even without that fact, it's easy to be drawn deeply into the bakery's orbit, with its cases and cases of pastries and cakes; look for breads, sandwiches—and the Piquant Truffé, a many-peaked concoction dusted with chocolate. In the rest of the market, more than a dozen butchers and cheese shops do business, along with boutiques that sell chocolates, *bonbons au miel* (honey drops), gourmet packaged goods, and high-end condiments. Eat your snacks at one of the small Parisian-style tables or outdoors. Even the pizza is worth traveling for, piled high with fresh mozzarella and veggies. And of course, in the warm months, the market is flush with fresh fruit and vegetables.

The Lionel-Groulx Métro stop is only 3 blocks away, north on rue Atwater toward downtown Montréal. The paths of the Lachine Canal are just a few blocks south, where kayak and pedal boat rentals are available in summer (p. 128).

celebration. Some 12,000 children ages 6 to 12 filled the capsule with messages and drawings depicting their visions for the city in the year 2142, when Montréal will be 500 years old and the capsule will be opened.

To return to downtown Montréal, go back along the path to the chalet terrace. On the left, just before the terrace, is another path. It leads to the staircase described in no. 3 and descends to where the tour began. The walk down by this route takes about 15 minutes. The no. 11 bus also runs from the summit to the Mont-Royal Métro, and there are buses at Beaver Lake and along chemin de la Remembrance.

Montréal Shopping

You can shop in Montréal until your feet swell and your eyes cross. Whether you view shopping as the focus of your travels or simply as a diversion, you won't be disappointed. Among natives, shopping ranks right up there with dining out as a prime activity. Most Montréalers are of French ancestry, after all, and seem to believe that impeccable taste bubbles through the Gallic gene pool. The city has produced a thriving fashion industry, from couture to ready-to-wear, with a history that reaches back to the earliest trade in furs and leather. More than 1,700 shops populate the underground city alone, and many more than that are at street level and above. It is unlikely that any reasonable consumer need—or even outlandish fantasy—cannot be met here.

The Visitor Rebate Program, which used to allow nonresident visitors to apply for a tax rebate on items purchased in Québec, was eliminated in April 2007.

---

1 THE SHOPPING SCENE

When you're making purchases with a credit card, the charges are automatically converted at the going bank rate before appearing on your monthly statement. In most cases, this is the best deal of all for visitors. Visa and MasterCard are the most popular credit cards in this part of Canada; shops accept Discover less frequently.

Most stores are open from 9 or 10am to 6pm Monday through Wednesday, to 9pm on Thursday and Friday, and to 5pm on Saturday. Many stores are now also open on Sunday from noon to 5pm.

THE BEST BUYS

While not cheap, **Canadian Inuit sculptures** and 19th- to early-20th-century **country furniture** are handsome and authentic. Less expensive crafts than the intensely collected Inuit works are also available, including quilts, drawings, and carvings by Amerindian and other folk artists.

The province's daring **clothing** designers produce some appealing fashions at prices that are often reasonable. And while demand has diminished somewhat due to animal-rights and environmental concerns, **furs and leather goods** remain high-ticket items.

Ice cider (*cidre de glace*) and **ice wines** made in Québec province from apples and grapes left on trees and vines after the first frost are unique, inexpensive products to bring home. They're sold in duty-free shops at the border in addition to the stores listed at the end of this chapter.

Most international clothing items, including those by such big names as Burberry and Ralph Lauren, cost approximately what they would in their countries of origin.

THE BEST SHOPPING AREAS

In downtown, **rue Sherbrooke** is a major shopping street, with international and domestic designers, luxury shops, art galleries, and the Holt Renfrew department store.

Also downtown, **rue Ste-Catherine** is home to the city's top department stores and myriad satellite shops from international chains such as H&M and Tommy Hilfiger. An excursion along the 12-block stretch can keep a diligent shopper busy for hours. Nearby, **rue Peel** is known for its men's fashions.

In Vieux-Montréal, the western end of **rue St-Paul** has an ever-growing number of art galleries, clothing boutiques, and jewelry shops. **Marché Bonsecours** is home to a dozen art galleries, as well as boutiques selling high-end crafts and clothing.

In Plateau Mont-Royal, **rue St-Denis** north of Sherbrooke has blocks of shops filled with fun, funky items. **Boulevard St-Laurent** sells everything from budget practicalities to off-the-wall handmade fashions. And further north, **avenue Laurier,** between boulevard St-Laurent and avenue de l'Epée, is where to go for French boutiques, furniture and accessories shops, and products from the minds of young Québécois designers.

SHOPPING COMPLEXES

A unique shopping opportunity in Montréal is the **underground city,** a warren of passageways connecting more than 1,700 shops in 10 shopping malls that have levels both above and below street level (p. 66). Typical is the **Complexe Desjardins** (*(C)* **514/845-4636**), a downtown mall that's both at street level and underground, and is bounded by rues Ste-Catherine, St-Urbain, and Jeanne-Mance and boulevard René-Lévesque. It has waterfalls and fountains, trees and hanging vines, music, lanes of shops going off in every direction, and elevators whisking people up to one of the four tall office towers.

You're also likely to end up in downtown's **Place Ville-Marie,** opposite Fairmont The Queen Elizabeth hotel, between boulevard René-Lévesque and Cathcart (*(C)* **514/861-9393;** www.placevillemarie.com), which was Montréal's first major post-World War II shopping complex and is known locally as "PVM." It has some 80 boutiques and eateries. A plaque honoring Vincent Ponte, who designed the underground city and died in 2006, is on the PVM esplanade.

The Montréal tourist office's *Official Tourist Guide,* available at tourist offices (p. 24), lists the underground city's other complexes. The main thing to remember is that when you enter a street-level shopping emporium downtown, it's likely that you'll be able to head to a lower level and connect to the tunnels and shopping hallways that lead to another set of stores.

2 SHOPPING FROM A TO Z

ANTIQUES

Some of the city's quirkier antiques shops have disappeared in recent years, thanks, probably, to eBay. But there are dozens of tempting shops along **"Antique Alley,"** as it's nicknamed, on rue Notre-Dame west of Vieux-Montréal. They're especially concentrated between rue Guy and avenue Atwater. See p. 148 in chapter 9 for more information.

Antiques can also be found downtown along rue Sherbrooke near the Musée des Beaux-Arts, on the little side streets near the museum, and in the Village (the gay neighborhood described on p. 64) on rue Amherst.

ARTS & CRAFTS

Some of Montréal's best crafts stores are in museums. See p. 158. for a listing of museum stores.

Guilde Canadienne des Métiers d'Art ★ In English, it's called the Canadian Guild of Crafts. A small but choice collection of craft items is displayed in a meticulously arranged gallery setting. Among the objects are blown glass, silk paintings, pewter, tapestries, and ceramics. The store is particularly strong in avant-garde jewelry and Inukjuak sculpture. A small carving might be had for C$100 to C$300 (£50–£150), while larger, more important pieces go for hundreds, even thousands, more. 1460 rue Sherbrooke ouest (near rue Mackay), downtown. (C) 866/477-6091. www.canadianguild.com.

La Guilde Graphique Contemporary artists are represented here, working with a variety of media and techniques, but primarily producing works on paper, including drawings, serigraphs, etchings, lithographs, and woodcut prints. 9 rue St-Paul ouest (at bd. St-Laurent), Vieux-Montréal. (C) 514/844-3438. www.guildegraphique.com.

L'Empreinte This is a *coopérative artisane* (a craftspersons' collective). The ceramics, textiles, glassware, and other items on sale often occupy that vaguely defined territory between art and craft. Quality is uneven but usually tips toward the high end. 272 rue St-Paul est (next to Marché Bonsecours), Vieux-Montréal. (C) 514/861-4427. www.lempreintecoop.com.

Les Artisans du Meuble Québécois A mix of crafts, jewelry, and other objects—some noteworthy, others mediocre—makes this an intriguing stop in Vieux-Montréal. Among the possibilities are handmade clothing and accessories for women, greeting cards, woven goods, and items for the home. 88 rue St-Paul est (near Place Jacques-Cartier), Vieux-Montréal. (C) 514/866-1836.

Salon des Métiers d'Art du Québec Since the 1950s, the Salon has brought together masses of artisans into one space for the Christmas season; in 2009, it celebrates its 54th year. Some 450 exhibitors set up to sell original, handmade, and exclusive creations for gift-givers, and nearly 250,000 people visit every year. It takes place daily for about 2 weeks in mid-December. Place Bonaventure, downtown. No phone number. www.salondesmetiersdart.com.

BATH & BODY

Lush Freshly installed on the ground floor of a pretty Queen Anne Victorian in the heart of the Plateau's St-Denis shopping district, this U.K.-based chain displays its rough-hewn chunks of soap like wheels of cheese. They're scented with olive oil, fig, mint, coriander, orange, and many other mellifluous odors. A fist-size chunk costs about C$8 (£4). 4067 rue St-Denis (near av. Duluth), Plateau Mont-Royal. (C) 514/849-5333. www.lush.com.

Spa Dr. Hauschka This chichi spa is for high-end pampering and getting "in touch with your inner beauty," as the promotional materials put it. On-site treatments include facials, lavender baths, mud baths, and more. You can also buy the Dr. Hauschka products and indulge at home. 1444 rue Sherbrooke ouest (at rue Redpath), downtown. (C) 514/286-1444. www.spadrhauschka.com.

BOOKS

As is the case with arts and crafts, some of Montréal's best bookstores are in the city's museums.

Canadian Centre for Architecture Bookstore A comprehensive selection of books about architecture, with an emphasis on Montréal in particular and Canada in general. Volumes are also available on landscape and garden history, photography, preservation,

conservation, design, and city planning. 1920 rue Baile (at rue du Fort), downtown. ℭ 514/939-
7028. www.cca.qc.ca/bookstore.

Champigny (Kids)   For those who know French or want to brush up, this two-level bookstore with a primarily French-language stock is a valuable resource. It also sells tapes, CDs, and newspapers and magazines from all over the world. Most English-language books are on the upper floor. There's a large children's section, too. 4380 rue St-Denis (at rue Marie-Anne), Plateau Mont-Royal. ℭ **514/844-2587.**

Chapters   The flagship store of a chain with many branches is the result of a merger between Smithbooks and Coles booksellers. Thousands of titles are available in French and English. 1171 rue Ste-Catherine ouest (at rue Stanley), downtown. ℭ **514/849-8825.** www. chapters.indigo.ca.

Indigo Livres, Musique & Café   Occupying a street-level space in the Place Montréal Trust, this very complete store sells music, books, magazines, and gifts, and operates a cafe upstairs. 1500 av. McGill College (at rue St-Catherine), downtown. ℭ **514/281-5549.**

Paragraphe   This long storefront is popular with students from the McGill campus, which is a block away. The store hosts frequent author readings. 2220 av. McGill College (south of rue Sherbrooke). ℭ **514/845-5811.** www.paragraphbooks.com.

CLOTHING
For Men
Eccetera & Co.   Favoring ready-to-wear attire from such higher-end manufacturers as Baldessarini and Canali, this store lays out its stock in a soothing setting with personalized service. As it says on the door: GOOD CLOTHES OPEN ALL DOORS. 2021 rue Peel (near bd. de Maisonneuve), downtown. ℭ **514/845-9181.** www.eccetera.ca.

Harry Rosen ★   For more than 50 years, this well-known retailer of designer suits and accessories has been making men look good in Armani, Versace, and its own "Harry Rosen Made in Italy" line. The store's website features a nifty "What should I wear?" interactive page. Les Cours Mont-Royal, 1455 rue Peel (at bd. de Maisonneuve), downtown. ℭ **514/284-3315.** www.harryrosen.com.

L'Uomo Montréal ★   A top men's clothing boutique founded in 1980, L'Uomo mostly deals in Italian and other European menswear by such forward-thinking designers as Ermenegildo Zegna Couture, Kiton, Prada, AvonCelli, and Borrelli. 1452 rue Peel (near rue Ste-Catherine), downtown. ℭ **514/844-1008.** www.luomo-montreal.com.

For Women
Montréal Fashion Week happens every March. The 2008 event took place at the Marché Bonsecours and featured 20 Canadian designers; photos and links are online at www. mfw.ca. Each June, the **Montréal Fashion & Design Festival** happens on McGill College Avenue. For more information about it and to see the artistic creations on display at the last event, go to www.sensationmode.com/fmdm.

Aime Com Moi   If you're heading north to the hipster bar Bílý Kůň (p. 169), leave some time to stroll av. du Mont-Royal, which is chock-full of new and used clothing. Among the shops is this one, which features fabulously funky designer dresses by Québecois designers. 150 av. du Mont-Royal est (3 blocks from bd. St-Laurent), Mile End. ℭ **514/982-0088.**

Ambre Fashionable suits, cocktail dresses, and casual wear made of linen, rayon, and cotton are featured in this small, centrally located shop. To go with the clothes, there are bold accessories. 201 rue St-Paul ouest (at rue St-François-Xavier), Vieux-Montréal. ℂ 514/982-0325.

Artéfact Montréal Sold here are moderate to expensive articles of clothing by up-and-coming Québécois designers and artists. 4117 rue St-Denis (near rue Rachel), Plateau Mont-Royal. ℂ 514/842-2780.

Collection Méli Mélo (Finds) This shop used to focus on a mix of exotica and furniture from Morocco down into sub-Saharan Africa. There's still some of that, but a shift in spring 2007 brought a new concentration: women's fashion by Montréal's chic designers, as well as international names like Yumi London. During your visit, you might just see a Montréal actress finding just the right dress to wear to the Cannes Film Festival. 205 St-Paul ouest (at rue St-François-Xavier), Vieux-Montréal. ℂ 514/285-5585.

Giorgio Femme Ursula B This boutique features cutting-edge fashion from around the world, as well as jeans and shoes. Les Cours Mont-Royal, 1455 rue Peel (at bd. de Maisonneuve), downtown. ℂ 514/282-0294. www.ursulab.com.

Harricana ★ One designer taking a unique cue from the city's long history with the fur trade is Mariouche Gagné, who was born on Ile d'Orleans in 1971. Her company recycles old fur into funky patchwork garments. The slogan: "Made from your mother's old coat." She also recycles silk scarves, turning them into tops and skirts. Her boutique is outside of the other districts mentioned here, but it's close to the Marché Atwater and the Lionel-Groulx Métro station. 3000 rue St-Antoine ouest (at ave. Atwater), west of Vieux-Montréal. ℂ 877/894-9919. www.harricana.qc.ca.

Kaliyana ★ Vaguely Japanese and certainly minimalist, these free-flowing garments sold here are largely asymmetrical separates. Made by a Canadian designer, they come in muted tones of solid colors. Simple complementary necklaces are available to buy, too. 4107 rue St-Denis (near rue Rachel), Plateau Mont-Royal. ℂ 514/844-0633. www.kaliyana.com.

La Cache Clothes designed by Montréal-born April Cornell, with flowers, leaves and birds as the recurring motifs, are among the offerings of this national Canadian chain, as are housewares and bedding. Many of the clothes are produced in India. 3941 rue St-Denis (near rue Roy), Plateau Mont-Royal. ℂ 514/842-7693. www.lacache.ca.

Mango This is the first downtown outlet of a Spanish-owned international chain. Much of its merchandise consists of upmarket jeans and tees. The dressier separates intrigue with quiet tones and jazzy cuts—very Euro. 1000 rue Ste-Catherine ouest (at rue Metcalfe), downtown. ℂ 514/397-2323. www.mango.com.

Tag Cuir (Finds) You have to check this out: Suede jeans that are washable! They're made in Canada, of course. Also on display in this small *cuir* (leather) shop are bomber jackets and other leather items. 1325 rue Ste-Catherine ouest (at rue Crescent), downtown. ℂ 514/499-1180.

For Men & Women

Montréal's fur-trading past buttresses the many wholesale and retail furriers, which maintain outlets downtown and in Plateau Mont-Royal. Nowhere, though, are fur shops more concentrated than on the "fur row" of **rue Mayor,** downtown between rue de Bleury and rue City Councillors. If you're buying, watch out for PETA protesters.

Club Monaco   Awareness of this expanding international chain is growing, as is appreciation of its minimalist, largely monochromatic garments for men and women, along with silver jewelry, eyewear, and cosmetics. Think Prada but more affordable, with a helpful young staff. In Les Cours Mont-Royal shopping complex, 1455 rue Peel (north of rue Ste-Catherine), downtown. ℭ 514/499-0959. www.clubmonaco.com.

Crocs   Who knew that Crocs, the pillowy, marshmallowy, bright-colored clogs that took the world by storm a few years ago, came out of Québec? Indeed they do. The company has branched into more normal-looking (read: less childlike) shoes, and it opened its first Montréal store in the heart of downtown in summer 2008. 1382 rue Ste-Catherine ouest (near rue Crescent), downtown. ℭ 514/750-9796. www.crocs.com.

Kanuk   One of the top Canadian manufacturers of high-end winter jackets makes its clothes right in Montréal and has a warehouse-like factory store in the heart of Plateau Mont-Royal. Like LL Bean in the U.S, Kanuk's first customers for the heavy parkas were outdoor enthusiasts. Today, their clientele includes the general public. The jackets aren't cheap—the heavy-duty ones cost upwards of C$700 (£350)—but they're extremely popular. 485 rue Rachel est (near rue St-Denis), Plateau Mont-Royal.ℭ 514/284-4494. www.kanuk.com.

Roots   The company whose berets and uniforms were such a hit at the 2006 Winter Olympics has a three-floor store here, in addition to other locations throughout Canada. Along with clothing, the store sells table settings, perfume, books, and CDs. 1035 rue Ste-Catherine ouest (at rue Peel), downtown. ℭ 514/845-7995. www.roots.com.

DEPARTMENT STORES

Montréal's major downtown shopping emporia stretch along rue Ste-Catherine from avenue Union westward to rue Guy. Most of the big department stores here were founded when Scottish, Irish, and English families dominated the city's mercantile class, so most of their names are identifiably English, albeit shorn of their apostrophes. The principal exception is La Baie, French for "the Bay," itself a shortened reference to an earlier name, the Hudson's Bay Company.

Henry Birks et Fils ★   Across from Christ Church Cathedral at the corner of rue Ste-Catherine stands Henry Birks et Fils, a highly regarded jeweler since 1879. This beautiful old store, with its marble pillars and ornamental ceiling, is a living part of Montréal's Victorian heritage. The valuable products on display go well beyond jewelry to encompass pens, desk accessories, watches, ties, leather goods, belts, glassware, and china. 1240 Phillips Square (at rue Ste-Catherine), downtown. ℭ 514/397-2511. www.birks.com.

Holt Renfrew ★   This store began as a furrier in 1837 and is now a showcase for the best in international style. Wares are displayed in mini-boutiques and focus on fashion for men and women. Brands, including Giorgio Armani, Prada, Gucci, and Stuart Weitzman, are displayed with a tastefulness bordering on solemnity. The marquee outside just reads HR. 1300 rue Sherbrooke ouest (at rue de la Montagne), downtown. ℭ 514/842-5111. www.holtrenfrew.com.

La Baie ★   No retailer has an older or more celebrated name than the Hudson's Bay Company, a name shortened in recent years to "the Bay," then transformed into "La Baie" by the language laws that decreed French the lingua franca. The company was incorporated in Canada in 1670. Its main store focuses on clothing, but also offers crystal, china, and Inuit carvings. Its signature Hbc line features variations on the famous Hudson's Bay blankets. The company was bought by an American investor in 2006, an event that understandably caused consternation among many Canadians. 585 rue Ste-Catherine ouest (near rue Aylmer), downtown. © 514/281-4422. www.hbc.com.

Ogilvy ★★   The most vibrant of a classy breed of department store that appears to be fading from the scene was established in 1866. Ogilvy has been at this location since 1912. A bagpiper still announces the noon hour, and special events, glowing chandeliers, and wide aisles enhance the shopping experience. Ogilvy has always had a reputation for quality merchandise and now contains more than 60 boutiques, including Louis Vuitton, Anne Klein, and Burberry. It's also known for its eagerly awaited Christmas windows. The basement-level **Café Romy** sells quality sandwiches, salads, and desserts. 1307 rue Ste-Catherine ouest (at rue de la Montagne), downtown. © 514/842-7711. www.ogilvycanada.com.

Simons   This branch was the first expansion for Québec City's long-established family-owned department store. Most Montréalers had never heard of it, but that changed fast given the fairly priced fashions. 977 rue Ste-Catherine ouest (at rue Mansfield), downtown. © 514/282-1840. www.simons.ca.

EDIBLES

The food markets described in "Picnic Fare" at the end of chapter 7 carry abundant assortments of cheeses, wines, and packaged food products that can serve as gifts or delicious reminders of your visit when you get home.

Canadian Maple Delights (Kids)   Everything maple-y is presented here by a consortium of Québec producers: pastries, gift baskets, truffles, and, of course, every grade of syrup. A cute cafe serves sweets and gelato; on nearly any day, a cone of maple-raspberry gelato is a good thing. 84 rue St-Paul est (near Place Jacques-Cartier), Vieux-Montréal. © 514/765-3456. www.mapledelights.com.

La Tomate   Inside a brick building painted on the outside with a two-story tomato, this shop is filled with quirkily packaged pastes, jellies, sauces, salsas, and ketchups, all made from the most humble of fruits. 4347 rue de la Roché (2 blocks north of rue Rachel), Plateau Mont-Royal. © 514/523-0222.

La Vieille Europe   In this compact storehouse of culinary sights and smells, you can choose from wheels of pungent cheeses, garlands of sausages, pâtés, *jamón ibérico,* cashews, honey, fresh peanut butter, and dried fruits. Coffee beans are roasted in the back, adding to the mixture of maddening aromas. 3855 bd. St-Laurent (north of rue Roy), Plateau Mont-Royal. © 514/842-5773.

Les Chocolats de Chloé (Finds)   If you approach chocolate the way aficionados approach wine or cheese—that is, on the lookout for the best of the best—then this teeny shop will bring great delight. Chocolates are made on-site, and tastes can be had for C$2.50 (£1.25). Especially adorable: a hollow chocolate fish filled with three little chocolate fishes, for C$9 (£4.50). 375 rue Roy est (at St-Denis), Plateau Mont-Royal. © 514/849-5550. www.leschocolatsdechloe.com.

Marché Atwater ★   This indoor-outdoor farmer's market west of Old Town is open daily. French in flavor, it features the freshest fruits, vegetables, and flowers, and has several *boulangeries* and *fromageries,* plus shops with every kind of easy-to-travel-with food under the sun. There are also specialty shops like Chocolats Geneviève Grandbois. You can walk there by heading down rue Notre Dame, where you'll pass Antique Alley (about 45 min.; p. 148), or take the Métro to Lionel-Groulx. 138 ave. Atwater (at rue Notre Dame ouest), west of Vieux-Montréal. © 514/937-7754. www.marchespublics-mtl.com.

Suite 88 Chocolatier More fancy chocolates. These are displayed in cases like fine jewelry, and flavors include jalapeño, chili-cayenne, ouzo, sake, and mojito. Gelato costs C$3 (£1.50) and chocolate boxes start at C$18 (£9), though you can buy single pieces for less. There's a cafe in the back. 3957 rue St-Denis (near rue Roy), Plateau Mont-Royal. (C) 514/844-3488. www.suite88.com.

HOME DESIGN & HOUSEWARES
Also see "Arts & Crafts" and "Department Stores," earlier in this chapter.

Arthur Quentin ★ Doling out household products of quiet taste and discernment for more than 25 years, this St-Denis stalwart is divided into departments specializing in tableware, kitchen gadgets, and home decor. That means lamps and Limoges china, terrines and tea towels, mandolins and mezzalunas, and just about any related items that might be imagined. Clay jugs for making vinegar? *Naturellement.* 3960 rue St-Denis (south of av. Duluth), Plateau Mont-Royal. (C) 514/843-7513. www.arthurquentin.com.

Les Touilleurs Kitchenware of the highest order is sold here, meticulously arranged like museum pieces in a minimalist setting (the shop earned design honors shortly after it opened). Stock includes only superior versions of cooking essentials, including small appliances that strike high new standards. Now it has doubled its size, incorporating a full kitchen where **cooking classes** are conducted by local chefs. 152 rue Laurier ouest (near rue St-Urbain), Mile End. (C) 514/278-0008. www.lestouilleurs.com.

Option D Option D sells high-end housewares, candy-colored and steel, in the heart of Old Town. Brands include Alessi, Iittala, Alexandre Turpault, and Bodum. 50 rue St-Paul ouest (near rue St-Sulpice), Vieux-Montréal. (C) 514/842-7117. www.optiond.ca.

Senteurs de Provence The sunny south of France is evoked in pottery that's hand-painted in Provence's creamy-bright colors, complemented by cunning collections of bath soaps and gels, printed linens, and lightly perfumed lotions and creams. There are several locations throughout the city. 363 rue St-Paul est (opposite Marché Bonsecours), Vieux-Montréal. (C) 514/395-8686.

12° en Cave This store is dedicated to the good life, with an emphasis on the passions of wine aficionados. Reidel crystal and a variety of mostly high-end wine-related paraphernalia are for sale. Especially notable is the Schott Zwiesel Tritan line, which features nearly unbreakable wine glasses for C$14 to C$18 (£7–£9); a salesperson tapped a goblet right on the metal shelf to demonstrate. If you need a custom wine cellar built anywhere in North America, they'll do that, too. 367 rue St-Paul est (opposite Marché Bonsecours), Vieux-Montréal. (C) 514/866-5722. www.12encave.com.

JEWELRY & ACCESSORIES
Also see "Arts & Crafts," earlier in this chapter.

Château D'Ivoire When you absolutely, positively have to buy a Rolex *right now,* this store carries jewelry and watches from that brand plus other top luxury names: Raymond Weil, Omega, Cartier, Piaget, et al. 2020 rue de la Montagne (at rue de la Montagne), downtown. (C) 514/845-4651. www.chateaudivoire.com.

Clio Blue, Paris This little rue Peel shop of the Paris-based international chain features spare displays in a narrow modernist storefront (the store is a design-competition winner). Custom jewelry tastefully incorporates Middle Eastern and South Asian motifs, often with carefully spaced semiprecious stones on silver strands and more festively designed bracelets. A sister store, **bleu comme le ciel,** is just down the block at no. 2000 and stocks costume jewelry that's worth a visit for women looking to shake up their image. 1468 rue Peel (near bd. de Maisonneuve), downtown. ✆ **514/281-3112.** www.clioblue.com.

MUSEUM STORES

Musée d'Art Contemporain Boutique   The contemporary art museum's boutique sells much of what might be expected, including poster-size reproductions of paintings and prints, postcards, and art books. Added to the mix are tasteful design pieces and unusual gifts as well as souvenirs that eschew the lowest-common-denominator standards of too many Vieux-Montréal shops. The museum's bookstore has a wide selection, in both French and English, of monographs about Canadian and international artists since the 1950s. 185 rue Ste-Catherine ouest (at rue Jeanne-Mance), downtown. ✆ **514/847-6904.** www.macm.org.

Musée des Beaux-Arts Boutique   An unusually large and impressive shop that sells everything from folk art to furniture. The expected art-related postcards and prints are at hand, along with ties, watches, scarves, address books, toys, games, clocks, jewelry, and other crafts, with special focus on work by Québec artisans. 1390 rue Sherbrooke ouest (at rue Crescent), downtown. ✆ **514/285-1600.** www.mbam.qc.ca.

Musée McCord Boutique   Part of an expanded museum that relates the province's history, this shop stocks a small, carefully chosen selection of Native and Canadian arts and crafts, china, rustic pottery, books with an emphasis on history, jewelry, and clothing, including moccasins. There's also a nice cafe inside the museum. 690 rue Sherbrooke ouest (at rue Victoria), downtown. ✆ **514/398-7100,** ext. 274. www.mccord-museum.qc.ca.

Pointe-à-Callière Gift Shop   Located in the Old Customs House at the end of the Museum of Archaeology and History's underground tour (and with a separate entrance on rue St-Paul), this boutique sells collectibles for the home, gift items, paper products, souvenirs, toys, and books (in French). Particularly nice are the maple spoons and spatulas made by Québec artist Tom Littledeer. 150 rue St-Paul ouest (at Place Royale), Vieux-Montréal. ✆ **514/872-9150.** www.pacmusee.qc.ca.

MUSIC

Archambault Musique   This is a premier spot at which to find CDs by French-Canadian singers, the Montréal Symphony Orchestra, I Musici, and others. Many of the recordings can be difficult to get outside of Québec, so stock up here. 500 rue Ste-Catherine est (at rue Berri), downtown. ✆ **514/849-6201.** www.archambault.ca.

Inbeat   The decor is plain, but the stock includes CDs and vinyl that just aren't available elsewhere. The staff describes the store's offerings as "deep house, progressive, tribal, techno, trance, old skool, Afro-Latin nu jazz, U.S. & U.K. garage," and there are albums and singles that don't even fit into *those* categories. 3814 bd. St-Laurent (near rue Roy), Plateau Mont-Royal. ✆ **514/499-2063.** www.inbeatstore.com.

WINES & SPIRITS

The food markets described in "Picnic Fare" at the end of chapter 7 carry a good variety of wines, which are also sold in supermarkets and convenience stores. Beer is also available in these venues.

Liquor and other spirits, on the other hand, can only be sold in stores operated by the provincial **Société des Alcools du Québec (SAQ).** Though it was once as bureaucratic as most state-run agencies, successful upgrade efforts have made its stores more inviting and given differently named stores different personalities. The SAQ website, www.saq. com, provides a wealth of information about Québec wines and area outlets.

One of the largest outlets is the downtown **SAQ Selection** at 440 bd. de Maisonneuve ouest west of rue de Bleury (© **514/873-2274**), a veritable supermarket of wines and liquors, with thousands of labels. Prices run from C$10 (£5) to way, way up for Bordeaux vintages. The downtown **SAQ Signature** at 677 Ste-Catherine west in the Complexe Les Ailes (© **514/282-9445**) is one of SAQ's boutique shops, featuring a smaller selection of rarer wines and fine liquors.

The VQA logo, for Vintners Quality Alliance, is given to wines that meet the state's quality standards.

Québec's unique **ice cider** *(cidre de glace),* made from apples left on trees after the first frost, can be purchased in duty-free shops at the border in addition to the stores listed above. One top producer is **Domaine Pinnacle** (© **450/298-1222;** www. domainepinnacle.com), based about an hour and a half from the city; it's a regular gold medalist in international competitions.

MONTRÉAL SHOPPING

10

SHOPPING FROM A TO Z

Montréal After Dark

Montréal's reputation for effervescent nightlife reaches back to the Roaring Twenties—specifically to America's 13-year Prohibition from 1920 to 1933. Americans streamed into Montréal for temporary relief from alcohol deprivation (while Canadian distillers and brewers made fortunes). Montréal already enjoyed a sophisticated and slightly naughty reputation as the Paris of North America, which added to the allure.

Nearly a century later, clubbing and barhopping remain popular activities, with nightspots keeping much later hours in Montréal than in arch-rival Toronto, which still heeds Calvinist notions of propriety and early bedtimes.

Nocturnal pursuits are often as cultural as they are social. The city boasts its own outstanding symphony, dozens of French- and English-language theater companies, and the incomparable Cirque du Soleil. It's also on the standard concert circuit that includes Chicago, Boston, and New York, so internationally known entertainers, music groups, and dance companies pass through frequently.

A decidedly French enthusiasm for film, as well as the city's ever-increasing reputation as a movie-production center, ensures support for cinemas showcasing experimental, offbeat, and foreign films.

A ticket office for Montréal cultural events opened in summer 2007. Called **Vitrine Culturelle de Montréal (Cultural Window of Montréal; ② 866/924-5538 or 514/285-4545;** www.vitrineculturelle.com), it's at 145 rue Sainte-Catherine ouest in Place des Arts. It sells last-minute deals as well as full-price tickets.

In summer, the city becomes even livelier. Many of the events and festivals are listed in "Montreal & Quebec City Calendar of Events" in chapter 3. The biggest of the bunch is the 3-day Grand Prix du Canada, the country's only Formula 1 auto race. In June, it roars onto Ile Notre-Dame and the partying overflows into downtown.

Concentrations of pubs and discos underscore the city's linguistic dichotomy. While there's much crossover, the parallel blocks of **rue Crescent, rue Bishop,** and **rue de la Montagne** north of rue Ste-Catherine have a pronounced Anglophone (English-speaking) character, while Francophones (French speakers) dominate the **Quartier Latin,** with college-age patrons most evident along the lower reaches of rue St-Denis; their yuppie elders gravitate to the nightspots of the slightly more uptown blocks of the same street. **Vieux-Montréal,** especially along rue St-Paul, has a more universal quality, and many of its bars and clubs showcase live jazz, blues, and folk music. In **Plateau Mont-Royal,** boulevard St-Laurent, parallel to St-Denis and known locally as "the Main," has become a miles-long haven of hip restaurants and clubs, roughly from rue Sherbrooke up to rue Laurier. It's a good place to wind up in the wee hours, as there's always someplace with the welcome mat still out, even after the official 3am closings.

Most bars and clubs don't charge cover, and when they do, it's rarely more than C$10 (£5). Beer is usually in the C$4 to C$7 (£2–3.50) range, while cocktails typically cost C$7 to C$12 (£3.50–£6).

Smoking has been banned in bars and restaurants since 2006.

Tips **Finding Out What's On**

For details about performances or special events when you're in town, pick up a free copy of *Montréal Scope* (www.montrealscope.com), a weekly ads-and-events booklet usually available in hotel lobbies, or the free weekly papers *Mirror* (www.montrealmirror.com) and *Hour* (www.hour.ca), both in English, or *Voir* (www.voir.ca) and *Ici* (www.icimontreal.com), both in French, available all over town. Also in French is the free monthly *Nightlife* magazine (www.nightlifemagazine. ca). *Fugues* (www.fugues.com) provides news and views of gay and lesbian events, clubs, restaurants, and activities. One particularly fun blog about city happenings is **Midnight Poutine** (www.midnightpoutine.ca), a self-described "delicious high-fat source of rants, raves and musings." Extensive listings of mainstream cultural and entertainment events are posted at **www.canada.com** and **www.montrealplus.ca**.

1 THE PERFORMING ARTS

CIRCUS

The extraordinary circus company **Cirque du Soleil** (p. 123) is based in Montréal. Each show is a celebration of pure skill and nothing less than magical, with acrobats, clowns, trapeze artists, and people costumed to look like creatures not of this world—iguanas crossed with goblins, or peacocks born of trolls. Cirque performs internationally, with as many as 18 shows simultaneously, but there isn't a permanent show in Montréal. Check **www.cirquedusoleil.com** for the schedule.

Pavillon de la TOHO Value   Adjacent to Cirque du Soleil's training complex and company offices, TOHO is a performance space devoted to the circus arts. Acrobats and performers from Québec's Productions à Trois Têtes and the Imperial Acrobats of China have performed here, and the annual June shows by students of the National Circus School present many of the top rising stars. TOHO features an intimate in-the-round hall done up like an old-fashioned circus tent, and an exhibit space displays more than 100 circus artifacts. The entire venue was built with recycled pieces of an amusement-park bumper-car ride and wood from a dismantled railroad. The venue is in the lower-income Saint-Michel district well north of downtown, and accessible by Métro and bus, but you'll probably want to take a taxi. 2345 rue Jarry est (where Jarry crosses Autoroute 40). ✆ **888/376-TOHU** (376-8646). www.tohu.ca. Free to view the facility and exhibits daily 9am–5pm. Performance tickets from C$21 (£11) adults, C$15 (£7.50) children 12 and younger. 8km (5 miles) from downtown. Métro: Jarry or Iberville and then bus.

CLASSICAL MUSIC & OPERA

L'Opéra de Montréal ★★★   Founded in 1980, this outstanding opera company mounts five productions per year in Montréal, with artists from Québec and abroad participating in such shows as Bizet's *The Pearl Fishers,* Verdi's *Macbeth,* and Pucci's *La Fanciulla del West.* Video translations are provided from the original languages into

French and English. Performances are held from September to April at Place des Arts. Place des Arts, Salle Wilfrid-Pelletier, 260 bd. de Maisonneuve ouest, downtown. © 514/985-2258 for tickets. www.operademontreal.com. Tickets from C$46 (£23). Métro: Place des Arts.

L'Orchestre Symphonique de Montréal (OSM) ★★ Kent Nagano was brought on as conductor in 2005 and has focused this world-famous orchestra's repertoire on programs featuring works by Bach, Brahms, Mahler, and Messiaen. All is not staid: The orchestra performs at Place des Arts and the Notre-Dame Basilica and offers a few free concerts in the parks each summer. Place des Arts, Salle Wilfrid-Pelletier, 260 bd. de Maisonneuve ouest, downtown. © 514/842-9951 for tickets. www.osm.ca. Tickets from C$26 (£13). Métro: Place des Arts.

Orchestre Métropolitain du Grand Montréal This orchestra performs during its regular season at Place des Arts. Its 2009 schedule includes **Mahler's The Song of the Earth and Bruckner's Symphony No. 8.** In summer, this talented group presents free outdoor concerts at Théâtre de Verdure in Parc La Fontaine. Place des Arts, Maisonneuve Theatre, 260 bd. de Maisonneuve ouest, downtown. © 514/842-2112. www.orchestre metropolitain.com. Tickets from C$22 (£11). Métro: Place des Arts.

CONCERT HALLS & AUDITORIUMS

Montréal has a score of venues; check newspapers, magazines, and websites to find out who's playing where.

Centre Bell Seating up to 21,500, Centre Bell is the home of the Montréal Canadiens hockey team and host to the biggest international rock and pop stars traveling through the city, including Janet Jackson, Coldplay, and Montréal local Céline Dion, as well as Disney on Ice. 1260 rue de la Gauchetière ouest, downtown. © 514/989-2841. www.centrebell. ca. Métro: Bonaventure.

Métropolis After starting life as a skating rink in 1884, the Métropolis is now a prime showplace for traveling rock groups, especially for bands on the way up or retracing their steps down. It has recently hosted the Black Crowes, Ladytron, and the "Ethnic Heroes of Comedy" comedy tour. There's also a small attached lounge, **Le Savoy.** 59 Ste-Catherine est, downtown. © 514/844-3500. www.montrealmetropolis.ca/metropolis. Métro: St-Laurent or Berri-UQAM.

Place des Arts ★★ Since 1992, Place des Arts has been the city's central entertainment complex, presenting performances of musical concerts, opera, dance, and theater in five halls: **Salle Wilfrid-Pelletier** (2,982 seats), where l'Orchestre Symphonique de Montréal (see above) often performs; **Théâtre Maisonneuve** (1,458 seats), where the Orchestre Métropolitain du Grand Montréal (see above) and Les Grands Ballets Canadiens (p. 163) perform; **Théâtre Jean-Duceppe** (755 seats); **Cinquième Salle** (417 seats); and the small **Studio-Théâtre Stella Artois** (138 seats). Portions of the city's many arts festivals are staged in the halls and outdoor plaza here, as are traveling productions of Broadway shows. 260 bd. de Maisonneuve ouest, downtown (ticket office). © 514/842-2112 for information and tickets. www.pda.qc.ca. Métro: Place des Arts.

Pollack Concert Hall In a landmark building dating from 1899 and fronted by a statue of Queen Victoria, this McGill University venue is in nearly constant use, especially during the school year with concerts and recitals by university students and music faculty. Recordings of some concerts are available on the university's label, McGill Records. Concerts are also given in the campus's smaller **Redpath Hall,** 861 Sherbrooke

St. ouest (✆ **514/398-4547**). On the McGill University campus, 555 rue Sherbrooke ouest, downtown. ✆ **514/398-4547**. www.music.mcgill.ca. Performances are usually free. Métro: McGill.

Théâtre de Outremont   Opened in 1929, the Outremont started a new life in 2001, with a larger stage and terraced seating. Its calendar incorporates all manner of French-language music, comedy, theater, and film, but non-Francophones will enjoy the dance shows, especially performances during the Montréal International Festival of Tango. 1248 av. Bernard ouest (at av. Champagneur), Mile End. ✆ **514/495-9944**. www.theatreoutremont.ca/ outremont. Métro: Outremont.

Théâtre de Verdure ⟨Value⟩   Tango nights in July are especially popular at this open-air theater nestled in a popular park in Plateau Mont-Royal. Everything is free: music, dance, and theater, often with well-known artists and performers. Many in the audience pack picnics. Performances are held from June to August; check with the tourism office (p. 24) for days and times. Parc La Fontaine, Plateau Mont-Royal. Métro: Sherbrooke.

Théâtre St-Denis   Recently refurbished, this theater complex in the heart of the Latin Quarter hosts a variety of shows by the likes of Norah Jones and Alice Cooper, as well as segments of the Juste pour Rire (Just for Laughs) comedy festival in July. One hall seats 2,218 and the other fits 933. 1594 rue St-Denis (at Emery), Quartier Latin. ✆ **514/849-4211**. www.theatrestdenis.com. Métro: Berri-UQAM.

DANCE
Montréal hosts frequent appearances by notable dancers and troupes from other parts of Canada and the world—among them Paul Taylor, the Feld Ballet, and Toronto's Le Ballet National du Canada—and has accomplished resident companies as well.

Les Grands Ballets Canadiens ★★   This prestigious touring company, performing both a classical and a modern repertoire, has developed a following far beyond national borders in its 50-plus years (it was founded in 1957). In the process, it has brought prominence to many gifted Canadian choreographers and composers. The troupe's production of *The Nutcracker* is always a big event each winter. Performances are held October through May. Place des Arts, 175 Ste-Catherine ouest (main entrance), downtown. ✆ **514/842-2112**. www.grandsballets.qc.ca. Tickets from C$26 (£13). Métro: Place des Arts.

THEATER
Centaur Theatre   The city's principal English-language theater is housed in a former stock-exchange building (1903). Presented here are a mix of classics, foreign adaptations, and works by Canadian playwrights. It was here that famed playwright Michel Tremblay's Forever Yours, Marie-Lou received its first English-language staging in 2008. 453 rue St-François-Xavier (near rue Notre-Dame), Vieux-Montréal. ✆ **514/288-3161**. www. centaurtheatre.com. Tickets from C$32 (£16). Métro: Place d'Armes.

Segal Centre for Performing Arts at the Saidye   From about 1900 to 1930, Yiddish was Montréal's third most common language. That status has since been usurped by any number of languages, but its dominance lives on here. The Centre presents theater performed in both Yiddish and English and is one of the few North American theaters that still presents plays in Yiddish. Recent productions have included Neil Simon's The Odd Couple and the Dora Wasserman Yiddish Theatre's production of The Wise Men of Chelm. Note that this is located at a considerable distance from downtown. 5170 Côte-Ste-Catherine (near bd. Décarie), Plateau Mont-Royal. ✆ **514/739-2310**. www.said yebronfman.org. Tickets from C$35 (£18). Métro: Côte-Ste-Catherine. Bus: 29 ouest.

2 MUSIC & DANCE CLUBS

A note to walkers: Montréal is one of the safest cities to visit, but a pocket of streets right in the middle of the neighborhoods described here is very quiet and something of a no-man's land at night. It's the area just north of Vieux-Montréal and the convention center, and south of rue Sherbrooke (the Quartier International is part of it). You may want to take a cab or the Métro when traveling through this area in the late evening.

DOWNTOWN/RUE CRESCENT

Hard Rock Cafe   No surprises here, not with all of its clones scattered around the world. The formula still works, though, and this outpost in the heart of the rue Crescent party strip gets crowded at lunch and on weekend evenings. A terrace seats about 30 patrons. Open Sunday through Thursday from 11am to 11pm, Friday and Saturday 11am to midnight, with a big dance floor that's hopping in the evenings. 1458 rue Crescent (near bd. de Maisonneuve). *C* **514/987-1420.** Métro: Guy-Concordia.

Hurley's Irish Pub   In front is a street-level terrace, and there are several semi-subterranean rooms in back. Celtic instrumentalists perform nightly, usually starting around 9:30pm. There are 19 beers on tap and more than 50 single-malt whiskeys from which to choose. 1225 rue Crescent (at rue Ste-Catherine), downtown. *C* **514/861-4111.** www.hurleys irishpub.com. Métro: Guy-Concordia.

Maison de Jazz ★   Right downtown, this New Orleans–style jazz venue has been on the scene for decades. Lovers of barbecued ribs and jazz, most of them well past the bloom of youth, start early in filling the room, which is decorated in mock Art Nouveau style with tiered levels. Live music starts around 8pm most nights and continues until closing time. The ribs are okay and the jazz is of the swinging mainstream variety, with occasional digressions into more esoteric forms. 2060 rue Aylmer (south of rue Sherbrooke). *C* **514/842-8656.** www.houseofjazz.ca. Cover C$5 (£2.50). Métro: McGill.

Newtown   Huge fanfare trumpeted this tri-level club's 2001 opening in the white-hot center of rue Crescent nightlife, and it's still a sought-after destination. One of the owners is Formula 1 race car driver and local hero Jacques Villeneuve—whose last name can be translated as "New Town." The square bar in the middle of the main barroom is a friendly place, even if you're on your own. A specialty of the house is the French Kiss Martini: vodka, framboise liquor, pineapple juice, and lime—try it. There's a disco in the basement, a restaurant one floor up, and, most prominently, a rooftop terrace in summer. The bar and restaurant are open daily, and the disco is open Friday and Saturday. 1476 rue Crescent (at de Maisonneuve), downtown. *C* **514/284-6555.** www.newtown.ca. Métro: Peel.

Time Supper Club   Though food is served, it isn't the prime attraction—after dinner, Time's fabulous crowd gets up from the tables and works off the calories to rock, house, and hip-hop that thumps on until closing at 3am. The waitstaff is startlingly sexy. Dress well, look good, and approach the door with confidence. The club is in a dreary industrial neighborhood south of the downtown core, so you might want to arrive by car or taxi. 997 rue St-Jacques ouest (near rue Peel), downtown. *C* **514/392-9292.** Métro: Bonaventure.

Upstairs Jazz Bar & Grill   Its name notwithstanding, this club is *down* a few steps from the street. Big names are infrequent, but the jazz groups appearing every night are more than competent. Performances usually begin at 9pm. Decor is largely vintage, with record-album covers and fish tanks. Pretty good food ranges from bar snacks to more

VIEUX-MONTREAL

Les Deux Pierrots ★   This is perhaps the best-known of Montréal's *boîtes-à-chansons* (song clubs), but its more visible personality these days is as a sports bar. The athletic-style posters are certainly what you'll see when you walk by, and that's how the operation appears to make most of its money. But on Friday and Saturday nights, an intimate French-style cabaret still brings in singers who interact animatedly, and often bilingually, with the crowd. 104 rue St-Paul est (west of place Jacques-Cartier). ✆ 514/861-4311. www. lespierrots.com. Métro: Place d'Armes.

Modavie   Set aside an evening for dinner with jazz at this popular Vieux-Montréal bistro (p. 112) and wine bar. Music is usually mainstream jazz by duos or trios, and there's no fee for the show. In addition to tables, there are about a dozen seats at a handsome horseshoe-shaped bar just inside the door. Choose from 10 scotches; a long wine list; and some 30 cognacs, grappas, and ports. Even when there's snow outside, the female waitstaff still show a lot of flesh. It's a friendly place and the food is good, too. 1 rue St-Paul ouest (corner of rue St-Laurent). ✆ 514/287-9582. Métro: Place d'Armes.

PLATEAU MONT-ROYAL

Casa del Popolo   This is the CBGB of the Montréal jazz and indie music scene. It's set in a scruffy storefront, serves vegetarian food, and operates a laid-back bar. Across the street, a sister performance space, **La Sala Rosa,** offers a bigger stage and a full calendar of interesting rock music as diverse as the American band Shellac and the Argentinian trip-hop artist Federico Aubele. **Sala Rosa Restaurant,** also across the street, has a Spanish menu with a big card of tapas and paella and, every Thursday, presents live flamenco music with dancing and singing. 4873 and 4848 bd. St-Laurent (near bd. St-Joseph). ✆ 514/284-3804. www.casadelpopolo.com. Cover C$6–C$15 (£3–£7.50). Métro: Laurier.

Club Balattou   This club on the Main is a premiere venue for seeing African music and performers from the West Indies and Latin America. An infectious, sensual beat issues from it, a happy variation from the prevailing grunge and dance music of mainstream clubs. 4372 bd. St-Laurent (at rue Marie-Anne). ✆ 514/845-5447. www.lucubrium.com/balattou. Cover C$10–C$20 (£5–£10). Métro: Mont-Royal.

Le Divan Orange   A hopping club with a good, hipster vibe, bands and combos here include indie rock, jazz, country, and traditional North African. There are also events best described as performance art. Shows start around 9:30pm. Open every night. 4234 bd. St-Laurent (near rue Rachel), ✆ 514/840-9090. www.ledivanorange.org. Cover C$4–C$10 (£2–£5) Métro: Mont-Royal.

Les Bobards   There's music here every night (except Mon) in a wide variety of forms—swing, jazz, blues, salsa, sync-pop, and Brazilian. Live shows start around 9pm. Foosball and billiards can fill the time until then. 4328 bd. St-Laurent (at rue Marie-Anne). ✆ 514/987-1174. www.lesbobards.qc.ca. Cover $5 (£2.50). Métro: Mont-Royal.

Orchid   Wonder where Montréal's young, black, and fabulous crowd is? Their hands-down choice is the Orchid nightclub, and the line to get in here is bigger than anywhere else on the Main. The demographic: superfine young professionals and college kids dressed to impress. The R&B and hip-hop starts up around 10pm. Ladies drink for free

> ## ⓂMoments Late Night Montréal, when the Street Festivals Subside
>
> Montréal closes streets to car traffic with the blink of an eye for music festivals, sidewalk sales, street fairs, and everything in between. One recent June night, we walked the Main—boulevard St-Laurent—from av. du Mont-Royal in the north to rue Sherbrooke in the south, at 1am. Normally a busy, main thoroughfare, the road had become pedestrian-only because of the afternoon fair earlier that day. Most of the food vendors were packed up, although a few were still selling the last of their food—crepes and strawberries from one, meat on a stick from another. On every block, bars and restaurants had set up impromptu outdoor cafes jutting into the street, and most were thick with people drinking, chatting, and flirting. Some of the thumping music clubs had lines out the door and bouncers manning velvet ropes. Bicyclists slalomed through the walkers. On the northern end of the street, the attire was more casual, more T-shirt than high fashion. Closer to rue Sherbrooke, there was a sharp spike in the number of men dressed in all-black suits and women teetering in superhigh heels and wrapped in teeny, tight dresses. The crowds were French speaking, English speaking, Spanish speaking, black, white, brown, dressed up, dressed down. It was a snapshot of the hodgepodge that is this city's nightlife, all in 8 blocks.

until midnight on Friday. Photos are posted regularly on the club's zippy website. 3556 bd. St-Laurent (1 block north of rue Sherbrooke). ✆ **514/848-6398.** www.orchidnightclub.com. Métro: Sherbrooke.

THE VILLAGE & QUARTIER LATIN

Chez Mado The glint of the sequins here can be blinding! Inspired by 1920s cabaret theater, this determinedly trendy place in the Village has performances and a dance floor; it's considered a premiere venue these days. Friday and Saturday feature festive drag shows, which, on a given night, may honor the likes of the Spice Girls or ABBA. Look for the pink-haired drag queen on the retro marquee. 1115 rue Ste-Catherine est (near rue Amherst). ✆ **514/525-7566.** www.mado.qc.ca. Métro: Beaudry.

Club Soda This long-established rock club's current quarters in a seedy part of the Latin Quarter are larger than its old location on avenue du Parc. Club Soda remains one of the prime destinations for performers just below the star level —Stereolab, Ariane Moffatt, and Ron Sexsmith have all come through recently—and also hosts several of the city's comedy festivals and acts for the annual jazz festival. Check the website for show times. 1225 bd. St-Laurent (at rue Ste-Catherine), Quartier Latin. ✆ **514/286-1010.** www.club soda.ca. Tickets from C$22 (£11). Métro: St-Laurent.

Gotha Salon Bar Lounge For a quieter venue in the Village, this cozy lounge has a fireplace, live piano on Sunday nights, and a relaxed vibe. It's at street level below the **Aubergell Bed & Breakfast** (www.aubergell.com) on rue Amherst, a road chockablock with antiques shops sporting vintage and collectible goodies from the 1930s to 1980s. 1641 rue Amherst. ✆ **514/597-0878.** Métro: Beaudry.

Jello Bar Lava lamps and other fixtures make Jello Bar look like the rumpus room of a suburban ranch house in the 1960s. But central to this goofy throwback that draws folks in their mid-20s to late 30s is the menu of more than 50 kinds of martinis. Most are flavored excuses for people who don't really like liquor, but the classic gin and vodka versions are stalwarts to be savored. There's often live music—merengue, salsa, swing—to fuel the rollicking good mood that pervades. 151 rue Ontario est (near bd. St-Laurent). ℂ 514/285-2621. www.jellobar.com. Métro: St-Laurent.

Les Foufounes Electriques From the outside, this Latin Quarter club looks like something out of a *Mad Max* movie; a spider the size of a Smart Car hangs over the front gate. Inside, it's a multilevel rock club that features hard-core and industrial bands like Agnostic Front and Gang Green. If you're within 2 blocks, you'll hear the emanating music. Open daily from 4pm to 3am. 87 Ste-Catherine est (near bd. St-Laurent). ℂ 514/844-5539. www.foufounes.qc.ca. Métro: St-Laurent.

Sky Club & Pub ★ A complex that includes drag performances in the cabaret room, a pub serving dinner daily from 4 to 9pm, a hip-hop room, a spacious dance floor that's often set to house music, and a popular roof terrace, Sky is thought by many to be the city's hottest spot for the gay, young, and fabulous. It's got spiffy decor and pounding music. 1474 rue Ste-Catherine est (near rue Plessis). ℂ 514/529-6969. www.complexesky.com. Métro: Beaudry.

Stéréo This hyperhip after-hours disco doesn't start up with its jaw-dropping sound system until 3am, but then it roars until noon. Club kids, drag queens, hipsters, and students gay and straight all come out to play on Friday, Saturday, and Sunday nights. Passionate devotees have been known to tattoo the club's audio-wave logo on their bodies. 858 rue Ste-Catherine est (near rue Berri). ℂ 514/286-0325. Métro: Berri-UQAM.

Unity The former dance club Unity II was one of the biggest and most popular gay discos in town before it was severely damaged in an April 2006 fire. It reopened as Club Unity Montréal a few months later (now known again just as Unity) and once more draws well-dressed, friendly, mixed crowds. The large outdoor roof terrace is especially popular. 1171 Ste-Catherine est. ℂ 514/523-2777. www.clubunitymontreal.com. Métro: Beaudry.

3 BARS

There are four main drags to keep in mind for a night on the town. Downtown's **rue Crescent** hums with activity from late afternoon until far into the evening, especially on summer weekend nights, when the street swarms with people careening from bar to restaurant to club. In the Plateau Mont-Royal neighborhood, **boulevard St-Laurent,** or the Main, as it's known, has blocks and blocks of bars and clubs, most with a distinctive French personality, as opposed to rue Crescent's Anglo flavor. In Vieux-Montréal, **rue St-Paul** west of Place Jacques-Cartier falls somewhere in the middle on the Anglophone-Francophone spectrum. And in the Village, **rue Catherine** closes in summer to cars and becomes flush with people; the cafes and bars that line the street build temporary terraces that fill with people in the afternoons and evenings.

In all cases, bars tend to open around 11:30am and stay open until 2am or 3am. Many of them have *heures joyeuses* (happy hours) from as early as 3pm to as late as 9pm, but usually for a shorter period within those hours. You'll see signs that read BIERES EN FUT; this means "beer on draft."

Brutopia   This pub pulls endless pints of its own microbrews to go with the rock and pop music it plays. With several rooms on two levels, a terrace in back, and a street-side balcony, it anchors rue Crescent's raucous southern end. Bands perform here, too, with an open-mic night on Sunday. 1219 rue Crescent (north of bd. René-Lévesque). ✆ 514/393-9277. Métro: Lucien L'Allier.

Le Cabaret   In L'Hôtel de la Montagne (p. 71) and within sight of the trademark lobby fountain with its nude bronze sprite sporting stained-glass wings, this appealing piano bar draws a crowd of youngish to middle-aged professionals after 5:30pm. In summer, the hotel's **La Terrasse Magnétic** on the roof offers meals, drinks, dancing, and use of the outdoor pool until 3am. 1430 rue de la Montagne (north of rue Ste-Catherine). ✆ 514/288-5656. Métro: Guy-Concordia.

Le Tour de Ville   Memorable and breathtaking. We're talking about the view, that is, from Montréal's only revolving restaurant and bar (the bar part doesn't revolve, but you still get a great view). The best time to go is when the sun is setting and the city lights are beginning to blink on. Open Tuesday through Saturday from 5:30pm to 11pm, and on Sunday for brunch at two seatings: 10:30am to 12:30pm and 1pm to 3pm. In the Delta Centre-Ville Hôtel, 777 rue University. ✆ 514/879-4777 for reservations. Métro: Square Victoria.

Sir Winston Churchill Pub ★   The three levels of bars and cafes here are rue Crescent landmarks, and they got a recent makeover, too. The New Orleans–style sidewalk and first-floor terraces (open in summer and enclosed in winter) make perfect vantage points from which to check out the pedestrian traffic. Inside and down the stairs, the pub, with English ales on tap, attempts to imitate a British public house and gets a mixed crowd of young professionals. Open daily to 3am, with DJs every day. 1459 rue Crescent (near rue Ste-Catherine). ✆ 514/288-3814. Métro: Guy-Concordia.

Thursday's   In existence too long to be considered "hot," this remains another prime watering hole for Montréal's young, professional set. The pubby bar spills out onto a terrace that hangs over the street, and there's a glittery disco in back. It was voted "Best Pick-Up Spot" by the *Montréal Mirror* in 2007 for its third year running. In L'Hôtel de la Montagne, 1449 rue Crescent (north of rue Ste-Catherine). ✆ 516/288-5656. Métro: Guy-Concordia.

W Hotel   With its Plateau Lounge, W Bartini, and Wunderbar open daily until 3am, W attracts some of the best-looking partiers in town. 901 Victoria Square (at rue McGill). ✆ 516/395-3100. Métro: Square-Victoria.

VIEUX-MONTREAL

Aszú (Finds)   This classy wine bar features hundreds of labels. Better still, on any given night, some 40 of them are available by the glass. A menu of oysters, risotto, bison tartar, and the like provides accompaniment to the main event. With room for about 30 people at the bar, 40 at inside tables, and 75 on an attractive side terrace, this is a cozy find—get here before the crowds catch on. Daily noon to 10 pm (until 11pm Thursday through Satuday). An upstairs cafe is open from 7am to 4pm daily. 212 rue Notre Dame ouest (at rue St-François-Xavier). ✆ 514/845-5436. www.aszu.ca. Métro: Place d'Armes.

Le Jardin Nelson   Near the foot of Place Jacques Cartier, a passage leads into a tree-shaded garden court in the back of a stone building dating from 1812. A pleasant hour or two can be spent listening to live jazz every afternoon or evening. Food takes second place, but the kitchen does well with its pizzas and crepes; the latter can be filled with either sweet or savory fillings (including lobster). There's a covered people-watching porch in front, and dining rooms and a bar inside. When the weather's nice, it's open until 2am. Closed November through mid-April. 407 Place Jacques-Cartier (at rue St-Paul). ℂ 514/861-5731. Métro: Place d'Armes or Champ de Mars.

Suite 701 When Le Place d'Armes Hôtel (p. 79) converted its old lobby and wine bar into a spiffy lounge, yuppies got the word fast. The so-called *cinq-à-sept* (5-to-7) set fills the space after work each night, especially on Thursday. Upscale bar food comes from the same kitchen as the restaurant's high-end operation, **Aix Cuisine du Terroir** (p. 90). At the corner of rue St-Jacques and côte de la Place d'Armes. ℂ 514/904 1201. Métro: Place d'Armes.

PLATEAU MONT-ROYAL & MILE END

Bifteck This perennially popular bar jumps, with a grungy crowd aging from barely legal (18) to early 30s. Most quaff beer by the pitcher, but attention is also given to shooters, including classy evergreens such as the Kamikaze and the Windex. Despite the bar's name, food isn't served, apart from popcorn. Late at night, it's one of the Main's most packed bars. 3702 bd. St-Laurent (near rue Prince Arthur). ℂ 514/844-6211. Métro: Sherbrooke.

Bílý Kůň Pronounced "Billy Coon," this popular bar is a bit of Prague right in Montréal, from the avant-garde decor to the full line of Czech beers (alongside local microbrews). Students, 30ish journalists, and leftie professionals all jam in for the relaxed atmosphere in the narrow space with honeycomb floor tiles, twirling ceiling fans, and big picture windows that open to the street. There's live jazz early evenings Tuesday through Friday from 6 to 8pm, and DJs Wednesday through Saturday 8pm until 3am. Get here early to do a little shopping in the hipster boutiques along the street. 354 av. Mont-Royal est (near rue St-Denis). ℂ 514/845-5392. www.bilykun.com. Métro: Mont-Royal.

Champs Montréalers are no less enthusiastic about sports, especially hockey, than other Canadians, and fans both avid and casual drop by this three-story sports emporium to catch up with their teams and hoist a few. Games from around the world are fed to walls of TVs, more than a dozen athletic events might be showing at any given time. Food is what you'd expect—burgers, steaks, and such. 3956 bd. St-Laurent (near rue Duluth). ℂ 514/987-6444. Métro: Sherbrooke.

Koko New in 2008, this chic bar and restaurant is part of the Opus Hotel, which took over the Hôtel Godin in 2007. It includes a spectacular terrace and an Asian-influenced menu with options such as green-tea soba noodles with poached chicken and prawn, and beef tataki. As befits its positioning as a premier venue for urban glamour, a bouncer stands watch at the door. 8 rue Sherbrooke ouest (at bd. St-Laurent). ℂ 514/657-5656. www.kokomontreal.com. Métro: Saint-Laurent.

Laïka Amid the plethora of St-Laurent watering stops, this bright little *boîte* offers tasty sandwiches and tapas and a popular Sunday brunch. DJs spin house, funk, electronica, and whatnot from mid-evening until 3am for a mostly 18- to 35-year-old crowd. 4040 bd. St-Laurent (near rue Duluth). ℂ 514/842-8088. www.laikamontreal.com. Métro: Sherbrooke.

Le Pistol Get here early, because this spot on The Main gets packed in no time. Catering to the post-collegiate T-shirt-and-jeans crowd, this bar offers ample attractions, including high-definition plasma TVs showing hockey, and tasty food, including sandwiches named for Bond flicks—Goldfinger, Moonraker, and so on. Music moves from jazz to house to rock. The ground-floor front is open in decent weather. Drinks and eats are mostly less than C$10 (£5). 3723 bd. St-Laurent (near rue Prince Arthur). ℭ **514/847-2222.** Métro: Sherbrooke.

Whisky Café Those who enjoy scotch, particularly single-malts like Laphraoig and Glenfiddich, will find more than 150 different labels to sample at this handsome bar. Decor is sophisticated, with exposed beams and vents, handmade tiled tables, and large wood-enclosed columns. Another decorative triumph: The men's urinal has a waterfall acting as the *pissoir*. Attached is a separate cigar lounge with leather armchairs and Cubans. 5800 bd. St-Laurent (at rue Bernard). ℭ **514/278-2646.** Métro: Laurier.

4 MORE ENTERTAINMENT

GAMBLING

The **Casino de Montréal** (ℭ **800/665-2274** or 514/392-2746; www.casino-de-montreal. com), Québec's first, is housed in recycled space: The complex reuses what were the French and Québec pavilions during Expo 67. Asymmetrical and groovy, the buildings provide a dramatic setting for games of chance. Four floors contain more than 115 game tables, including roulette, craps, blackjack, baccarat, and varieties of poker, and there are more than 3,200 slot machines.

Its four restaurants get good reviews, especially the elegant **Nuances** (p. 105). There are also live shows in the Cabaret.

No alcoholic beverages are served in the gambling areas, and patrons must be at least 18 years old and dressed neatly (the full dress code is posted online). The casino is entirely smoke-free, though it offers outside smoking areas; it's open 24 hours a day, 7 days a week, with overnight packages available at nearby hotels.

The casino is on Parc Jean-Drapeau; you can drive there or take the Métro to the Parc Jean-Drapeau stop and then walk or take the casino shuttle bus (no. 167, labeled CASINO). From May through October, a free shuttle bus *(navette)* leaves on the hour from the downtown Infotouriste Centre at 1001 rue du Square-Dorchester (it makes other stops downtown, too).

CINEMA

In Montréal, English-language films are usually presented with French subtitles. However, when the initials "VF" (for *version française*) follow the title of a non-Francophone movie, it means that the movie has been dubbed into French. Policies vary regarding English subtitles on non-English-language films, so ask about this at the box office. Besides the many first-run movie houses that advertise in the daily newspapers, look for "ciné-clubs," which tend to be slightly older and show second-run, foreign, and art films.

Admission to films is usually about C$10 (£5) for adults, and less for students, seniors, and children. There are usually special afternoon rates for matinees.

Foreign-language and independent films are on the billboard at **Ex-Centris**, 3536 bd.
St-Laurent (© **514/847-2206**; www.ex-centris.com), and the architectural surroundings
are at least as interesting—the venue sort of looks like a post-machine-age spaceship. Go
inside and try to find the ticket booth to ask about showtimes just to see what we mean.
A nifty bar-cafe, **Café Méliès** (p. 100), is on the premises. Films are in English about half
the time.

The **National Film Board of Canada**, 1564 rue St-Denis (© **514/496-6887**; www.
nfb.ca), shows classic Canadian and international films, primarily in English and French.
Also there is the unique **CinéRobothèque**, a high-tech screening center that lets visitors
browse a multimedia catalog and then watch a film at a personal viewing station.

Imposing, fantastically huge images confront viewers of the five-story **IMAX Theatre**
screen in the Centre des Sciences de Montréal (Montréal Science Centre;) © **877/496-
4724**; www.montrealsciencecentre.com). Many of the films are suitable for the entire
family. See "Especially for Kids," in chapter 8.

COMEDY

The once red-hot market for comedy clubs across North America may have cooled off in
most places, but it lives on in Montréal, mostly because the city is the home to the highly
regarded **Juste pour Rire (Just for Laughs) Festival** (© **888/244-3155**; www.hahaha.
com) every summer. Those who have so far avoided the comedy-club experience should
know that profanity, bathroom humor, and ethnic slurs are common fodder. To avoid
becoming the object of comedians' barbs, sit well back from the stage. Check before
buying tickets whether the show you're interested in is in French or English.

There's a full array of comedy at **Comedyworks**, a long-running club at 1238 rue
Bishop (© **514/398-9661**; www.comedyworksmontreal.com). Monday is open-mic
night, Tuesday and Wednesday are improv nights (a comedy troupe works off the audience's suggestions), and Thursday through Saturday nights feature international headlin-
ers. No food is served, just drinks. Reservations are recommended, especially on Friday,
when it may be necessary to arrive early to secure a seat. Shows are in English and happen
nightly at 8:30pm, with additional shows at 11pm on Friday and Saturday.

Side Trips from Montréal

You don't have to travel far from Montréal to reach mountains, parks, or bike trails; in fact, enjoyable touring regions are a mere 30-minute drive from the city.

The **Laurentians** (to the north) and the **Cantons-de-l'Est** (to the southeast) have both seen the development of year-round vacation retreats, with skiing in winter, biking and boating in summer, maple sugaring in spring, and vineyard-touring and leaf-peeping in fall.

The pearl of the Laurentians (also called the Laurentides) is **Mont-Tremblant,** eastern Canada's highest peak and a winter mecca for skiers and snowboarders from all over North America. Development has been particularly heavy in the resort town here.

The region has dozens of other ski centers, too, with scores of trails at every level of difficulty, and many are less than an hour from Montréal. The area loses none of its charm in summer (and in fact gains some with thinned-out traffic); that's when ski resorts become attractive, green mountain properties close to biking, fishing, and golfing. It's even possible to participate in cattle roundups.

The bucolic Cantons-de-l'Est were known as the Eastern Townships when they were a haven for English Loyalists and their descendants; some Anglophones still refer to the region by that name by today. It's blessed with memorable country inns, former homes of early 1900s aristocracy, and the beautiful Lake Massawippi. As with the Laurentians, many of the same trails developed for winter sports are used for parallel activities in summer. The mountain of **Bromont,** for example, has marked paths for mountain biking, and **Mont-Orford Park** is the focal point for hiking trails linking six regional parks. Rock climbing, whitewater kayaking, sailing, and fishing are additional options, with equipment readily available for rent.

Because the people of both regions rely heavily on tourism for their livelihoods, knowledge of at least rudimentary English is widespread, even outside such obvious places as hotels and restaurants.

1 NORTH INTO THE LAURENTIANS (LAURENTIDES)

55–129km (34–80 miles) N of Montréal

Don't expect spiked peaks or high, ragged ridges. The Laurentian Shield's rolling hills and rounded mountains are among the world's oldest, worn down by wind and water over eons. They average between 300m and 520m (984 ft. and 1,706 ft.) in height, with the highest being Mont-Tremblant, at 968m (3,176 ft.). In the lower area, closer to Montréal, the terrain resembles a rumpled quilt, its folds and hollows cupping a multitude of lakes large and small. Farther north, the summits are higher and craggier, with patches of snow persisting well into spring, but these are still not the Alps or the Rockies. They're welcoming and embracing as opposed to awe inspiring.

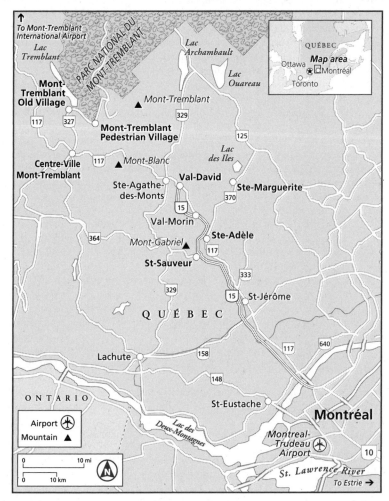

Half a century ago, the first ski schools, rope tows, and trails began to appear. Today, there are 14 ski centers within a 64km (40-mile) radius, and cross-country skiing has as enthusiastic a following as downhill. Sprawling resorts and modest lodges and inns are packed in winter with skiers, some of them through April. Trails for those with advanced skills typically have short pitches and challenging moguls, with broad, hard-packed avenues for beginners and the less experienced. Skiers can usually expect reliable snow from early December to mid-April; in 2008, the area enjoyed record snow falls.

But skiing is only half the story. As transportation improved, people took advantage of the obvious warm-weather opportunities for watersports, golf (courses in the area now total more than 30), tennis, mountain biking, hiking, and the like. Before long, the region gained a sometimes-deserved reputation for fine dining and a convivial atmosphere.

Bird-watchers of both intense and casual bent can be fully occupied. Loon lovers, in particular, know that the lakes of Québec province's mountains are home to the native waterfowl that gives its name to the dollar coin. Excellent divers and swimmers, the birds are unable to walk on land, which makes nesting a trial. They're identified by a distinctive call that might be described as an extended, mournful giggle.

At any time of year, a visit to any of the villages or resorts in the Laurentians is likely to yield pleasant memories. The busiest times are February and March for skiing, July and August for summer vacation, and during the Christmas-to-New Year's holiday period.

In March and April, the maple trees are tapped, and *cabanes à sucre* (sugar shacks) open up everywhere, some selling just maple syrup and candies, others serving full meals and even staging entertainment. May is often characterized by warm days, cool nights, and just enough people that the streets don't seem deserted. September is the same way, and in the last 2 weeks of that month, the leaves put on a stunning show of autumnal color.

In May and June, it must be said, the indigenous black flies and mosquitoes can seem as big and as ill-tempered as buzzards, so be prepared. Some of the resorts, inns, and lodges close down for a couple of weeks in spring and fall, so be sure to check ahead if you're traveling during that time.

Prices can be difficult to pin down. The large resorts have so many types of rooms, suites, cottages, meal plans, discounts, and packages that you may need a travel agent to pick through the thicket of options. Prices listed for hotels in this chapter are the rack rate for double occupancy during the busy skiing and summer-vacation months, unless otherwise noted. At other times of the year, reservations are easier to get and prices for virtually everything are lower. Most hotels and resorts offer package deals with meals or activities, so consult their websites for options. Many also offer discounts to AAA members.

Remember that Montréalers fill the highways when they "go up north" on weekends, particularly during the top skiing months, so make reservations early if that's when you'll be traveling.

See p. 68 for general information about hotel rates and the Frommer's star system.

ESSENTIALS
Getting There

BY CAR The fast and scenic **Autoroute des Laurentides,** also known as **Autoroute 15,** goes straight from Montréal to the Laurentians. Just follow the signs to St-Jérôme. The exit numbers represent the distance in kilometers that the village lies from Montréal.

Though the pace of development is quickening, flanking the highway with water parks, condos, and chain restaurants, this is still a pretty drive once you're out of the clutches of the tangle of expressways surrounding Montréal and past St-Jérôme. You'll quickly get a sweeping, panoramic introduction to the area, from lower Laurentians' rolling hills and forests to the mountain drama of the upper range.

Those with the time to meander can exit at St-Jérôme and pick up the older, parallel **Route 117,** which plays tag with the autoroute all the way to Ste-Agathe-des-Monts. Many of the region's more appealing towns are along or near this route. (Beware in winter, however, when parts of Rte. 117 can become riddled with potholes large enough to

On the Road: A Quick Guide

Canada is on the metric system, so distances are measured in kilometers (1 kilometer = .62 miles). Many U.S. cars have a secondary speedometer that gives speed in kilometers. The maximum posted speed limit on most highways is 100kmph (62 mph).

At gas stations, *avec service* means full-service, and *libre service* means self-service. The directions on the pump are usually in French and English, especially at name-brand stations. Gas is sold by the liter, and 3.78 liters equals 1 gallon. It's expensive by U.S. standards, with recent prices of C$1.40 per liter (70p) translating to about US$5.30 per gallon.

Road signs are always in French; *arret* means stop, *demi tour* means U-turn.

seriously damage your car; the extreme weather does a job on the state of the roads.) North of Ste-Agathe, the autoroute ends and Rte. 117 becomes the major artery for the region. It continues well past Mont-Tremblant and deep into Québec's north country, finally ending at the Ontario border hundreds of miles from Montréal.

Québec's equivalent of the highway patrol, Sûreté de Québec, maintains a presence along the stretch of Autoroute 15 between St-Faustin and Ste-Adèle. While enforcement of speed limits is loose, if you're pulled over, remember that radar detectors are illegal in the province (even if they're not turned on) and can be confiscated.

BY PLANE Mont-Tremblant International Airport (✆ 819/275-9099; www.mtia.ca), 39km (24 miles) north of Mont-Tremblant, began receiving direct flights from Newark, New Jersey, in 2007 (Continental Airlines; winter months only). It also gets direct flights from Toronto. Car rentals are available from Hertz and Budget by reservation only. An airport shuttle bus delivers guests directly to 18 hotels in Mont-Tremblant and the ski mountain, and taxis are available. The ride takes about 40 minutes.

Aéroport International Pierre-Elliot-Trudeau de Montréal (airport code YUL; ✆ 800/465-1213 or 514/394-7377; www.admtl.com), known more commonly as Montréal-Trudeau Airport, is 30 to 60 minutes from the Laurentians, depending on how far north you're headed. Skyport (✆ 800/471-1155; www.skyportinternational.com) runs a shuttle to Mont-Tremblant. There are also taxis and limousines that will take you to any Laurentian hideaway—for a price. Ask about the best options when making accommodations reservations.

BY BUS From Montréal, Galland buses (✆ 514/333-9555; www.galland-bus.com) depart Terminus Voyageur, 505 bd. de Maisonneuve est, stopping in the larger Laurentian towns, including Ste-Sauveur, Ste-Adèle, and Mont-Tremblant. The ride to Mont-Tremblant takes just less than 3 hours.

Another option is the nonprofit **Allo Stop;** it's an alternative program that coordinates rideshares to help reduce the numbers of cars on the road. Travelers help pay for gas. Call ✆ 514/985-3032 for the Montréal office or visit www.allostopmontreal.com.

Tourist offices are plentiful throughout the Laurentians. Look for the blue "?" signs along the highways or in towns. For an orientation to the entire region, stop in at the major information center, well marked from the highway, at Exit 51 off Autoroute 15. It shares a building with a 24-hour McDonald's, and there's a gas station next door. Called **Tourisme Laurentides** (© **800/561-6673;** www.laurentides.com), it has racks of brochures and a helpful staff that can, for no charge, make reservations for lodging throughout the Laurentides. It's open daily from 8:30am to 5pm (until 9pm in summer).

ST-SAUVEUR

Only 60km (37 miles) north of Montréal, the village of St-Sauveur (pop. 8,470) can easily be a day trip. The area is flush with outlet malls and the carloads of shoppers they attract, but a few blocks farther north, the older village square is dominated by a handsome church, and the streets around it bustle with a less frenzied activity for much of the year. Be prepared to have difficulty finding a parking place in season (try the large lot behind the church). Dining and snacking on everything from crepes to hot dogs are big activities here, evidenced by the many beckoning cafes. In summer, there's a tourist kiosk on the square.

In summer, **Parc Aquatique du Mont St-Sauveur,** 350 ave. St-Denis (© **450/227-4671;** www.mssi.ca), Canada's largest water park, features rafting, a wave pool, a tidal-wave river, and slides, including one which you go up in a chairlift and ride down in a tube. Admission is C$33 (£17) ages 13 and older, C$27 (£14) ages 6 to 12, C$15 (£7.50) ages 3 to 5, free for 2 and younger.

Ten days in early August are dedicated to St-Sauveur's annual **Festival des Arts** (© **450/227-0427;** www.fass.ca), with an emphasis on music and dance, including jazz and chamber concerts and ballet troupes. The schedule always includes a number of free events.

Where to Stay & Dine

If the idea of a picnic appeals—and in this town of ordinary restaurants, it well might—drive west on the main street, rue Principale, to **Chez Bernard,** 411 rue Principale (© **450/240-0000;** www.chezbernard.com). Inside the pretty little house behind the iron fence, you'll find a store selling fragrant cheeses, crusty breads, wines, savory tarts, pâtés, sausages, smoked meats, and a variety of prepared meals. There are three small tables. Prices range from C$4 to C$16 (£2–£8). The store opens daily at 10am.

Le Petit Clocher　At the end of a residential cul-de-sac at the top of a hill, tucked in the woods and looking out to the mountains in the distance, this converted monastery is an intriguing B&B. The decor is a riot of styles: English country-cottage braided rugs, wood roosters, medieval tapestries, and knights' armor. Each room has a French-Catholic theme (La Chapelle, La Divine), and La Cardinale features a red double whirlpool in the bedroom corner. In winter, the antique piano in the main room gets covered with miniature houses to make a multi-leveled village tableau. All but one room look out at the mountains; the last faces the woods where deer wander by. Have a light dinner to take full advantage of the opulent breakfast: fresh croissants, French cheeses, quiche, just-tapped maple water, individual soufflés. This could be the best breakfast in all the Laurentians.

216 av. de l'Eglise, St-Sauveur, PQ J0R 1R7. (C) **450/227-7576.** Fax 450/227-6662. www.bbcanada.com/ lepetitclocher. 7 units. C$185–C$215 (£93–£108) double. Rates include huge breakfast. Packages available. AE, MC, V. Exit 60 from Autoroute 15, left at the traffic light (364 west), right on Chemin de la Gare, right on rue Principale, left on av. de l'Eglise. Watch for sign after 1km (²/₃ mile) and turn left up driveway. **Amenities:** Outdoor hot tub. *In room:* A/C, TV, Wi-Fi, Internet access, hair dryer.

Manoir Saint-Sauveur   Just minutes off the autoroute and in the heart of the outlet shopping frenzy, Manoir Saint-Sauveur offers a monster outdoor pool and a comprehensive roster of four-season activities. The on-site spa, **Le Spa du Manoir,** specializes in body treatments and massage therapy. Rooms are spacious and comfortable, blandly modern with light-wood furnishings that hint vaguely of 19th-century Gallic inspirations. Units in the condo section have kitchenettes. The main building, with its many dormers, is easily spotted from the road. Like most properties in the region, the front desk adjusts prices up or down according to season, demand, and occupancy rate on any given night, so ask if they have anything less expensive when you book or arrive.

246 Chemin du Lac Millette, St-Sauveur, PQ J0R 1R3. (C) **800/361-0505** or 450/227-1811. Fax 450/227-8512. www.manoir-saint-sauveur.com. 280 units. C$129–C$299 (£65–£150) double; from C$189 (£95) suite. 2 children 17 and younger stay free in parent's room. Packages available. AE, MC, V. Indoor parking C$10 (£5); outdoor parking free. Take exit 60 off Autoroute 15. **Amenities:** 2 restaurants; bar; large indoor and outdoor pools; substantial health club; spa; room service; babysitting. *In room:* A/C, TV, Wi-Fi, high-speed Internet, hair dryer.

STE-ADELE & MONT-GABRIEL

In winter, the ski mountain of **Mont-Gabriel** is a popular destination (for information, see Hôtel Mont-Gabriel, p. 178). To get there, follow Autoroute 15 to Exit 64 and turn right at the stop sign. In addition to offering downhill skiing, the mountain is wrapped in cross-country trails that range through the surrounding countryside.

The adjacent village, Ste-Adèle (pop. 10,662), only 67km (42 miles) north of Montréal, is a near-metropolis compared to the other Laurentian villages. What makes it seem big are its services: police, doctors, ambulances, a shopping center, cinemas, art galleries, and a larger collection of places to stay and dine. As rue Morin mounts the hill to Lac Rond, Ste-Adèle's resort lake, it's easy to see why the town is divided into a lower part *(en bas)* and an upper part *(en haut).*

To get to the village, either take Route 117, which swings directly into its main street, boulevard Ste-Adèle, or get off Autoroute 15 at Exit 67.

Exploring Ste-Adele

Ste-Adèle's main street, **rue Valiquette,** is a busy one-way thoroughfare lined with cafes, galleries, and bakeries.

Lac Rond is the center of summer activities: Canoes, sailboats, and *pédalos* (pedal-powered watercraft), which can be rented from several docks, glide over the placid surface, while swimmers splash and play near shore-side beaches.

Where to Stay & Dine

Hôtel Le Chantecler ★ (Value)   Sprawled across steep slopes cupping Lac Rond, this resort draws families in both summer and winter. Housing is comprised of two- and three-story stone buildings, their roofs bristling with steeples and dormers. The hotel is directly on a ski mountain with 16 runs for all levels of skiers. A chalet up top has a cafeteria and bar, and cross-country skiing and ice-skating are available. Warm weather brings the possibilities of windsurfing and boating on the lake, as well as rounds on two golf courses. Rooms renovated in 2006 have pine furniture; most also have air-conditioning and many have whirlpools. A bountiful buffet breakfast is served in a dining room overlooking the slopes and the lake.

1474 Chemin Chantecler, Ste-Adèle, PQ J8B 1A2. ✆ 888/916-1616. www.lechantecler.com. 215 units. From C$115 (£58) double. Packages and meal plans available. AE, DC, DISC, MC, V. Free parking. Take exit 67 off Autoroute 15, turn left at the 4th traffic light onto rue Morin, and then turn right at the top of the hill onto Chemin Chantecler. **Amenities:** Restaurant; bar; indoor pool; lake beach; golf; 6 lit tennis courts; racquetball and badminton; health club w/squash; whirlpool and saunas; watersports equipment; bike rental; room service; babysitting; hiking trails; horseback riding. *In room:* A/C, TV, free Wi-Fi, high-speed Internet, hair dryer.

Hôtel Mont-Gabriel ★ **(Kids)**   Perched high atop Mont-Gabriel and looking like the rambling log cottages of the turn-of-the-20th-century wealthy, this kid-friendly resort is set on a 480-hectare (1,186-acre) forest estate and features golf and tennis programs in summer and ski and spa packages in winter. The spacious rooms in the Tyrol section were renovated in 2006 and are the most modern and desirable, and many provide views of the surrounding hills. One luxury suite and two chalets offer the option for more space still. The hotel is a ski-in-ski-out facility, with night-skiing available on more than a dozen runs. Dog sledding and snowmobiling are also available in season. The hotel is only 45 minutes from Montréal's Trudeau Airport.

1699 Chemin Mont-Gabriel, Ste-Adèle, PQ J8B 1A5. ✆ 800/668-5253 or 450/229-3547. Fax 450/229-7034. www.montgabriel.com. 128 units. C$96–C$195 (£48–£98) double. Children 16 and younger stay free in parent's room. Meal plans and packages available. AE, MC, V. Take exit 64 from Autoroute 15. **Amenities:** Restaurant; bar; heated indoor and outdoor pools; 18-hole golf course; 6 night-lit clay tennis courts; health club; spa; Jacuzzi; sauna; babysitting; alpine skiing on-site. *In room:* A/C, TV, Wi-Fi, hair dryer.

L'Eau à la Bouche ★   The owners leave no doubt as to where their priorities lie. While the hotel, directly on busy Route 117, is entirely satisfactory, the restaurant is their beloved baby, and has the glowing reviews to prove it. False modesty isn't a factor—*l'eau à la bouche* means "mouthwatering"—and the kitchen uses native ingredients with nouvelle presentations. Full advantage is taken of seasonal products, as with one summer starter of a poached half-lobster with chanterelles and gathered wild vegetables. Desserts are impressive, and the cheese plate—pungent nubbins delivered with warm baguette slices—is truly special. There are two meal options, both pricey: the C$150 (£75) discovery menu, and the C$67 (£34) *table d'hôte*, with extra charges for potatoes (C$9/£4.50) and vegetables (C$12/£6). A spa with massage rooms, a pretty outdoor hot tub, and a small waterfall was added in 2006; nonguests can come for C$40 (£20).

3003 bd. Ste-Adèle (Rte. 117), Ste-Adèle, PQ J8B 2N6. ✆ 888/828-2991 or 450/229-2991. Fax 450/229-7573. www.leaualabouche.com. 17 units. C$155–C$255 (£78–£128) double. Packages and meal plans available. AE, DC, MC, V. **Amenities:** Restaurant; spa; room service; babysitting. *In room:* A/C, TV, Wi-Fi, Internet access, hair dryer.

STE-MARGUERITE-DU-LAC-MASSON

Ste-Marguerite (pop. 2,581), about 12 km (7¹⁄₂ miles) east of Autoroute 15, is alongside the large Lac Masson and home to **Bistro à Champlain,** one of the region's prime restaurants (see below). To get there, take exit 69 off of Autoroute 15 onto Route 370. Or, if you're driving from Ste-Adèle, look for a street heading northeast named Chemin Pierre-Péladeau (which is Route 370). It becomes a narrow road that crosses the 9m-wide

Biker's Paradise: The 4,000km Route Verte

Québec is bike crazy, and it's got the goods to justify it. In summer 2007, the province officially inaugurated the new **Route Verte (Green Route),** a 4,000km (2,485-mile) bike network that stretches from one end to the other and links all regions and cities. The idea started in 1995 and is modeled on the Rails-to-Trails program in the U.S. and cycling routes in Denmark, Great Britain, and along the Danube and Rhine rivers. It was initiated by the nonprofit biking organization Vélo Québec with support from the Québec Ministry of Transportation. Route Verte won the prestigious Prix Ulysse, one of the grand prizes given annually by the Québec tourist office, right out of the gate. To boot, the National Geographic Society declared it one of the 10 best bicycle routes in the world.

Included in the network is the popular **P'tit Train du Nord** bike trail that goes north into the Laurentians to Mont-Tremblant and beyond. It's built on a former railway track and passes through the villages of Ste-Adèle, Val David, and Ste-Agathe-des-Monts. Cyclists can get food and bike repairs at renovated railway stations along the way and hop on for a day trip or a longer tour. Access fees have been eliminated—since 2008, use of the trail is free of charge.

The Route Verte website (www.routeverte.com) provides maps of all the paths and links to places to rent bikes as well as B&Bs, campsites, and hotels that are especially focused on serving bikers. Accredited accommodations display a BIENVENUE CYCLISTES! sticker and provide a covered and locked place for overnight bicycle storage, access to high-carb meals with lots of fruits and veggies, a bike pump and tools, and information about where to make repairs nearby. The guidebook *Cycling in Québec: Official Guide to Bicycling on Québec's Route Verte* is available from the site.

Also look for the free *Official Tourist Guide to the Laurentians,* published by the regional tourist office (www.laurentides.com); it always has a big section on biking. And if you decide to plan a big trip, keep in mind **Transport du Parc Linéaire** (© **888/686-1323** or 450/569-5596; www.transportduparclineaire. com), which provides baggage transport from inn to inn.

(30-ft.) Rivière du Nord, then winds through evergreen forests past upscale vacation homes. The road dead-ends at the lake, with the restaurant at the intersection.

In summer, information about the area is available from Pavillon du Parc, a kiosk alongside Lac Masson, and across from the restaurant.

Where to Dine

Bistro à Champlain ★ FRENCH   On Lac Masson's shore is one of the most honored restaurants in the Laurentians. The 37,000-bottle cellar is the reason most people make gastronomic pilgrimages here from Montréal. In fact, it can be fairly said that the tail wags the dog—this is a place to have some food with your wine. The vintage list is as thick as the A-to-D volume of an encyclopedia and is posted as a 120-page PDF on the restaurant's website. Everyone is invited to visit the cellar. If you're feeling giddy, try a 2-ounce pour of Château d'Yquem with a serving of seared duck foie gras for C$79

(£40). It goes without saying that waiters are readily equipped to discuss even the humblest bottles at length. The 1864 building used to be a general store, and it retains the exposed beams and original cash register. Abstract paintings and prints, some of them by prominent artists including Jean-Paul Riopelle, adorn the rough-hewn board walls.

75 Chemin Masson, Ste-Marguerite-du-Lac-Masson. ℂ **450/228-4988.** www.bistroachamplain.com. Reservations recommended. Main courses C$19–C$44 (£9.50–£22); *table d'hôte* C$46 (£23); menu degustation C$82 (£41). AE, MC, V. Summer Tues–Sun from 6pm; winter Wed–Sat from 6pm but call to confirm.

VAL-DAVID

At exit 76 of Autoroute 15 (and also along Route 117) is Val-David, the region's faintly bohemian enclave (pop. 4,439). About 80km (50 miles) north of Montréal, it conjures up images of cabin hideaways set among hills rearing above ponds and lakes, and creeks tumbling through fragrant forests.

The **tourist office** is on the main street at 2525 rue de l'Eglise (ℂ **888/322-7030,** ext. 235, or 819/322-2900, ext. 235; www.valdavid.com). Another possibility for assistance is **Centre d'Exposition de Val-David,** a cultural center that mounts art exhibits in a two-story wooden building at 2495 rue de l'Eglise (ℂ **819/322-7474;** www.culture. val-david.qc.ca).

Note that this far north into the Laurentians, the telephone area code changes to 819.

Exploring Val-David

Val-David is small, so park anywhere and meander at leisure. There are many artist studios, and the village sponsors a huge **ceramic art festival** (ℂ **819/322-6868;** www. 1001pots.com) from mid-July to mid-August that it claims is "the largest exhibition of ceramics in North America." Sculptors and ceramicists, along with painters, jewelers, pewter smiths, and other craftspeople display their work; at the same time, there are concerts and other outdoor activities. There are pottery workshops for children every Saturday and Sunday; reserve a spot online.

Also look for the organic **farmer's market** every Saturday morning from late June to late September.

Val-David is one of the villages along the bike path called **Parc Linéaire le P'Tit Train du Nord,** built on a former railroad track (p. 179). For a relaxing picnic, get fixings at the **Metro Supermarket** across from the tourist office. Then turn left onto the bike path just around the corner from the tourist office. Walk 5 minutes to the North River and the teeny **Parc des Amoureux.** There are plenty of benches (and some parking spaces). Look for the sign that says SITE PITTORESQUE.

STE-AGATHE-DES-MONTS

With a population of 9,024, Ste-Agathe-des-Monts, 103km (64 miles) north of Montréal, has as its main thoroughfare **rue Principale,** which is lined with shops, restaurants, and cafes. The town marks the end of Autoroute 15.

Exit from the autoroute and follow the signs for CENTRE-VILLE and then QUAI MUNICIPAL. The town dock on the lake, **Lac des Sables,** and the pretty **waterfront park** make Ste-Agathe a good place to pause in warm months. If you like, rent a bicycle from **Intersport Jacque Champoux,** 74 rue St-Vincent (ℂ **819/326-3480**), for the 5km (3-mile) ride around the lake. Lake cruises, beaches, and watercraft rentals seduce many visitors into lingering for days.

ute lake cruises that depart from the dock at the foot of rue Principale from mid-May to late-October. A running commentary explains the sights (in English and/or French, with Spanish and Italian available upon request), and provides information about the water-ski competitions and windsurfing that Ste-Agathe and the Lac des Sables are famous for. The Alouette cruise costs C$12 (£6) for adults, C$10 (£5) for seniors 60 and older, C$5 (£2.50) for children 6 to 15, and free for children 5 and younger.

VILLE DE MONT-TREMBLANT

The Mont-Tremblant region is a kind of Aspen-meets-Disneyland. It's beautiful country, with great skiing and an ever-expanding resort village on the slope—a prime destination in the province in all four seasons.

In 2005, the villages of St-Jovite and Mont-Tremblant and the pedestrian area at the base of the mountain, which had all been independent, combined to become the single entity called Ville de Mont-Tremblant. Note that many maps, hotels, and residents still refer to the areas as distinct "sectors," which can cause some confusion.

In fact, the abundant use of the name "Tremblant" makes things difficult to keep straight. Here's a primer: There is Mont-Tremblant, the mountain. At the base of its slope is Tremblant, a growing resort village of hotels, restaurants, and shops sometimes called Mont-Tremblant Station or "the pedestrian village" (see "Mont-Tremblant's Pedestrian Village," p. 188). Just adjacent to the pedestrian village is Lac (Lake) Tremblant. About 5km (3 miles) northwest of the resort is a small village which long ago was the region's center and which is now known as the old village of Mont-Tremblant. A cute commercial district about 12km (7½ miles) south of the mountain that used to be called St-Jovite is now called Centre-Ville (Downtown) Mont-Tremblant. Oh, and don't forget the large national park: Parc National du Mont-Tremblant.

Clear as mud?

Getting There

There are two exits from the main roadway, Route 117. The first is exit 122, labeled MONT-TREMBLANT CENTRE-VILLE. Watch closely: Last time we visited, it was barely marked and consisted of a small, inconspicuous sign directing cars to bear right off the highway onto the small rue de St-Jovite. If you miss it, turn into the gas stations on the right directly after the turnoff and pass through them onto the smaller road.

This exit takes visitors through Centre-Ville Mont-Tremblant, formerly the village of St-Jovite, a pleasant community with most of the expected services. The main street, rue de St-Jovite, is lined with cafes and shops, including the women's clothing boutique **Mode Plus** (no. 813), the folk-art and country-antiques store **Le Coq Rouge** (no. 821), and the restaurant **Antipasto** (no. 855; p. 189). From the center of town, Route 327 heads to the mountain.

The second exit from Route 117 bypasses Centre-Ville and goes directly to the mountain and most of the properties listed here. Take exit 119 to Montée Ryan and follow the blue signs for 10km (6¼ miles). Also watch for signs with the resort's logo, which turns the "A" in "Tremblant" into a graphic of a ski mountain.

Mont-Tremblant International Airport (© 819/275-9099; www.mtia.ca) is 24 miles north of the mountain. See p. 175 for more information.

Tourist information, including maps of local ski trails, is available at © **877/425-2434** and two **Visitor Information Centres:** one in Centre-Ville Mont-Tremblant at 48 Chemin de Brébeuf (© **819/425-3300**), open daily 9am to 5pm, and another closer to the ski mountain, at 5080 Montée Ryan (© **819/425-2434**), open daily 9am to 5pm.

You can also check **www.tourismemonttremblant.com**, an official tourism site, and **www.tremblant.ca**, the Mont-Tremblant ski resort's website.

Skiing, Watersports & More

Mont-Tremblant, the mountain, is the highest peak in the Laurentians at 968m (3,176 ft.). In 1894, the provincial government began setting aside land for a "government forest preserve," establishing Parc Mont-Tremblant. The foresight of this early conservation effort has afforded outdoor enjoyment to hikers, skiers, and four-season vacationers ever since: The park is the largest in the province, at 1,510 sq. km (583 sq. miles). It has 400 lakes and 6 rivers, along with 196 bird species and a forest primarily of sugar maple and yellow birch as far as the eye can see. The mountain's name comes from a legend of the area's first inhabitants: Amerindians named the peak after the god Manitou, and say that when humans disturbed nature in any way, Manitou became enraged and made the great mountain tremble—*montagne tremblante.*

The **Mont-Tremblant ski resort** (www.tremblant.ca) draws the biggest downhill crowds in the Laurentians, and is repeatedly ranked as the top resort in eastern North America by *Ski Magazine.* Founded in 1939 by a Philadelphia millionaire named Joe Ryan, it's one of the oldest in North America. It pioneered creating trails on both sides of a mountain and was the second mountain in the world to install a chairlift. The vertical drop is 650m (2,133 ft.).

When the snow is deep, skiers here like to follow the sun around the mountain, making the run down slopes with an eastern exposure in the morning and down the western-facing ones in the afternoon. There are higher mountains with longer runs and steeper pitches, but something about Mont-Tremblant compels people to return time and again.

Today, the resort has snowmaking capability to cover 253 hectares (625 acres). Of its 94 downhill runs and trails, half are expert terrain, about a third are intermediate, and the rest beginner. The longest trail, Nansen, is 6km (almost 4 miles).

There is plenty of **cross-country** action on maintained trails and another 112km (70 miles) of ungroomed trails in the adjacent national park. Many enthusiasts maintain that some of the best cross-country trails are on the grounds of the Mont-Tremblant monastery **Domaine du St-Bernard,** 545 Chemin St-Bernard (© **819/425-3588;** www.domainesaintbernard.org).

In warm weather, watersports are almost as popular as the ski slopes are in winter, thanks to the opportunities surrounding the base of Mont-Tremblant. They include Lac Tremblant, a gorgeous stretch of lake, and another dozen lakes, as well as rivers and streams. From June until October, **Croisières Mont-Tremblant,** 2810 Chemin du village (© **819/425-1045;** www.croisierestremblant.com), offers a 70-minute narrated cruise of Lac Tremblant, focusing on its history, nature, and legends. Fares are C$18 (£9) for adults, C$15 (£7.50) for seniors, C$5 (£2.50) for children ages 6 to 15, and free for children 5 and younger.

Other summer options include **golf** at the renowned **Le Diable** and **Le Géant** courses, as well as tennis, boating, swimming, biking, and hiking.

There are some well-regarded cultural offerings here, too. Right in the pedestrian village, the **Tremblant Film Festival** (www.tremblantfilmfestival.org) spans 5 days in June. Also in the pedestrian village, the **Tremblant International Blues Festival** (ww1.tremblant.ca/blues), which celebrated its 15th year in 2008, hosts up to 150 free shows for 10 days with artists such as Johnny Winter, Keb'Mo, Ana Popovic, and Pinetar Perkins. Five stages are set up throughout the village.

A new summer diversion is the downhill dry-land alpine **luge run** right at the pedestrian village. The engineless sleds are gravity-propelled, reaching speeds of up to 48kmph (30 mph), if you so choose (it's easy to go down as a slowpoke, too). Rides cost C$10 (£5). The village has other games and attractions that can keep visitors occupied for days.

There's also the opportunity to participate in a real **cattle roundup.** The adventure lasts 5 hours and takes place at **Ranch Mont-Tremblant** (☎ **819/681-4848;** www.ranch-mont-tremblant.qc.ca), 40 minutes from the mountain. Cost is C$150 (£75). Teens and young adults tend to love it.

Where to Stay

There are abundant options for housing in the area. In addition to the listings below, **B&Bs** are listed at **www.bbtremblant.com.** For **camping** options within the national park, visit **www.parcsquebec.com.** Also see the sidebar "Mont-Tremblant's Pedestrian Village," on p. 188.

Of the accommodations listed below, the following are in or just adjacent to the pedestrian village: Ermitage du Lac, Fairmont Mont Tremblant, Homewood Suites by Hilton, and Quintessence.

Of the accommodations listed below, Auberge La Porte Rouge and Hôtel Mont-Tremblant are in the old village.

And of the accommodations listed below, the following are a short driving distance from both the pedestrian village and the old village: Château Beauvallon, Gray Rocks, Hôtel du Lac, Le Grand Lodge, and Wyndham Cap Tremblant.

Auberge La Porte Rouge ⓥalue

This unusual motel-inn, run by a third-generation owner, is in the old village of Mont-Tremblant. Wake to a view of Lake Mercier through your picture window (every unit has one), or take in the vista from a little balcony. Some rooms have both fireplaces and whirlpool tubs. There is a terrace facing the lake and a small cocktail lounge. Rooms accommodate two to three people, while cottages have space for 10. Rowboats, canoes, and pedal boats are all available, and the motel is directly on the regional bike and cross-country ski linear park, Le P'tit Train du Nord. Rates listed here include dinner and breakfast for two.

1874 Chemin du Village, Mont-Tremblant. J8E 1K4. ☎ **800/665-3505** or 819/425-3505. Fax 819/425-6700. www.aubergelaporterouge.com. 26 units. C$160–C$210 (£80–£105) double. Rates include dinner and breakfast. Packages available. AE, MC, V. **Amenities:** Restaurant; heated outdoor pool; watersports equipment; bike rental. *In room:* A/C, TV, free Wi-Fi.

Château Beauvallon ★★ ⓚids

Since opening in 2005, Château Beauvallon has become the region's premiere property for families who want to stay off the mountain. A member of Small Luxury Hotels of the World, the 70-suite, three-story property has positioned itself as an affordable luxury retreat for seasoned travelers, and it delivers with a relaxed elegance. Every suite has two bathrooms, a small bedroom with a plush California-king-size bed, a queen-size Murphy bed, a pullout couch, a patio, a gas fireplace,

Tips **With Apologies to Monty Python: "SPA, spa, spa, spa . . ."**

Spas are big business around here: They're probably the most popular new features at hotels, especially in the Mont-Tremblant area, where people have money to burn and are looking for other things to do (and new ways to pamper themselves) beyond dropping a lot of money on skiing.

At some hotels, innkeepers might say they have a "spa" on-site when what they've got is an outdoor hot tub. What we're talking about here, though (and what we mean in the hotel listings when we say a facility has a spa), is a complex that features therapeutic services, particularly ones that involve water.

The spa industry, it turns out, has some clear definitions of what constitutes a spa. In Québec province, the organization **Spas Relais Santé** (www.spas relaissante.com) distinguishes between facilities like *day spas* and *hotel spas,* which offer massages and *estétique* services such as facials and pedicures; *destination spas,* which often involve overnight stays and healthy cuisine; and *Nordic spas,* which are built around a natural water source and include outdoor and indoor spaces.

In the Mont-Tremblant region, many hotels have an on-site spa. The facility at **Quintessence** (℘ **819/425-3400;** www.hotelquintessence.com) is open only to guests and includes an option for a four-hands Swedish massage conducted by two therapists. Fairmont Mont-Tremblant houses **Amerispa** (℘ **819/681-7680;** www.amerispa.ca), which offers rain massages and aromatherapy, and at Hôtel du Lac's **Spa-sur-le-Lac** (℘ **819/425-2731;** www.

a 32-inch high-definition flatscreen TV (with a smaller TV in the bedroom), and an equipped kitchenette. The building is crescent-shaped so that all rooms face the pool and the year-round outdoor hot tub or the lake behind the property. A large central fireplace lounge provides a warm gathering place, and the staff is friendly and competent.

6385 Montée Ryan, Mont-Tremblant, PQ J8E 1S5. ℘ **888/681-6611** or 819/681-6611. Fax 819/681- 1941. www.chateaubeauvallon.com. 70 units. C$179 (£90) 1-bedroom suite. Packages available. AE, DC, MC, V. Free self-parking. **Amenities:** Restaurant; bar; 2 pools (outdoor heated pool w/terrace, indoor heated); golf adjacent; exercise room; all-year outdoor hot tub; concierge; room service; babysitting. *In room:* A/C, TV, free Wi-Fi, kitchenette, hair dryer.

Ermitage du Lac **Kids** Convenient to the ski mountain and the pedestrian village without being directly upon either, this hotel offers a little more peace and quiet than larger properties closer to the action. It's also agreeably close to Parc Plage, the beach on Lac Tremblant, which makes for an enjoyable summer stay. All units are large studios or one- to three-bedroom suites, with kitchenettes or full kitchens equipped with oven ranges, microwaves, unstocked fridges, and necessary cookware and crockery (not all have dishwashers, though). Most have fireplaces and balconies, too. There is a secure underground parking garage.

hoteldulac.ca), you can try the "chocolate package"—a truffle bath, exfoliation with Dead Sea salts, a chocolate body wrap, and a back massage with vanilla oil.

If you've never experienced a European-style Nordic spa before, try to set aside 3 hours for a visit to **Le Scandinave Spa,** at 4280 Montée Ryan, Mont-Tremblant (© **891/425-5524;** www.scandinave.com). It's a tranquil complex of small buildings tucked among evergreen trees on the Diable River shore, and is as chic as it is rustic. A C$43 (£22) fee gives visitors (18 and older only) the run of the facility. Options include outdoor hot tubs designed to look like natural pools (one is set under a man-made waterfall); a Norwegian steam bath thick with eucalyptus scent; indoor relaxation areas with super-comfortable, low-slung chairs; and the river itself, which the heartiest of folk dip into even on frigid days. The idea is to move from hot to cold to hot, which supposedly purges toxins and invigorates your skin. Bathing suits are required and men and women share all spaces except the changing rooms. For extra fees, massages and yoga classes are offered.

Couples, mothers and daughters, groups of friends, and folks on their own all come to "take the waters." The spa is year-round, and few activities are more relaxing than being in a warm outdoor pool as snow falls, the sun sets, and the temperature plummets. (That stroll back to the locker room is another story, though.)

150 Chemin du Curé-Deslauriers, Mont-Tremblant, PQ J8E 1C9. © **800/461-8711** or 819/681-2222. Fax 819/681-2223. www.tremblant.ca. 69 units. C$249 (£125) double; from C$329 (£180) suites. Rates include breakfast. Packages available. Children 11 and younger stay free in parent's room. AE, DC, DISC, MC, V. Parking C$10 (£5). **Amenities:** Breakfast room; outdoor pool in summer; exercise room; outdoor hot tub year-round; locker area for skis. *In room:* A/C, TV, CD players, free Wi-Fi, free high-speed Internet, kitchenette or kitchen, hair dryer.

Fairmont Mont Tremblant ★★★ (Kids)   The high-end resort for families who want to stay directly on the mountain's slopes was built in 1996. The luxury property stands on a crest above the pedestrian village, as befits its stature among the Tremblant hostelries. It hews closely to the high standards of its Fairmont siblings across Canada (Château Frontenac in Québec City, the Queen Elizabeth in Montréal), with 13 levels of rooms including the appealing Fairmont View, which overlook the slope and the fairy-tale resort, and Fairmont Gold, which have access to a private lounge. Families can take advantage of arts-and-crafts programs, year-round indoor and outdoor pools, the 38-person outdoor Jacuzzi, and ski-in-ski-out accessibility to the chairlifts. An on-site **Amerispa** offers body wraps, facials, and a variety of massages. Even vacationers staying elsewhere come for the C$39–C$49 (£20–£25) dinner buffet of in-house restaurant **Windigo.**

3045 Chemin de la Chapelle, Mont-Tremblant, PQ J8E 1E1. ☎ **800/257-7544** or 819/681-7000. Fax 819/681-7099. www.fairmont.com/tremblant. 314 units. Winter C$299–C$349 (£150–£175) double; summer from C$199 (£100). Children 17 and younger stay free in parent's room. Packages available. AE, DC, DISC, MC, V. Pets accepted, C$25 (£13) additional per day. Valet parking C$20 (£10). **Amenities:** Restaurant; cafe in ski season; bar; indoor lap pool and heated outdoor pools; exercise room; spa; access to watersports equipment; children's programs; concierge; Wi-Fi in lobby; room service; babysitting; executive-level rooms. *In room:* A/C, TV, high-speed Internet, minibar, hair dryer.

Gray Rocks ★ Kids A century old as of 2006, the area's dowager resort continues to hold charm for family vacations. Beside Lake Ouimet, the rambling main building has most of the guest rooms, while condo units—which feature full kitchens, air-conditioning, beds for six, and washers and dryers—are in the forest across the lake, a drive or free shuttle ride from the lodge. Rooms are well designed for families, with open closets and ample space for luggage, coat hooks along a front hall, and separate toilet and sink areas. Breakfast buffets are bountiful; eat up to prepare for on-site summer activities such as tennis (22 courts), golf (two 18-hole courses), horseback riding, or boating. Motorboats have been banned on the lake, a fact that irks longtime locals but is a boon to guests seeking peace and quiet. In winter, Grey Rocks has its own mountain with 22 trails and a ski school.

2322 rue Labelle, Mont-Tremblant, PQ J8E 1T8. ☎ **800/567-6767** or 819/425-2771. Fax 819/425-9156. www.grayrocks.com. 207 units. C$300 (£150) double; C$225 (£113) condo. Dinner and breakfast for 2 is included in room rate, but not in condo rate. Children stay free in parent's room but pay an extra fee for meals. Packages and meal plans available. AE, DC, DISC, MC, V. Free parking. **Amenities:** Restaurant; bar; indoor pool w/hot tub and sauna; 36 holes of golf; 22 tennis courts; exercise area; spa; watersports equipment; family programs; babysitting; on-site horseback riding; on-site ski mountain. *In room:* A/C, TV, dial-up Internet, hair dryer.

Homewood Suites by Hilton Directly on the pedestrian village at Place St-Bernard, a central gathering space, the Hilton offers direct access to the resort's restaurants, bars, and shops which ring the plaza. It has ski-in-ski-out access to the mountain's slopes, which are just out the door, and ski lockers are available to guests. Renovations in 2008 were expected to add a pool to the complex. The hotel is made up of several buildings decorated on the outside to look like candy-colored row houses, and all accommodations are crisply furnished suites with fireplaces and equipped kitchens—useful when you want to avoid the village's expensive food venues.

3035 Chemin de la Chapelle, Mont-Tremblant, PQ J8E 1E1. ☎ **888/288-2988** or 819/681-0808. Fax 819/681-0331. www.homewoodsuitestremblant.com. 102 units. From C$200 (£100) suite. Rates include breakfast and afternoon snack and beverages every Mon–Thurs. Children 17 and younger stay free in parent's room. Packages available. AE, DISC, MC, V. Self-parking C$10 (£5). **Amenities:** Pool; babysitting. *In room:* A/C, TV, free high-speed Internet, kitchen, hair dryer.

Hôtel du Lac ★★ Kids Value About 3km (2 miles) from ski mountain's base, this resort is a quieter option than being directly in the pedestrian village hubbub, and has a good variety of on-site activities: private lake access, kayaks and paddleboats, a day camp, the hushed Spa-sur-le-Lac. A needed renovation of rooms and public spaces started in 2008 and is continuing into 2009. The complex is terraced into a hillside that slopes toward Lac Tremblant and consists of several lodges in muted alpine style. Accommodations represent an excellent value and that greatest of luxuries: space. Most rental units are suites of one or two bedrooms, with prices about equivalent to a single room at many other area resorts. Because the hotel is tucked away, most people take a dinner and breakfast plan (call or go online for details about this). There are no elevators, so ask for a lower level if stairs present an issue. There are a lot of families, conventions, and weddings here.

121 rue Cuttle, Mont-Tremblant, PQ J8E 1B9. © **800/567-8341** or 819/425-2731. Fax 819/425-5617. www.club-tremblant.com. 122 units. C$179 (£90) suite. Children 4 and younger stay free in parent's room. Packages available. AE, DC, DISC, MC, V. Free parking. Pets accepted, C$25 (£13) additional per day. Take Lac Tremblant north and follow signs for less than a mile. **Amenities:** Restaurant; bar; small indoor/outdoor pool; 3 tennis courts; exercise room; spa; hot tub; watersports equipment; bike rental; concierge; babysitting; day camp in summer. *In room:* A/C, TV, high-speed Internet, kitchen, hair dryer.

Hôtel Mont-Tremblant (Value)

A modest hotel in the old village of Mont-Tremblant, this 25-room property (founded in 1902) is popular both with skiers who want to avoid the resort village's higher prices (there's a shuttle bus stop to the slopes across the street) and, in summer, with cyclists who appreciate the location directly on Le P'tit Train du Nord cycling path (p. 179). Most rooms have twin or double beds, and a few have sitting areas. What's more, the inn houses the popular restaurant **Le Bernardin,** which has a covered front terrace and dinner main courses that cost C$12 to C$37 (£6–£19). Room prices include dinner and breakfast for two.

1900 Chemin du Village, Mont-Tremblant, PQ J8E 1K4. © **888/887-1111** or 819/425-3232. Fax 819/425-9755. www.hotelmonttremblant.com. 25 units. C$140–C$190 (£70–£95) double. Rates include dinner and breakfast. MC, V. **Amenities:** Restaurant; bar; bike storage; Wi-Fi in restaurant. *In room:* A/C, TV, hair dryer.

Le Grand Lodge ★★ (Kids)

At a quiet distance from the main resort's frequent clamor, this handsome hotel, which consists mostly of suites, is on the bank of Lake Ouimet and draws families, small conventions, and weddings. It was built in 1998 with the palatial log construction of the north country and units leave little to be desired—what with full kitchens, gas fireplaces, and balconies. Dog sledding directly from the hotel and snowshoeing flesh out the more obvious winter pursuits (i.e., skiing), and, in summer, guests partake in tennis, mountain biking, and canoeing and kayaking on the lake. There are events for kids every night in the height of the summer and winter ski seasons. A big bar area overlooks the lake, and inside you'll find what the hotel claims is Mont-Tremblant's largest pool. Like it enough and you can buy one of the condos in the complex.

2396 rue Labelle (Rte. 327), Mont-Tremblant, PQ J8E 1T8. © **800/567-6763** or 819/425-2734. Fax 819/425-9725. www.legrandlodge.com. 112 units. C$120–C$200 (£60–£100) studio or suite. Children 17 and younger stay free in parent's room. Packages available. AE, DC, DISC, MC, V. Free self-parking; valet parking C$10 (£5). Pets accepted, C$25 (£13) additional per night. **Amenities:** Restaurant; bar; 20m (66-ft.) indoor pool; 2 tennis courts; easy access to golf; exercise room; spa; Jacuzzi; sauna; watersports equipment; children's programs and arcade room; concierge; babysitting. *In room:* A/C, TV, free Wi-Fi, kitchen, hair dryer.

Quintessence ★★★

This is the region's luxury property. Go assuming that virtually every service you might find in a much larger deluxe hotel will be available to you—then concentrate on the extras. The hugely comfortable beds have 10cm-thick (4-in.) feather mattress covers. Bathroom floors are heated, showers are of the drenching rainforest variety, and every unit has a wood-burning fireplace and balcony. All suites have views of Lake Tremblant, and if it's warm, you can book a picnic and a ride on the hotel's gorgeous 1910 mahogany powerboat. There's an outdoor infinity pool, and a spa that limits the number of guests to ensure an unhurried atmosphere. Lavish dinners can include wine from the 18m-long (60-ft.), 5,000-bottle wine cellar, taken in the 80-seat dining room

Mont-Tremblant's Pedestrian Village

The pedestrian-only resort village (see www.tremblant.ca/village) on Mont-Tremblant's slope is the social hub of winter (and, increasingly, summer) tourism in the Laurentians. From the bottom of the village near the parking lots and bus shuttle, small lanes lead up past clothing shops and more than three dozen restaurants and bars. Along the paths and spread off in all directions are hotels, several of which are described in this chapter.

The village has the prefabricated look of a theme park, but at least planners used the Québécois architectural style of pitched or mansard roofs in bright colors, not ersatz Tyrolean or Bavarian Alpine flourishes. For a sweeping view, take the free gondola from the bottom of the village to the top; it zips over the walkways, candy-colored hotels, and outdoor swimming pools.

Year-round, the village hosts outdoor concerts and barbecues and events like the goofy spring Caribou "Splash" Cup, where skiers dress in Halloween costumes, ski down an alpine trail into a pool of cold water, then run through the village, stopping for shooters and a full glass of beer. Dude!

The resort is owned by Intrawest, a real-estate giant headquartered in Vancouver. The company plans to add two additional villages, a conference center, and 1,200 housing units to the resort within the next 10 years.

Make reservations for lodgings in the resort by contacting the establishments directly, through a central number (© **888/738-1777**), or online at www.tremblant.ca. There are options, too, to rent fully equipped condos and single-family residences.

La Quintessence, the intimate Jardin des Saveurs, or outdoors near the pool. Nature lovers should consider booking the rustic cabin, which comes with a brick fireplace and a four-poster bed.

3004 Chemin de la Chapelle, Mont-Tremblant, PQ J8E 1E1. © **866/425-3400** or 819/425-3400. Fax 819/425-3480. www.hotelquintessence.com. 31 units. Late June to early Sept C$371–C$1,685 (£186–£842) suite. Rates include breakfast. Weekends require a 2-night minimum stay. Children 5 and younger stay free in parent's room. Packages available. AE, MC, V. Valet parking C$12 (£6). **Amenities:** Restaurant; bar; heated outdoor pool and hot tub; health club w/sauna and steam rooms; spa; concierge; room service; babysitting; private shoreline; 1910 mahogany powerboat. *In room:* A/C, TV (upon request), CD player, Wi-Fi, high-speed Internet access, minibar, hair dryer.

Wyndham Cap Tremblant ★   The Wyndham is a sprawl of handsome condos, both residential and rental, built high into a mountainside with terrific views of Mont-Tremblant, Lake Mercier below, and distances far into the horizon. Units were built in the last few years and rentals suites have one to five bedrooms and all the amenities needed for an extended stay: a kitchen, a fireplace, a washer and dryer, a private balcony with a barbecue in summer, and a locker for skis or golf clubs. Outdoor pools include one with a long slide that's popular with kids. The resort's restaurant, **Il Pinnacolo,** is surprisingly good. It's housed in a building at the top of the mountain along with the reception desk, a steep walk from the condos. (The driving isn't easy, either.) There's a shuttle bus to the ski mountain. This is a fine choice if you're looking to be tucked away and left on your own.

400 rue du Mont-Plaisant, Mont-Tremblant, QC J8E 1L2. © **888/996-3227** or 819/681-8043. Fax 819/681-8086. www.wyndham.com. 170 units. From C$161 (£82) suite. Packages available. AE, DC, MC, V. Up the hill from the old village of Mont-Tremblant, off Chemin du Village. **Amenities:** Restaurant; bar; outdoor pools in summer; 3 tennis courts; exercise room; hot tubs; concierge; trails for hiking and cross-country skiing. *In room:* A/C, TV/DVD, CD player, free Wi-Fi, kitchen, hair dryer, washer/dryer.

Where to Dine

Though most Laurentian inns and resorts have their own dining facilities and often require that guests use them (especially in winter), the area does have some good independent dining options for casual lunches or the odd night out. Also keep in mind **La Quintessence** in Quintessence (p. 187), **Le Bernardin** in Hôtel Mont-Tremblant (p. 187), and **Il Pinnacolo** in the Wyndham Cap Tremblant (p. 188).

For coffee and sandwiches, **Au Grain de Café** (© **819/681-4567;** www.augrain decafe.com), tucked into a corner of the upper pedestrian village just off Place St-Bernard, is a favorite. It's open daily from 7:30am until 11pm during ski season, 6pm during the rest of the year.

Antipasto ITALIAN Antipasto is housed in an old train station in Centre-Ville Mont-Tremblant. So there's the expected railroad memorabilia on the walls, but the owners have resisted the temptation to play up the theme to excess. Captain's chairs are drawn up to big tables with green Formica tops. The César salad (their spelling) is dense and strongly flavored—the half portion is more than enough as a first course. Individual pizzas are cooked in brick ovens with an enormous range of toppings, including scallops and crabmeat, on a choice of regular or whole-wheat crust; pastas are available in even greater variety. There are outdoor tables in summer.

855 rue de St-Jovite (in Centre-Ville Mont-Tremblant). © **819/425-7580.** Main courses C$11–C$36 (£5.50–£18). AE, MC, V. Daily 11am–10pm.

Aux Truffes ★ FRENCH CONTEMPORARY The management and kitchen here are more ambitious than just about any on the mountain, evidenced by a wine cellar that sails through Canadian, Californian, Argentine, Australian, Spanish, and many admirable French bottlings, up to a Château Latour [']86 for C$900 (£450). (In 2007, *Wine Spectator* magazine gave Aux Truffes its award of excellence for its wine list.) Put yourself in the hands of the knowledgeable sommelier and go from there. Imaginative mains include ostrich in a chai-green-tea rub and smoked wild boar with nutmeg and molasses sauce. Close with selections from the *plateau* of raw-milk Québec cheeses.

Place Saint-Bernard, 3035 Chemin de la Chapelle (in the pedestrian village). © **819/681-4544.** www. auxtruffes.com. Main courses C$32–C$46 (£16–£23). AE, MC, V. Daily 6–10pm.

Le Cheval de Jade FRENCH Chef Oliver Tali is what is known in the culinary world as a maître canardier, or master chef, in the preparation of duck. In fact, there is only one maître canardier in all of Canada recognized by France's *l'ordre des canardiers,* and he's the one. Normally, that would mean that there's really only one choice: the house specialty, duckling *à la rouennaise.* But, surprise: The bouillabaisse is also a standout. This is a modest-looking roadside restaurant in Centre-Ville Mont-Tremblant with a dozen tables and country decor. If you're interested in having the duck, you have to call in advance to make a special reservation.

688 rue de St-Jovite (in Centre-Ville Mont-Tremblant). © **819/425-5233.** www.chevaldejade.com. Reservations recommended. Main courses C$28–C$35 (£14–£18); *table d'hôte* from C$36 (£18); 7-course gastronomic menu for 2 C$176 (£88). AE, MC, V. Tues–Sat 5:30–10pm.

Patrick Bermand ★ FRENCH/SEAFOOD   If you cherish seafood and have been disappointed by the paucity of finned offerings in the pedestrian village, make dinner reservations here on a Friday or Saturday night. Other nights, it's still a marked improvement over other eateries in Tremblant. Appetizers are especially satisfying and have included garlicky, buttery escargot served in individual ceramic pots, and cool chunks of tuna rolled in black sesame seeds accompanied by cold sesame noodles. Main courses are good, too, and large—a lot of leftovers leave the building. Opened in 2003 in a roadside log-cabin-style house, the restaurant is in Mont-Tremblant's old village, a short drive from the base of the ski mountain.

2176 Chemin du Village (Rte. 327 in the old village). ℂ **819/425-6333.** www.patrickbermand.com. Main courses C$25–C$40 (£13–£20); *table d'hôte* from C$25 (£13). AE, MC, V. Daily 5–10pm; sometimes closed Mon in off season.

---

2 CANTONS-DE-L'EST

20–160km (12–99 miles) SE of Montréal, toward Sherbrooke

The rolling countryside of Cantons-de-l'Est has long served as Québec province's breadbasket. Still referred to by most Anglophones as the **Eastern Townships** (and, less frequently, as Estrie), the region is largely pastoral, marked by billowing hills, small villages, a smattering of vineyards, and the 792m (2,598-ft.) peak of Mont-Orford, the centerpiece of a provincial park. Cantons-de-l'Est's southern edge borders Vermont, New Hampshire, and Maine, and just past the Knowlton exit, at Km 100, there's an especially beguiling vista of the Appalachian Mountains that stretches toward New England, not far over the horizon.

Sherbrooke is the gritty, industrial capital at the center of the region, but the highlights noted below are located before you reach it, in an upside-down triangle approximately bordered by the villages of **Bromont** and **North Hatley** in the north (with 62km/38 miles between them) and **Dunham** in the south.

Serene glacial lakes attract summer swimmers, boaters, and fishers. Bicyclists zip along rural roads, passing day-trippers touring the region's grape and apple orchards (for wine and cider, natch). Except for a few disheartening signs for fast-food stops, the region is largely advertisement-free.

In winter, skiers who don't head north to the Laurentians come this direction; the Ski Bromont center (p. 194), just 45 minutes from Montréal, offers 50 illuminated trails for night skiing. (Fun fact: In 1922, Armand Bombardier, who was born near Sherbrooke, invented the prototype for the Ski-Doo, the first snowmobile, to get through the region's unplowed rural roads.)

The Cantons-de-l'Est kick into another gear when spring warmth thaws the ground; crews penetrate every sugar-maple stand to tap the sap and "sugar off." The result? Maple festivals and farms hosting sugaring parties, with guests wolfing down prodigious country repasts capped by traditional maple-syrup desserts. Montréal newspapers and local tourist offices (p. 24) keep up-to-date lists of what's happening and where during the sugaring; most spots are within an hour's drive from the city.

Autumn has its special attractions, too. In addition to the glorious fall foliage (usually best from early Sept until early Oct), the orchards around here sag under the weight of apples of every variety, and cider mills hum day and night to produce Québec's "wine." Particularly special are the ice-cider aperitifs produced by vineyards such as Domaine

Pinnacle (p. 195) from apples that have frosted over. Visitors are invited to help with the harvest and can pay a low price to pick their own baskets of fruit. Cider mills open their doors for tours and tastings.

English town names such as Granby, Sutton, and Sherbrooke are vestiges of the time when Americans loyal to the Crown migrated here during and shortly after the Revolutionary War. Now, however, the population of Cantons-de-l'Est is about 90% French-speaking, with a name to reflect that demographic. A few words of French and a little sign language are sometimes necessary outside hotels and other tourist facilities, since the area draws fewer Anglophone visitors than do the Laurentides.

Best of all for tourists, the Cantons are one of Québec's best-kept secrets: It's mostly Québécois who occupy rental houses here. Follow their lead. For extended stays, consider making your base in one of the several luxury inns along the shores of Lac Massawippi and take day trips from there.

ESSENTIALS
Getting There
BY CAR   Leave Montréal by Pont Champlain, a bridge which funnels into arrow-straight Autoroute 10. Go east toward Sherbrooke, and within 30 minutes, you'll be passing silos and fields, clusters of cows, and meadows strewn with wildflowers. The exit numbers represent the distance in kilometers that the exit is from Montréal.

BY BUS   Limocar (which is actually a bus service) offers about 10 trips a day from Montréal through Cantons-de-l'Est as far north as Sherbrooke. Most of the trips are express, while some make stops at Granby, Bromont, Magog, and other towns. Call © 866/692-8899 or visit www.limocar.ca for schedules and prices.

Visitor Information
Tourisme Cantons-de-l'Est (© 800/355-5755; fax 819/566-4445; www.cantonsdelest. com) provides a slew of information, including updates regarding special packages and promotions.

Driving from Montréal, the first regional **tourist information office** (© 866/472-6292; www.granby-bromont.com) is at exit 68 off Autoroute 10. It's open Monday through Friday 8:30am to 4:30pm and Saturday and Sunday 9am to 5pm (shorter hours in winter).

Telephone area codes in Cantons-de-l'Est are 450 and 819, depending on where you're calling. Towns with a 450 area code are closer to Montréal.

GRANBY
About an hour out of Montréal, north of Autoroute 10 at exit 68, this largely unassuming city (pop. 58,390) offers a few fun activities for children.

First is the **Zoo de Granby,** 525 rue St-Hubert (© 877/472-6299 or 450/372-9113; www.zoodegranby.ca). Take exit 68 (or, if you're coming from the east, exit 74) off Autoroute 10 and follow the signs. Two roller coasters were added in 2008, and other recent additions include a hippo's river, an outside gorilla park, a "Mayan temple" with jaguars and spectacled bears, a lemur's island, and a tiger's habitat, which can be toured by elevated train. There is also a shark petting area (called a "touch tank" and overseen by an educator), bumper cars, and a Ferris wheel. There's also a water park with a massive wave pool. The zoo is open daily June through early September and weekends through mid-October, from 10am to 7pm in peak summer months and until 5pm the rest of the season. Admission is C$30 (£15) for 13 and older, C$24 (£12) for 65 and older,

C$19.50 (£9.75) for children 3 to 12, and free for 2 and younger. The fee includes entry to both the zoo and the water park.

Granby is also home to **Parc de la Yamaska** (© 800/665-6527; www.sepaq.com), with the longest beach in the area, and opportunities for such activities as swimming, canoeing, hiking, and biking. This is the northern part of the Appalachian mountain range, and it's lush and verdant in summer.

MONT-ORFORD

Also on the north side of Autoroute 10 is one of Québec's most popular provincial parks. From mid-September to mid-October, **Parc du Mont-Orford** (© 800/665-6527 or **819/843-9855;** www.sepaq.com/pq/mor/en) blazes with autumnal color. Visitors come to try the 18-hole golf course and the 80km (50 miles) of short and long hiking trails in summer; the Route Verte cycling network also passes through the park. In winter, people flock to the slopes to ski, snowboard, or traverse the network of cross-country ski and snowshoe trails. From Autoroute 10, take exit 118 north.

The mountain itself, Mont-Orford, is a veteran ski area. It has long provided the preferred slopes of local moneyed families.

The resort is composed of contiguous Mont-Giroux, Mont-Desrochers, and Mont-Orford, which is one of the three highest peaks in Québec. Combined, the mountains provide four faces with seven lifts and 56 trails. Information is at © **866/673-6731** and www.orford.com.

The area's other ski resorts—**Owl's Head** (© 800/363-3342; www.owlshead.com) and **Mont-Sutton** (© 866/538-2545; www.montsutton.com)—are more family-oriented and less glitzy.

Orford has another claim to fame in the warm months: **Centre d'Arts Orford,** 3165 Chemin du Parc (© 800/567-6155 or 819/843-3981; www.arts-orford.org), is a world-class music academy set on an 89-hectare (222-acre) estate. From late June to mid-August each year, the **Festival Orford** presents a series of classical and chamber music concerts. Most tickets are C$35 (£18) for professional concerts, with student ("rising-star") performances for just C$5 (£2.50). Concert and dinner packages are available. The center also has an **auberge** with rooms starting at C$36 (£18). It's also off exit 118 north from Autoroute 10.

Where to Stay

Manoir des Sables ★★ This contemporary facility is one of the region's most complete resort hotels, serving couples, families, golfers, skiers, skaters, fitness enthusiasts, tennis players, kayakers, and business groups. They enjoy snowshoeing trails, snowmobiling, toboggan rides, and Saturday-night horse-drawn sleigh rides in winter, and tube slides and fishing in the hotel's lake in summer. An 18-hole expert golf course and 9-hole, par-3 executive course are both on-site, as is a spa offering algae wraps, "pressotherapy" detoxification, and more. Bedrooms have all big-city gadgets and niceties, which is to be expected, since the hotel began life as a Sheraton. About a third of the rooms have fireplaces. The newer Château section contains 24 upscale suites and its own lounge. A huge number of packages allow guests to pick and choose amenities and the cost of their trip in advance.

90 av. des Jardins, Orford, PQ J1X 6M6. © **800/567-3514** or 819/847-4747. Fax 819/847-3519. www. manoirdessables.com. 141 units. C$178 (£89) and up double. Children 16 and younger stay free in parent's room. AE, DC, MC, V. Packages and meal plans available. Take exit 118 from Autoroute 10 and follow Rte. 141 north to the hotel, on the right. **Amenities:** 2 restaurants; bar; indoor and outdoor pools; 27-hole golf course; tennis courts; health club; spa; bike rental; children's programs; room service; babysitting. *In room:* A/C, TV, free Wi-Fi, hair dryer.

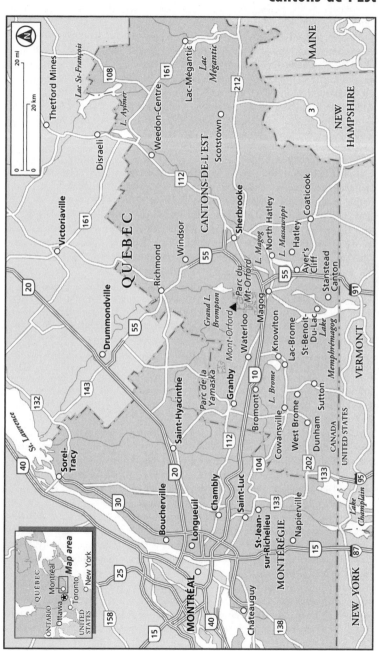

The rest of the towns and attractions in this chapter are all on the southern side of Autoroute 10. Medium-size country roads connect many of them.

Founded in 1964 primarily to accommodate an industrial park and other commercial enterprises, this town of 6,049 at exit 78 is now a popular destination for **Ski Bromont** (*©* **866/276-6668;** www.skibromont.com). In winter, the mountain offers day and night skiing. In summer, it has mountain biking (rent bikes at the town's entrance, opposite the tourist office), hiking, and the Ski Bromont Water Park.

Bromont is also home to the area's largest **flea market** *(marché aux puces),* with more than 1,000 vendors set up in the local drive-in from 9am to 5pm weekends from April to October. It's at 16 rue Lafontaine (*©* **450/534-0440**).

Where to Stay & Dine

Château Bromont ★ Kids A landscaped panoramic terrace looks up at the ski mountain across the way, giving this valley hotel a most attractive setting. It sits adjacent to the Royal Bromont golf course, making this a particularly choice spot for a golf getaway. The hotel coordinates packages with horseback riding or a day at the Granby Zoo (p. 191), making this also a good choice for families. For those who just want to relax, an on-site spa features mud and algae baths, a Turkish hammam (sauna), and a restaurant that serves healthy lunches. About a quarter of the rooms have fireplaces. The interior decor gets a trifle gaudy here and there, but it's not jarring.

90 rue Stanstead, Bromont, PQ J2L 1K6. *©* **800/304-3433** or 450/534-3433. Fax 450/534-0514. www. chateaubromont.com. 160 units. From C$149 (£75) double. Rates include breakfast. Some dates require 2-night minimum stay. Packages available. AE, MC, V. **Amenities:** 2 restaurants; bar; heated indoor and outdoor pools; golf; racquetball court; exercise room; hot tubs; spa; babysitting. *In room:* A/C, TV, Wi-Fi, minibar, hair dryer.

KNOWLTON & WEST BROME

For a good confluence of countryside, cafes, and antiquing, head to the town of Knowlton, at Brome Lake's southeast corner; it's part of the seven-village municipality known as **Lac Brome** (pop. 5,078). From Autoroute 10, take exit 90, heading south on Route 243 toward Lac Brome.

In the summer season, the Lac Brome **tourist center** is open on Route 243 shortly after you've left Autoroute 10. Knowlton is about 8km (5 miles) past the tourist center, and you'll hug the lake's eastern side for most of the trip. (Be careful: Bikers share the road with nary a shoulder to fall back on.) There is a public parking area and a lake beach, **Plage Douglass,** about 5km (3 miles) into the route, just before Knowlton. You can park to take a dip or do some easy lakeside hiking.

Knowlton is compact, but its two main shopping streets (Lakeside and Knowlton) have about three dozen boutiques and antiques stores that reveal the creeping chic influence of refugees from Montréal. Stores sell toys, gourmet items, quilts, jewelry, pottery, chocolate, and clothing. One shop sells outdoor gear and whimsically refers to itself as "L.L. Brome."

Knowlton is one of the last towns in the region where a slim majority of the residents keep English as their mother tongue. Paul Holland Knowlton, a Loyalist from Vermont, settled here in the early 1800s, establishing a farm, general store, and sawmill. He was a member of Parliament for Lower Canada from 1830 to 1834.

(Finds) **Cantons-de-l'Est:**
Wine (& *Cidre de Glace*) Country

Canada is generally known more for its beers and ales than its wines, but that hasn't stopped agriculturists from planting vines and transforming the fruit into drinkable clarets, chardonnays, and sauternes. So far, the most successful efforts have blossomed along southern Ontario's Niagara Frontier and in British Columbia's relatively warmer precincts.

Cantons-de-l'Est enjoys the mildest microclimates in the province, and where apples grow, as they do in these parts, so will other fruits, including grapes. Most vintners and fruit-growers are concentrated around **Dunham,** about 103km (64 miles) southeast of Montréal, with several vineyards along Route 202. A stop for a snack or a facility tour makes for a pleasant afternoon. If you're really gung-ho, follow the established **Route des Vins,** which passes 16 vintners (find the map at www.laroutedesvins.ca).

One of the vineyards on the route is Vignoble de l'Orpailleur, at 1086 Rte. 202 in Dunham (© **450/295-2763;** www.orpailleur.ca). It has four guided tours per day from June through October for C$5 (£2.50). Its white wines, such as L'Orpailleur Classique, are popular on Montréal restaurant menus.

Ice cider and ice wine are two regional products that may be new to visitors: They're made from apples and grapes, respectively, left on the trees and vines past the first frost, and served ice-cold with foie gras, cheese, or dessert. One top producer is **Domaine Pinnacle,** at 150 Richford Rd. in Frelighsburg (© **450/298-1222;** www.icecider.com), about 13 km (8 miles) south of Dunham. Its *cidre de glace* is a regular gold medalist in international competitions: It's delightfully smooth and not cloyingly sweet. The farm's tasting room and boutique are open daily from 10am to 5pm May through December.

Other credible wines come out of **Le Cep d'Argent,** at 1257 Chemin de la Rivière in Magog (© **819/864-4441;** www.cepdargent.com). Many of the vintages produced here are also prizewinners, including the dry white Le Cep d'Argent and the maple-tinged dessert wine L'Archer. There are several tour options, including a "privilege tour" of the champagne cellar that describes the méthode champenoise and includes tastings of six wines with regional products. Cost is C$15 (£7.50) for the 90-minute exploration. Reservations are required.

The major local sight is **Musée Historique du Comté de Brome (Brome County Historical Museum)** at 130 rue Lakeside (Rte. 243; © **450/243-6782).** It occupies five historic buildings, including the town's first school. Exhibits focus on various aspects of town life, with re-creations of a general store and courthouse. The Martin Annex (1921) is dominated by a 1917 Fokker single-seat biplane, the foremost German aircraft in World War I. Also on the premises are collections of old radios and 18th- to early-20th-century weapons. The museum sells books about the area. Admission is C$5 (£2.50) adults, C$3 (£1.50) seniors, and C$2.50 (£1.25) children. It's open mid-May through

Biking the Cantons-de-l'Est: Easy on, Easy Off

The Québec province's new **Route Verte (Green Route),** a 4,000km (2,485-mile) bike network (www.routeverte.com), stretches southeast into the Cantons-de-l'Est on a new 200km (124-mile) circuit called **Véloroute des Cantons** (© **800/ 355-5755;** www.cantonsdelest.com/velo).

The website offers details about where to find picnic areas, restaurants, and bathrooms near the trail; maps; and lists parking areas, bike rental and repair shops, and accommodations catering to cyclists. Day-tripping is easy, but all-inclusive 3- and 4-day bike tours are available for beginners and more advanced bikers. Find current programs on the website by clicking on the "Cycling planners" tab.

mid-September Monday to Saturday 10am to 5pm, Sunday 11am to 5pm. Allow about an hour.

For a quick snack, the funky, barnlike **Station Knowlton Country Store** at 7 Mount Echo Rd. (© **450/242-5862;** www.stationknowlton.com) sells fruit smoothies and healthy sandwiches for less than C$5 (£2.50). You can also buy a variety of handmade soaps and pick up free copies of the English-language paper *The Townships Outlet,* whose tagline is "Linking the Eastern Townships' 41,000-member English-speaking community."

Where to Stay & Dine

Auberge Lakeview The core structure of this Victorian inn dates from 1874, and a 19th-century flavor has been sustained through many renovations. Leather chairs are arranged around the fireplace in the lobby, tin ceilings prevail, and much of the furniture was crafted in Québec country style. The bedrooms come in several categories of relative comfort—if you go for the best ("Deluxe Studio," C$462/£231 in high season), you get access to a veranda, a heart-shaped whirlpool bathtub, and a sitting area. Since rates include dinner in the dining room, this is the place to sample the area's gourmet treat, Lake Brome duck. The auberge is about a half km (about a third of a mile) from downtown Knowlton and its many boutiques and antiques shops.

50 rue Victoria, Knowlton (Lac Brome), PQ J0E 1V0. © **800/661-6183** or 450/243-6183. Fax 450/243-0602. www.aubergelakeviewinn.com. 28 units. May–Dec C$312–C$462 (£156–£231) double; about C$40 (£20) less off season. Rates include dinner, breakfast, and gratuities for 2. Packages available. AE, MC, V. **Amenities:** Restaurant; bar; heated outdoor pool. *In room:* A/C, TV, dial-up Internet, hair dryer.

Auberge & Spa West Brome Out in the country, beyond town limits, this quiet property is made up of a grouping of creamy-yellow buildings amid rolling hills. A 1898 farmhouse at the roadside contains the reception desk and restaurant. About 90m (295 ft.) back are more modern structures, where the bedrooms are. A spa with therapeutic baths, massage rooms, and pedicure chairs was added in 2005. Rooms are in three categories: Classic, on the small side but not cramped; Deluxe, with full kitchens, fireplaces, and decks; and Suite, which can accommodate four. The complex is close to the Route des Vins (www.laroutedesvins.ca; p. 195), with many of the vineyards near Dunham. The auberge recycles 80% of all glass, metal, and paper items; uses only recycled-paper

(Moments) Maple Heaven in Cabanes à Sucre

For a purely Québec experience that shouldn't be missed, get yourself to a sugar shack. Called *cabanes à sucre* or *érablières* in French, they were once places that merely processed sap from maple trees. When producers realized that they were drawing large audiences, some began offering wider experiences to keep the customers reaching for their wallets, putting in bars and dining rooms where bountiful spreads of simple country food are served at long communal tables. Some even put in dance floors and booked live entertainment.

Originally open only during sugaring-off season, roughly February through April, a few now stay open much longer, even all year. There are hundreds across the province, with small directional signs often positioned at roadsides or on highways.

At most shacks, you can see the rendering room, where sap gathered from maple-tree taps is boiled in a trough called an evaporator, then cooked further on a stove. After that, the syrup is filtered and poured into cans or bottles.

You can often get your taste at the long, narrow tray of snow that has a wiggly stream of syrup pouring down the middle. This forms a sort of maple taffy, which is rolled up onto popsicle sticks for lollipop-like eating.

At the restaurants, there usually isn't a menu. If there's not a buffet, just sit down at a table and food will start coming. Thick pea soup is standard, as are baked beans, loaves of fragrant bread, sausages, ham slices, home fries, coleslaw, and stacks of pancakes. At the ready are preserves, pickles, and all the maple syrup you can ingest. Total cost rarely exceeds C$25 (£13).

Signature products are available in a variety of sizes and forms, primarily syrup and candy. Some folks consider the best syrup to be the clearer and lighter Grade A from the first run of sap, while others prefer the darker, denser Grade B from later in the season.

products and compact fluorescent light bulbs; and bans fertilizers and pesticides from its gardens and lawns.

128 Rte. 139, West Brome, PQ J0E 2P0. (℃) **888/902-7663** or 450/266-7552. Fax 450/266-2040. www.awb. ca. 26 units. C$165–C$215 (£83–£108) double; suites from C$215 (£108). Rates include full breakfast. Packages available. 2-night minimum stay during peak summer months. AE, MC, V. **Amenities:** Restaurant; bar; heated outdoor pool and hot tub; fitness room; spa. *In room:* A/C, TV, dial-up Internet, hair dryer.

MAGOG & LAC MEMPHREMAGOG

As with countless other North American town names, Magog (pop. 23,540) came by its handle through corruption of a Native Canadian word. The Abenaki name *Memrobagak* ("great expanse of water") somehow became Memphrémagog, which was eventually shortened to Magog (pronounced *May*-gog).

> ## (Fun Facts   Québec's Own Nessies?
>
> Lac Memphrémagog is known locally for more than just its annual international swimming marathon: Eagle eyes scan the ripples for **Memphre** (pronounced Mem-*phree*), the lake's legendary sea creature. Like the Loch Ness monster, which was first spotted in the Scottish waters in the year 565, Memphre supposedly surfaced for the first time in 1798 but left no hard evidence. Other sightings, it will come as no surprise, have been claimed since then.
>
> Locals in North Hatley whisper about a creature of their own in Lake Massawippi, whom they have dubbed **Wippi.** Like Loch Ness, Lake Massawippi has pockets that go very deep—up to 150m (500 ft.) in some spots. Unlike Loch Ness, however, neither Memphrémagog nor Massawippi has been subjected to teams of scientists bouncing sonar signals to search out the water's depths. Memphre and Wippi are free to surface and retreat again in peace.

Confusingly, the town of Magog is not adjacent to Lac Magog, which is about 13km (8 miles) north. Instead, it's positioned at the northernmost end of the large, long Lac Memphrémagog (pronounced Mem-*phree*-may-gog), which spills across the U.S.-Canadian border into Vermont on its southern end.

The helpful **Bureau d'Information Touristique Memphrémagog** (© 800/267-2744 or 819/843-2744; www.tourisme-memphremagog.com), at 55 rue Cabana (via Rte. 112), in Magog, is open daily 8:30am to 7pm in summer, and 9am to 5pm the rest of the year.

Magog has a fully utilized waterfront, and in late July to early August each year, the **Lac Memphrémagog International Swimming Marathon** (© 818/847-3007; www.traversee-memphremagog.com) creates a big splash. From 1979 until 2003, competitors started out in Newport, Vermont, at 6am and swam 42km (26 miles) to Magog, arriving in midafternoon. Since 2004, the event has become a 34km (21-mile) race, beginning and ending in Magog.

To experience the lake without such soggy exertion, board a boat. Croisière Memphrémagog (© 819/843-8068; www.croisiere-memphremagog.com) offers lake cruises; one option is a 2½-hour trip to Abbaye-Saint-Benoît-du-Lac (see below). Boats leave from Point Merry Park, the focal point for many of the town's outdoor activities. Cruises off season depend upon demand; call for times and prices.

Several firms rent sailboats, motorboats, kayaks, and windsurfers, including **Marina Le Merry Club,** 201 rue Merry sud (© 819/843-2728; www.lemerryclub.com).

Abbaye de Saint-Benoît-du-Lac   There's no mistaking the abbey, with its granite steeple that thrusts into the sky above Lac Memphrémagog's western shore. Although Saint-Benoît-du-Lac dates only from 1912, its serenity is timeless. Some 50 monks live here largely in silence, keeping the art of Gregorian chant alive in their liturgy, which can be attended by outsiders. For the 45-minute service, walk to the rear of the abbey and down the stairs; follow signs for the *oratoire* and sit in back to avoid the otherwise obligatory standing and sitting during the service.

A blue cheese known as L'Ermite, among Québec's most famous, is produced here, along with a creamy version and Swiss and cheddar cheeses. They are on sale in a little shop, which also sells honey, books, tapes of religious chants, and a nonalcoholic cider produced from fruit from the property's orchard. Visitors that come mid-September to mid-October may want to help pick apples. And be sure to peek into the tiny stone chapel to the left of the property's entrance, opposite the small cemetery.

The abbey maintains **hostels** for men and women (*©* **819/843-4080** for men, *©* **819/843-2340** for women) who are seeking a quiet retreat and spiritual reflection. Suggested donation is C$40 (£20) per person for room and board. Room reservations must be made in advance by phone.

Saint-Benoît-du-Lac. *©* **819/843-4080.** www.st-benoit-du-lac.com. Free admission; donations accepted. Daily 5am–9pm; Mass with Gregorian chant daily at 11am; vespers with Gregorian chant at 5pm (7pm Thurs). No vespers Tues July–Aug. Shop: Mon–Sat 9–10:45am and 11:45am–4:30pm (until 6pm July–Aug). Exit 106 from Autoroute 10, Rte. 245 south to Bolton center, left on Nicolas Austin Rd. to village of Austin, follow signs 2km (1¼ mile) to lake and abbey.

Where to Stay

There are a number of modest B&Bs and small hotels along the blocks of rue Merry, immediately north and south of its intersection with the main street, rue Principale. Many are listed with Tourisme Cantons-de-l'Est (*©* **800/355-5755;** fax 819/566-4445; www.cantonsdelest.com). Also consider the hostels at the **Abbaye de Saint-Benoît-du-Lac,** described above. Otherwise, look for accommodations in one of the nearby towns described in this section.

LAKE MASSAWIPPI

Set among rolling hills and fertile farm country, 19km-long (12-mile) Lake Massawippi, with its scalloped shoreline, is easily Cantons-de-l'Est's most desirable resort area. It was settled in the late 19th century by people of wealth and power, including many U.S. Southerners trying to escape their sultry summers (they came up by train and are said to have pulled down their window shades while they crossed through Yankee territory). They built grand estates with verandas and formal gardens on slopes along the lakeshore, with enough bedrooms to house their friends and extended families for months at a time. Several homes have been converted into inns, including the lavish **Auberge Ripplecove & Spa** (p. 200) and **Manoir Hovey** (p. 200). For an escape from intensive travel or work, it's difficult to do better than here.

The jewel of Lake Massawippi (which means "deep water" in Abenaki) is the town of **North Hatley** (pop. 780). Only 148km (92 miles) from Montréal and just 34km (21 miles) from the U.S. border, it has a river meandering through it that empties into the lake. See the impressive sunsets over the lake, try the town's very fine restaurants, take advantage of access to 54km (33 miles) of good bike paths, and partake in a summertime program of Sunday-afternoon band concerts. A full listing of activities is online at www.northhatley.net.

Horse lovers will want to know about **Randonnées J. Robidas** at 32 Chemin McFarland (*©* **888/677-8767** or 819/563-0166; www.randonneesjrobidas.qc.ca). Guides lead trail rides through forest and meadow beside the Massawippi in summer, with rates starting at C$51 (£26) for a 1½-hour ride with two to four people. Buggy and winter sleigh rides are possibilities as well, and there's a discovery farm and nature school on-site.

Where to Stay

The acclaimed gastronomic resort Auberge Hatley burned to the ground in early 2006, and the Groupe Germain, which owned the property, announced later that year that it will not be rebuilding. There are, however, many other lodging options, including the three listed below. These full-service inns won't refuse children, but they have serious dining rooms that can test youngsters' patience. Other meal arrangements should be made for children 12 and younger.

Auberge Ripplecove & Spa ★★★   The staff extends a warm welcome at this handsome inn, and impeccable housekeeping standards are observed throughout. With 4.8 hectares (12 acres) directly on Lake Massawippi's southern end, the auberge is a grand miniresort, with a private beachfront and equipment for sailing, water-skiing, and canoeing. In winter, there is cross-country skiing on the property and, on Saturdays, horse-drawn sleigh rides. The core structure dates from 1945, but subsequent expansions have added well-appointed rooms, suites, cottages, and, in 2003, a spa with a full range of therapies and an outdoor hot tub with a view of the lake. About half the rooms have private balconies and whirlpools. The award-winning lakeside restaurant fills up in season with diners drawn to the kitchen's reputation for creativity. Members of the same family run **Manoir Hovey,** below. At what's nearly Québec province's most southeastern corner, the inn is only 378km (235 miles) from Boston.

700 Chemin Ripplecove, Ayer's Cliff, PQ J0B 1C0. ✆ **800/668-4296** or 819/838-4296. Fax 819/838-5541. www.ripplecove.com. 35 units. Late June to mid-Oct C$316–C$630 (£158–£315) double; rest of the year from C$266 (£133) double. Rates include dinner, breakfast, gratuities for 2, and use of most recreational facilities. AE, MC, V. Exit 121 from Autoroute 10, take Autoroute 55 south to exit 21, then Rte. 141 south 5 min. to Ayer's Cliff; follow signs to auberge. **Amenities:** Restaurant; pub; heated outdoor pool; lit tennis court; exercise room; spa; bikes for guests' use (free); concierge; room service. *In room:* A/C, TV, high-speed Internet, hair dryer.

Le Tricorne   At the end of a long dirt-and-gravel road deep in the countryside, this family-run inn offers spectacular views of Lake Massawippi and the rolling Canadian Appalachians. While the core of the main house is 145 years old, it looks as if it could have been erected only a few years ago—the exterior is dusty rose and white, and the interior is decked out in *Good Housekeeping* manner, with equestrian-print wallpaper and tartans. A newer building 45m (148 ft.) up the hill has five larger bedrooms decorated in a more sophisticated corporate style. With 37 hectares (92 acres), three small ponds, and a heated outdoor pool, this property offers the peace and quiet of being tucked away in the woods. Some units have wood fireplaces, and about half have jet bathtubs.

50 Chemin Gosselin, North Hatley, PQ J0B 2C0. ✆ **819/842-4522.** Fax 819/842-2692. www.manoirle tricorne.com. 17 units. C$125–C$200 (£63–£100) double. Rates include full breakfast. AE, MC, V. From North Hatley, take Rte. 108 west; follow the signs. Bringing children younger than age 9 is discouraged. **Amenities:** Heated outdoor pool. *In room:* A/C, no phone.

Manoir Hovey ★★★   Built in 1898 by the owner of paper manufacturer Georgia Pacific, this lakeside manor house, with its broad veranda and ivy-covered white pillars, was inspired by George Washington's home in Mount Vernon, Virginia. This manor manages to maintain a magical balance of feeling like both a genteel estate for a private getaway and a grand resort for a weekend's pampering; it's a member of the exclusive Relais & Châteaux group. Aristocratic touches include tea and scones in the afternoon, a carefully manicured English garden with fresh herbs (used by cooks in the kitchen), and a massive stone hearth in a library lounge with deep chairs and floor-to-ceiling bookshelves. Sumptuously appointed rooms have touches like Italian bathroom tiles and antique sink basins; all feature high-end bedding and CD players with classical discs. Dinner is included; consider the extraordinary caribou with crystallized foie gras taboule that melts into the meat.

www.manoirhovey.com. 41 units. Late June to mid-Oct and Christmas week C$300–C$590 (£150–£295) double, rest of the year from C$260 (£130) double; suites from C$660 (£330) double. Rates include 3-course dinner, full breakfast, gratuities, and use of most recreational facilities for 2. Packages available. AE, DC, MC, V. From Autoroute 55, exit 29, take Rte. 108 east, follow the signs. **Amenities:** Restaurant; bar; heated outdoor pool; lit tennis court; fitness room; bikes (free to borrow); concierge; room service. *In room:* A/C, TV, free Wi-Fi, hair dryer.

Where to Dine

Café Massawippi ★ FRENCH CONTEMPORARY   It was daring to open a restaurant in the same small town as the multistarred inns described above, but chef-owner Dominic Tremblay has pulled it off. Contained in a small roadside house with a plain, unassuming interior, the true art appears on the plate. Think seared scallops with blackened watermelon, cilantro pesto, and cantaloupe froth, or veal sweetbread with roasted peaches and orange-cardamom tapioca. All evening meals are served as one of three *table d'hôtes,* and served leisurely (plan 2$^1/_2$ hr.).

3050 Chemin Capelton. © **819/842-4528.** www.cafemassawippi.com. Reservations recommended. *Table d'hôte* dinner C$42–C$56 (£21–£26). AE, DC, MC, V. Late May to early Oct daily 6–10pm, with lunch in July–Aug daily 11:30am–3pm; rest of year Wed–Sun 6–10pm.

Pilsen Restaurant & Pub INTERNATIONAL   For food less grand and less expensive than that at the establishments described above, head to Pilsen in the center of North Hatley. Housed in a former horse-carriage manufacturing shop from 1900, the restaurant has a narrow deck with tables over a narrow river, the better to watch boats setting out or returning. The place fills up quickly on warm days with patrons who snaffle renditions of quesadillas, burgers, pastas, and fried calamari, as well as more adventurous fare, such as the Ploughman's Platter with wild game terrine, St-Benoit-du-Lac blue cheese pâté, onion confit, and apples. There's an extensive choice of beers, including local microbrew Massawippi Blonde and the Czech Pilsner Urquel, for which the restaurant was named. Most nights, the bar stays open well past midnight.

55 rue Main. © **819/842-2971.** www.pilsen.ca. Reservations recommended on weekends. Main courses C$10–C$30 (£5–£15). AE, MC, V. Daily 11:30am–10:30pm.

Stanstead & Beebe Plain

For a brief detour on the drive south to Vermont, explore the border villages that compose the town of Stanstead, at the end of Route 143.

Stanstead (pop. 3,162) was settled in the 1790s and, as a border town, became a commercial center for the Québec-Boston stagecoach route. Many of the society homes from the late 1800s have been preserved.

Fans of geographical oddities will want to stop by the **Haskell Opera House** (© **819/ 876-2020;** www.haskellopera.org). Dating from 1904, it's literally and logistically half-Canadian and half-American: The stage and performers are in Canada, while the audience watches from the U.S. Ticket information is at © **802/334-2216** and www.qnek. com.

What makes the township of **Beebe Plain** notable is 1km-long (²/₃-mile) **Canusa Street.** The north side is in Canada, the south side in the U.S.—hence the name, CAN-USA. Check the car license plates on either side. Here, it's long-distance to call a neighbor across the street, and, while folks are free to walk across for a visit, they are expected, at least technically, to report to the authorities if they drive that same distance.

Getting to Know Québec City

Québec City seduces from first view. Situated along the majestic Fleuve Saint-Laurent (St. Lawrence River), much of the oldest part of the city—Vieux-Québec—sits atop Cap Diamant, a rock bluff that once provided military defense. Fortress walls still encase the upper Old City, and the soaring Château Frontenac, a hotel with castlelike turrets, dominates the landscape. Hauntingly evocative of a coastal town in the motherland of France, the tableau is as romantic as any in Europe.

Québec City is, in fact, the soul of New France, and it holds fast to that history. Founded in 1608, 400 years ago, by Samuel de Champlain, it was the first significant settlement in Canada. Major sprucing up took place all over the city in 2007 and 2008 for the 400th-anniversary celebrations, including additional pedestrian-friendly access to the waterfront and a new waterside pavilion called Espace 400e that serves as a Parks Canada discovery center.

The city is almost entirely French in feeling, spirit, and language. Almost everyone—95% of the population—is Francophone, or French speaking. But many of its 622,000 residents do know some English, especially those who work in hotels, restaurants, and shops. Although it's more difficult in Québec City than in Montréal to get by without French, the average Québécois goes out of his or her way to communicate—in halting English, sign language, simplified French, or a combination of all three. Most of the Québécois are uncommonly gracious.

Because of its beauty, history, and unique stature as the only walled city north of Mexico (Campeche), Québec City's historic district was named a UNESCO World Heritage Site in 1985—the only city so designated in North America.

Ile d'Orléans, an agricultural island within sight of Vieux-Québec, is less than 20 minutes from downtown and an easy day or overnight trip. Consider, too, a trip along the St. Lawrence's northern coast past the shrine of Ste-Anne-de-Beaupré (p. 277), the waterfalls near Mont Ste-Anne (p. 278), and on to pastoral Charlevoix (p. 281) and the Saguenay River, where whales come to play.

---

1 ORIENTATION

Almost all of a visit to Québec City can be spent on foot in the old Lower Town, which hugs the river below the bluff, and in the old Upper Town, atop Cap Diamant (Cape Diamond); many accommodations, restaurants, and tourist-oriented services are based in these places.

The colonial city was first built right down by the St. Lawrence; it was here that the earliest merchants, traders, and boatmen earned their livelihoods. Unfriendly fire from the British and Amerindians in the 1700s moved residents to safer houses atop the cliffs that form the rim of the Cap. The tone and atmosphere of the 17th and 18th centuries still suffuse these areas today.

Basse-Ville (Lower Town) became primarily a district of wharves and warehouses. That trend has been reversed, with new auberges (inns), small hotels, and many attractive bistros and shops bringing life to the area—though it maintains the architectural feel of its origins, reusing old buildings and maintaining the narrow cobbled streets.

Haute-Ville (Upper Town) turned out to not be immune to cannon fire either (as the British General James Wolfe proved in 1759 when he took the city from the French). Nevertheless, the division into Upper and Lower towns persisted for obvious topographical reasons. Upper Town remains enclosed by fortification walls, with a cliff-side elevator *(funiculaire)* and several steep streets connecting it to Lower Town.

ARRIVING

BY PLANE **Jean-Lesage International Airport** (airport code YQB; © 418/640-2700; www.aeroportdequebec.com) is small, despite the grand name. Bus service is no longer available between the airport and the city. A taxi to downtown Québec City is a fixed-rate C$30 (£15).

BY TRAIN The handsome train station in Québec City, **Gare du Palais,** 450 rue de la Gare-du-Palais, was designed by architect Bruce Price, who is also responsible for the magnificent Château Frontenac. Its Lower Town location isn't central, though, so plan on a strenuous uphill hike or a cab ride to Upper Town or other areas of Lower Town.

BY BUS The bus terminal, at 320 rue Abraham-Martin (© 418/525-3000), is just beside the train station. As from the train station, it's an uphill climb or short cab ride to Upper Town or other parts of Lower Town.

BY CAR For driving directions to Québec City, see "Getting There & Getting Around," in chapter 3.

VISITOR INFORMATION

There are several tourist information centers. The most central is in Upper Town, across from the Château Frontenac and directly on Place d'Armes. **Centre Infotouriste de Québec,** 12 rue Ste-Anne (© 877/266-5687; www.bonjourquebec.com), is run by Québec province's tourism department and is open from 8:30am to 7:30pm daily from June 21 to early September and from 9am to 5pm daily the rest of the year. It has brochures, a lodging reservation service, a currency-exchange office, and information about tours by foot, bus, or boat.

Also in front of the Château is the independent **Kiosque Frontenac** (© 418/692-5483), which sells tour tickets and exchanges currency. It's open daily from 9am until 8 or 9pm in summer and is in a small kiosk next to the entrance of the cliff-side elevator to Lower Town.

Just outside the Old City walls on Parc des Champs-de-Bataille's northern edge, the **Greater Québec Area Tourism and Convention Bureau** has an information office in the Discovery Pavilion at 835 av. Wilfrid-Laurier (© 877/783-1608 or 418/641-6290; www.quebecregion.com). You'll find rack after rack of brochures, as well as attendants who can answer questions and make hotel reservations. It's open daily 8:30am to 7:30pm from June 24 to Labour Day; 8:30am to 6:30pm Labour Day (the first Monday in September, as in the U.S.) to mid-October; and the rest of the year 9am to 5pm Monday through Saturday, 10am to 4pm Sunday. On the outside, the building is marked with a large, blue question mark.

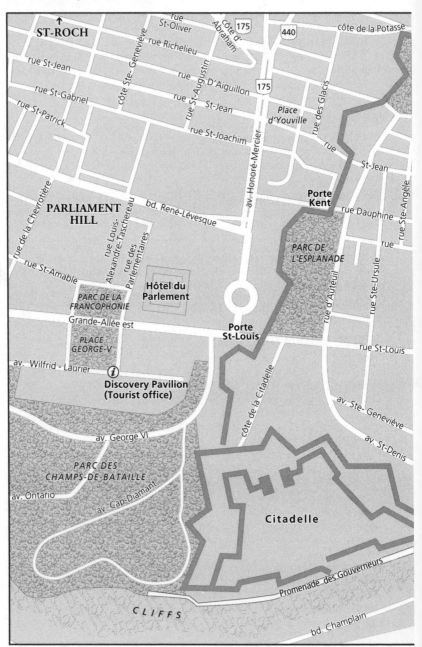

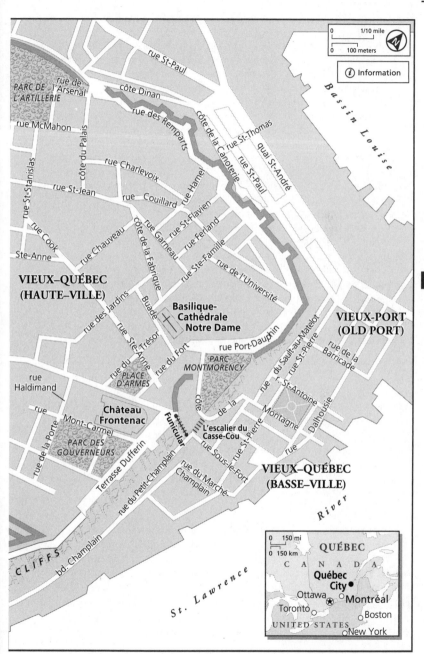

Long May They Wave: The Flags of Canada

With a relatively small population spread over a territory larger than the continental U.S., Canadians' loyalties have always tended to be directed to the cities and regions in which they live, rather than to the nation at large. Part of this comes from the semi-colonial relationship the nation retained with England after the British North America Act made it self-governing in 1867 (Queen Elizabeth II is still on all the currency). The rest comes from the fact that Canada's citizens speak two different major languages. Canadians didn't even have a national anthem until *O, Canada!* was given the honor in 1980.

All this is reflected in the flags. Québécois began asserting themselves and declaring their regional pride after World War II, and officially adopted their "national" flag, the Fleurdelisé, in 1950. It employs blue-and-white crossbars with four fleurs-de-lis (one in each resulting quadrant), and is flown prominently in Québec City.

In 1965, the red-and-white maple leaf version of the Canadian flag was introduced, replacing a previous ensign that featured a Union Jack in the upper-left corner.

In the face of decades of hurt and outright hostilities between French and English Canada, there must be occasional sighs of longing in some quarters for the diplomatic display of the flag of Montréal. Adopted way back in 1832, it has red crossbars on a white background. The resulting quadrants have depictions of a rose, a fleur-de-lis, a thistle, and a shamrock. They stand, respectively, for the founding groups of the new nation—the English, French, Scots, and Irish.

From early June to Labour Day, the tourist office's student staff pilot motor scooters through the tourist districts of Upper and Lower towns, making themselves available for questions; they're also in force on foot during the Winter Carnival season. In French, they're called the *service mobile,* and their blue mopeds bear flags with a large question mark. Just hail them as they approach; they're bilingual.

When you're driving in or near the city, tune into 89.7 FM on your radio. It's the city's tourism station, and it provides a continual update of current events along with evergreen information about the city.

CITY LAYOUT

MAIN AVENUES & STREETS   Within the walls of Haute-Ville (Upper Town), the principal streets are **rues St-Louis** (which becomes **Grande-Allée** outside the city walls), **Ste-Anne,** and **St-Jean.** In Basse-Ville (Lower Town), major streets are **St-Pierre, Dalhousie, St-Paul,** and, parallel to St-Paul, **St-André.** Useful maps of Upper and Lower towns and the metropolitan area are available at any tourist office (see above).

FINDING AN ADDRESS   If it were larger, the historic district's winding and plunging streets might be confusing to negotiate. However, it's very compact. Most streets are only a few blocks long, making it fairly easy to find a specific address.

THE NEIGHBORHOODS IN BRIEF

Vieux-Québec: Haute-Ville Old Québec's Upper Town, surrounded by thick ramparts, occupies the crest of Cap Diamant and overlooks the Fleuve Saint-Laurent (St. Lawrence River). It includes many of the sites for which the city is famous, among them the **Château Frontenac, Place d'Armes,** the **Basilica of Notre-Dame,** and the **Québec Seminary and Museum.** At a still higher elevation, to the south of the Château and along the river, is the **Citadelle,** a partially star-shaped fortress built by the French in the 18th century and augmented often by the English (after their capture of the city) well into the 19th century.

With most buildings at least 100 years old and made of granite in similar styles, Haute-Ville is visually harmonious, with few jarring modern intrusions. When they added a new wing to the Château Frontenac, for instance, they modeled it after the original—standing policy here.

Terrasse Dufferin is a pedestrian promenade atop the cliffs that attracts crowds in all seasons for its magnificent views of the river and its water traffic, which includes ferries gliding back and forth, cruise ships, and Great Lakes freighters putting in at the harbor below.

Vieux-Québec: Basse-Ville and Vieux-Port Old Québec's Lower Town encompasses **Vieux-Port,** the old port district; the impressive **Museum of Civilization,** a highlight of any visit; **Place Royale,** perhaps the most attractive of the city's many small squares and home of the **Notre-Dame-des-Victoires** church; and the restored **Quartier du Petit-Champlain,** including pedestrian-only rue du Petit-Champlain,

which is undeniably touristy, but not unpleasantly so, and has many agreeable cafes and shops. Visitors travel between Lower and Upper towns by the cliff-side elevator *(funiculaire)* at the north end of rue du Petit-Champlain, or by the adjacent stairway.

Parliament Hill Once you pass through the walls at St-Louis Gate, you're still in Haute-Ville (Upper Town), but no longer in Vieux-Québec. Rue St-Louis becomes **Grande-Allée,** a wide boulevard that passes the stately Parliament building and runs parallel to the broad expanse of the Plains of Abraham, where one of the most important battles in the history of North America took place between the French and the British for control of the city. This is also where the lively Carnaval de Québec is held each winter. Two blocks after Parliament, Grande-Allée becomes lined on both sides with terraced restaurants and cafes. The city's large modern hotels are in this area, too, and the **Musée National des Beaux-Arts** is a pleasant 20-minute walk up the Allée from the Parliament. Here, the neighborhood becomes more residential and flows into the Montcalm district.

St-Roch Northwest of Parliament Hill and enough of a distance from Vieux-Québec to warrant a cab ride, this newly revitalized neighborhood has some of the city's trendiest restaurants and bars. A dreary indoor pedestrian mall on the main strolling street, **rue St-Joseph est,** was gutted—the roof removed, the sidewalks widened, new benches added—and artists were hired to renovate the interiors and exteriors of their industrial buildings. It has all brought a youthful pop and an influx of new technology and media companies to the neighborhood.

Much of St-Roch, however, including what's referred to as Québec's "downtown" shopping district, remains nondescript and a little grubby. But the blocks near the corner of rue St-Joseph and **rue du Parvis** (where Hugo Boss moved in with a massive store) are increasingly home to top-notch restaurants and cute boutiques. *Note:* On older maps, rue du Parvis was called rue de l'Eglise.

2 GETTING AROUND

See "Getting Around Québec City" on p. 36.

Where to Stay in Québec City

Staying in one of the small hotels within or below the walls of Vieux-Québec can be one of your trip's most memorable experiences. It's important, though, to keep in mind that standards of amenities fluctuate wildly from one small hotel to another—even from room to room within a single establishment. From rooms with private bathrooms, luxury bedding, flatscreen TVs, and free Wi-Fi, to walk-up accommodations with linoleum floors and shared toilets down the hall, Québec City has a wide enough variety of lodgings to suit most tastes and budgets.

With the less expensive hotels, even with an advance reservation, always ask to see two or three rooms before making a decision to stay there.

If cost is a prime consideration, note that prices drop significantly from November to May, with the exception of the Christmas holiday and winter Carnaval de Québec in February. Many hotels offer special deals through their websites or offer AAA discounts.

Unless otherwise noted, all rooms in the lodgings listed below have private bathrooms—*en suite,* as they say in Canada. Note that some properties use the word "spa" to mean an outdoor hot tub; in this book, it means an indoor facility offering massages and other therapeutic treatments. Also, many of the hotels listed here are completely nonsmoking; if you smoke, check before booking.

Vieux-Québec has about a dozen bed-and-breakfasts. With rates mostly in the C$80-to-C$120 (£40–£60) range, they don't represent substantial savings over the small hotels, but do give you the opportunity to get to know some of the city dwellers. Many will post signs that say *complet,* meaning full, or *vacant,* which means that rooms are available.

When calling to make arrangements at a B&B, be very clear about your needs and requirements. A deposit is often required, as are minimum stays of 2 nights. Credit cards may not be accepted.

The *Official Accommodation Guide* put out by Québec City Tourism and revised annually is helpful in this regard. Available at tourist offices (p. 24), it lists every member of the Greater Québec Area Tourism and Convention Bureau, from B&Bs to five-star hotels, and provides details about number of rooms, prices, and facilities.

If you prefer the conveniences that large chain hotels can provide, the Fairmont Le Château Frontenac (p. 210) is your most central option. High-rise hotels outside the ancient walls in the younger part of town, Parliament Hill, are within walking distance or a quick taxi ride away from the Old City's attractions. The clutch of upscale boutique hotels in Lower Town has greatly enhanced the lodging stock, too.

Important note: The prices in the listings below represent rack rates for a double-occupancy room in high season (which includes the warm months, Christmastime, and Carnaval).

See p. 68 for information about the Frommer's star-rating system, price rankings, categories, and taxes.

1 BEST HOTEL BETS

- **Best Historic Hotel: Fairmont Le Château Frontenac,** 1 rue des Carrières (© **800/ 441-1414** or 418/692-3861), is the visual star of this city. It was built more than a century ago as one of the first hotels to serve railroad passengers and to encourage tourism at a time when most people stayed close to home. Nothing can beat it for proximity to all the sights. In fact, "the Château" *is* one of the sights. See p. 210.

- **Most Romantic Boutique Hotels: Auberge Saint-Antoine,** 8 rue St-Antoine (© **888/692-2211** or 418/692-2211), features a grand wing and archaeological displays from lobby to bedside, and it's hard to beat curling up with a glass of wine beside the fire in one of the cozy lobby alcoves. See p. 215. The sleek **Dominion 1912,** 126 rue St-Pierre (© **888/833-5253** or 418/692-2224), is also a favorite, infusing a pre–World War I building with a cunning modernist flavor, continuing a trend in Basse-Ville's designer hotels and inns. See p. 216.

- **Best Location for Peace and Quiet:** The Parc des Gouverneurs, just south of the Château, is a green space just steps from Upper Town's streets, restaurants, and shops. It's quiet, giving visitors a respite from activity at the end of the day. Dozens of B&Bs and small hotels are directly on the park or farther down av. Ste-Geneviève, including **Cap Díamant,** 39 ave. Ste-Geneviève (© **888/694-0303** or 418/692-0303); **Hôtel Château Bellevue,** 16 rue de la Porte (© **800/463-2617** or 418/692-2573); and **Manoir Sur-le-Cap,** 9 av. Ste-Geneviève (© **418/694-1987**). See p. 214, 214, and 215.

- **Best Hotel for Business Travelers:** The **Hilton Québec,** 1100 bd. René-Lévesque est (© **800/447-2411** or 418/647-2411), has beautiful new executive floors, a satisfactory fitness center, and guest rooms with ergonomic chairs at their desks. It's adjacent to the convention center, too. See p. 217.

- **Best Hotel in a Touristy Area That Doesn't Feel Touristy:** Fans of spare, vaguely Asian-Scandinavian room design who want to stay in Upper Town should consider **Hôtel Sainte-Anne,** 32 rue Ste-Anne (© **877/222-9422** or 418/694-1455). Beds are low and comfortable, decor is simple, and bathrooms are sleek. See p. 215.

- **Best Location for Proximity to Fine Dining:** Lower Town, hands down. You could have a satisfying visit just eating your way across the neighborhood without ever once traveling to Upper Town. The walk up the steep cliff-side stairs, though, would probably do you some good.

- **Most Memorable Hotel:** How many chances do you get to sleep in a hotel built completely of ice, on a bed of ice, near a chandelier and disco and front hallway all made of ice, ice, ice? The **Hôtel de Glace,** Station touristique Duchesnay, 30 minutes outside the city (© **877/505-0423;** www.icehotel-canada.com), is open from January to late March or the first thaw, whichever comes first. See p. 219.

2 VIEUX-QUEBEC: HAUTE-VILLE (UPPER TOWN)

VERY EXPENSIVE

Fairmont Le Château Frontenac ★★★ (Kids) Québec's magical "castle" opened in 1893 and has been wowing visiting royalty and other guests ever since. Luxurious rooms are outfitted with elegant château furnishings, bathrooms have marble touches, and more than 500 rooms were renovated in a 3-year project that finished in 2008. Anyone can stay on the more princely (and pricey) Fairmont Gold floors, which have a separate concierge and a lounge with an honor bar in the afternoons and breakfast in the mornings. Room prices depend on size, location, how recently the room was renovated, and view, with river views garnering top dollar, but lower-priced rooms overlooking the inner courtyard are appealing, too: The gabled roofs they look onto are quite romantic, and children might imagine Harry Potter swooping by in a Quidditch match. Known locally as "the Château," the hotel was built in phases, following the landline, so the wide halls take crooked paths. Santrol, a trained guide dog, is the hotel's new "canine ambassador" and greets guests in the lobby. The **Véranda Saint-Laurent** is a casual piano bar with dancing on Friday nights.

1 rue des Carrières (at Place d'Armes), Québec City, PQ G1R 4P5. ✆ **800/441-1414** or 418/692-3861. Fax 418/692-1751. www.fairmont.com/frontenac. 618 units. May–Oct C$259–C$499 (£130–£250) double, Nov–Apr from C$189 (£90) double; suites from C$499 (£250) and way up. Children 17 and younger stay free in parent's room. Children 5 and younger eat free; ages 6–12 get 50% off meals. Packages available. AE, DC, DISC, MC, V. Valet parking C$31 (£16), self-parking C$26 (£13). Pets accepted, C$25 (£13) per night. **Amenities:** 3 restaurants; bar; indoor pool and kiddie pool w/outdoor terrace; expansive health club and spa; children's programs; concierge; room service; babysitting; concierge-level rooms. *In room:* A/C, TV, high-speed Internet, minibar, hair dryer.

EXPENSIVE

Hôtel du Vieux-Québec (Kids) This century-old brick hotel is centrally located and has been renovated with care. Some guest rooms are equipped with sofas and two double beds, and six have kitchenettes. With these homey layouts, the hotel is understandably popular with families, skiers, and groups of visiting high school students who descend upon the city in late spring. In addition to its French bistro, **Les Frères de la Côte** (✆ **418/692-5445**) on the ground floor, many moderately priced restaurants and nightspots are nearby. In July and August, the hotel offers complimentary walking tours of the area.

1190 rue St-Jean (at rue de l'Hôtel Dieu), Québec City, PQ G1R 1S6. ✆ **800/361-7787** or 418/692-1850. Fax 418/692-5637. www.hvq.com. 50 units. May to late Oct C$144–C$264 (£72–£132) double; late Oct to Apr C$94–C$214 (£47–£107) double. Continental breakfast included with advance bookings. Packages available. AE, MC, V. Pets accepted, C$25 (£13) additional per night. *In room:* A/C, TV, free Wi-Fi, fridge, hair dryer.

Hôtel Manoir Victoria ★ With its lobby of stained glass and maroon curtains, this hotel has an air of a grand old-timer. It sprawls all the way from the main entrance on Côte de Palais to adjacent St-Jean, zigzagging around a couple of stores. The proximity to the rue St-Jean restaurant-and-bar scene is a plus for many, and the small F-shaped indoor pool, rare in this city, is an added extra. A spa, added in 2004, increased the hotel's appeal. Body wraps in mud or algae or chocolate (!), along with Swedish massages and sea-salt exfoliations, are administered in the eight treatment rooms. There's a long staircase to get to the lobby, but elevators make the trip to most guest rooms.

44 Côte du Palais (at rue St-Jean), Québec City, PQ G1R 4H8. ✆ **800/463-6283** or 418/692-1030. Fax 418/692-3822. www.manoir-victoria.com. 156 units. May to mid-Oct C$165–C$400 (£83–£200) double; mid-Oct to Apr C$125–C$325 (£63–£163) double. Packages available. AE, DC, DISC, MC, V. Valet parking C$20 (£10). **Amenities:** 2 restaurants; bar; heated indoor pool; exercise room; expansive spa; concierge; room service; babysitting. *In room:* A/C, TV, free Wi-Fi, free high-speed Internet, minibar, hair dryer.

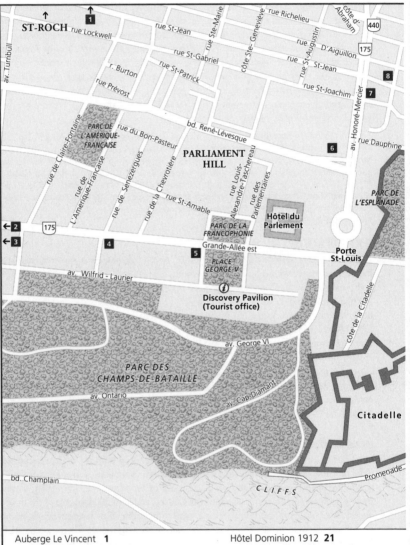

Auberge Le Vincent **1**
Auberge Saint-Antoine **20**
Cap Diamant **13**
Fairmont Le Château Frontenac **16**
Hilton Québec **6**
Hôtel Château Laurier Québec **5**
Hôtel Courtyard Marriott de Québec **7**

Hôtel Dominion 1912 **21**
Hôtel Champlain Vieux-Québec **9**
Hôtel Château Bellevue **14**
Hôtel du Vieux-Québec **11**
Hôtel Le Priori **17**
Hôtel Manoir Victoria **10**
Hôtel Sainte-Anne **12**

213

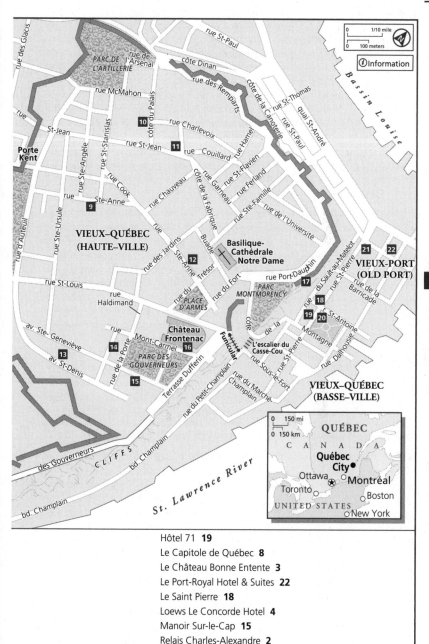

WHERE TO STAY IN QUÉBEC CITY

14

VIEUX–QUÉBEC: HAUTE–VILLE (UPPER TOWN)

Hôtel 71 **19**
Le Capitole de Québec **8**
Le Château Bonne Entente **3**
Le Port-Royal Hotel & Suites **22**
Le Saint Pierre **18**
Loews Le Concorde Hotel **4**
Manoir Sur-le-Cap **15**
Relais Charles-Alexandre **2**

Cap Díamant   There are a lot of B&Bs in this corner of Vieux-Québec—the quiet, pretty part in back of the Château Frontenac. Owner Florence Guillot has turned this 1826 home into something of a Victoriana showpiece, with antiques and old photos richly decorating common areas and bedrooms. The whole thing is quite grand and romantic. Many of the rooms feature ornate fireplaces, mantles, heavy gold-edged mirrors, oriental rugs, and glass lamps. There's a small all-season back porch where breakfast is served, and a summer garden. All rooms have private baths. Ask to see the industrial-size dumb waiter that descends from a secret trap door in the front hall ceiling to carry luggage up to the top floors; the controls are behind a painting that slides to the right, like something out of a James Bond movie. Mindboggling!

39 ave. Ste-Geneviève (at Ste-Ursule), Québec City, PQ G1R 4B3. (℃ 888/694-0303 or 418/692-0303. www.hotelcapdiamant.com. 9 units. Summer C$154–C$179 (£77–£90) double; rest of the year from C$124 (£62). Continental breakfast included. AE, MC, V. Parking C$14 (£7). *In room:* A/C, TV, free Wi-Fi, fridge, hair dryer.

Hôtel Champlain Vieux-Québec (Value)   In 2006, new owners gave this property a total overhaul, from decor to bathrooms to beds. Even the smallest rooms have silk curtains, king or queen beds, 300-count cotton sheets, flatscreen TVs, and *space:* Rooms here are advertised at 50% larger than others in Vieux-Québec. A midpriced room, no. 13, allows views of stone buildings across the street and feels very French, while guests in no. 47 can see the Château Frontenac from their bed. Windows open in every room, an unusual feature in this city. A self-serve Nuovo Simonelli espresso machine by the front desk ensures free cappuccinos any time of day or night, and there's a computer that's free for guests to use. Don't be alarmed when you arrive; the bleh 1960s façade hasn't been updated and doesn't reflect the pizzazz inside.

A nearby sister property, **Auberge Place d'Armes,** 24 rue Ste-Anne (℃ 866/333-9485), was renovated in 2008 and offers 12 sumptuous rooms with 17th-century stone walls and handmade furniture.

115 rue Ste-Anne (near rue Ste-Ursule), Québec City, PQ G1R 3X6. (℃ 800/567-2106 or 418/694-0106. Fax 418/692-1959. www.champlainhotel.com. 54 units. Summer C$179–C$209 (£90–£110) double; rest of the year C$109–C$149 (£55–£75) double. Continental breakfast included. AE, DISC, MC, V. Limited on-site parking. **Amenities:** Concierge. *In room:* A/C, TV/DVD, free Wi-Fi, fridge, hair dryer.

Hôtel Château Bellevue   Occupying several row houses at the top of the Jardin des Gouverneurs in one of Vieux-Québec's prettiest areas, this minihotel has a helpful staff as well as some of the creature comforts typical of larger facilities. Though the rooms are small and unspectacular, they are quiet for the most part, have private bathrooms, and offer one or two double beds or a queen. Many were renovated in 2008, so ask for a newer room. A few higher-priced units overlook the park. The lobby features a wine machine offering selections by the glass (think soda machine, but classier). If this place is full, there are about a dozen other small lodgings within a block in any direction. A sister hotel, **Château Laurier** (p. 219), is outside the walls on Parliament Hill.

16 rue de la Porte (at av. Ste-Geneviève), Québec City, PQ G1R 4M9. (℃ 800/463-2617 or 418/692-2573. Fax 418/692-4876. www.hotelchateaubellevue.com. 58 units. May–Oct 15 C$105–C$239 (£53–£120) double; Oct 16–Apr C$89–C$179 (£45–£80) double. Continental breakfast included during the non-summer months. Packages available. AE, DC, DISC, MC, V. Valet parking C$18 (£9). *In room:* A/C, TV, free Wi-Fi, hair dryer.

Hôtel Sainte-Anne ★ This find for fans of modern, European-style design is housed in a 19th-century row house that fronts a pedestrian block of rue Ste-Anne in the center of Upper Town's historic district. Exposed stone and brick walls are common, and each guest room contains a tall, narrow, free-standing cabinet with a TV near the top, an unstocked fridge, a coffeemaker, and a closet. The effect is spare but clean, and unusual light fixtures add drama. Beds are comfortable, and swank, high-design bathrooms feature satisfyingly drenching showers (most rooms have just showers; specify if you want one of the few with a bathtub). Breakfast and room service are provided from the adjacent restaurant **Le Grill**, a high-end joint which offers meals throughout the day and evening.

32 rue Ste-Anne (near rue des Jardins), Québec City, PQ G1R 1X3. ✆ **877/222-9422** or 418/694-1455. Fax 418/692-4096. www.hotelste-anne.com. 28 units. Mid-June to mid-Oct C$189–C$229 (£90–£115) double; rest of year from C$149 (£75) double. AE, DISC, MC, V. **Amenities:** Room service; in-room massage. *In room:* AC, TV, free Wi-Fi, fridge, hair dryer.

INEXPENSIVE

Manoir Sur-le-Cap Continual renovations and sprucing up of units keep this inn on the Parc des Gouverneurs, opposite the Château Frontenac, looking spiffy. All the guest rooms have gleaming floors and many feature exposed stone or brick walls. The price is right, though if you require air-conditioning, be sure to request one of the seven units that have it. Know, too, that these four floors have no elevator. Room no. 8 is one of the least expensive but has a small balcony; room no. 10 is more expensive and features a king bed and a view of the Château. There's one condo unit, which has a fireplace and a kitchenette with a microwave oven and basic crockery.

9 av. Ste-Geneviève (near rue de la Porte), Québec City, PQ G1R 4A7. ✆ **418/694-1987.** Fax 418/627-7405. www.manoir-sur-le-cap.com. 14 units. C$100–C$265 (£50–£135) double. AE, MC, V. *In room:* TV, free Wi-Fi, hair dryer.

3 VIEUX-QUEBEC: BASSE-VILLE (LOWER TOWN)/VIEUX-PORT

EXPENSIVE

Auberge Saint-Antoine ★★★ This uncommonly attractive property began life as an 1830 maritime warehouse. It kept the soaring ceilings, dark beams, and stone floors, and is now one of the city's landmark luxury boutique hotels (and a member of the prestigious Relais & Chateaux luxury group). Ancient walls remain in view, and artifacts unearthed during the development are on display throughout the hotel—in public areas, at the door to each room, and bedside, lit with an underwater-blue glow. Bedrooms are modern and sleek with luxury linens, plush robes, Bose sound systems, heated bathroom floors, and bathing nooks with rain-shower nozzles directly overhead. Many have balconies, terraces, fireplaces, or kitchenettes; ask when booking if you want to ensure having any of these features in your room. A striking lounge serves breakfast, lunch, snacks, and drinks, while a high-end restaurant, **Panache** (p. 228), occupies the original warehouse lobby.

8 rue St-Antoine (next to the Musée de la Civilisation), Québec City, PQ G1K 4C9. ✆ **888/692-2211** or 418/692-2211. Fax 418/692-1177. www.saint-antoine.com. 94 units. C$169–C$399 (£86–£200) double; from C$299 (£150) suite. AE, DC, MC, V. Valet parking C$22 (£11). **Amenities:** Restaurant; bar; exercise room; concierge; Wi-Fi in public areas; room service; babysitting. *In room:* A/C, TV, free high-speed Internet, hair dryer.

Dominion 1912 ★★★   Old Québec meets new in one of the city's most romantic boutique hotels. The owners stripped the 1912 building down to the studs and started over, keeping the angular lines and adding soft touches. Québec-made beds are topped with mattresses that are deep, soft, and enveloping, heaped with pillows and feather duvets. Custom-made bedside tables swing into place or out of the way, and even the least expensive rooms are large. About a third of the rooms have only showers, while the rest include tubs. Room no. 206 is a dandy, with a shower that shares a glass wall with the bedroom and views of the city's centuries-old, formerly industrial buildings. A hearty continental breakfast is set out along with morning newspapers near the fireplace in the handsome lobby, and a machine that dispenses free espresso is available round the clock. A fitness room has been rigged up in the basement.

126 rue St-Pierre (at rue St-Paul), Québec City, PQ G1K 4A8. ℂ **888/833-5253** or 418/692-2224. Fax 418/692-4403. www.hoteldominion.com. 60 units. C$169–C$425 (£85–£213) double. Rates include breakfast. AE, DC, MC, V. Parking C$18 (£9). Pets accepted, additional C$30 (£15) per night. **Amenities:** Espresso bar; exercise room; concierge; room service; babysitting. *In room:* A/C, TV, CD player, free Wi-Fi, high-speed Internet, minibar, hair dryer.

Hôtel 71 ★★   Owned by the same people as the adjacent **Le Saint-Pierre** (see below), the two properties share a bar, but Hôtel 71 is slicker and ultra-contemporary. Room no. 620 is typical, with 4.5m (15-ft.) crème-colored walls and curtains that extend nearly floor to ceiling, warmed up with deep-red velveteen chairs and cloth panels that serve as closet doors. Bathrooms are in the open style common to the area's boutique hotels, with seafoam-green glass separating the shower from the sink area and shower nozzles of the big-disk variety (all rooms have showers; four have bathtubs as well). Rooms are on floors four to seven and many feature bird's-eye views of the tops of the 19th-century buildings of Old Québec, the St. Lawrence River, or the ramparts of the fortress wall. The small but stylish **Café 71,** on the first floor, is open for breakfast and for snacks during the day.

71 rue St-Pierre (near rue St-Antoine), Québec City, PQ G1K 4A4. ℂ **888/692-1171** or 418/692-1171. Fax 418/692-0669. www.hotel71.ca. 40 units. C$200–C$290 (£100–£145). Rates include breakfast. Packages available. AE, MC, V. Valet parking C$18 (£9). **Amenities:** Cafe; bar; exercise room w/spectacular river view; concierge; room service; babysitting. *In room:* A/C, TV/DVD, CD player, free Wi-Fi, free high-speed Internet, hair dryer.

MODERATE

Hôtel Le Priori ★   A playful Art Deco interior livens up the somber façade of a 1726 house—you'll find conical stainless-steel sinks in the bedrooms and, in four units, claw-foot tubs beside duvet-covered queen-size beds. Several units, including no. 10, are quite masculine, with brown walls, an animal-skin rug, and fur throws. Suites include sitting rooms with wood-burning fireplaces, kitchens, and Jacuzzis. Rooms face either the small street out front or a leafy, pretty, inner courtyard (some units are upstairs with no elevator). The inventive restaurant **Toast!** (p. 229) is off the lobby and moves into the courtyard in summer.

15 rue Sault-au-Matelot (at rue St-Antoine), Québec City, PQ G1K 3Y7. ℂ **800/351-3992** or 418/692-3992. Fax 418/692-0883. www.hotellepriori.com. 26 units. Summer C$199–C$269 (£100–£135) double, winter C$139–C$209 (£70–£105) double; suites from C$299 (£150). Rates include breakfast. Packages available. AE, MC, V. **Amenities:** Restaurant; bar; concierge; room service; babysitting. *In room:* A/C, TV/DVD, CD player, free Wi-Fi, hair dryer.

Le Port-Royal Hotel & Suites (Kids) Open since 2005, this bright corner near the water is giving serious competition to Basse-Ville's best hotels. Its 18th-century structure was hollowed out to make 40 suites, the smallest of which is 37 sq. m (398 sq. ft.), and all of which have well-equipped kitchenettes with microwave ovens and range tops. Four to six people can be accommodated in each unit, making this an excellent choice for families as well as long-stay businesspeople. From May through October, the hotel operates at near-total capacity, so book early. The owner is hoping to build a condo complex in the parking lot in front of the hotel, but no construction is expected in 2009. **Le 48,** a restaurant under separate management with an entrance from the lobby, provides appetizing food via room service.

144 rue St-Pierre (rue St-Andre), Québec City, PQ G1K 8N8. (*)(*) **866/417-2777** or 418/692-2777. Fax 418/692-2778. www.hotelportroyalsuites.com. 36 units. May–Oct C$209–C$419 (£105–£220) suite; Nov–Apr C$159–C$289 (£80–£145) suite. Packages available. AE, MC, V. Parking C$15 (£7.50). Pets accepted. **Amenities:** Restaurant; bar; room service. *In room:* A/C, TV/DVD, CD player, kitchenette, microwave, free Wi-Fi, hair dryer.

Le Saint-Pierre ★ One of the city's country-cozy auberge options—though recent renovations have sleeked up the hotel and, with rebranding, dropped the word "auberge" from the name. Most rooms are surprisingly spacious. The even more commodious suites are a luxury on a longer visit, especially since they have modest kitchen facilities. The made-to-order furnishings suggest traditional Québec style, and units have wood floors and original brick or stone walls. All rooms are on the fourth to seventh floors, and some have a river view. The full breakfasts, included in the price, are cooked to order.

79 rue St-Pierre (behind the Musée de la Civilisation), Québec City, PQ G1K 4A3. (*)(*) **888/268-1017** or 418/694-7981. Fax 418/694-0406. www.le-saint-pierre.ca. 41 units. C$229–C$289 (£115–£145) double. Rates include full breakfast. Packages available. AE, DC, DISC, MC, V. Valet parking C$20 (£10). **Amenities:** Bar; concierge; babysitting. *In room:* A/C, TV, free Wi-Fi, hair dryer.

4 PARLIAMENT HILL/ON OR NEAR GRANDE-ALLÉE

EXPENSIVE

Hilton Québec ★★ (Kids) Superior on virtually every count to the other midrise hotels nearby, this Hilton is entirely true to the breed and the clear choice for executives and leisure travelers who want their amenities dependable. Renovations in 2008 spruced up the lobby, the swank executive lounge, the pool, and about half of the rooms, which now feature luxe bedding, big desks, ergonomic work chairs, and bland, sand-colored walls. The idea: less clutter, more Zen. The best rooms face the St. Lawrence River and Vieux-Québec, where you can watch the sun rise over the Citadelle. The busy boulevard René-Lévesque provides a steady hum of cars but is not overly distracting. Nonguests can come for a Sunday brunch that includes free admission to the heated outdoor pool, which is open year-round (there's nothing quite like swimming in a snowstorm). The hotel is connected to the large Place Québec shopping complex (p. 265) and the convention center.

1100 bd. René-Lévesque est, Québec City, PQ G1K 7K7. ☎ **800/447-2411** or 418/647-2411. Fax 418/647-6488. www.hiltonquebec.com. 571 units. Summer C$169–C$299 (£85–£150) double; winter from C$109 (£55) double. Children stay free in parent's room. Packages available. AE, DC, DISC, MC, V. Valet parking C$21 (£11). Pets accepted, C$25 (£13) additional for stay. **Amenities:** Restaurant; bar; heated outdoor pool (year-round); well-equipped health club w/sauna; concierge; Wi-Fi in common areas; room service; babysitting; executive-level floors. *In room:* A/C, TV, high-speed Internet, hair dryer.

Hôtel Courtyard Marriott de Québec ★

Sidestepping its parent chain's conventional template by renovating a handsome building from the 1930s, the Marriott makes a substantial contribution to the ongoing enhancement of Place d'Youville, Upper Town's central plaza. Beds here got a deluxe upgrade in 2006; now they're piled with five pillows, plus sheet covers on the duvets. All rooms have either a sofa bed or an oversized chair that pulls out into a single bed, and all feature ergonomic chairs at the desks. The lobby sets a handsome tone with a balustraded second floor above a fireplace flanked by leather sofas, and a first-floor bar leads to a full-service restaurant, **Que Sera Sera.**

850 Place d'Youville (near rue St-Jean), Québec City, PQ G1R 3P6. ☎ **866/694-4004** or 418/694-4004. Fax 418/694-4007. www.marriott-quebec.com. 111 units. C$175–C$299 (£88–£150) double. Packages available. AE, DC, DISC, MC, V. Valet parking C$20 (£10), self-parking C$16 (£8). **Amenities:** Restaurant; bar; exercise room and whirlpool; Wi-Fi in lobby; room service. *In room:* A/C, TV, free high-speed Internet, fridge, hair dryer.

Le Capitole de Québec ★

In the heart of Place d'Youville, Le Capitole is as gleefully eccentric as the business hotels it competes with are conventional. Rooms are all curves and obtuse angles, borrowing from Art Deco, and feature stars on the carpets and painted clouds on the ceiling. Beds have down duvets, and some rooms feature a bathtub in the corner. Mostly this works to its advantage, though some of the angles and funky furniture are tests to practicality. The owner runs the adjacent music and theater venue, also called **Le Capitole** (p. 267) and **Ristorante Il Teatro.** The hotel's entrance is squeezed almost to anonymity between the theater and restaurant—just head for the theater marquee. Unlike many business hotels nearby, prices are higher rather than lower on the weekends because of theater business.

972 rue St-Jean (1 block outside the Old City walls), Québec City, PQ G1R 1R5. ☎ **800/363-4040** or 418/694-4040. www.lecapitole.com. 40 units. C$165–C$235 (£83–£118) double; suites from C$225 (£113). Packages available. AE, DC, DISC, MC, V. Valet parking C$19 (£9.50). **Amenities:** Restaurant; bar; concierge; room service. *In room:* A/C, TV/VCR, free Wi-Fi, free high-speed Internet, minibar, hair dryer.

Loews Le Concorde Hotel ★ (Kids)

The skyscraper that houses this hotel rises discordantly from a neighborhood of late-Victorian town houses. But for guests, no matter: With all rooms on the fifth floor and above, the hotel offers spectacular views of the river and the Old City. To boot, every guest room was renovated in 2006 so that now the furniture, mattresses, curtains, marble bathrooms, plush robes, and flatscreen TVs are that much better. Kids can borrow from a selection of toys. **L'Astral** (p. 223), the hotel's revolving rooftop restaurant with a bar and live piano music on weekends, has way better food than usually can be expected of sky-high venues. The hotel is adjacent to the Grande-Allée restaurant and party scene on one side, and the pristine Joan of Arc garden in Parc des Champs-de-Bataille on the other.

1225 cours du Général de Montcalm (at Grande-Allée), Québec City, PQ G1R 4W6. ☎ **800/463-5256** or 418/647-2222. Fax 418/647-1773. www.loewshotels.com. 406 units. Summer C$209–C$299 (£105–£150) double; rest of year C$119–C$199 (£60–£100) double. Packages available. AE, DC, DISC, MC, V. Self-parking C$25 (£13), valet parking C$28 (£14). Pets accepted, C$25 (£13) additional per stay. **Amenities:** Restaurant (revolving rooftop); 2 bars; heated outdoor pool; well-equipped health club w/sauna; Jacuzzi; concierge; room service; babysitting. *In room:* A/C, TV, Wi-Fi, high-speed Internet, minibar, hair dryer.

Moments — Québec's Ice Hotel: The Coldest Reception in Town

For C$15 (£7.50) you can visit, but for C$299 (£150) per person (and way up) you can have dinner and spend the night. Tempted? Québec's **Ice Hotel** (© **877/505-0423;** www.icehotel-canada.com) is built each winter at the Station touristique Duchesnay, a woodsy resort a half-hour outside of Québec City.

It's crafted from 500 tons of ice, and nearly everything is clear or white, from the ice chandelier in the 5.4m (18-ft.) vaulted main hall to the thick, square ice shot glasses in which vodka is served to the pillars and arches and furniture. That includes the frozen slabs they call beds; deer skins and sleeping bags provide insulation.

Nighttime guests get their rooms after the last tours at 8pm and have to clear out before the next day's arrivals at 10am. Some rooms are themed and vaguely grand: The chess room, for instance, features solid-ice chess pieces the size of small children at each corner of the bed. Other rooms bring the words "monastic" or "cell block" to mind.

Bear in mind that except for in the hot tub, temperatures everywhere hover between 23° and 28°F (−5° to −2°C); refrigerators are used not to keep sodas cold but to keep them from freezing. And to whomever dreamed up the luxury suite with a real fireplace that somehow emits no heat: There is a special circle in hell for you.

In 2008, the hotel had 36 rooms and suites, a wedding chapel, two small art galleries, and a disco where guests could shake the chill from their booties. Open each January, the Hôtel de Glace takes guests until late March or the first thaw, whichever comes first—at that point, it's destroyed.

Locals have a bemused reaction to all the fuss. A waitress down the road told one guest, "I would have charged you half as much and let you sleep in a snowbank behind the pub."

MODERATE

Hôtel Château Laurier Québec ★★ Right on action-filled Grande-Allée, this property has perked up considerably in recent years. A saltwater pool and Finnish sauna opened in 2007, and the health center and restaurant were renovated that same year. Eight categories of rooms and suites are available, thanks to nearly continual expansion in recent years. The newer rooms, such as those on the executive floors, are more desirable than those in the plainer and more cramped original wing; the former come with sizable desks and leather sitting chairs with reading lamps. Some units feature working fireplaces, whirlpools, and king beds; all enjoy the comforts and doodads of a first-class hotel. Many rooms on the higher floors have views of the Citadelle and the St. Lawrence River. The hotel is 2 blocks west of the fortress wall and St-Louis Gate.

1220 Place Georges V ouest (at Grande-Allée), Québec City, PQ G1R 5B8. ℂ **800/463-4453** or 418/522-8108. Fax 418/524-8768. www.oldquebec.com. 291 units. May–Oct C$114–C$309 (£57–£155) double; Nov–Apr C$99–C$269 (£50–£135) double; suites from C$189 (£95). Children 17 and younger stay free in parent's room. Packages available. AE, DC, MC, V. Parking C$19 (£9.50). **Amenities:** Restaurant; indoor saltwater pool; exercise room; sauna; concierge; room service; babysitting; executive-level floors. *In room:* A/C, TV, CD player, free Wi-Fi, hair dryer.

INEXPENSIVE

Relais Charles-Alexandre (Value)   This little hotel is a 10-minute walk from the fortress walls and St-Louis Gate and a few blocks from Parc des Champs-de-Bataille and the Musée des Beaux-Arts du Québec. In addition to the restaurants on Grande Allee, the pleasant residential shopping street avenue Cartier is just around the corner. Rooms are basic, crisply maintained, and decorated with eclectic antique and wicker pieces and reproductions. They are quiet, for the most part. Spend the extra C$10 (£5) for one of the nicer rooms.

91 Grande-Allée est (2 blocks east of av. Cartier), Québec City, PQ G1R 2H5. ℂ **418/523-1220.** Fax 418/523-9556. www.quebecweb.com/rca. 23 units. May–Oct and Carnaval C$124–C$134 (£62–£67) double; Nov–Apr C$89–C$99 (£45–£50) double. Rates include breakfast. MC, V. Parking C$8 (£4). **Amenities:** Breakfast room. *In room:* A/C, TV, hair dryer.

5 ST-ROCH

Until about 2000, there were few reasons for travelers to include Québec's St-Roch neighborhood in their plans, but that's changing. Young restaurateurs, artists, and media techies have settled in and dubbed the area "Le Nouvo St-Roch" (proper spelling would be too traditional).

MODERATE

Auberge Le Vincent ★ (Value)   The emerging Le Nouvo St-Roch neighborhood has restaurants worth going out of your way for (four are listed in chapter 15) and joining the neighborhood of tech companies, skateboard punks, and well-heeled hipsters is the Van Gogh–inspired Le Vincent, which opened its 10 rooms in August 2006. Housed in a renovated 100-year-old building, the sophisticated accommodations represent a brilliant value, considering all the luxe features: goose duvets, 400-count sheets, custom-made dark cherry-wood furniture, generous lighting options, and local art. Breakfast (included in your rate) is served in a brick-walled seating area off the lobby; as you walk through the lobby, take note if its floor, which is painted in Van Gogh–style sunbursts and roiling blue curves. Bike storage and repair is available. Rooms are up either one or two flights of stairs.

295 rue St-Vallier est (corner of rue Dorchester), Québec City, PQ G1K 3P5. ℂ **888/523-5005** or 418/523-5000. Fax 418/523-5999. www.aubergelevincent.com. 10 units. C$129–C$179 (£65–£90) double. Rates include breakfast. Packages available. AE, MC, V. Valet parking C$16 (£8). *In room:* A/C, TV/DVD, CD player, free Wi-Fi, free high-speed Internet, fridge, hair dryer.

MODERATE

Le Château Bonne Entente ★★ (Kids)   In summer, cast a line for trout in the pond out front; in winter, twirl around the skating rink; year-round, get swaddled in seaweed—and still be only a 20-minute drive from the city. Bushels of dollars have elevated this hotel far beyond the folksy boardinghouse that it was a half-century ago. Accordingly, it's now a member of the prestigious consortium Leading Hotels of the World. Aiming to attract some of the design aficionados who head to Vieux-Québec's boutique hotels, the owners put a boutique hotel right on the facility. Called **Urbania,** the hotel-within-a-hotel offers loft rooms with tall ceilings, leather headboards, and chic bathrooms. The on-site **AmeriSpa** serves up an apple-ice-cider body wrap and a maple-sugar body scrub along with standard massages. There's a supervised play area for children, with toys, videos, and a nap space.

3400 Chemin Ste-Foy, Québec, PQ G1X 1S6. (C) **800/463-4390** or 418/653-5221. Fax 418/653-3098. www.chateaubonneentente.com. 163 units. C$189–C$339 (£95–£170) double; suites from C$359 (£180). Packages available. AE, DC, DISC, MC, V. Free parking. Rte. 40 west, exit onto Autoroute Duplessis, shortly turning right onto Chemin Ste-Foy; at the light, turn right into the main hotel entrance. **Amenities:** 2 restaurants; bar; large outdoor pool in summer; extensive health club and spa; concierge; room service; babysitting. *In room:* A/C, TV, CD player, Wi-Fi, minibar, hair dryer.

Where to Dine in Québec City

With a little research, it's possible to eat extraordinarily well in Québec City. It used to be that this gloriously scenic town had no *temples de cuisine* comparable to those of Montréal. That has changed. There are now restaurants comparable in every way to the most honored establishments of any North American city, with surprising numbers of creative, ambitious young chefs and restaurateurs bidding to achieve similar status.

By sticking to any of the many competent bistros and a couple of jazzy fusion eateries, you'll likely be more than content. Another step up, a half-dozen enterprises tease the palate with hints of higher achievement.

Even the blatantly touristy restaurants along rue St-Louis in Upper Town and around the Place d'Armes, many of them with hawkers outside and accordion players and showy tableside presentations inside, can produce decent meals. The less extravagant among them are entirely satisfactory for breakfast or lunch.

The best dining deals are the *table d'hôte* (fixed-price) meals. Nearly all full-service restaurants offer them, if only at lunch. As a rule, they include at least soup or salad, a main course, and a dessert. Some places add in an extra appetizer and/or a beverage. The total price ends up being approximately what you'd pay for the main course alone.

At the better places, and even at some that might seem inexplicably popular, reservations are all but essential during traditional holidays and the festivals that pepper the social calendar. Other times, it's necessary to book ahead only for weekend evenings. In the listings below, where no mention is made of reservations, they aren't necessary. Dress codes are rarely stipulated, but "dressy-casual" works almost everywhere.

The evening meal tends to be served earlier in Québec City than in Montréal, at 6 or 7pm rather than 8pm.

Smoking in restaurants, bars, and most other public places in the Québec province has been prohibited since 2006.

1 BEST DINING BETS

- **Best Bistros:** In a city that specializes in the informal bistro tradition, **L'Echaudé,** 73 rue Sault-au-Matelot, near rue St-Paul (© **418/692-1299**), is a star. The classic dishes are all in place, from confit de canard to steak frites. The dining terrace, just a block from the waters of Vieux-Port, is on a street that's pedestrian-only in summer. See p. 228. The spiffed-up **Café du Clocher Penché,** 203 rue St-Joseph est (© **418/640-0597**), offers a cozy atmosphere and a good reason to explore the trendy St-Roch neighborhood. See p. 232.

- **Best New(ish) Restaurant:** Amid the cluster of innovative new restaurants, St-Roch's **Utopie,** 226¹/₂ rue St-Joseph est (© **418/523-7878**), is the one most likely to equal the current champs. It recently added a new tapas and wine bar called **Le Cercle** right next door. See p. 232 and 267.
- **Best Rockin' Hot Spot with Good Food:** You don't have to be young and gorgeous to get into the **Voo Doo Grill,** 575 Grande-Allée est (© **418/647-2000**), but there seems to be a lot of self-selection going on. In a complex that includes the Maurice disco, the noise level gets brutal and the pace frantic, making the surprisingly good food all the more remarkable. See p. 231.
- **Best Seafood: Le Marie-Clarisse,** 12 rue du Petit-Champlain (© **418/692-0857**), touts just-off-the-boat seafood served in comfortable bistro environs at the bottom of Breakneck Stairs (next to the funicular). In warm weather, enjoy the terrace; in the cold months, the fireplace and 300-year-old walls. See p. 229.
- **Best Sugar Pie:** Québec's favorite dessert reaches its apogee at **Aux Anciens Canadiens,** 34 rue St-Louis (© **418/692-1627**), in central Upper Town. Think smooth maple sugar with a crust, or pecan pie without the pecans. See p. 224.
- **Best Big View:** Revolving rooftop restaurants rarely dish out food as elevated as their lofty venues. **L'Astral** in the Loews Le Concorde hotel, 1225 Cours du Général de Montcalm (© **418/647-2222**), is an exception. The food is above average and the revolving view one of a kind. See p. 269.
- **Best People-Watching:** The few outdoor tables at **Le Marie-Clarisse,** 12 rue du Petit-Champlain (© **418/692-0857**)—perched above Quartier du Petit-Champlain's main pedestrian intersection—monopolize an unsurpassed observation point. See p. 229.
- **Best Idyllic Terrace:** The main room, all crimson glow and retro lighting, is nice enough, but try to get onto the leafy enclosed back terrace of Lower Town's **Toast!,** 17 rue Sault-au-Matelot (© **418/692-1334**); it's a haven. See p. 229.
- **Best Afternoon Bargain:** Dinners at **Aux Anciens Canadiens,** 34 rue St-Louis (© **418/692-1627**), can easily set you back C$50 (£25) or more, but from noon until 5:45pm daily, the purveyor of classic Québécois fare offers a three-course meal with a glass of wine or beer for just C$17 (£8.50). See p. 224.
- **Best Place for a Family Holiday Meal:** Large (it seats more than 200) and jovial, **Le Café du Monde,** 84 rue Dalhousie (© **418/692-4455**), manages the nearly impossible: fast service without compromising quality even on crowded holiday weekends. See p. 230.
- **Best Breakfast with Locals:** Just outside the tourist orbit in the residential neighborhood of Montcalm (and not far from the Musée des Beaux-Arts du Québec), **Café Krieghoff,** 1091 av. Cartier (© **418/522-3711**), has an outdoor terrace and gets a mix of families, singles, and artsy folks of all ages. See p. 231.
- **Best Restaurants, Period: Laurie Raphaël,** 117 rue Dalhousie (© **418/692-4555**), is sophisticated and endlessly eclectic; you never know what Daniel Vézina's kitchen will have in store. See p. 228. **Initiale,** 54 rue St-Pierre (© **418/694-1818**), is more hushed and classic with less sizzle but equally top-notch cuisine. See p. 225. These stellar restaurants are just blocks from each other in Lower Town.

2 RESTAURANTS BY CUISINE

French Bistro
Café du Clocher Penché ★
   (St-Roch, $$, p. 232)
L'Ardoise (Basse-Ville/Vieux-Port, $$,
   p. 230)
L'Echaudé ★★ (Basse-Ville/
   Vieux-Port, $$$, p. 228)
Mistral Gagnant ★ (Basse-Ville/
   Vieux-Port, $$, p. 230)

French Contemporary
Initiale ★★★ (Basse-Ville/
   Vieux-Port, $$$$, p. 225)
Le Pain Béni ★ (Haute-Ville, $$,
   p. 225)
Panache ★★ (Basse-Ville/
   Vieux-Port, $$$$, p. 228)
Restaurant Paris Brest ★
   (Parliament Hill, $$$, p. 230)

French/International
Le Café du Monde ★ (Basse-Ville/
   Vieux-Port, $$, p. 230)

Fusion
Laurie Raphaël ★★★ (Basse-Ville/
   Vieux-Port, $$$$, p. 228)
Toast! ★ (Basse-Ville/Vieux-Port, $$$,
   p. 229)
Utopie ★ (St-Roch, $$$, p. 232)
Versa (St-Roch, $$, p. 232)
Voo Doo Grill ★ (Parliament Hill,
   $$$, p. 231)

Light Fare
Café Krieghoff (Parliament Hill, $,
   p. 231)
Paillard (Haute-Ville, $, p. 225)

Quebecois
Aux Anciens Canadiens ★
   (Haute-Ville, $$$, p. 224)

Seafood
Le Marie-Clarisse ★ (Basse-Ville/
   Vieux-Port, $$$, p. 229)
Poisson d'Avril (Basse-Ville/
   Vieux-Port, $$$, p. 229)

Sushi/Japanese
Yuzu Sushi ★ (St-Roch, $$, p. 233)

Key to Abbreviations: $$$$ = Very Expensive $$$ = Expensive $$ = Moderate $ = Inexpensive
The prices within each review refer to the cost in Canadian dollars of individual main courses, using the
following categories: Very Expensive ($$$$), main courses at dinner average more than C$40, Expensive
($$$), C$25 to C$40; Moderate ($$), C$12 to C$25; and Inexpensive ($), C$12 and less.
Restaurants are listed alphabetically at the end of the index in the back of this book.

3 VIEUX-QUEBEC: HAUTE-VILLE (UPPER TOWN)

EXPENSIVE
Aux Anciens Canadiens ★ QUEBECOIS Inundated by travelers during peak
months, this venerable restaurant with costumed servers is in what's probably the city's
oldest (1677) house; its front windows are small because their original glass came over from
France packed in barrels of molasses. Surprisingly, it's one of the best places in La Belle
Province at which to sample cooking that has its roots in New France's earliest years; ancient
Québécois recipes are done well here, if well short of extraordinary. Caribou figures into
many of the dishes, as does maple syrup, which goes into, for example, the duckling,

goat-cheese salad, and luscious sugar pie. Servings are large enough to ward off hunger for a week. The restaurant's afternoon special, from noon to 5:45pm, is a terrific bargain: soup, a main course, a dessert, and a glass of beer or wine for just C$17 (£8.50).

34 rue St-Louis (at rue des Jardins). ✆ **418/692-1627.** www.auxancienscanadiens.qc.ca. Reservations recommended. Main courses C$31–C$55 (£16–£28); *table d'hôte* dinner C$46–C$69 (£23–£35); *table d'hôte* lunch C$17 (£8.50). AE, DC, MC, V. Daily noon–9pm.

MODERATE

Le Pain Béni ★ FRENCH CONTEMPORARY   You know the moment. You're in the mood for adventurous eating, a dip into the local cuisine, and the fanciful taste combinations of a creative chef. But the person you're traveling with wants pizza. Or a steak. Put Pain Béni on your itinerary and everyone ends up happy. There are pizzas— three-cheese and tomato, vegetarian, grilled chicken—and pastas, and a filet mignon with scalloped potatoes. But there are also Québécois classics with modern twists, like blood pudding and Mamirolle cheese in puff pastry with star-anise sauce, or sweetbreads and red tuna caramelized in honey and soy with a vanilla-perfumed artichoke purée. Even the desserts are kicked up a notch, as with the rum-flambéed banana crème brûlée with grilled coconut. This newish restaurant in the heart of Upper Town is handsome and fairly priced.

24 rue Ste-Anne (at rue du Trésor). ✆ **418/694-9485.** Main courses C$15–C$35 (£7.50–£18). AE, DC, MC, V. Daily 11:30am–11:30pm in high-season summer months, until 10pm the rest of the year.

INEXPENSIVE

Paillard LIGHT FARE   Keep this bright, cavernous sandwich shop in mind when you're looking for healthy, fast food to eat in or take out. Hot and cold sandwiches on hearty ciabatta, baguettes, or croissants are the main event, and natural sodas, satisfying espresso drinks, and a yummy selection of pastries and gelato fill out the menu. There's communal seating at big tables and smaller tables as well.

1097 rue St-Jean (near rue St-Stanislas). ✆ **418/692-1221.** www.paillard.ca. All items cost less than C$10 (£5). MC, V. Daily 7:30am–7pm; until 10pm in summer.

---

4 VIEUX-QUEBEC: BASSE-VILLE (LOWER TOWN)/VIEUX-PORT

VERY EXPENSIVE

Initiale ★★★ FRENCH CONTEMPORARY   Initiale is not only one of the elite restaurants of Québec City, but one of the best in the entire province. The palatial setting of tall windows, columns, and a deeply recessed ceiling sets a gracious tone, and the welcome is both cordial and correct. Subdued lighting and the muffled noise level help, too. This is a good place to cast economy to the winds and go with one of the prix-fixe menus. Dinner might start with a buckwheat crepe folded around an artichoke, a round of crabmeat with a creamy purée of onions, and a flash-fried leaf of baby spinach that adds a delicate crackle, all arrayed on the plate as on an artist's palette. It might continue with grilled tuna supported by sweet garlic, salsify, and lemon marmalade, and a swirl of pasta with marguerite leaves. Québec cheeses are an impressive topper. Men should wear jackets; women can pull out the stops.

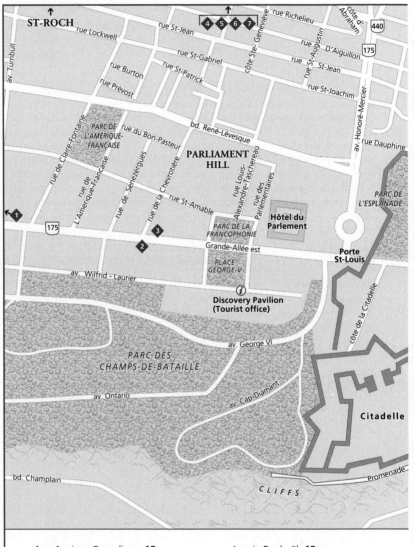

Aux Anciens Canadiens **18**

Café du Clocher Penché **4**

Café Krieghoff **1**

Initiale **16**

L'Ardoise **10**

Laurie Raphaël **12**

Le Café du Monde **13**

Le Pain Béni **19**

L'Echaudé **11**

Le Marie-Clarisse **15**

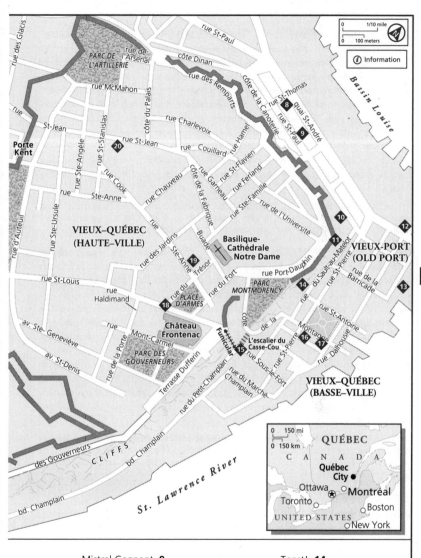

Mistral Gagnant **9**
Paillard **20**
Panache **17**
Poisson d'Avril **8**
Restaurant Paris Brest **3**

Toast! **14**
Utopie **5**
Versa **6**
VooDoo Grill **2**
Yuzu Sushi **7**

54 rue St-Pierre (corner of Côte de la Montagne). ℰ **418/694-1818.** www.restaurantinitiale.com. Reservations recommended on weekends. Main courses C$42–C$46 (£21–£23); *table d'hôte* dinner C$69 (£35); tasting menu C$97 (£49). AE, DC, MC, V. Tues–Fri 11:30am–2pm; Tues–Sat 6–9pm.

Laurie Raphaël ★★★ FUSION   The owners of this smashingly creative restaurant tinker relentlessly with their handiwork. An overhaul of the space a couple of years ago gave it a more sophisticated look, tempered by decorating dashes of eye-popping red and electric pink. From what has long been one of the city's most accomplished kitchens, silky-smooth foie gras arrives on a teeny ice cream paddle, drizzled with a port-and-maple-syrup reduction. Alaskan snow crab is accompanied by a bright-pink pomegranate terrine. An egg-yolk "illusion" of thickened orange juice encapsulated in a pectin skin is served in a puddle of maple syrup in an Asian soup spoon. And so on. It's as if Willy Wonka was in the kitchen. Service is friendly and correct, and the meal's pace is spot-on. A second locale of the same name opened Montréal in fall 2007. At the Québéc location, though, there's a fancy public kitchen where chef/owner Daniel Vézina gives cooking classes.

117 rue Dalhousie (at rue St-André). ℰ **418/692-4555.** www.laurieraphael.com. Reservations recommended. Main courses C$38–C$48 (£19–£24); 3-course chef's inspiration C$60 (£30); gourmet dinner C$94 (£47). AE, DC, DISC, MC, V. Tues–Fri 11:30am–2pm; Tues–Sat 5:30–10pm.

Panache ★★ FRENCH CONTEMPORARY   The restaurant of the superb **Auberge Saint-Antoine** (p. 215) started life in 2004 with a big advantage: It's housed in a former 19th-century warehouse delineated by massive wood beams and rough stone walls. A wrought-iron staircase winds up to a second dining level, creating the feel of a secret attic with tables tucked into its eves. Flickering candles, a center fireplace, velvet couches, generous space between tables, and good acoustics—not loud, not churchlike—enhance the inherent romantic aura. Aiming to serve *cuisine Québécoise revisitée*—French-Canadian cuisine with a twist—the frequently changing menu is heavy on locally sourced game, duck, fish, and vegetables. Descriptions are simple and border on the austere: "Atlantic cod, ginger, beet, Jerusalem artichoke, C$40," or "Gaspor Farm piglet, winter squash, celeriac, raspberries." A slip of a bar inside the restaurant seats about a dozen. **Café Artefact,** a separate lounge just off the Auberge's main lobby, provides a casual pre-meal meeting spot.

10 rue St-Antoine (in Auberge Saint-Antoine). ℰ **418/692-1022.** www.saint-antoine.com. Reservations recommended at dinner. Main courses C$40–C$49 (£20–£25); 7-course tasting menu C$149 (£75); lunch main courses from C$17 (£8.50). AE, DC, MC, V. Mon–Fri 6:30–10:30am; Sat–Sun 7–10am; Mon–Fri noon–2pm; daily 6–10pm.

EXPENSIVE

L'Echaudé ★★ FRENCH BISTRO   The most polished of the necklace of restaurants adorning this Vieux-Port corner, L'Echaudé is like a well-worn cashmere sweater—it goes well with both silk trousers and your favorite pair of jeans. Sit at the stainless-steel bar or at tables covered with butcher paper. Grilled meats and fishes and the seafood stews are satisfying and an excellent value, even if they blaze no new trails. Lunch deals range from fish and mussel soup to steak tartare served with appetizer, dessert, and coffee. Among classics on the menu are steak frites, duck confit, and salmon tartare. Less expected are the shrimp with coconut milk, or the smoked chicken carpaccio. The owner keeps an important cellar with 300 wine varieties; about 20 of them are available by the glass. The bistro is frequented mostly by locals of almost all ages (the very young are rarely seen) and they're attended to by a highly efficient staff. In summer, the small street in front of the patio becomes pedestrian only.

73 rue Sault-au-Matelot (near rue St-Paul). ℭ **418/692-1299.** www.echaude.com. Reservations suggested on weekends. Main courses C$18–C$42 (£9–£21); *table d'hôte* dinner cost of the main course plus C$15 (£7.50). AE, DC, MC, V. Mon–Sat 11:30am–2:30pm; Sun 10:30am–2:30pm; daily 5–10pm.

Le Marie-Clarisse ★ SEAFOOD   This spot, at the bottom of Breakneck Stairs and perched overlooking the pedestrian-only rue du Petit-Champlain, sits where the streets are awash with day-trippers and shutterbugs. It serves what many consider to be the best seafood in town. The menu changes often, so look closely at the long list of specials posted on chalkboards. A more pleasant hour cannot be passed anywhere in Québec City than here, over a platter of shrimp or pâtés, out on the terrace on a summer afternoon. In winter, cocoon by the stone fireplace inside, indulging in the dense bouillabaisse—a stew of mussels, scallops, tuna, tilapia, and shrimp, with a boat of saffron mayo to slather on croutons. Try a Québec wine to wash it down, maybe L'Orpailleur from Dunham. The inside rooms are formed of rafters, brick, and stone walls that are more than 300 years old, evoking the feel of a small country inn.

12 rue du Petit-Champlain (at the funicular). ℭ **418/692-0857.** www.marieclarisse.qc.ca. Main courses C$30–C$35 (£15–£18); *table d'hôte* dinner C$48–C$56 (£24–£28). AE, MC, V. Daily 11:30am–10pm in summer; dinner only the rest of the year.

Poisson d'Avril SEAFOOD   Nautical trappings that include model ships, marine prints, and mounted sailfish make the intention clear here: The menu is packed with seafood, including some combinations of costly crustaceans responsible for the stiffer prices. A crowded bouillabaisse Provençal fits in calamari, scallops, shrimp, mussels, and *rouille*. Mixed grills and pastas are also available. In good weather, there's a covered dining terrace. It's almost directly across from Espace 400e (p. 241), the port-side interpretation center that opened in 2008.

115 quai Saint-André (in Vieux-Port). ℭ **418/692-1010.** www.poissondavril.net. Reservations recommended. Main courses C$13–C$67 (£6.50–£34); *table d'hôte* C$30–C$80 (£15–£40). AE, DC, MC, V. Daily 5–10pm.

Toast! ★ FUSION   This zesty restaurant adjoins **Hôtel Le Priori** (p. 216) and occupies the space where Laurie Raphaël (p. 228) started before it went on to become the city's gastronomic flag bearer. There must be good karma here, because Toast! continues to impress. As is true of most important restaurants in the province, the kitchen has its base in the French idiom, but it takes off from there in many directions. Experience that in a pecan-crusted rack of rabbit with a cold purée of potato, cream, and horseradish, perked with a basil foam and Parmesan. Or try the fennel soup followed by chopped tuna, spiced with ginger and lemon zest, shaped into a burger and then grilled—but on just one side. Every dish is like that: audacious, sprightly, and attentive to joined tastes and textures. The interior room glows crimson from a wall of fire-engine-red tiles, retro-modern lights, and red Plexiglas window paneling. The outdoor dining terrace in back, with wrought-iron furniture and big leafy trees overhead, is an oasis.

17 rue Sault-au-Matelot (at rue St-Antoine). ℭ **418/692-1334.** www.restauranttoast.com. Reservations recommended on weekends. *Table d'hôte* dinner C$65 or C$75 (£33–£38); lunch C$17 (£8.50); brunch C$15 (£7.50). AE, DC, MC, V. Mon–Fri 7–10am and 11:30am–2pm; Sat–Sun 7:30–10am; Sun 11am–2pm; Wed–Sun 6–10pm (until 10:30pm Thurs–Sat).

L'Ardoise FRENCH BISTRO   One of several appealing bistros that wrap around the intersection of rues St-Paul and Sault-au-Matelot in Vieux-Port, L'Ardoise is a place to sip a double espresso, leaf through a book, and maybe meet the neighbors. A new owner took over in 2006 but has kept the Van Gogh–bright orange swirls and cobalt-blue ceiling overhead, and jaunty Piaf- and Sinatra-style voices on the stereo. The menu, though, has been tinkered with and is now a little more sleeked down. For instance, mussels, a staple at Québec restaurants, used to be offered with 11 sauce options; now there are three options (and a plate that offers a selection of each). An additional brunch menu is an option on weekends.

71 rue St-Paul (near rue du Sault-au-Matelot). ✆ **418/694-0213.** Reservations recommended for dinner. Main courses C$17–C$30 (£8.50–£15). AE, DC, MC, V. Mon–Fri 11:30am–3pm; Sat–Sun 10:30am–3pm; daily 5:30–10pm (closing earlier in winter).

Le Café du Monde ★ ⓥalue FRENCH/INTERNATIONAL   A longtime and entirely convivial eating venue, Café du Monde moved in 2002 to its current location adjoining Le Terminal de Croisières—the cruise terminal. It's a rather large, Parisian-style space, seating more than 100 inside and nearly that number on a terrace overlooking the St. Lawrence River. The staff is as amiable as ever, the food a touch more creative but still within bistro conventions. The menu continues to feature classic French preparations of pâtés, duck confit, onion soup, smoked salmon tartare, and three versions of mussels with frites. Even on busy holiday weekends, brunch plates—scrambled eggs with salmon, dill, potatoes, fruit, and a croissant—are served fast and with a smile.

84 rue Dalhousie (next to the cruise terminal). ✆ **418/692-4455.** www.lecafedumonde.com. Reservations recommended. Main courses C$12–C$20 (£6–£10); table d'hôte add C$14 (£7) to cost of main course. AE, DC, MC, V. Mon–Fri 11:30am–11pm; Sat–Sun and holidays 9:30am–11pm.

Mistral Gagnant ★ ⓥalue FRENCH BISTRO   This "restaurant Provençal" channels the spirit of a modest village cafe in France, in both its sunny decor and its friendly atmosphere. Better yet, the food is modestly priced and tasty. A main course at lunch, a *duo de poissons a l'huile de basilica,* turns out to be a full plate of flakey white sea bass with pesto, salmon, scalloped potatoes, carrot mousse, and cauliflower—all fresh and well seasoned. With gazpacho to start, a slice of sublime lemon pie to close, and a price of less than C$15 (£7.50), a meal here can be the best bargain in the area. "Le Mistral" attracts locals of a certain age and, it appears, nearly no tourists.

160 rue St. Paul (near rue Rioux). ✆ **418/692-4260.** www.mistralgagnant.ca. Main courses C$13–C$29 (£6.50–£14); table d'hôte dinner C$22–C$35 (£11–£17); lunch and 3-course early-bird special 5:30–6:30pm C$11–C$15 (£5.50–£7.50). AE, MC, V. Tues–Sat 11:30am–2pm and 5:30–9pm.

---

5 PARLIAMENT HILL/ON OR NEAR GRANDE-ALLÉE

EXPENSIVE

Restaurant Paris Brest ★ FRENCH CONTEMPORARY   Named for a French dessert (an almond-topped pastry filled with butter cream), this is one of the best restaurants outside the walls, tendering a polished performance from greeting to check. It

(Finds) Picnic Fare

Le Petit-Cartier is a mall for foodies: About a dozen merchants in open-fronted shops purvey cheeses, pâtés, terrines, glistening produce, pastries, confections, fresh meats, fish, sushi, deli products, and fancy picnic items. A few counters make sandwiches to order and there's a small grocery store in back. It's open 7 days a week and located just outside the tourist orbit: west of Parliament Hill, in the Montcalm residential neighborhood, at 1191 av. Cartier (1 block off Grande Allée).

draws a fashionable crowd wearing everything from bespoke suits to designer jeans. The menu doesn't change much, so pay attention to the daily specials, which are more likely to demonstrate the kitchen's creativity. Wapiti with raspberry sauce and spiced pear was a recent highlight, as was roasted salmon with tomatoes and balsamic vinaigrette. The restaurant is an easy stroll from the St-Louis gate of the Old City walls.

590 Grande-Allée est (at rue de la Chevrotière). (C) **418/529-2243.** Reservations recommended. Main courses C$15–C$28 (£7.50–£14); *table d'hôte* dinner C$23–C$36 (£12–£13). AE, DC, MC, V. Mon–Fri 11:30am–3pm; daily 5–11pm.

Voo Doo Grill ★ FUSION   Of all the unlikely places to expect a decent meal, let alone one that surpasses most of what can be found at more conventional local restaurants, Voo Doo takes the laurels. Waitstaff are clad in all black (women in sleeveless halter tops—even when temperatures are arctic outside), African carvings adorn the walls, thumping music sets the pace, and conga drummers circulate nightly, beating out rapid, insistent rhythms—a tremendous distraction. It is all loud, young, and casual. Options range from a plate featuring shrimps, scallops, and Chinese ravioli stuffed with seafood to General Tao's chicken, which is presented Québec-style. The cover charge for the disco upstairs, **Maurice** (p. 268), is waived with proof that you ate at Voo Doo. There's also an attached cigar lounge, the **Société Cigare.**

575 Grande-Allée est (corner of rue de la Chevrotière). (C) **418/647-2000.** www.voodoogrill.com. Reservations recommended. Main courses C$14–C$58 (£7–£29), with most costing less than C$30 (£15). AE, DC, MC, V. Mon–Fri 11am–2am; Sat–Sun 5pm–2am.

INEXPENSIVE

Café Krieghoff LIGHT FARE   Walk down Grande-Allée about 10 minutes from Parliament, and turn right on avenue Cartier. This 5-block strip is the heart of the Montcalm residential neighborhood, with bakeries, boutiques, an Indian restaurant, and a mini-mall of food shops (see "Picnic Fare," below). In the middle of it all is this cheerful cafe, which features an outdoor terrace a few steps up from the sidewalk. On weekend mornings, it's packed with artsy locals of all ages, whose tables get piled high with bowls of café au lait and huge plates of egg dishes, sweet pastries, or steak frites. Service is efficient and good-natured.

1091 av. Cartier (north of Grande-Allée). (C) **418/522-3711.** www.cafekrieghoff.qc.ca. Most items cost less than C$11 (£5.50). MC, V. Mon–Fri 7am–10pm; Sat 8am–11pm; Sun 8am–9pm.

EXPENSIVE

Utopie ★ (Finds) FUSION   Utopie continues to have the essential ingredients for its considerable success: The clientele has a stylish sheen, the interior is almost painfully chic, the food isn't same-old, and the location is sufficiently out of the way to require that customers are those in the know. Stands of birch trunks march down the middle of the high-ceilinged space, and blown-up photos of bark align on one wall. The chef is a co-owner and clearly ambitious. Daïkon vanilla cream soup opened one meal; at another, sautéed *lotte* (monkfish) was joined with translucent baby bok choy and wild asparagus no thicker than bean sprouts took center stage. There are two all-out meal options: an eight-course degustation menu with wine pairing for C$135 (£68), and the *menu bouteille*, in which the chef creates a meal around a wine you pick. A new tapas and wine bar right next door, **Le Cercle** (p. 267), is run by the chef and two others and serves food until 1am.

226½ rue St-Joseph est (near rue Caron). ℰ **418/523-7878.** www.restaurant-utopie.com. Reservations recommended on weekends. Main courses C$28–C$32 (£14–£16); 8-course tasting dinner C$85 (£43); *menu bouteille* C$50 (£25) per person plus C$65 (£33) for the wine; *table d'hôte* lunch C$19 (£9.50). AE, MC, V. Thurs–Fri noon–2pm; Tues–Sun 6–9pm.

MODERATE

Café du Clocher Penché ★ (Finds) FRENCH BISTRO   Open since 2000, the development of this unpretentious neighborhood bistro parallels the polishing up the overall neighborhood has seen during the same period. With its caramel-toned woods, tall ceilings, and walls serving as gallery space for local artists, Clocher Penché maintains a laid-back European sophistication. A huge wine list features nearly 200 choices, with three quarters of the bottles organic or "biodynamic"; about a dozen wines are sold by the glass. The short menu changes regularly and can include duck confit and wild boar. A terrific rich blood sausage *(boudin noir)* is served on a delicate pastry bed with caramelized onions and yellow beets. The menu touts that nearly everything is sourced locally. Service reflects the food—amiable and without flourishes.

203 rue St-Joseph est (at rue Caron). ℰ **418/640-0597.** Reservations recommended. Main courses C$18–C$25 (£9–£13); *table d'hôte* lunch and weekend brunch C$14 (£7). AE, MC, V. Mon–Fri 11:30am–3pm; Sat–Sun 9am–2pm; daily 5–10pm.

Versa FUSION   Looking more like a club than a restaurant, Versa is a destination to remember when with a group in a partying mood. A communal table sits beneath a teak oval ceiling illuminated by pin lights and a basketball-size disco ball, seats have a '60s Swedish mien, and the translucent panels behind the back bar pulse with a rainbow of colors, highlighting the pride of the barkeeps, their inventive roster of cocktails. A wide selection of appetizers invites grazing: mini salmon tartar burgers, perhaps, or maybe duck *poutine*. The windows along the front open in good weather, and the evening action floats between here and the **Boudoir Lounge** (p. 268) across the street, a busy nightspot in the heart of what locals call "Le Nouveau St-Roch."

432 rue du Parvis (at rue St-Françoise). ℰ **418/523-9995.** www.versarestaurant.com. Main courses C$13–C$36 (£6.50–£18); *table d'hôte* dinner C$21–C$33 (£11–£17), lunch C$9–C$18 (£4.50–£9). MC, V. Mon–Fri 11am–midnight; Sat–Sun 5pm–midnight.

Yuzu Sushi ★ SUSHI/JAPANESE   At the epicenter of the renovated portion of St-
Roch, an area that's slowly getting a youthful pop amid otherwise dreary office buildings
and low-key retail, Yuzu focuses on sushi and Japanese preparations. But authenticity isn't
paramount, not with foie gras on the card (yes, it's as expensive as you'd expect). Individual sushi rolls run from C$4 to C$15 (£2–£7.50) each, but you can opt for tasting
menus of C$65 (£33) for five courses and C$85 (£43) for seven.

438 rue du Parvis (at bd. Charest). ✆ **418/521-7253.** www.yuzu.ca. Reservations recommended. Main
courses C$12–C$22 (£6–£11). AE, DC, MC, V. Mon–Fri 11:30am–2:30pm; daily 5–10pm.

Exploring Québec City

Wandering at random through the streets of Vieux-Québec is a singular pleasure, comparable to exploring a provincial capital in Europe. You might happen upon an ancient convent, blocks of gabled houses with steeply pitched roofs, a battery of 18th-century cannons in a leafy park, or a bistro with a blazing fireplace on a wintry day.

The Old City, Upper and Lower, is so compact that it's hardly necessary to plan precise sightseeing itineraries. Start at Terrasse Dufferin alongside the Château Frontenac and go off on a whim, down Breakneck Stairs (L'Escalier du Casse-Cou) to the Quartier du Petit-Champlain and Place-Royale, or out of the walls to the military fortress of the Citadelle that overlooks the mighty St. Lawrence River and onto the Plains of Abraham, where generals James Wolfe of Britain and Louis-Joseph, marquis de Montcalm of France, fought to their mutual deaths in a 20-minute battle that changed the continents' destiny.

Most of the historic sights are within the city walls of Vieux-Québec's Haute-Ville (Upper Town) and Basse-Ville (Lower Town). While Upper Town is hilly, with sloping streets, it's nothing like, say, San Francisco, and only people with physical limitations are likely to experience difficulty. Other sights are outside Upper Town's walls, along or just off the boulevard called Grande-Allée. If rain or ice discourages exploration on foot, tour buses and horse-drawn *calèches* are options.

If you're planning to visit several museums, consider buying a **Québec City Museum Card.** Good for 3 consecutive days, the pass gives entry to 20 museums and attractions, including many mentioned in this chapter, and includes two 1-day bus passes. The price is C$50 (£25); there are no discounts for seniors or children. It's available at all participating attractions and at the Québec City Tourism Information Bureau at 835 av. Wilfrid-Laurier, in the Discovery Pavillion. To find out more, call ⓒ **418/641-6290** or visit www.museocapitale.qc.ca.

1 THE TOP ATTRACTIONS

VIEUX-QUEBEC: BASSE-VILLE (LOWER TOWN)

Musée de la Civilisation ★★★ (Kids)   Try to set aside at least 2 hours for a visit to this special museum, one of the most engrossing in all of Canada. Open since 1988, it's an innovative presence on the waterfront of historic Basse-Ville—but its precise mission has never been entirely clear. Recent temporary exhibits, for example, have included the science and fiction of dragons, 110 years of Québec cinema, and the opportunity to solve a faux murder. No matter. Through highly imaginative display techniques, hands-on devices, holograms, and even an ant farm, curators have ensured that visitors will be so enthralled by the experience that they won't pause to question its intent.

A dramatic atrium-lobby sets the tone with a representation of the St. Lawrence River with an ancient ship beached on the shore. If time is short, definitely take in "*People of Québec . . . Then and Now,*" a permanent exhibit that is a sprawling examination of Québec history, moving from the province's roots as a fur-trading colony to the present, providing visitors with a rich sense of Québec's daily life over the generations. Another permanent exhibition, "Encounter with the First Nations," examines the visions and products of the aboriginal tribes that inhabited the region before the Europeans arrived and still maintain a presence.

Exhibit texts are in French and English, and there's a ground-floor cafe. Through the glass wall in the back, you can see the 1752 Maison Estèbe, now restored to contain the museum shop.

85 rue Dalhousie (at rue St-Antoine). ℭ 418/643-2158. www.mcq.org. Admission C$10 (£5) adults, C$9 (£4.50) 65 and older, C$7 (£3.50) students older than 16, C$4 (£2) children 12–16, free for children 11 and younger; free to all on Tues Nov 1–May 31 and Sat 10am–noon Jan–Feb. Late June to early Sept daily 9am–7pm; rest of the year Tues–Sun 10am–5pm.

Place-Royale ★★★ Ⓚⓘⓓⓢ This small but picturesque plaza is considered by Québé-cois to be the literal and spiritual heart of Basse-Ville—in grander terms, the birthplace of French America. There's a **bust of Louis XIV** in the center. In the 17th and 18th centuries, Place-Royal, or "Royal Square," was the town marketplace and the center of business and industry and was populated by many rich merchants.

Eglise Notre-Dame-des-Victoires dominates the plaza. It's Québec's oldest stone church, built in 1688 after a massive fire in Lower Town destroyed 55 homes in 1682. The church was restored in 1763 and again in 1969. Its paintings, altar, and large model boat suspended from the ceiling were votive offerings brought by early settlers to ensure safe voyages. The church is open daily to visitors May through October; admission is free. Sunday Masses are held at 10:30am and noon.

Commercial activity here began to stagnate around 1860, and by 1950 this was a poor, rundown district. Rehabilitation began in 1960, and all the buildings on the square have now been restored, though only some of the walls are original.

For years, there was an empty lot behind the stone façade on the west side, which now is a whole building again housing the **Centre d'Interprétation de Place-Royale** on the ground floor. Inside, a 20-minute multimedia show and other exhibitions detail the city's 400-year history. Guided tours explaining the plaza's role are available in both English and French. When you exit, turn left and at the end of the block, turn around to view a *trompe l'oeil* mural depicting citizens of the early city.

Centre d'Interprétation de Place-Royale, 27 rue Notre-Dame. ℭ 418/646-3167. www.mcq.org. Free admission to the Place-Royale and Eglise Notre-Dame-des-Victoires; Center d'Interprétation admission C$5 (£2.50) adults, C$4.50 (£2) seniors, C$3.50 (£2) students, C$2 (£1) ages 12–16, free for children 11 and younger. June 24–Sept 1 daily 9:30am–5pm; Sept 2–June 23 Tues–Sun 10am–5pm.

VIEUX-QUEBEC: HAUTE-VILLE (UPPER TOWN)

La Citadelle ★★ The duke of Wellington had this partially star-shaped fortress built at the south end of the city walls in anticipation of renewed American attacks after the War of 1812. Some remnants of earlier French military structures were incorporated into the Citadelle, including a 1750 magazine. Dug into the Plains of Abraham high above Cap Diamant (Cape Diamond), the rock bluff adjacent to the St. Lawrence River, the

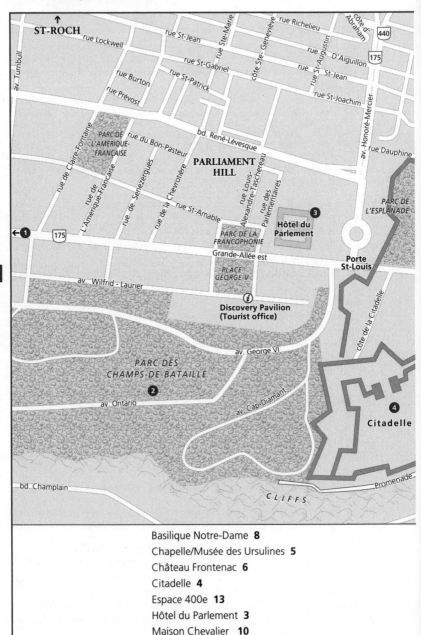

EXPLORING QUÉBEC CITY

16

THE TOP ATTRACTIONS

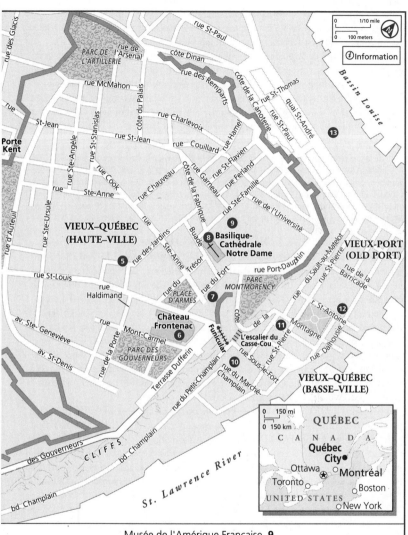

Musée de l'Amérique Française **9**

Musée de la Civilisation **12**

Musée des Beaux-Arts du Québec **1**

Musée du Fort **7**

Parc de l'Artillerie **14**

Parc des Champs-de-Bataille **2**

Place-Royale **11**

fort has a low profile that keeps it all but invisible until walkers are actually upon it. The facility has never actually exchanged fire with an invader but continues its vigil for the state. It's now a national historic site, and since 1920 has been home to Québec's Royal 22e Régiment, the only fully Francophone unit in Canada's armed forces. That makes it North America's largest fortified group of buildings still occupied by troops.

You can only go in by guided tour, which provides access to the Citadelle and its 25 buildings, including the small regimental museums in the former powder house and prison. The hour-long walk and dry narration are likely to test the patience of younger visitors and the legs of many older people. For them, it might be better simply to attend the ceremonies of the **changing of the guard** (daily at 10am in summer) or **beating the retreat,** a sunset ceremony to call in the troops (Fri, Sat, and Sun at 7pm in summer). Walk or drive up the Côte de la Citadelle; there are many free parking spaces.

Côte de la Citadelle (enter off rue St-Louis). ✆ **418/694-2815.** www.lacitadelle.qc.ca. Admission C$10 (£5) adults, C$9 (£4.50) older students and senior citizens (65 and up), C$5.50 (£4) students 17 and younger. Apr daily 10am–4pm; May–June daily 9am–5pm; July to Labour Day daily 9am–6pm; Sept (after Labour Day) daily 9am–4pm; Oct daily 10am–3pm; Nov–Mar, 1 bilingual tour per day at 1:30pm. Changing of the guard (30 min.) June 24 to Labour Day daily at 10am; beating the retreat (20 min.) July to early Sept Fri at 7pm (and Sat–Sun at 7pm at the Esplanade Park). May be canceled in the event of rain.

PARLIAMENT HILL/NEAR GRANDE-ALLEE

Musée National des Beaux-Arts du Québec ★★★ Kids Toward the southwestern end of Parc des Champs-de-Bataille (Battlefields Park) and a half-hour walk from Upper Town, the Musée du Québec, as it's known, is the city's major art museum. It occupies a former prison, a soaring glass-roofed Grand Hall, a stylish cafe, and a shop.

The best reason to visit is to see the Inuit art collected over the years by Québécois **Raymond Brousseau.** In 2005, the museum acquired his major collection, which was assembled over many years. The art and artifacts here are decidedly non-kitschy, especially when compared to the goods passed off as art in inexpensive souvenir shops all over town. Much of what's in this collection has been produced in the last 20 years, and 285 works from the 2,635-piece collection are on display. (Look for the small, whimsical statue called "Woman Pulling out Grey Hairs.")

The original 1933 **Gérard-Morisset Pavilion** houses much of the rest of the museum's permanent collection—North America's largest aggregation of Québécois art fills eight galleries with works produced from the beginning of the colony to the present. The museum tilts to the modern and the indigenous, with a permanent exhibition, for instance, of works by famed Québec abstract expressionist and surrealist Jean-Paul Riopelle. Included is his *L'Hommage à Rosa Luxemburg,* a triptych made up of 30 individual paintings that include spray-painted outlines of birds and handyman tools.

The second building is the 1867 **Charles-Baillairgé Pavilion,** a former prison with one cellblock left intact as an exhibit. Keep climbing until you reach the tower room; it's the museum's highest point, a small widow's walk accessible only by spiral staircase. In addition to housing the massive wooden sculpture of a body in motion by Irish artist David Moore, the petite space offers terrific views of the city in every direction.

Several spots in the museum focus on children, including a craft-projects room. An accomplished cafe serves lunch Monday through Friday, brunch on Saturday and Sunday, and dinner on Wednesday.

www.mnba.qc.ca. Free admission to permanent collection. Admission for special exhibitions C$15 (£7.50) adults, C$12 (£6) 65 and older, C$7 (£3.50) students 18 and older, C$4 (£2) ages 12–17, free for children 11 and younger. June 1 to Labour Day daily 10am–6pm (until 9pm Wed); day after Labour Day to May 31 Tues–Sun 10am–5pm (until 9pm Wed). Bus: 11.

Parc des Champs-de-Bataille ★★ (Kids) Covering 108 hectares (267 acres) of grassy hills, sunken gardens, monuments, fountains, and trees, Québec's Battlefields Park was Canada's first national urban park. It also goes by the name the **Plains of Abraham,** and is where Britain's General James Wolfe and France's Louis-Joseph, marquis de Montcalm, engaged in their short but crucial battle in 1759 which resulted in the British defeat of the French troops—and in the deaths of both military leaders. Today, it's a favorite place for Québécois when they want sunshine or a bit of exercise.

From spring through fall, see the **Jardin Jeanne d'Arc (Joan of Arc Garden),** just off avenue Wilfrid-Laurier near the Loews le Concorde Hotel. This spectacular garden combines French classical style with British-looking flower beds. Through the rest of the park, nearly 6,000 trees representing more than 80 species blanket the fields. Prominent among these are sugar maple, silver maple, Norway maple, American elm, and American ash. Also in the park are two Martello towers, cylindrical stone defensive structures built between 1808 and 1812 when Québec feared an American invasion.

In summer, free concerts are given at the park's bandstand, **Kiosque Edwin-Bélanger.** Fittingly, the national anthem, *O Canada,* was first performed here.

The **Discovery Pavilion of the Plains of Abraham,** at 835 av. Wilfrid-Laurier (ⓒ **418/648-4071**), near the Citadelle, has a gift shop, bathrooms, racks of brochures, and a multimedia exhibit called "Odyssey: A Journey through History on the Plains of Abraham," which is presented in English, French, Spanish, and Japanese.

Parc des Champs-de-Bataille. www.ccbn-nbc.gc.ca. Discovery Pavilion, 835 av. Wilfrid-Laurier. ⓒ **418/ 648-4071.** Odyssey show C$10 (£5) adults, C$7 (£3.50) seniors and ages 13–17, C$3 (£1.50) 12 and younger; discount prices mid-Sept to mid-June. Summer daily 8:30am–5:30pm; winter Mon–Fri 8:30am– 5pm, Sat 9am–5pm, Sun 10am–5pm.

---

2 MORE ATTRACTIONS

VIEUX-QUEBEC: HAUTE-VILLE (UPPER TOWN)
Basilique Notre-Dame ★ Notre-Dame Basilica, representing the oldest Christian parish north of Mexico, has weathered a tumultuous history of bombardment, reconstruction, and restoration. Parts of the existing basilica date from the original 1647 structure, including the bell tower and portions of the walls, but most of today's exterior is from the reconstruction completed in 1771. The interior, a re-creation undertaken after a fire in 1922, is flamboyantly neo-baroque, with glinting yellow gold leaf and shadows wavering by the fluttering light of votive candles. Paintings and ecclesiastical treasures still remain from the time of the French regime, including a chancel lamp given by Louis XIV. More than 900 people are buried in the crypt, including four governors of New France (Frontenac, Vaudreuil, Callières, and Jonquière). The basilica is connected to the group of old buildings that make up Québec Seminary.

16 rue Buade (at Côte de la Fabrique). (C) **418/694-0665.** Free admission for those who come for prayers and services, but donations are encouraged. Daily 8am–4pm. Guided tours May–Oct daily. Tour C$2 (£1) adults, free for children 16 and younger. Crypt C$2 (£1) adults, C$1 (50p) children 16 and younger.

Chapelle/Musée des Ursulines   Marie de l'Incarnation arrived in Québec City in 1639 and her Ursuline convent, originally built as a girls' school in 1642, is North America's oldest. The museum tells the story of the nuns, who were also pioneers and artists. On display are vestments woven with gold thread and a cape made of the drapes from the bedroom of Anne of Austria, which was given to the 40-year-old Marie de l'Incarnation when she left for New France. There are also musical instruments and Amerindian crafts, including the *flèche,* or arrow sash, which is still worn during the winter carnival. Some of the docents are nuns of the still-active order.

The chapel is notable for the sculptures in its pulpit and two richly decorated altarpieces, created by Pierre-Noël Levasseur between 1726 and 1736. Although the present building dates only from 1902, much of the interior decoration is nearly 200 years older. Marie de l'Incarnation's tomb is to the right of the entry. Pope John Paul II beatified her in 1980.

12 rue Donnacona (des Jardins). (C) **418/694-0694.** http://museocapitale.qc.ca/014a.htm. Free admission to chapel. Museum C$6 (£3) adults, C$5 (£2.50) seniors, C$4 (£2) students, C$3 (£1.50) ages 12–16, free for children 11 and younger. Museum May–Sept Tues–Sat 10am–noon and 1–5pm, Sun 1–5pm; Oct–Apr Tues–Sun 1–5pm. Chapel May–Oct Tues–Sat 10–11:30am and 1:30–4:30pm, and Sun 1:30–4:30pm.

Château Frontenac ★   This monster version of a Loire Valley palace is Québec City's emblem, its Eiffel Tower. Visitors curious about the interior can take a 50-minute guided tour, which is led by a costumed guide. The hotel opened in 1893 to house railroad passengers and encourage tourism; it's visible from almost every quarter of the city, commanding its majestic position atop Cap Diamant, the rock bluff that once provided military defense. Tour reservations are recommended. See p. 210 for accommodation details.

1 rue des Carrières, at Place d'Armes. (C) **418/691-2166.** Tours C$8.50 (£4) adults, C$8 (£4) for seniors, C$6 (£3) children 6–16, free for children 5 and younger. May 1–Oct 15 daily 10am–6pm; Oct 16–Apr 30 Sat–Sun noon–5pm. Departures on the hour.

Musée de l'Amérique Française   Located at the Québec Seminary, which dates from 1663, the "Museum of French America" focuses on, as one might guess from the name, the evolution of French culture in North America. Its collections include paintings by European and Canadian artists, engravings from the early French regime, rare books, early scientific instruments, even mounted animals and an Egyptian mummy. The mix makes for a mostly engrossing visit, though parts of the museum can be rather dry. The museum is in three parts of the large seminary complex, and the beautiful François-Ranvoyze section has extensive *trompe l'oeil* ornamentation and served as a chapel for the seminary priests and students. Concerts are often given in the chapel, which Pope Jean-Paul II visited in 1984.

2 Côte de la Fabrique (next to Basilique Notre-Dame). (C) **418/692-2843.** www.mcq.org. Admission C$6 (£3) adults, C$5 (£2.50) seniors, C$3.50 (£2) students, C$2 (£1) children 12–16, free for children 11 and younger; free to all Tues Nov–May. Late June to Labour Day daily 9:30am–5pm; Sept to mid-June Tues–Sun 10am–5pm. Guided tours at 10am and 3:30pm daily; the language of the tour is determined by the first registered visitor.

Musée du Fort A long-running but still effective multimedia show combines film, light, stirring music, and a 36-sq.-m (400-sq.-ft.) scale model of the city and environs to tell the story of several battles that flared here in the 18th century. At 30 minutes, it's a sufficiently engrossing presentation during which only the very young are likely to grow restless. Check in advance to find out when English-language shows are scheduled.

10 rue Ste-Anne, Place d'Armes. (✆ **418/692-2175.** www.museedufort.com. Admission C$8 (£4) adults, C$6 (£3) seniors, C$5 (£2.50) students. Apr–Oct daily 10am–5pm; Nov–Mar Thurs–Sun 11am–4pm (except Dec 26–1st Sun in Jan, when it's open daily 11am–4pm). Open to groups with reservations in winter months.

Parc de l'Artillerie A complex of defensive buildings erected by the French in the 17th and 18th centuries make up Artillery Park, including an ammunition factory that was functional until 1964 (it was staffed by Canadian Rosie the Riveter–type women during World War II). On view are the iron foundry, officers' mess and quarters, and a scale model of the city created in 1806. (It may be a blow to romantics and history buffs to learn that the nearby St-Jean Gate in the city wall was built in 1940, the fourth in a series that began with the original 1693 entrance, which was replaced in 1747, and then replaced again in 1867.)

2 rue d'Auteuil (near Porte St-Jean). (✆ **418/648-4205.** www.pc.gc.ca/artillerie. Admission C$4 (£2) adults, C$3.50 (£2) age 65 and older, C$2 (£1) ages 6–16, free for age 5 and younger. Additional fees for audio guide and special activities. Apr–Oct 7 daily 10am–5pm; by reservation only the rest of the year.

VIEUX-QUEBEC: BASSE-VILLE (LOWER TOWN)

L'Escalier du Casse-Cou These stairs connect Terrasse Dufferin at the top of the cliff with rue Sous-le-Fort at the base. The name translates to **"Breakneck Stairs,"** which is self-explanatory as soon as you see them. They lead—very steeply—from Haute-Ville to the Quartier du Petit-Champlain in Basse-Ville. A stairway has existed here since the settlement began. In fact, in 1698, the town council forbade citizens from taking their animals up or down the stairway; if they didn't comply, they were punished with a fine.

Espace 400e At the site of what used to be an old-fashioned interpretation center, this all-new waterfront pavilion opened in June 2008 as the central location for Québec's 400th-anniversary celebrations. Purposely raw-looking, it's a vast concrete, metal, and glass space ideal for avant-garde, dreamlike exhibits. Its initial offering was a smashingly innovative work that featured whispered audio, dim lighting, stories from dozens of "regular-folk" Québecois about their family histories, and a clever, interactive motif that allowed visitors to imagine what it might have been like to arrive here as an immigrant. From 2009 on, Espace will be a Parks Canada discovery center, with exhibits to be determined.

100 quai St-Andre (at rue Rioux). www.pc.gc.ca. (Further information not yet available at press time.)

Maison Chevalier Built in 1752 for ship owner Jean-Baptiste Chevalier, the existing structure incorporated two older buildings dating from 1675 and 1695. It was run as an inn throughout the 19th century, and after the Québec government restored the house, it became a museum in 1965. The interior has exposed wood beams, wide-board floors, and stone fireplaces. A permanent exhibit, "A Sense of the Past," shows how people lived in the 18th and 19th centuries. While exhibit texts are in French, guidebooks in English are available at the sometimes-unattended front desk. The house also serves as an air-conditioned refuge on hot days.

50 rue du Marché-Champlain (near rue Notre-Dame). ℂ **418/646-3167.** www.mcq.org. Free admission. Late June to Labour Day daily 9:30am–5pm; rest of the year Tues–Sun 10am–5pm.

PARLIAMENT HILL/NEAR GRANDE-ALLEE

Hôtel du Parlement   Since 1968, what the Québécois call their "National Assembly" has occupied this imposing Second-Empire château constructed in 1886. Twenty-two bronze statues of some of the most prominent figures in Québec province's tumultuous history gaze out from the façade. Inside, highlights include the Assembly Chamber and the Legislative Council Chamber, where parliamentary committees meet. Throughout the building, representations of the fleur-de-lis and the initials VR (for Victoria Regina) remind visitors of Québec's dual heritage. The building can be toured unaccompanied, but guided tours are available weekdays year-round from 9am to 4:30pm, and weekends in summer from 10am to 4:30pm. Go to door no. 3 to enter.

The grand Beaux-Arts style restaurant **Le Parlementaire** (ℂ **418/643-6640**) is open to the public as well as parliamentarians and visiting dignitaries. Featuring Québec products and cuisine, it serves breakfast and lunch Monday through Friday most of the year.

Entrance at corner of Grande-Allée est and av. Honoré-Mercier. ℂ **418/643-7239.** www.assnat.qc.ca. Free admission. Guided tours in summer Mon–Fri 9am–4:30pm, Sat–Sun and holidays 10am–4:30pm; in winter Mon–Fri 9am–4:30pm.

3 ESPECIALLY FOR KIDS

If military sites are appealing to your children, take them to see the colorful ceremonies at **La Citadelle:** the changing of the guard and beating retreat (p. 235).

To allow them to run off excess energy, head for **Parc des Champs-de-Bataille (Battlefields Park,** also called the **Plains of Abraham;** p. 239), adjacent to the Citadelle. Acres of grassy lawn give kids room to roam and are perfect for a family picnic.

Children who have responded to Arthurian tales of fortresses and castles or to Harry Potter's adventures will delight in simply walking around this storybook city. Start at **Terrasse Dufferin** in Upper Town, where there are coin-operated telescopes, street entertainers, and ice-cream stands.

A few steps away, at Place d'Armes, is the **Musée du Fort** (see above), at 10 rue Ste-Anne which is a kid-friendly presentation of the city's military history. Also at Place d'Armes is the top of **Breakneck Stairs** (see above). Halfway down, across the road, are giant **cannons** ranged along the battlements on rue des Ramparts. The gun carriages are impervious to the assaults of small humans, so kids can scramble all over them at will. At the bottom of Breakneck Stairs, on the left, is a glass-blowing workshop, the **Verrerie la Mailloche.** It's somewhat less impervious to the assaults of small humans, but still kid-friendly: In the downstairs room, craftsmen give intriguing and informative glass-blowing demonstrations.

In Lower Town, at 86 rue Dalhousie, the terrific **Musée de la Civilisation** (p. 234) presents child-friendly exhibits as well as a shop and cafe.

When in doubt, though, head to the water. **Montmorency Falls** (p. 276) makes a terrific day trip for kids of all ages; it's just 10 minutes north of the city by car. On Wednesdays and Saturdays from late July to mid-August, the city hosts a grand fireworks competition, **Les Grands Feux Loto-Québec** (p. 30), at the falls, during which international pyrotechnic teams presents their own programs.

Canyon Ste-Anne (p. 278), about a 45-minute drive northeast, offers thrilling bridge walks over a rushing waterfall, which is particularly spectacular in spring when the snow begins to melt.

Village Vacances Valcartier (© 888/384-5524) in St-Gabriel-de-Valcartier, about 40 minutes northwest of the city, is a major manmade water and snow park. In summer, it boasts 35 slides, a huge wave pool, a faux Amazon River to go tubing down, and diving shows. In winter, the same facilities are put to use for snow rafting on inner tubes, trips down ice slides, and skating.

Québec City is also close to where whales come out to play each summer. To take a **whale-watching cruise,** go north about 207km (129 miles) along the St. Lawrence River into the Charlevoix region; boats leave from the towns of Baie Ste-Catherine and Tadoussac and typically spend 2¹/₂ hours out with the giants. Buses from the city can take you up and back in a (long) day. Or, if you have a car, consider booking an overnight stay at Hôtel Tadoussac (p. 288) and get a package that includes a cruise. See p. 287 for more information.

---

4 ORGANIZED TOURS

Québec City is small enough to get around with a good map and a guidebook, but a tour is tremendously helpful for getting background information about the city's history and culture, for grasping the lay of the land, and, in the case of bus tours, for seeing those attractions that are a bit of a hike or require wheels to reach.

Below are some agencies and organizations that have proved to be reliable. Arrange tours by calling the companies directly or by stopping by the large tourist center at the Place d'Armes in Upper Town.

BUS TOURS

Buses are obviously convenient if extensive walking is difficult, especially in hilly Upper Town. Among the established tour operators, **Dupont,** which also goes by the name **Old Québec Tours** (© 800/267-8687 or 418/664-0460; www.tourdupont.com), offers English-only tours, which are preferable to bilingual tours since twice as much information is imparted in the same amount of time. The company's city tours are in small coaches, while day trips out of the city are in full-size buses. To take a **whale-watching cruise,** go about 3 hours north into the Charlevoix region; Dupont offers a 10-hour whale-watching excursion that includes a cruise in Baie-Ste-Catherine. Buses from the city can take you up and back in a day—inquire at the tourist office.

HORSE-DRAWN CARRIAGE TOURS

A romantic but expensive way to see the city at a genial pace is in a horse-drawn carriage, called a *calèche*. Carriages will pick you up or can be hired in places throughout the city, including at Place d'Armes. The 40-minute rides of **Calèches du Vieux-Québec** (© 418/683-9222; www.calecheduvieuxquebec.com), **Calèches de la Nouvelle-France** (© 418/692-0068; www.calechesquebec.com), and **Calèches Royales du Vieux-Québec** (© 418/687-6653) cost C$80 (£40) plus tip for four people maximum. Carriages operate year-round, rain or shine.

Croisières AML (② **800/563-4643** or 418/692-1159 in season; www.croisieresaml.
com) offers a variety of cruises. Weighing in at 900 tons, M/V *Louis Jolliet* is a three-deck
1930s ferry-turned–excursion vessel. It carries 1,000 passengers and is stocked with
bilingual guides, full dining facilities, and a bar. The basic cruise, "Stories of an Explorer,"
lasts 1¹/₂ hours, and three times daily in peak summer months and once a day in spring
and fall. Prices are C$30 (£15) for adults, C$27 (£14) for seniors and students, C$16
(£8) for children 6 to 16, and free for children 5 and younger. Board the boats at quai
Chouinard, 10 rue Dalhousie, in Lower Town.

WALKING TOURS

Times and points of departure for walking tours change, so get up-to-date information
at any tourist office (addresses are listed on p. 203). Many tours leave from the Place
d'Armes in Upper Town, just in front of the **Château Frontenac.**

Tours Voir Québec (② **866/694-2001;** www.toursvoirquebec.com) specializes in
English-only guided tours of the Old City and limits groups to 15 people. "The Grand
Tour," which is available year-round, focuses on the history of the French in North
America and the variety of cultures that make up the province. Cost is C$20 (£10)
adults, C$17 (£8.50) students, C$11 (£6) children 6 to 12., and free for children 5 and
younger. The company also offers private tours for families, small groups, or even a single
person; call or go online to inquire about rates.

One way to split the difference between being out on your own and signing up for a
tour is to use **Map Old Québec** (www.oldquebecmap.com), a website which offers a
beautifully designed map and MP3 files, so that you can download a tour onto your iPod
(or any other MP3 player) and go at your own pace.

A new option, inaugurated in spring 2008, is a self-guided tour called **VivaCité Trail**
(www.parcoursvivacite.com). The route is marked throughout the city with signs and
colored markers embedded in sidewalks. Plaques provide written information about the
parks, public squares, and attractions along the way.

5 SPECTATOR SPORTS

Québec has not had a team in any of the major professional leagues since the NHL Nor-
diques left in 1995, but since 1999, it has been represented by **Les Capitales de Québec**
(**Québec Capitales;** www.capitalesdequebec.com), a baseball club in the Can-Am League.
Home games happen at Stade Municipal (Municipal Stadium), 100 rue du Cardinal
Maurice-Roy (② **877/521-2244** or 418/521-2255), not far beyond the St-Roch neighbor-
hood. General-admission tickets cost C$8 (£4), and the top loge seat is C$14 (£7).

Horse races were set to take place at the refurbished and renamed **Sulky Québec,** 250
bd. Wilfrid-Hamel (② **418/524-5283;** www.attractionshippiques.com). Its parent company, Attractions Hippiques, invested more than C$23 million into the facility, which
was inaugurated in December 2007. But financial troubles suspended racing at the track
in 2008. Check to find out what's going on there before making plans to visit.

6 OUTDOOR ACTIVITIES

Right inside the city, **Parc des Champs-de-Bataille (Battlefields Park)** is the most popular park for bicycling and strolling.

Outside the city, the waters and hills provide countless opportunities for outdoor recreation, including swimming, rafting, fishing, skiing, snowmobiling, and sleigh riding. There are three centers in particular to keep in mind for most winter and summer activities, all within a 45-minute drive from the capital. The provincial **Parc de la Jacques-Cartier** (© **418/848-3169** in summer, 418/528-8787 in winter; www.sepaq.com/pq/jac/en) is off Route 175 north; **Station Touristique Duchesnay** (© **800/665-6527;** www.sepaq.com/duchesnay) is a resort in the town of Ste-Catherine-de-la-Jacques-Cartier; and **Parc Mont Ste-Anne** (© **888/827-4579** or 418/827-4561; www.mont-sainte-anne.com) is northeast of the city toward Charlevoix. All three are mentioned in the listings below. See p. 280 for details about Parc Mont Ste-Anne.

From mid-November to late April, the **Taxi Coop Québec** shuttle service picks up passengers at hotels in the morning to take them to Parc Mont Ste-Anne and Station Stoneham (where Parc de la Jacques-Cartier is) and return them to Québec City in the late afternoon. Call © **418/525-5191** to check rates, make a reservation, or ask if your hotel participates when booking a room. More information is at www.taxicoop-quebec.com.

WARM-WEATHER ACTIVITIES
Biking
Given Upper Town's hilly topography, biking isn't a particularly attractive option in that area. But there are lots of places to go for a couple hours right in the city, either along the river or up in Parliament Hill in Parc des Champs-de-Bataille (Battlefields Park). Rentals are available at a shop next to the Marché du Vieux-Port (Old Port Market) in flatter Lower Town: **Cyclo Services,** 289 rue St-Paul (© **418/692-4052;** www.cycloservices.net) rents bikes for C$25 (£13) for 4 hours, with other increments available. The company also conducts guided bicycle tours with several route options.

A marked path for cyclists (and in-line skaters) along the waterfront follows the second half of the route described in "Walking Tour 2: Lower Town (Vieux-Québec: Basse-Ville & Vieux-Port)" (p. 255). Tourist information centers provide bicycle trail maps and can point out a variety of routes depending on your timing and interests.

Camping
The greater Québec City area has 24 campgrounds, some with as few as 25 campsites, and several with hundreds (Camping Valcartier has 700). Most have showers and toilets. For a list of all the sites and their specs, go to **www.quebecregion.com** and click on "Camping."

Canoeing
Parc de la Jacques-Cartier's several lakes and rivers are fairly easy to reach, yet seem to be in the midst of wilderness; you can rent canoes in the park.

The **Station Touristique Duchesnay** resort (www.sepaq.com/ct/duc/en), 45km (28 miles) from Québec City, is on the shores of Lac Saint-Joseph and rents out canoes, kayaks, and pedal boats.

Anglers can wet their lines in the river that flows through **Parc de la Jacques-Cartier;** catches are mostly trout and salmon. Permits are absolutely required and can be purchased at many sporting-goods stores. Information about fishing regulations is available from the **Minstère des Ressources naturelles et de la Faune** (© 866/248-6936; www. mrnf.gouv.qc.ca/faune).

Golf

A new 18-hole course, **Golf de la Faune** (© 418/627-1576; www.golfdelafaune.com), opened in June 2008, 10 minutes from downtown, at the **Sheraton Four Points Hotel Québec** (© 418/627-8008; www.fourpoints.com/quebec). The course has eight water hazards and 45 sand traps. Green fees start at C$35 (£18).

Outside the city, **Le Grand Vallon** (© 888/827-4579 or 418/827-4653; www. legrandvallon.com) at Parc Mont Ste-Anne is an 18-hole, par-72 course with tree-lined stretches, wide-open midcourse sections, four lakes, and 40 sand traps. Rates are C$36 to C$88 (£18–£44) and include use of a golf cart, access to the driving range, and practice balls.

Swimming

Those who want to splash around during their visit should plan to stay at one of the handful of hotels with pools. **Fairmont Le Château Frontenac** has one, as do **Manoir Victoria, Hilton Québec, Loews Le Concorde, Château Laurier,** and **Château Bonne Entente.** They're all listed in chapter 14. **Village Vacances Valcartier** (p. 243), an all-season recreational center a half-hour from the city, has an immense wave pool and water slides.

COLD-WEATHER ACTIVITIES
Cross-Country Skiing

Parc des Champs-de-Bataille (Battlefields Park), where Carnaval de Québec establishes its winter playground during February, has a network of groomed cross-country trails. Equipment can be rented at the **Discovery Pavilion** (© 418/648-2586; www. ccbn-nbc.gc.ca), at 835 av. Wilfrid-Laurier, near the Citadelle. Thirty minutes outside the city, **Station Touristique Duchesnay** (©877/511-5885; www.sepaq.com/ct/duc/ en) offers extensive trails and ski rentals. This is where the **Ice Hotel** (p. 219) is built each winter, making it well worth a trip. The resort also has a spa, nightly accommodations, and a bistro, Le Quatre-Temps. The **Association of Cross-Country Ski Stations** (www. rssfrq.qc.ca) maintains a website that proffers a list of maps and other options.

Dog Sledding

Aventure Inukshuk (© 418/875-0770; www.aventureinukshuk.qc.ca), at 143 route de Duchesnay in Ste-Catherine-de-la-Jacques-Cartier, is in Station Touristique Duchesnay, near where the Ice Hotel is built each winter. Guides show you how to lead a sled pulled by six dogs. Even on the short 1-hour trip, you go deep into a hushed world of snow and thick woods, past rows of Christmas trees, and over a beaver pond. The company's 200-plus dogs live in a field of individual pens and houses under evergreen trees and work up an enormous cacophony of howls whenever a team of dogs is harnessed up and set to go. Guides work with the same dogs every day, training and caring for their teams themselves. Overnight camping trips are available, too. The 1-hour trip, which includes an additional half-hour of training, costs C$88 (£44) in December, January, and March, and C$97 (£ 49) in February. Children ages 6 to 12 are half price, and ages 2 to 5 go free (children younger than 2 aren't allowed). It's expensive, especially for families, but the memory stays with you.

Ice-Skating

In winter, outdoor rinks (with skate rentals) are set up in Place d'Youville just outside the Upper Town walls. (Until 1931, Place d'Youville was a public market.) Check with the tourist office for more information.

Skiing

Foremost among the nearby downhill centers is **Mont Ste-Anne,** containing eastern Canada's largest total skiing surface, with 66 trails (17 are lit for night skiing). See p. 280 for more information.

Tobogganing

From December to mid-March, an old-fashioned toboggan run is set up on the steep wooden staircase at Terrasse Dufferin's south end; the run extends almost to the Château Frontenac. Tickets for Les Glissades de la Terrasse are sold at a temporary booth and include the use of a four-person toboggan; cost is C$2 (£1) per person. Call © **418/829-9898 for information.**

Québec City Strolls

The many pleasures of walking in picturesque French Québec are entirely comparable to walking in similar *quartiers* in northern European cities. Stone houses rub shoulders with each other; carriage wheels creak behind muscular horses; sunlight filters through leafy canopies; drinkers and diners lounge in sidewalk cafes; childish shrieks of laughter echo down cobblestone streets. Not common to other cities, however, is the bewitching vista of river and mountains that the higher elevations bestow.

In winter especially, Vieux-Québec takes on a Dickensian quality, with a lamp glow flickering behind curtains of falling snow. The man who should know—

Charles Dickens himself—described the city as having "splendid views which burst upon the eye at every turn."

An alternative to these guided strolls is to simply "walk the walls" of the city, an endeavor which takes about an hour. In some sections, you are literally on top of the fortress wall; in most spots, you're on a path alongside it. There's a little creative guesswork involved in figuring out how to follow the route. Because of the number of stairs and occasional .6m (2-ft.) gap to traverse, walking the wall rates as moderately strenuous and isn't for young children. But it's easy to get on and off the path, and the trek offers wonderful views of the city.

WALKING TOUR 1	UPPER TOWN (VIEUX-QUEBEC: HAUTE-VILLE)

START:	Château Frontenac, the castle-like hotel that dominates the city.
FINISH:	Hôtel du Parlement, on Grande-Allée, just outside the walls.
TIME:	2 to 3 hours, depending on whether you take all the optional diversions.
BEST TIMES:	Anytime, although early morning when the streets are emptier is most atmospheric.
WORST TIMES:	None.

The Upper Town (Haute-Ville) of Old Québec (Vieux-Québec) is surrounded by fortress walls. This section of the city overlooks the St. Lawrence River and includes much of what makes Québec so beloved. Buildings and compounds along this tour have been carefully preserved, and most are at least a century old. We start at the grand Château Frontenac, the visual heart of the city.

❶ Château Frontenac

The original section of the famous edifice that defines the Québec City skyline was built as a hotel from 1892 to 1893 by the Canadian Pacific Railway Co. The architect, an American named Bruce Price, raised his creation on the site of the governor's

mansion and named it after Louis de Buade, comte de Frontenac. Monsieur le Comte was New France's governor general who, in 1690, was faced with the threat of an English fleet under Sir William Phips during King William's War. Phips sent a messenger to demand Frontenac's surrender, but

Frontenac replied, "Tell your lord that I will reply with the mouths of my cannons." He did, and Phips sailed away. Known locally as "the Château," the hotel today has 618 rooms (p. 240). Guided tours are available.

Walk around to the river side of the Château, where there is a grand boardwalk called:

❷ Terrasse Dufferin

With its green-and-white-topped gazebos in warm months, this boardwalk promenade looks much as it did 100 years ago, when ladies with parasols and gentlemen with top hats and canes strolled along it on sunny afternoons. It offers vistas of river, watercraft, and distant mountains, and is particularly romantic at sunset.

Walk south on Terrasse Dufferin, past the Château. If you're in the mood for some exercise, continue up the stairs—there are 310 of them—walking south along the:

❸ Promenade des Gouverneurs

This path was renovated in 2007 and skirts the sheer cliff wall, climbing up and up past Québec's military Citadelle, a fort built by the British army between 1820 and 1850 that remains an active military garrison. The promenade/staircase ends at the grassy Parc des Champs-de-Bataille, about 15 minutes away. If you go to the end, return back along the path to Terrasse Dufferin.

Walk back on the terrace as far as the battery of ancient (but not original) cannons on the left, which are set up as they were in the old days. Climb the stairs toward the obelisk into the:

❹ Parc des Gouverneurs

Just southwest of the Château Frontenac, this park stands on the site of the mansion built to house the French governors of Québec. The mansion burned in 1834 and the ruins lie buried under the great bulk of the Château.

In summer, shows and musical programs sponsored by the municipal government are held here. B&Bs and small hotels border it on two sides.

The obelisk monument is dedicated to both generals in the momentous battle of September 13, 1759, when Britain's General James Wolfe and France's Louis-Joseph, marquis de Montcalm, fought for what would be the ultimate destiny of Québec (and, quite possibly, of all of North America). The French were defeated and both generals died; Wolfe, wounded in the fighting, lived only long enough to hear of England's victory. Montcalm died a few hours after Wolfe. Told that he was mortally wounded, Montcalm replied, "All the better. I will not see the English in Québec."

Walk up rue Mont-Carmel, which runs between the park and Château Frontenac; turn right onto rue Haldimand. At the next corner, rue St-Louis, stands a white house with blue trim. This is:

❺ Maison Kent

Built in 1648, this might be Québec's oldest building. It's most famous for being the building in which France signed the capitulation to the British forces. Its name comes from the duke of Kent, Queen Victoria's father. He lived here for a few years at the end of the 18th century, just before he married Victoria's mother in an arranged liaison. His true love, it is said, was with him in Maison Kent. Today, the building houses France's consulate general, as the tricolor over the door attests.

To the left and diagonally across from Maison Kent, at rue St-Louis and rue des Jardins, is:

❻ Maison Jacquet

This small, white dwelling with crimson roof and trim dates from 1677 and now houses a popular restaurant called Aux Anciens Canadiens (p. 224). Among the oldest houses in the province, it has sheltered some prominent Québécois, including Philippe Aubert de Gaspé, the author of *Aux Anciens Canadiens,* which recounts Québec's history and folklore. He lived here from 1815 to 1824.

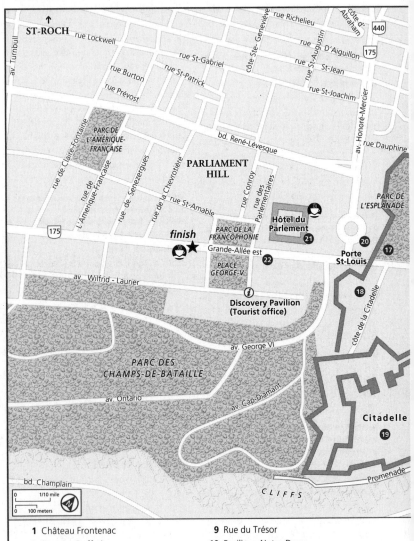

1 Château Frontenac
2 Terrasse Dufferin
3 Promenade des Gouverneurs
4 Parc des Gouverneurs
5 Maison Kent
6 Maison Jacquet
7 Maison Maillou
8 Place d'Armes

9 Rue du Trésor
10 Basilique Notre-Dame
11 Séminaire de Québec
12 Hôtel-de-Ville (City Hall)
13 Anglican Cathedral of the Holy Trinity
14 Chapelle/Musée des Ursulines
15 Cannonball
16 Hôtel d'Esplanade

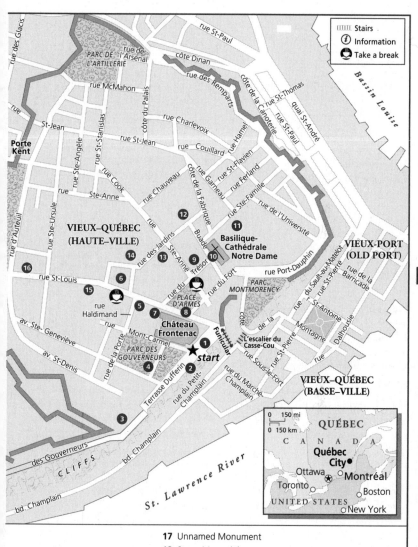

- **17** Unnamed Monument
- **18** Stone Memorial
- **19** Citadelle
- **20** Site of Winter Carnival
- **21** Hôtel du Parlement
- **22** Grand Allée

> **TAKE A BREAK**
> Try Québécois home cooking right here at the restaurant named for de Gaspé's book, **Aux Anciens Canadiens,** 34 rue St-Louis. Consider caribou in blueberry-wine sauce or duckling baked in maple syrup, and don't forget the sugar pie that floats in cream. See p. 224 for more information.

Leaving the restaurant, turn back toward Maison Kent and walk along rue St-Louis to no. 17:

⑦ Maison Maillou

This house's foundations date from 1736, though the house was enlarged in 1799 and restored in 1959. It's best seen from the opposite side of the street. Maison Maillou was built as an elegant luxury home and later served as headquarters of militias and armies. Note the metal shutters used to thwart weather and unfriendly fire.

Continue on rue St-Louis to arrive at the central plaza called:

⑧ Place d'Armes

This plaza was once the military parade ground outside the governors' mansion (which no longer exists). In the small park at the center is the fountain **Monument to the Faith,** which recalls the arrival of the Recollet monks from France in 1615. France's king granted them a large plot of land in 1681 on which to build their church and monastery.

Facing the square is the **monument to Samuel de Champlain,** who founded Québec in 1608. Created by French artists Paul Chevre and Paul le Cardonel, the statue has stood here since 1898. Its pedestal is made from stone that was also used in the Arc de Triomphe and Sacré-Coeur Basilica in Paris.

Near the Champlain statue is the diamond-shaped **UNESCO monument** designating Québec City as a World Heritage Site, the only North American city with that distinction. Installed in 1986, it's made of bronze, granite, and glass.

A **tourist information center** faces the plaza, at 12 rue Ste-Anne.

> **TAKE A BREAK**
> This part of town is a great place to sit and watch the world go by. Grab a sidewalk table and enjoy something to drink or eat at **Restaurant Le Relais,** a red-roofed building with a mock-Tudor façade at 16 rue Ste-Anne.

Just adjacent to the Restaurant Le Relais is the narrow pedestrian lane called:

⑨ Rue du Trésor

Artists hang their prints and paintings of Québec scenes on both sides of the walkway. In decent weather, it's busy with browsers and sellers. Most prices are within the means of the average visitor.

Follow rue du Trésor down to rue Buade and turn left. On the right, at the corner of rue Ste-Famille is the:

⑩ Basilique Notre-Dame

The basilica's interior is ornate and its air rich with the scent of burning candles. Many artworks remain from the time of the French regime. The chancel lamp was a gift from Louis XIV, and the crypt is the final resting place for most of Québec's bishops. Notre-Dame, which dates back to 1647, has suffered a tumultuous history of bombardment and reconstruction; see p. 239 for more information.

As you exit the basilica, turn a sharp right to enter the grounds and down into the all-white inner courtyard of the historic:

⑪ Séminaire de Québec

Founded in 1663 by North America's first bishop, Bishop Laval, this seminary had grown into Laval University by 1852. During summer only, visitors can take a 1-hour tour of the old seminary's grounds and some of its stone and wood buildings, which reveal lavish decorations of stone, tile, brass, and gilt-framed oil paintings. The language of the tour is determined by the first registered visitor; more information is available by calling the museum at ✆ 418/643-2158.

The Musée de l'Amérique Française, open year-round, is tucked inside the seminary.

Head back to the basilica. Directly across the small park from the church is:

⑫ Hôtel-de-Ville (City Hall)

The park next to City Hall is often converted into an outdoor show area in summer, especially during the **Festival d'Eté (Summer Festival)** with concerts and other staged programs.

In the distance, up behind City Hall, you can see **Édifice Price,** Old City's tallest building at 18 stories. It was built in 1929 in Art Deco style with geometric motifs and a steepled copper roof. (When it was built, it inadvertently gave a bird's-eye view into the adjacent Ursuline Convent, and a "view tax" had to be paid to the nuns to ameliorate them.)

An apartment on the 16th and 17th floors has been the official residence of the premier of Québec since 2001.

Facing the front of Hôtel-de-Ville, walk left on rue des Jardins and across rue Ste-Anne. On the left are the spires of the:

⑬ Anglican Cathedral of the Holy Trinity

Said to be modeled after London's St-Martin-in-the-Fields, this building dates from 1804 and was the first Anglican cathedral to be built outside the British Isles. The interior is simple but spacious and bright, with pews of solid English oak from the Royal Windsor forest and a latticed ceiling with a gilded-chain motif. Visitors may happen upon an organ recital or choral rehearsal.

One block up rue des Jardins, turn right at the small square (triangle-shaped, actually) and go a few more steps to 12 rue Donnacona, the:

⑭ Chapelle/Musée des Ursulines

This museum displays the Ursuline nuns' handiwork from the 17th, 18th, and 19th centuries. There are also Amerindian crafts and a cape that was made for Marie de

l'Incarnation, a founder of the convent, when she left for New France in 1639.

Peek into the restored chapel if it's open (May–Oct). It shelters the remains of French General Montcalm, who was buried here after he fell in the 1759 battle that marked the end of French rule in Québec. Montcalm's tomb is under the chapel and not accessible to the public. His skull, on the other hand, is on display in the Ursuline Museum next door. The tomb of Marie de l'Incarnation, who died in 1672, also is here. The altar was created by sculptor Pierre-Noël Levasseur between 1726 and 1736 and is worth a look.

From the museum, turn right on rue Donnacona and walk to the Ursuline Convent, originally built in 1642. The present complex is actually a succession of different buildings added and repaired at various times until 1836, as frequent fires took their toll. A statue of founder Marie de l'Incarnation is outside. The convent is now a private girls' school and not open to the public.

Continue left up the hill along rue du Parloir to rue St-Louis. Cross the street and turn right. At the next block, rue du Corps-de-Garde, note the tree with a:

⑮ Cannonball

Lodged at the base of the trunk, one story says that the cannonball landed here during the War of 1759 and over the years became firmly embraced by the tree. Another story says that it was placed here on purpose to keep the wheels of horse-drawn carriages from bumping the tree when making tight turns.

Continue along St-Louis another 1½ blocks to rue d'Auteuil. The house on the right corner is now the:

⑯ Hôtel d'Esplanade

Notice that many of the windows in the façade facing rue St-Louis are blocked by stone. This is because houses were once taxed by the number of windows they had, and the frugal homeowner who lived here found this way to get around the law, even though it cut down on his view.

Continue straight on rue St-Louis toward the Porte St-Louis, a gate in the walls. Before the gate on the right is the Esplanade powder magazine, part of the old fortifications. Just before the gate is an:

⑰ Unnamed Monument

This monument commemorates the 1943 meeting in Québec of U.S. President Franklin D. Roosevelt and British Prime Minister Winston Churchill. It remains a soft-pedaled reminder to French Québécois that it was the English-speaking nations that rid France of the Nazis.

Still on this side of the gate, cross over St-Louis and go up the hill along Côte de la Citadelle toward La Citadelle. On the right are headquarters and barracks of a militia district, arranged around an inner court. Near its entrance is a:

⑱ Stone Memorial

This marks the resting place of 13 soldiers of General Richard Montgomery's American army, felled in the unsuccessful assault on Québec in 1775. (Obviously, the conflicts that swirled for centuries around who would ultimately rule Québec didn't end with the British victory after its fateful 1759 battle with French troops.)

Continue up the hill to:

⑲ La Citadelle

The impressive star-shaped fortress just beyond view keeps watch from a commanding position on a grassy plateau 108m (354 ft.) above the banks of the St. Lawrence. It took 30 years to complete, by which time it had become obsolete. Since 1920, the Citadelle has been the home of the French-speaking Royal 22e Régiment, which fought in both world wars and in Korea. A pedestrian walkway tunneling into the hill has posted historical information. With good timing and weather, it's possible to visit the regimental museum and watch **the changing of the guard** ceremony, or, as it's called, "beating the retreat." See p. 235 for more details.

Return to rue St-Louis and turn left through Porte St-Louis, which was built in 1873 on the site of a gate dating from 1692. Here, the street broadens to become Grande-Allée. To the right is a park that runs alongside the city walls.

⑳ Site of Winter Carnival

One of the most captivating events on the Canadian calendar, the 17-day **Carnaval de Québec** happens every February and includes outdoor games, snow-tubing, dogsled races, canoe races, and more. A palace of snow and ice rises on this spot just outside the city walls, with ice sculptures throughout the field. Colorfully clad Québécois come to admire the palace and dance the nights away at outdoor parties. On the left side of Grande-Allée, a carnival park of games, food, and music is set up on Parc des Champs-de-Bataille. Teams of artists from around the world participate in the International Snow Sculpture Competition. See p. 28 for more about the festivities.

Fronting the park, on your right, stands Québec province's stately:

㉑ Hôtel du Parlement

Constructed in 1884, this government building houses what Québécois are pleased to call their "National Assembly." Along the façade are 22 bronze statues of prominent figures in Québec's tumultuous history. In the sumptuous Parliament chambers, the fleur-de-lis symbol and the initials VR (for Victoria Regina) are reminders of Québec's dual heritage. If the crown on top is lit, Parliament is in session.

Guided tours are available weekdays year-round from 9am to 4:30pm, and weekends in summer from 10am to 4:30pm. Go to door no. 3 to enter. Call ℭ **418/643-7239** for more information.

The massive fountain in front of the building, **La Fontaine de Tourny,** was commissioned by the mayor of Bordeaux, France, in 1857. Sculptor Mathurin Moreau created the dreamlike figures on the fountain's base. It was installed in 2007 as a gift from the Simons department store to the city for its 400th anniversary in 2008.

TAKE A BREAK
Le Parlementaire restaurant
(© **418/643-6640**), in the
Hôtel du Parlement at 1045 rue des Parle-
mentaires, is done up in regal beaux-arts
decor and open to the public (as well as
parliamentarians and visiting dignitaries)
for breakfast and lunch Monday through
Friday most of the year. Or, continue down
Grande-Allée to find plenty of other
options.

Continue down:

㉒ Grand-Allée

Just past Hôtel du Parlement is a park called
Place George-V; behind it are the charred
remains of the 1885 Armory. A major
visual icon and home to the country's oldest
French-Canadian regiment, the Armory
was all but destroyed in an April 2008 fire.
A few months after the fire, the city
appeared determined to try to save the parts
of the stone façade that were left standing.

To the left of the armory is a building
that houses **a tourist information office**
and the **Discovery Pavilion** (p. 239),
where a multimedia exhibit called "Odyssey: A Journey through History on the
Plains of Abraham" is presented.

After the park, the street becomes lined
with cafes, restaurants, and bars on both
sides. This strip really gets jumping at
night, particularly in the complex that
includes **Voo Doo** restaurant (p. 231) and
Maurice nightclub (p. 268), at no. 575.

One food possibility is **Chez Ashton,** at
640 Grande-Allée est. The Québec fast-
food restaurant makes what many consider
the town's best *poutine*—french fries with
fresh cheese curds and brown gravy. It's
open daily until 4am.

A great way to end the stroll is with a
stop at **L'Astral,** the restaurant and bar atop
Loews le Concorde Hotel, at the corner of
Grande-Allée est and cours du Général-De
Montcalm. The room spins slowly (it takes
about 1½ hours for a full rotation) and lets
you look back at all the places you've been
and all the places still to go.

The no. 11 bus along Grande-Allée can
return you to the Old City, or turn left at
Loews and enter the **Parc des Champs-de-
Bataille** (**Battlefields Park;** p. 239) at the
Joan of Arc Garden. If you turn left in the
park and continue along its boulevards and
footpaths, you'll end up at the Citadelle. If
you turn right, you'll reach the **Musée des
Beaux-Arts du Québec** (p. 238).

WALKING TOUR 2	LOWER TOWN (VIEUX-QUEBEC: BASSE-VILLE & VIEUX-PORT)

START:	Either in Upper Town at Terrasse Dufferin, the boardwalk in front of Château Frontenac, or, if you're already in Lower Town, at the funicular, the cable car that connects the two parts of the Old City.
FINISH:	Place-Royale, the restored central square of Lower Town.
TIME:	1½ hours.
BEST TIMES:	Anytime during the day. Early morning lets you soak up the visual history, though shops won't be open.
WORST TIMES:	Very late at night or when it's very cold.

The Lower Town (Basse-Ville) part of Old Québec (Vieux-Québec) encompasses the city's
oldest residential area—now flush with boutique hotels, high-end restaurants, and touristy
shops and cafes—and Vieux-Port, the old port district. The impressive Museum of Civilization is here, and if you have time, you may want to take a pause from the tour for a visit.
We start at the cliff-side elevator *(funiculaire)* that connects Upper and Lower towns.

If you're in Upper Town, descend to Lower Town by one of two options:

➊ Funicular (Option A)

This cable car's upper terminus is on Terrasse Dufferin near the Château Frontenac. As the car descends the steep slope, its glass front provides a broad view of Basse-Ville (Lower Town).

Or, if you prefer a more active (and free) means of descent, use the stairs to the left of the funicular, the:

➊ L'Escalier du Casse-Cou (Option B)

"Breakneck Stairs" is the self-explanatory name given to this stairway. Stairs have been in place here since the settlement began. In 1698, the town council had to forbid citizens from taking their animals up and down the stairway.

Breakneck Stairs and the funicular arrive at the intersection of rues Petit-Champlain and Sous-le-Fort. At the bottom of the last set of stairs on the left is the:

➋ Verrerie La Mailloche

In the downstairs room, craftsmen give glass-blowing demonstrations—intriguing and informative, especially for children who haven't seen that ancient craft. The glass is melted at 2,500°F (1,350°C) and is worked at 2,000°F (1,100°C). There are displays of the results and a small shop in which to purchase them.

Outside the glass-blowing shop, look at the building from which the funicular passengers exit:

➌ Maison Louis Jolliet

Built in 1683, this was home to Louis Jolliet, the Québec-born explorer who, with a priest, Jacques Marquette, was the first person of European parentage to explore Mississippi River's upper reaches. The building is now the funicular's lower terminus, and full of tourist trinkets and geegaws.

Walk down the pretty little street here:

➍ Rue du Petit-Champlain

Allegedly North America's oldest street, this pedestrian-only lane swarms with restaurant-goers, cafe-sitters, strolling couples, and gaggles of schoolchildren in the warm months. Many of the shops listed in chapter 18 are here. In winter, it's a snowy wonderland with ice statues and twinkling white lights.

TAKE A BREAK
Though it's early in the stroll, there are so many eating and shopping options here that you might want to pause for a while. Look for the sign with the flying rabbits for **Le Lapin Saute**, at 52 rue du Petit-Champlain, a country-cozy bistro with hearty food in generous portions. Smoked mackerel salad and grilled pork chop with maple syrup are both terrific. A lovely terrace overlooks a small garden and, in the warm months, street musicians serenade diners.

At the end of Petit-Champlain, turn left onto boulevard Champlain. A lighthouse from the Gaspé Peninsula used to stand across the street, but it has been returned to its original home, leaving just an anchor and cannons to stand guard (rather forlornly) over the river.

Follow the street's curve; this block offers pleasant boutiques and cafes. At the corner is the crimson-roofed:

➎ Maison Chevalier

Dating from 1752, this was once the home of merchant Jean-Baptiste Chevalier. Note the wealth of windows, more than 30 in front-facing sections alone. In 1763, the house was sold at auction to ship owner Jean-Louis Frémont, the grandfather of Virginia-born John Charles Frémont (1813–90). John Charles was an American explorer, soldier, and politician who mapped some 10 Western and Midwestern territories. He also was a governor of California and Arizona, a candidate for U.S. president in 1856, and a general during the U.S. Civil War.

The Chevalier House was sold in 1806 to an Englishman, who in turn rented it to

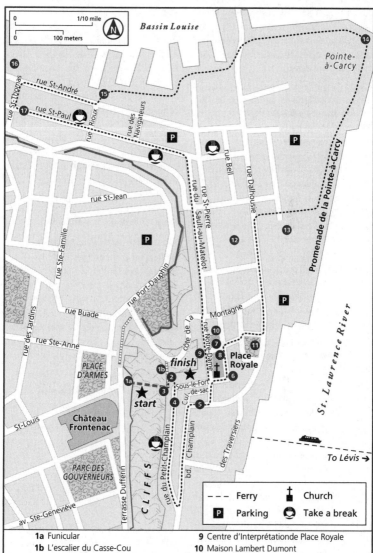

1a Funicular
1b L'escalier du Casse-Cou
2 Verrerie la Mailloche
3 Maison Louis Jolliet
4 Rue du Petit-Champlain
5 Maison Chevalier
6 Royal Battery
7 Place Royale
8 Église Notre-Dame-des-Victoires

9 Centre d'Interprétationde Place Royale
10 Maison Lambert Dumont
11 Place de Paris
12 Musée de la Civilisation
13 Vieux-Port (Old Port)
14 Pointe-à-Carcy
15 Espace 400ᵉ
16 Marché du Vieux-Port
17 Rue St-Paul and antique shops

a hotelier, who transformed it into an inn. In 1960, the Québec government restored the house, and it became a museum about 5 years later. It's overseen by the Musée de la Civilisation, which mounts temporary exhibitions here. Entrance is free. (See p. 241 for more details.)

Just past the Maison's front door, turn left and walk up the short block of rue Notre-Dame to rue Sous-le-Fort. Turn right, and walk 1 block to the:

❻ Royal Battery

Fortifications were erected here by the French in 1691 and the cannons added in 1712 to defend Lower Town from the British. The cannons got their chance in 1759, but the English victory silenced them and eventually, they were left to rust. Sunken foundations were all that remained of the battery by the turn of the 20th century, and when the time came for restorations, it had to be rebuilt from the ground up.

From the Royal Battery, walk back up rue Sous-le-Fort. You'll find a good photo opportunity at the imposing Château Frontenac framed between ancient houses.

Turn right on rue Notre-Dame. Half a block up the grade is the heart of Basse-Ville, the small:

❼ Place-Royale

Occupying the center of New France's first permanent colony, this small and still very much European-feeling enclosed square served as the town marketplace. It went into decline around 1860 and by 1950 had become a derelict, run-down part of town. Today, it has been restored to very nearly recapture its historic appearance. The prominent bust is of Louis XIV, the Sun King, a gift from the city of Paris in 1928 that was installed here in 1931. The striking 17th- and 18th-century houses once belonged to wealthy merchants. Note the ladders on some of the steep roofs used to fight fire and remove snow. See p. 235 for more information about the square.

Facing directly onto the square is:

❽ Eglise Notre-Dame-des-Victoires

Named for French naval victories over the British in 1690 and 1711, Québec's oldest stone church was built in 1688 after a massive Lower Town fire destroyed 55 homes in 1682. The church was restored in 1763 after its partial destruction by the British in the 1759 siege. The white-and-gold interior has a few murky paintings and a large model boat suspended from the ceiling, a votive offering brought by early settlers to ensure safe voyages. On the walls, small prints depict the stages of the Passion. The church is open to visitors 9am to 5pm from May through October. See p. 235 for more information.

Walk straight across the plaza, passing the:

❾ Centre d'Interprétation de Place-Royale

For decades, this space was nothing but a propped-up façade with an empty lot behind it, but it has been rebuilt to serve as an interpretation center with shows and exhibitions about this district's history; it's good for kids as well as adults (p. 235).

At the corner on the right is the:

❿ Maison Lambert Dumont

This building now houses Geomania, a store selling rocks and crystals. In earlier years, though, it was home to the Dumont family and one of several residences in the square. To the right as you're facing it once stood a hotel where U.S. President William Taft would stay as he headed north to vacation in the picturesque Charlevoix region.

Walk about 15m (50 ft.) past the last building on your left and turn around; the entire end of that building is a *trompe l'oeil* mural of streets and houses and depictions of citizens from the earliest colonial days to the present, an amusing splash of fool-the-eye trickery. Have your photo taken here—everyone else does!

Return to Place-Royale and head left toward the water, down two small sets of stairs to the:

⑪ Place de Paris

This plaza contains an undistinguished white sculpture that resembles three stacked Rubik's Cubes; it's called "Dialogue avec L'Histoire" and was a gift from the city of Paris in 1987.

Continue ahead to rue Dalhousie and turn left. A few short blocks up and on the left is the:

⑫ Musée de la Civilisation

This wonderful museum, which opened in 1988, may be housed in a nondescript gray-block building, but there is nothing bland or traditional about it once you enter. Spacious and airy, with ingeniously arranged multidimensional exhibits, it's one of Canada's most innovative museums. If there is no time now, put it at the top of your must-see list for later. See p. 234 for museum details.

Across the street from the museum is:

⑬ Vieux-Port (Old Port)

In the 17th century, this 29-hectare (72-acre) riverfront area was the port of call for European ships bringing supplies and settlers to the new colony. With the decline of shipping by the early 20th century, the port fell into precipitous decline. But since the mid-1980s, it has experienced a rebirth, becoming the summer destination for international cruise ships. It got additional sprucing up for Québec's 400th anniversary in 2008.

> **TAKE A BREAK**
> If you're doing this stroll in the colder months, you might want to head indoors at this point. **Le 48 Saint-Paul,** named after its address, is just steps from the corner of rue Dalhousie and rue St-Paul, 1 block from the museum. It's sleek and affordable, with creative burgers and pizzas, most costing less than C$10 (£5), and a good selection of local beer. To continue the tour, head back to rue Dalhousie and cross over toward Terminal de Croisières to the waterfront.

From the museum, head across the parking lot to the river and turn left at the water's edge. After Terminal de Croisières, the cruise terminal, you'll pass the **Agora,** an outdoor theater that has been under renovation, and, behind it, the city's **Customs House,** built between 1830 and 1839.

Continue along the river's promenade, past the Agora, to the small, landscaped:

⑭ Pointe-à-Carcy

The bronze statue of a sailor here is a memorial to Canadian merchant seamen who lost their lives in World War II. From the point, look out across Louise Basin to the Bunge of Canada grain elevator, which stores wheat, barley, corn, and soybean crops that are produced in western Canada before they are shipped to Europe.

The bridge to rural **Ile d'Orléans** can also be seen. Ile d'Orléans is the island that supplies Québec with much of its fresh fruits and vegetables and is an easy day trip from the city (p. 270).

The water below is the launch area for a wild canoe race across the ice floes during **Carnaval de Québec** (p. 28).

Follow the walkway left from Pointe-à-Carcy along the Louise Basin. You'll pass the free **Musée Naval de Québec,** renovated in 2007, and the city's Navy School. In the warm months, you can board a scenic river cruise here.

At the end of the basin, take a short jog left, then right along the water's edge. Up ahead is a modern glass building, the:

⑮ Espace 400e

Occupying the location that used to be the Vieux-Port Interpretation Center, this new, expanded pavilion was the central destination for Québec's 400th-anniversary celebrations. It's now a Parks Canada discovery center (p. 241).

From Espace 400e, go to the road that fronts it, rue St-André. Turn right and walk 1 block to:

⑯ Marché du Vieux-Port

This colorful market has jaunty teal-blue roofs and, in summer, rows of booths heaped with fresh fruits and vegetables, regional wines and ciders, soaps, pâtés, jams, handicrafts, cheeses, chocolates, fresh fish, and meat. Go to the cafes and kiosks inside to get a meal or sweet treat.

Farther down the street is the 1916 train station, designed by New York architect Bruce Price, who designed the Château Frontenac in 1893 and used his signature copper-turned-green spires here, too. You'll walk toward this landmark on your way to your next stop.

Leaving the market, cross rue St-André at the light and walk a short block to:

⑰ Rue St-Paul

Turn left onto this street, home to galleries, craft shops, and about a dozen antiques stores. They include **Maison Dambourgès,** at no. 155, which sells folk art and pine furniture, and **l'Héritage Antiquité,** at no. 109, which has old postcards,

bits of china sets, Hummel figurines, and the like. Rue St-Paul manages to maintain a sense of unspoiled neighborhood.

TAKE A BREAK
Mistral Gagnant, at 160 rue St-Paul, is a sunny Provençal restaurant that features hearty food from omelets to escargots to bouillabaisse to outrageously good lemon pie. **Café le Saint Malo,** at 75 rue St-Paul, has low ceilings, rough stone walls, and storefront windows that draw patrons in.

From here, return to the heart of Lower Town—Place-Royale and the funicular—by turning right off rue St-Paul onto either rue du Sault-au-Matelot or the parallel rue St-Pierre. Both are quiet streets with galleries and restaurants. Meander along and settle into the relaxed pace of this nook of the city.

Québec City Shopping

Vieux-Québec's compact size, with its upper and lower sections, makes it especially convenient for browsing and shopping, and much of the merchandise is of high quality.

1 THE SHOPPING SCENE

Vieux-Québec's Lower Town, particularly the area known as **Quartier du Petit-Champlain,** offers many possibilities—clothing, souvenirs, gifts, household items, collectibles—and is avoiding (so far) the trashiness that can afflict heavily touristed areas. The area is just around the corner from the funicular entrance.

In Upper Town, wander along **rue St-Jean,** both within and outside the city walls, and on **rue Garneau** and **Côte de la Fabrique,** which branch off the east end of St-Jean. For T-shirts, postcards, and other souvenirs, check out the myriad shops that line **rue St-Louis.**

If you're heading to St-Roch to eat, build in a little time to stroll **rue St-Joseph,** which, for a few blocks, has new boutiques alongside cafes and restaurants.

Outside the walls, just beyond the strip of eateries and nightspots that line Grande-Allée, **avenue Cartier** has shops and restaurants of some variety, from clothing and ceramics to housewares and gourmet foods. The 5 blocks attract crowds of youngish and middle-aged locals. The area remains outside the tourist orbit, but it's an easy walk: Head up wide, tree-lined Grande-Allée and turn right onto Cartier.

Most stores are open Monday through Wednesday from 9 or 10am to 6pm, Thursday and Friday from 9am to 9pm, and Saturday from 9am to 5pm. Many stores are now also open on Sunday from noon to 5pm.

THE BEST BUYS

Indigenous crafts, handmade sweaters, and **Inuit art** are among the desirable items specific to Québec. An official igloo trademark identifies authentic Inuit (Eskimo) art, though the differences between the real thing and the manufactured variety become apparent with a little careful study. Inuit artwork, which is usually in the form of carvings in stone or bone, is an excellent purchase not for its low price, but for its high quality. Expect to pay hundreds of dollars for even a relatively small piece.

You're bound to see a lot of the **Inukshuk** figurine, which looks like a human figure made of stacked rocks; it's the centerpiece of the logo of the 2010 Winter Olympics, which will be held in Vancouver (see www.vancouver2010.com).

Maple syrup products make sweet gifts, as do **regional wines, mustards,** and **jams.**

Apart from a handful of boutiques, Québec City does not offer the high-profile designer clothing showcased in Montréal.

2 SHOPPING FROM A TO Z

Listed with the address for each shop below is its neighborhood: Lower Town or Upper Town in Vieux-Québec, or Montcalm, the residential neighborhood just west of Parliament Hill.

ANTIQUES ROW

About a dozen antiques shops line rue St-Paul in Lower Town, near the water and not far from Espace 400e. They're filled with knickknacks, Québec country furniture, candlesticks, old clocks, Victoriana, Art Deco and Art Moderne objects, and the increasingly sought-after kitsch and housewares of the early post–World War II period.

ARTS & CRAFTS

Artisans Canada   Crafts predominate in the front of this shop, all a little on the expensive side. There are plenty of fur hats, slippers, coats, jewelry, toy soldiers, and soapstone carvings. Perhaps a chess set of French and British Generals Montcalm and Wolfe, so you can reenact the battle that sealed the political fate of all of Canada? 30 Côte de la Fabrique, Upper Town. ℭ 418/692-2109. www.artisanscanada.com.

Boutique Métiers d'Art   In a stone building at the corner of Place-Royale, this carefully arranged store displays works by more than 100 Québécois craftspeople, at least some of which are likely to appeal to almost any customer. Among these objects are wooden boxes, jewelry, graphics, and a variety of gifts. When departing, be sure to turn left, walk past the end of the building and turn around—it's a surprise! 29 rue Notre-Dame, Lower Town. ℭ 418/694-0267. www.boutiquemetiersdart.fr.

Dugal   One of the owners works in wood, carving sinuous and remarkably comfortable rocking chairs, while the other creates jewelry featuring black pearls set in gold and silver. 15 rue Notre-Dame, Lower Town. ℭ 418/692-1564.

Galerie Brousseau et Brousseau   In 2005, the important Inuit art collection assembled over 30 years by Québécois Raymond Brousseau was acquired by the Musée des Beaux-Arts du Québec, and 285 works from the 2,635-piece collection are on display at that museum. Here, you can buy Native Canadian carvings, mostly in stone, to take home. This is the city's most prominent art dealers, and a certificate of authenticity comes with each purchase. Prices are high, but competitive for merchandise of similar quality. The shop is set up like a gallery, so feel free to just browse. 35 rue St-Louis (at rue des Jardins), Upper Town. ℭ 418/694-1828. www.sculpture.artinuit.ca.

Galerie d'Art du Petit-Champlain   This shop features the superbly detailed carvings of Roger Desjardins, who applies his skills to meticulous renderings of waterfowl. The inventory has recently been expanded to include lithographs and paintings. 88½ rue du Petit-Champlain (near bd. Champlain), Lower Town. ℭ 418/692-5647. www.quartierpetit champlain.com.

Rue du Trésor Outdoor Gallery   Sooner or later, everyone passes this outdoor alley near the Place d'Armes. Artists gather along here much of the year to exhibit and sell their work. Most of the prints on view are of Québec scenes, and can make attractive souvenirs. The artists seem to enjoy chatting with interested passersby. Rue du Trésor (between rues Ste-Anne and Buade), Upper Town. No phone.

Sachem   Fur hats, baby moccasins, T-shirts, and dresses are all packed into this compact boutique. Foremost, though, is the wide variety of miniature Inukshuk human figurines, which look like they've been made of stacked rocks. The Inukshuk is part of the logo of the 2010 Winter Olympics being held in Vancouver, so stock up now and be ahead of the curve. 17 rue des Jardins (near Hôtel-de-Ville), Upper Town. ℂ 418/692-3056.

BATH & BODY

Fruits & Passion   A Québec-based chain that features lotions, shampoos, candles, foods, and even dog-care items. Its Cuchina hand-care line uses olive oil and olive leaf extract with scents ranging from fig to lime zest. 75 rue du Petit-Champlain, Lower Town. ℂ 418/692-2859. www.fruits-passion.com.

CLOTHING

Atelier La Pomme   Just steps from the funicular in Lower Town, this cute boutique of women's clothes specializes in chic dresses by Québécois designers and *vêtements de cuir,* or leather clothing. 47 Sous-Le-Fort (near rue du Petit-Champlain), Lower Town. ℂ 418/692-2875.

Crocs   It turns out that Crocs, the rubbery, marshmallowy, candy-colored clogs that took the world by storm a few years ago, are the product of a Québec company (though many of the shoes are made in China). The company now sells more adult-looking shoes, and opened this, its first Canada store, in 2008. 1071 rue St-Jean (at rue St-Stanislas), Upper Town. ℂ 418/266-0262. www.crocs.ca.

Fourrures du Vieux-Port   The fur trade underwrote the development and exploration of Québec and the vast lands west, and continues to be important to this day. This Lower Town merchant has as good a selection as any, including knit furs and shearlings, along with designer coats by Nicole Miller, Christia, and Olivieri. 55 rue St-Pierre, (at Côte de la Montagne), Lower Town. ℂ 866/692-6688. www.quebecfourrure.com.

La Maison Darlington   The popular emporium in this ancient house (it was built in 1775) comes on strong with both tony and traditional clothing for men and women produced by such makers as Ballantyne, Dale of Norway, and Geiger. Inventory includes high-quality and tasteful men's and women's hats, scarves, sweaters, and umbrellas. As appealing are the hand-smocked, locally made dresses for little girls. 7 rue de Buade (near the Hôtel-de-Ville), Upper Town. ℂ 418/692-2268.

LOGO Sport   The top spot for sports jerseys: soccer, baseball, and, of course, hockey. 1047 rue St-Jean (at rue Ste-Angèle), Upper Town. ℂ 418/692-1351.

Marie Dooley   A teeny boutique featuring the chic, youthful women's clothing of Dooley, a Québec-born designer. 3B bd. René-Lévesque est (1 block northeast of av. Cartier), Montcalm. ℂ 418/522-7597. www.mariedooley.com.

Michael   Fashionable women's clothing for work or for play featuring the chic Animale and Sandwich labels. A store by the same name for men is next door, at no. 1060. 1066 rue St-Jean (near rue Ste-Angèle), Upper Town. ℂ 418/692-5666.

Murmure   Off the tourist track on avenue Cartier, this small boutique features casual, middle-end dresses, jackets, and skirts, primarily for 30- to 50-something women. (For designer jeans and skimpy jackets for younger women, visit **Urbain,** directly across the street.) 989 av. Cartier (at bd. René-Lévesque), Montcalm. ℂ 418/522-1016.

Simons Old Québec's only department store opened here in 1840. Small by modern standards, Simons has two floors for men's and women's clothing, emphasizing sportswear for adults and teens. Most of it is pretty basic. 20 Côte de la Fabrique (near the Hôtel-de-Ville), Upper Town. ☎ 418/692-3630. www.simons.ca.

Boutique Zazou This little shop focuses primarily on casual and dressy fashions from Québécois designers, including wool sweaters with nature motifs. 31 Petit-Champlain (near the funicular), Lower Town. ☎ 418/694-9990. www.quartierpetitchamplain.com.

FOOD
Canadian Maple Delights (Kids) This maple-syrup foods boutique stocks everything from maple chocolate and maple crystals to gift bottles of syrup and freshly made pastries and cookies. Maple-sweetened gelatos come in flavors such as hazelnut, mocha, and—mmm—meringue. In French, the shop's name is Les Délices de l'Érable. 1044 rue St-Jean (near rue Ste-Angèle), Upper Town. ☎ 418/692-3245. www.mapledelights.com.

Epicerie Richard Keep this small, very French-looking shop in Upper Town in mind if you need a nibble and aren't quite hungry enough for a full meal, or if you're looking for picnic foods. A cross between a delicatessen and grocery store, the shop carries a high-end selection of meats, cheeses, pâtés, and sandwiches. There are vegetarian options, too, including lentil salad, couscous, and tabouli. Beer and wine are also available. It's open until 11pm daily. 42 rue des Jardins (near rue St-Louis), Upper Town. ☎ 418/692-1207.

La Petite Cabane à Sucre Canada is the biggest producer of maple syrup in the world, and Québec is the source of 75% of it. "The little sugar shack," which is what the name means in French, sells ice cream, honey, maple syrup, maple candy, and related products, including tin log cabins that pour syrup from their chimneys. 94 rue du Petit-Champlain (near bd. Champlain), Lower Town. ☎ 418/692-5875. www.quartierpetitchamplain.com.

Marché du Vieux-Port By the water near the train station, this market is a year-round operation that blossoms in spring and summer with farmers' bounty from Ile d'Orléans and beyond. In addition to fresh fruits and vegetables, you'll find relishes, jams, honey, meats, cheeses, and handicrafts. 160 Quai Saint-André (near Espace 400e), Lower Town. ☎ 418/692-2517. www.marchevieuxport.com.

HOUSEWARES
Zone In a more residential area, Zone is a nifty housewares store featuring colorful bowls and plates for the kitchen, clocks and frames for the office, and small lamps and vases for anywhere else. 999 av. Cartier (at the corner of bd. René-Lévesque), Montcalm. ☎ 418/522-7373. www.zonemaison.com.

LEATHER GOODS
Ibiza This leather store sells coats, hats, gloves, slippers, handbags, and knives. 57 Petit-Champlain (mid-block), Lower Town. ☎ 418/692-2103. www.quartierpetitchamplain.com.

MUSIC
Archambault Part of a Canadian chain, Archambault stocks two large floors with CDs, books, magazines, and some toys for children. 1095 rue St-Jean, Upper Town. ☎ 418/694-2088. www.archambault.ca.

Maison de la Presse Internationale   As its name implies, this large store in the midst of the St-Jean shopping and nightlife bustle sells magazines, newspapers, and paperbacks from around the world, in many languages. It also has adapter plugs and converters. It opens daily at 7am (except Sun, at 8am) and stays that way until 11pm. There's another branch in the Place Québec, the mall between the Hilton and Radisson hotels on Parliament Hill. 1050 rue St-Jean (at the corner of rue Ste-Angèle), Upper Town. © 418/694-1511.

SHOPPING COMPLEXES

Shopping malls on a grander scale aren't found in or near Old Town. For mall shopping, it's necessary to travel to the neighboring municipality of **Sainte-Foy.** The malls there differ little from their cousins throughout North America in terms of layout and available products.

Laurier Québec, at 2700 bd. Laurier in Sainte-Foy (© **418/651-7085;** www.laurier quebec.com), however, can't be beat for sheer size. It's got 350 shops, including 40 restaurants, and some 12 million shoppers per year.

Inside the city walls, **Les Promenades du Vieux-Québec,** at 43 rue Buade, in Upper Town across from the Basilique Notre-Dame, is a much smaller complex filled with upscale shops. You'll find a perfumery, shops selling Inuit carvings, cafes, a currency exchange, and clothing for men and women.

Place Québec, just outside the city walls, is attached to the convention center and the Hilton hotel, making it an easy-to-spot landmark. It has dozens of shops as well as a movie theater and restaurants.

WINES

Société des Alcools du Québec   Liquor and other spirits can only be sold in stores operated by this provincial agency. The SAQ outlets are veritable supermarkets of wines and spirits, with thousands of bottles in stock. Québec's unique ice cider *(cidre de glace),* made from apples left on trees after the first frost, can be purchased here for around C$26 (£13) as well as from duty-free shops at the border. Look for the VQA logo, for Vintners Quality Alliance, on wines that have received the state seal of approval for quality. 1059 av. Cartier (near rue Fraser), Montcalm. © 418/643-4334. www.saq.com.

Québec City After Dark

Though Québec City can't pretend to match the volume of nighttime diversions of exuberant Montréal, there are more than enough after-dark activities to occupy visitors' evenings during an average stay. Apart from theatrical productions, which are almost always in French, knowledge of the language is rarely necessary to enjoy nighttime entertainment.

The neighborhood for each venue below is listed with the address: Lower Town and Upper Town in Vieux-Québec; Vieux-Port, adjacent to Lower Town; Parliament Hill; Montcalm, the residential neighborhood just west of Parliament Hill; and St-Roch.

1 THE PERFORMING ARTS

CLASSICAL MUSIC, OPERA & DANCE

The region's premier classical groups are **Orchestre Symphonique de Québec** (© 418/643-8486; www.osq.org), Canada's oldest symphony; **Opéra de Québec** (© 418/529-0688; www.operadequebec.qc.ca); and **Les Violons du Roy** (© 418/692-3026; www.violonsduroy.com), a string orchestra established in 1985 that features young musicians in the early stages of their careers. It performs at the Raoul-Jobin hall in the centrally located Palais Montcalm (p. 267). The orchestra and opera both perform at Grand Théâtre de Québec (see below).

CONCERT HALLS & PERFORMANCE VENUES

Many of the city's churches host sacred and secular music concerts, as well as special Christmas festivities. Look for posters on outdoor kiosks around the city and check with the tourist office (p. 203) for listings.

Colisée Pepsi Rock concerts by name acts on the order of Nickelback and Def Leppard are held here, with events such as junior hockey (Les Remparts de Québec), and various expositions filling in other days. The stadium is about a 10-minute drive northwest of Parliament Hill. 250 bd. Wilfrid-Hamel (ExpoCité), north of St-Roch. © **418/691-7110.** www.expocite.com.

Grand Théâtre de Québec ★★★ Classical music concerts, opera, dance, jazz, blues, klezmer, and theatrical productions are presented in two halls, one of which contains Canada's largest stage. Visiting conductors, orchestras, and dance companies perform here when resident organizations are away. In addition to the **Orchestre Symphonique de Québec** and the **Opéra de Québec,** the **Trident Theatre** troupe performs in French with five productions per year, in the Salle Octave-Crémazie. 269 bd. René-Lévesque est (near av. Turnbull), Parliament Hill. © **418/643-8131.** www.grandtheatre.qc.ca.

Kiosque Edwin-Bélanger (Value)   The bandstand at the edge of Battlefields Park hosts a summer music season from about mid-June to late August. The outdoor performances generally happen Thursday through Sunday evenings at 8pm and range from chorales and classical recitals to jazz, pop, and blues. All concerts are free. 390 av. de Bernières (at the Plains of Abraham), Parliament Hill. (C) 418/648-4050. www.ccbn-nbc.gc.ca/_fr/edwinbelanger.php.

Le Capitole   In 2008, productions of *Les Misérables* and a 1980s musical tribute show, *Super Karma Kameleons*, were highlights on the calendar of this historic 1,262-seat theater on Place d'Youville. (Anglophones, take note: Dramatic productions are in French.) Musicians such as American Steve Earle and Québec rocker Marie-Chantal Toupin have performed recently in the attached cabaret. 972 rue St-Jean (near Porte St-Jean), Parliament Hill. (C) 800/261-9903 or 418/694-4444. www.lecapitole.com.

Palais Montcalm ★   Reopened in 2007 after renovations to make it bigger and more modern, this venue is home to the well-regarded Les Violons du Roy, as well as other groups. The main performance space is the 979-seat Raoul-Jobin Theatre, which presents a mix of classical music concerts, dance programs, and plays. More intimate recitals, including those by jazz groups, happen in a 125-seat cafe-theater. 995 Place d'Youville (near Porte Saint-Jean), Parliament Hill. (C) 418/641-6411. www.palaismontcalm.ca.

2 THE CLUB & MUSIC SCENE

Québec City's **Festival d'Eté (Summer Festival)** bills itself as Canada's largest outdoor arts festival. It's held in Vieux-Québec and St-Roch for 11 days each July. Highlights include the free jazz and folk combos who perform in an open-air theater next to City Hall. The festival brings in 200 groups of artists from Africa, Asia, Europe, and North America showcasing theater, music, and dance. For details, call (C) **888/992-5200,** or check www.infofestival.com.

BOITES A CHANSONS & OTHER MUSIC CLUBS

If you just want to stroll and see what you find, there are three principal streets to choose from for nightlife, all near or just beyond Parliament Hill: **rue St-Jean** inside the walls, **Grande-Allée** outside the walls, and **avenue Cartier** in the Montcalm neighborhood.

Largo (Finds) ★   This attractive restaurant and jazz club is one of a growing number of tourist-friendly businesses sprucing up a blocks-long strip of rue St-Joseph in the emerging St-Roch district. Largo combines the old and the new beautifully: High ceilings and chandeliers give it old-time class, while blond-wood floors, clean angles, and contemporary art make it modern. There's jazz on Thursday, Friday, and Saturday starting at 8pm. Main courses range from C$17 to C$39 (£8.50–£20). Most nights, the music is free for diners. If you don't want to eat here, come after 10pm and sit at the bar. 643 rue St-Joseph est, St-Roch. (C) 418/529-3111. www.largorestoclub.com.

Le Cercle   This new tapas and wine bar opened in 2008 adjacent to its sister restaurant, the worthy **Utopie** (p. 232). It's co-owned by Utopie's chef and features food until 1am. Stylish snacks are only half the deal, though. Three or four nights each week, there's live music in the space, which holds upwards of 300 people. Performers run the gamut from post-punk to post-modern. Music tends to start around 10pm, with the cover charge from about C$5 to C$20 (£2.50–£10). 228 St-Joseph Est (near rue Caron), St-Roch. ☎ 418/948-8648. www.lecerclesurst-joseph.com.

Le Pape-Georges (Finds) A cozy wine bar in a 325-year-old stone-and-beamed room features *chanson* (a French-cabaret singing style), along with other music genres, usually Thursday through Sunday at 9pm. Light fare—plates of mostly Québec cheeses, assorted cold meats, and smoked salmon—is served, along with up to 15 choices of wine by the glass. Although it's in the middle of a tourist district, most patrons appear to be locals. 8 rue Cul-de-Sac (near bd. Champlain), Lower Town. ☎ 418/692-1320. www.papegeorges.com.

Les Voûtes Napoléon Down a flight of stairs tucked behind the outdoor cafes and away from Grande-Allée's general bustle, this amicable *boîtes à chansons* has music 7 nights a week starting around 10:30pm and is always free. The stone arches and low ceiling give the front room a cavelike feel, and there's a postage-stamp-size stage for the Québécois singer-songwriters passing through town. 680 Grande-Allée, Parliament Hill. ☎ 418/640-9388.

Pub St-Patrick This Irish pub just keeps on getting on. Pints of Guinness are the steadiest pour, of course, and food is available, but the music of the Ould Sod is the big draw. For that, show up on Friday and Saturday starting at 9:30pm. 1200 rue St-Jean (at rue Couillard), Upper Town. ☎ 418/694-0618. www.pubsaintpatrick.com.

Théâtre du Petit-Champlain Québécois and French singers alternate with jazz and rock groups in this roomy cafe and theater in Lower Town. Have a drink on the patio before the show. Performances usually take place Tuesday through Saturday at 8pm. 68 rue du Petit-Champlain (near the funicular), Lower Town. ☎ 418/692-2631. www.theatrepetit-champlain.com. Tickets C$22–C$43 (£11–£22).

DANCE CLUBS

Boudoir Lounge ★ The hottest club so far in trendy St-Roch (and the bar of choice for much of the city's restaurant staff), Boudoir has DJs working sound systems Thursday, Friday, and Saturday 10pm to 3am, though the bar is open daily from noon to 3am. The Boudoir martini, by the way, features vodka, triple sec, ice wine, champagne, and peach syrup. 441 rue du Parvis (at bd. Charest est), St-Roch. ☎ 418/524-2777. www.boudoirlounge.com.

Le Drague Cabaret Club Catering to gay and lesbian clientele, "the Drag" has two dance rooms and a cabaret featuring drag shows on Sunday nights. Other nights bring live shows, karaoke, country-music dancing, and theater improv. 815 rue St-Augustin (just off rue St-Jean), Parliament Hill. ☎ 418/649-7212. www.ledrague.com.

Maurice Find this club in the triple-tiered enterprise that occupies a converted mansion at the thumping heart of the Grande-Allée scene. It includes a surprisingly good restaurant (**Voo Doo Grill;** p. 231), a couple of bars, and music that tilts heavily toward Latin. In winter, it has been known to set up a sidewalk-level "Icecothèque" with a bar made completely of ice, ice sculptures, and roaring music. Theme nights are frequent, and crowds of hundreds are not unusual. 575 Grande-Allée est, Parliament Hill. ☎ 418/647-2000. www.mauricenightclub.com.

3 BARS

If you're young and looking for fun, keep in mind the **Grande-Allée** strip just past Place George V, where a beery collegiate atmosphere can sometimes rule as the evening wears on. The bars listed here, however, are removed from Grande-Allée's melee. Note that smoking has been banned in bars throughout the province since 2006.

Aviatic Club   A good locale to visit when you're coming or going by train, as it's right in front of the train station. The theme is aviation (odd, given the venue), signaled by two miniature planes hanging from the ceiling. Food ranges from sushi to Tex-Mex, to go along with local and imported beers. 450 de la Gare-du-Palais (near rue St-Paul), Lower Town. ✆ 418/522-3555. www.aviatic-club.com.

D'Orsay   Visitors who are well into their mortgages will likely enjoy this dark but chummy pub-bistro; clientele is mostly older than 35, and they strike up conversations easily. In summer afternoons and evenings, music is piped to the decidedly unprecious terrace out back. There's a full menu of conventional international dishes, from meat pie and burgers to fajitas and mussels. 65 rue de Buade (opposite Hôtel-de-Ville), Upper Town. ✆ 418-694-1582.

L'Astral ★   Spinning slowly above a city that twinkles below like tangled necklaces, this restaurant and bar atop the Hôtel Loews le Concorde (p. 218) unveils a breathtaking 360-degree panorama. Many come for dinner at the high-quality restaurant (look for the classic French-Canadian dessert *pudding chômeur,* a pound cake soaked with maple syrup and brown sugar), but you can also just come for drinks and the view. It's open daily until 11pm. 1225 Cours du Général de Montcalm (at Grande-Allée), Parliament Hill. ✆ 418/647-2222.

Saint Alexandre Pub ★   Roomy and sophisticated, this is one of the best-looking bars in town. It's done in British-pub style: polished mahogany, exposed brick, and a working fireplace that's particularly comforting during the eight cold months. Bartenders serve more than 40 single-malt scotches and more than 200 beers, along with hearty victuals that complement the brews. Live music—rock, blues, sometimes jazz or Irish—is occasionally presented, but check before planning your night around that. 1087 rue St-Jean (near rue St-Stanislas), Upper Town. ✆ 418/694-0015. www.pubstalexandre.com.

4 SUMMER FIREWORKS

From late July to mid-August, the city hosts a grand fireworks competition, **Les Grands Feux Loto-Québec,** at scenic Montmorency Falls 10 minutes north of city center (p. 30).

Side Trips from Québec City

The first four excursions described below can be combined and completed in a day. Admittedly, it will be a morning-to-night undertaking, especially if much time is taken to explore each destination, but the farthest of the four destinations is only 42km (26 miles) from Québec City. Just over a bridge outside the city, bucolic **Ile d'Orléans,** with its maple groves, orchards, farms, and 18th- and 19th-century houses, is an unspoiled mini-oasis. The waterfalls of **Montmorency** and **Canyon Ste-Anne** make for dazzling fun, especially in the spring when winter thaws make them thunder. And **Ste-Anne-de-Beaupré** is home to one of Canada's most visited basilicas.

In 2 or more days, you can continue along the northern shore of the St. Lawrence River to **Charlevoix,** where the stunning expanse of the river, high-end inns, and a wide variety of outdoor activities, including whale-watching in summer and fall, invite an overnight stay. There's an option to take the ferry across the river so that you can explore different riverside villages as you make your way back to Québec City.

Although it's preferable to drive in this region, tour buses go to Montmorency Falls and the shrine of Ste-Anne-de-Beaupré, circle the Ile d'Orléans, and make the trek all the way up to **Tadoussac** for whale-watching cruises.

For more information, visit the Québec City website at **www.quebecregion.com**.

1 ILE D'ORLEANS

16km (10 miles) NE of Québec City

Ile d'Orléans was first inhabited by native people; the French settled it as one of their initial outposts of New France in the 17th century. Long isolated from the mainland, the island's 6,862 (or so) current residents firmly resist development, so far preventing it from becoming just another sprawling bedroom community. Many of the island's oldest houses are intact, and it remains a largely rural farming area. Notable are the many red-roofed homes.

Until 1935, the only way to get to Ile d'Orléans was by boat (in summer) or over the ice in sleighs (in winter). The highway bridge that was built that year has allowed the island's fertile fields to become Québec City's primary market garden. During harvest periods, fruits and vegetables are picked fresh on the farms and trucked into the city daily.

In mid-July, hand-painted signs posted by the main road announce FRAISES: CUEILLIR VOUS-MEME (STRAWBERRIES: YOU PICK 'EM). The same invitation is made during apple season, August through October. Farmers hand out baskets and quote the price, paid when the basket's full. Bring along a bag or box to carry away the bounty.

Look for the cookbook *Farmers in Chef Hats* (www.farmersinchefhats.com), which in 2008 received a Gourmand World Cookbook award for "Best in the World" in the local-growers category. The bilingual book has 50 recipes featuring 50 products from Ile d'Orléans, as well as an agrotourism map.

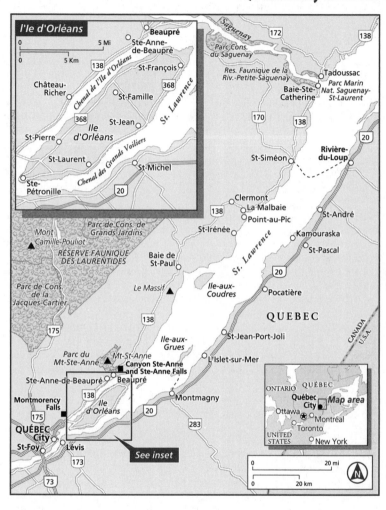

SIDE TRIPS FROM QUÉBEC CITY

20

ILE D'ORLÉANS

Thousands of migrating snow geese, ducks, and Canada geese stop by in April and May and again in late October. It's a spectacular sight when they launch in flapping hordes so thick that they almost blot out the sun.

ESSENTIALS

Getting There

BY CAR The drive from Québec City to the island is short. Get on Autoroute 440 east, in the direction of Ste-Anne-de-Beaupré. In about 15 minutes, the Ile d'Orléans bridge will be on your right. If you'd like a guide, **Maple Leaf Guide Services** (© **418/622-3677**) can provide one in your car or theirs.

While it's possible to bike over the bridge, it's not recommended: The sidewalk is narrow and precarious. But cyclists can park their cars at the tourist office (see below) for C$5 (£2.50) per day.

BY BUS   Dupont, which also goes by the name **Old Québec Tours** (*©* **800/267-8687** or 418/664-0460; www.tourdupont.com), offers a 6-hour tour with stops at a sugar shack, an apple orchard, and a *chocolaterie.*

Visitor Information

After arriving on the island, follow the **?** signs and turn right on Route 368 east toward Ste-Pétronille. **Bureau d'Accueil Touristique** (*©* 418/828-9411; www.iledorleans.com) is in the house on the right corner. Be sure to pick up the useful map that has most of the restaurants, farms, and accommodations marked. The bureau is open daily 9am to 5pm, with longer hours in summer and somewhat shorter hours in winter.

The tourist office offers a 2-hour audio tour on CD for rent, and brochures that detail a "Gourmet Route" driving tour, "Artists and Artisans" tour, and "Historic and Cultural Sites" tour.

A coast-hugging road—Route 368, also called chemin Royal and, in a few stretches, chemin de Bout-de-l'Ile—circles the island, which is 34km (21 miles) long and 8km (5 miles) wide; another couple of roads bisect it. Farms and picturesque houses dot its east side, and abundant apple orchards enliven the west side.

The island has six tiny villages, originally established as parishes, and each has a church as its focal point. Some are stone churches that date from the days of the French regime, and with fewer than a dozen such churches left in all of Québec province, this is a particular point of pride for the islanders.

It's possible to do a circuit of Ile d'Orléans in a half-day, but you can justify a full day if you eat a good meal, visit a sugar shack, do a little gallery hopping, or just skip stones from the beach. If you're strapped for time, loop around as far as St-Jean, and then drive across the island on route du Mitan ("middle road"). You'll get to the bridge by turning left onto Route 368 west.

The lodgings recommended below for Ile d'Orléans are of the auberge type, meaning they have six or more rooms and full-service restaurants open to both guests and nonguests. But there are also many B&Bs and *gîtes* (homes with a room or two available to travelers), which are less expensive and less elaborate. You can see brief details about many of these offerings on the tourist office's website, **www.iledorleans.com**. Many lodgings also provide leaflets to the tourist office.

For much of the year, you can meander at 40kmph (25 mph), pulling over only occasionally to let a car pass. There is no bike path, which means that bikers share the narrow rural roads, so cyclists might want to visit any month but July or August. Drive with care in the busiest summer months.

Important navigational note: Street numbers on the ring road "chemin Royal" start anew in each village, so that you could pass a no. 1000 chemin Royal in one stretch and then another no. 1000 chemin Royal a few minutes later. Be sure that you know not just the number of your destination, but which village it's in as well.

STE-PETRONILLE

The first village reached on the recommended counterclockwise tour is Ste-Pétronille, only 3km (2 miles) from the bridge (take a right turn off the bridge).

When the British occupied the island in 1759, General James Wolfe had his headquarters here before launching his successful attack on Québec City. At the end of the 19th century, this parish was a top vacation destination for the Québécois.

The village is now best known for its Victorian inn, **La Goéliche** (see below), and also claims North America's northernmost stand of **red oaks,** which dazzle in autumn. The houses were once the summer homes of wealthy English in the 1800s and the church dates from 1871. Even if you don't stay at the inn, drive down to the water's edge, where there's a small public area with benches and views of Québec City.

Where to Stay & Dine

La Goéliche ★ On a rocky point of land at the southern tip of Ile d'Orléans stands this romantic country inn and restaurant with a wraparound porch. The building is a virtual replica of the 1880 Victorian house that stood here until 1996. That one burned to the ground, leaving nothing but the staircase. This one recreates the period flavor with tufted chairs, Tiffany-style lamps, and antiques. All rooms are individually furnished and face the water, and first-floor units have small terraces. There are two apartments suitable for groups or longer stays. The river slaps at the foundation of the glass-enclosed terrace dining room, which is a grand observation point from which to watch cruise ships and Great Lakes freighters steaming past. A *goéliche,* by the way, is a small schooner; until the mid-1900s, they transferred goods from the St. Lawrence River's shore to larger schooners.

22 chemin du Quai, Ste-Pétronille, PQ G0A 4C0. ✆ **888/511-2248** or 418/828-2248. Fax 418/828-2745. www.goeliche.ca. 16 units. C$128–$208 (£64–£104) double. Rates include breakfast. Packages available. AE, DC, MC, V. Free parking. **Amenities:** Restaurant; bar; heated outdoor pool; golf and tennis nearby; babysitting. *In room:* Wi-Fi, minibar (some rooms), hair dryer.

ST-LAURENT

From Ste-Pétronille, continue on Route 368, which is called chemin de Bout-de-l'Ile for a few minutes here. After 7km (4¹⁄₃ miles), you'll arrive at St-Laurent, founded in 1679, once a boat-building center turning out ships that could carry up to 5,300 tons for Glasgow ship owners.

To learn about the town's maritime history, head down to the water and visit **Le Parc Maritime de St-Laurent** (✆ **418/828-9672**), an active boatyard from 1908 to 1967. Before the bridge was built, islanders journeyed across the river to Québec City by boat from here. The maritime park incorporates the old Godbout Boatworks and offers demonstrations of the art of building flat-bottomed schooners. It's open daily from 10am to 6pm mid-June through early September.

Where to Stay & Dine

Auberge Le Canard Huppé A roadside inn reminiscent of those in the motherland, this tidy establishment takes considerable pride in its kitchen. A gourmet four-course dinner, made almost entirely of local products, is served from 5 to 8pm and costs C$38 (£19); reservations are required. Guests can have their breakfast (included in the rate) in the bistro or on the terrace under the linden tree. Rooms are attractively decorated. Practice your French: The prickly owner/chef who took over the auberge in 2004 speaks English well but seems to begrudge having to.

2198 chemin Royal (Rte. 368), St-Laurent, PQ G0A 3Z0. ✆ **800/838-2292** or 418/828-2292. Fax 418/828-0966. www.canard-huppe.com. 10 units. C$128–C$170 (£64–£85) double. Rates include full breakfast. Packages available. AE, DC, MC, V. **Amenities:** Restaurant; bar. *In room:* A/C, CD player, Wi-Fi, hair dryer.

Le Moulin de Saint-Laurent ★ A former flour mill, in operation from 1720 to 1928, has been transformed into one of the island's most romantic restaurants. Rubble-stone walls and hand-wrought beams form the interior, with candlelight glinting off the hanging copper and brass pots. On a warm day, get a table on the shaded terrace beside the waterfall that tumbles down a small hill. Lunch can be light—maybe quiche or a plate of assorted pâtés or cheeses—and the ice cider made on the island is a refreshing alternative to wine. Main courses at dinner range from C$16 to C$27 (£8–£14). The restaurant is closed from November to April, but the owners rent 10 cottage chalets at the shore year-round. Each has a fully equipped kitchen and some have a fireplace and a washing machine, making them particularly appealing for bikers.

754 chemin Royal (Rte. 368), St-Laurent, PQ G0A 3Z0. ℂ **888/629-3888** or 418/829-3888. Fax 418/829-3716. www.moulinstlaurent.qc.ca. 10 units. Summer C$190–C$260 (£95–£130) double. Rates include dinner and breakfast. Packages available. AE, DC, MC, V. Pets allowed in some units for no additional charge. **Amenities:** Restaurant; small outdoor heated pool in summer; terrace next to waterfall. *In room:* TV, stereo, kitchen.

ST-JEAN

St-Jean, 6km (3³⁄₄ miles) from St-Laurent, was home to sea captains. That might be why the houses in the village appear more luxurious than others on the island. The creamy-yellow "Scottish brick" (as it's called) in the façades of several of the homes was ballast in boats that came over from Europe. The village **church** was built in 1734, and the walled **cemetery** is the final resting place of many fishermen and seafarers.

For a sweet treat, keep your eyes out for *cabanes à sucre,* traditional "sugar shacks," where maple syrup is made and casual all-you-can-eat meals are available. One that is regularly in business is **La Sucrerie Blouin,** 2967 chemin Royal (ℂ **418/829-2903;** www.sucrerieblouin.com), run by a family of bakers who have lived on the island for 300 years. They offer demonstrations of the syrup-making equipment and explanations about the process that turns tree sap into syrup.

If you're pressed for time, pick up route du Mitan here. It crosses Ile d'Orléans to St-Famille on the west side of the island, back near the bridge. The road is marked with a small sign on the left just past the church in St-Jean. Even if you're continuing the full loop, you might want to make a short detour down the road to see the farmland and forest here. To continue the tour, return to St-Jean and proceed east on Route 368.

A Manor House

Manoir Mauvide-Genest On the left as you enter St-Jean is the well-preserved manor home of Jean Mauvide, a French surgeon who settled here in 1720. Mauvide went on to acquire much of the western part of the island and built this small estate in 1752, becoming one of New France's leading figures. The teeny country castle, built right at the edge of the road, is unlike any other building on the island; take it in from across the street to really grasp its grandeur. It's filled with authentic and reproduction furnishings from Mauvide's era and is classified as a historic monument. Guided tours are available (call to reserve one if you're interested). The manor also has a gracious restaurant serving formal repasts of all-natural and local foods including quail and guinea hen, starting at C$33 (£17), by reservation only (ℂ **418/829-0236**).

ST-FRANÇOIS

St-François is at the island's most northeastern tip. The 9km (5²/₃-mile) drive from St-Jean to St-François exposes vistas of the Laurentian Mountains off to the left on the island's northern and western shores.

Mont Ste-Anne can be seen on the opposite side of the river in the distance, its slopes scored by ski trails. The St. Lawrence River is 10 times wider here than when it flows past Québec City and can be viewed especially well from the town's **observation tower,** which you'll pass on your right; you can park here and climb for a view. Regrettably, the town's original church (1734) burned in 1988. It was replaced in 1992.

After you've looped around the island's northern edge, the road stops being Route 358 east and becomes Route 368 west.

STE-FAMILLE

Founded in 1661, Ste-Famille is the island's oldest parish; it's 8km (5 miles) from St-François. Across the road from the triple-spired church (1743) is the convent of **Notre-Dame Congregation,** founded in 1685 by Marguerite Bourgeoys, one of Montréal's prominent early citizens (for more about her, see p. 116).

Maison de Nos Aïeux, 3907 chemin Royal (© **418/829-0330;** www.fondation francoislamy.org), is a genealogy center with minimovies about some of the island's oldest families and information about the island's history. It's open mid-June until mid-August daily from 10am to 6pm, and costs C$3 (£1.50). **Parc des Ancêtres,** a riverside green space with picnic tables, is adjacent.

For a satisfying low-key meal, stop into roadside **La Crêpe Cochonne,** 3963 chemin Royal (© **418/829-3656**). You'll find a wide selection of dessert crepes, filled with maple syrup, homemade chocolate, or fruit, and savory crepes, with make-your-own options from ham to cheese to asparagus. Crepes cost C$4 (£2) to C$9 (£4.50) each. A back deck has a river view.

ST-PIERRE

When you reach St-Pierre, you're nearly back to where you started. Its central attraction is the island's oldest church (1717). Services are no longer held there, but a large handicraft shop in the back, behind the altar, was founded in 1695, making it even older than the church.

If you haven't stopped at any of the above orchards that beckoned, **Bilodeau** at 2200 chemin Royal (© **418/828-9316;** www.cidreriebilodeau.qc.ca; daily 9am–5pm) makes a satisfying final stop. It produces some of Ile d'Orléans's regular ciders and *cidre de glace,* a sweet wine made from apples left on the trees until after the first frost. Visitors can partake of samples (try the hazelnut-and-apple-syrup mustard), guided facility tours, apple-picking (if you're there mid-Aug to mid-Oct), and a shop.

Buffet d'Orléans, 1025 Rte. Prévost (© **418/828-0013**) just at the bridge, is an old-time diner where the waitresses wear white skirts and black aprons and the bread comes in plastic wrap. Try the *tourtière maison,* a homemade meat pie in a crust, served with two scoops of mashed potatoes and vegetables, for C$12 (£6), or *cigare aux choux,* cabbage rolls with the same side dishes, for C$11 (£5.50). It's open daily 7am to 9pm year-round, and until 11pm in summer.

2 MONTMORENCY FALLS

11km (7 miles) NE of Québec City

Back on the mainland, the impressive **Montmorency Falls,** which were named by Samuel de Champlain for his patron, the duke of Montmorency, are visible from Autoroute 440. At 83m (272 ft.) tall, they're 30m (98 ft.) higher than Niagara—a boast no visitor is spared. These falls are, however, far narrower.

On summer nights, the plunging water is illuminated, and from late July to mid-August, an international fireworks competition, **Les Grands Feux Loto-Québec,** is held 2 nights per week (p. 30). In winter there's a particularly impressive sight: The freezing spray sent up by crashing water builds a mountain of white ice at the base, nicknamed *pain de sucre* (sugarloaf). It grows as high as 30m (98 ft.) and attracts ice climbers.

The water's yellowish tint is because of the riverbed's high iron content.

ESSENTIALS

Getting There

BY BUS   Dupont, which also goes by the name **Old Québec Tours** (*©* **800/267-8687** or 418/664-0460; www.tourdupont.com), offers tours to the falls.

BY CAR   Take Autoroute 440 east out of Québec City. After 10 minutes, watch for the exit for the falls and the parking lot. If you miss the exit, you'll see the falls on your left and will be able to U-turn.

VIEWING THE FALLS

The falls are surrounded by the provincial **Parc de la Chute-Montmorency** (*©* **418/663-3330;** www.sepaq.com/chutemontmorency), where visitors can take in the view and have a picnic. The grounds are accessible year-round.

Montmorency Falls ★   There are a couple ways to see the 83m (272 ft.) falls, which are visible from Autoroute 440. A path goes from the parking area to the very place where the water comes crashing down; the view is spectacular in all seasons from here. Stairs ascend from there to near the top, and there are viewing platforms along the way. At the top, a footbridge spans the water just where it flows over the cliff. If you don't want to walk, a cable car runs from the parking lot to a terminal above the falls. At that top terminal is **Manoir Montmorency,** a villa that contains an interpretation center, a cafe, and a restaurant. The dining room and porch have a side view of the falls; reservations are suggested. Parking is available at the top of the falls by the villa, too.

2490 ave. Royale, Beauport. *©* **418/663-3330.** www.sepaq.com/chutemontmorency. Admission to the falls is free, though parking costs C$9 (£4.50). Round-trip fares on the cable car cost C$11 (£6) for adults, C$5 (£2.50) for ages 6 to 16, and free for age 5 and younger. One-way fares are available, allowing you to walk the very steep side staircase in 1 direction. The cable car operates daily late Apr to late Aug, and on a more limited schedule the rest of the year.

3 STE-ANNE-DE-BEAUPRE

33km (21 miles) NE of Québec City; 22km (14 miles) NE of Montmorency Falls

The village of Ste-Anne-de-Beaupré is a religious destination, centered around a two-spired basilica that is one of Canada's most famous shrines. More than 1.5 million people make the pilgrimage each year to a complex that includes a major basilica and a museum.

Legend has it that French mariners were sailing up the St. Lawrence River in the 1650s when they ran into a terrifying storm. They prayed to their patroness, St. Anne, to save them, and when they survived, they dedicated a wooden chapel to her on the north shore of the St. Lawrence, near the site of their perils. Not long afterward, a chapel laborer was said to have been cured of lumbago, the first of many documented miracles. Since that time, believers have made their way here to pay their respects to St. Anne, mother of the Virgin Mary and grandmother of Jesus.

Route 138 travels along the river, which is tidal. At low tide, the beach can become speckled with hundreds of birds, such as purple sandpipers, pecking for food. Look for them behind the houses, gas stations, and garages that pepper the road.

ESSENTIALS
Getting There
BY BUS **Dupont,** also called **Old Québec Tours** (© 800/267-8687 or 418/664-0460; www.tourdupont.com) offers tours that include Ste-Anne-de-Beaupré.

BY CAR Autoroute 440 turns into Autoroute 40 at Montmorency Falls and then becomes Route 138 almost immediately. Continue on Route 138 to Ste-Anne-de-Beaupré. The church and exit are visible from the road.

A RELIGIOUS TOUR
Basilica and Shrine of Ste-Anne-de-Beaupré ★
The towering basilica that dominates this small village is the most recent building raised here in St. Anne's honor. After the French sailors' first modest wooden chapel (1658) was swept away by a flood, another chapel was built on higher ground. Floods, fires, and the ravages of time dispatched later buildings, until a larger structure was erected in 1887. In 1926, it, too, lay in ruins, gutted by fire. The present basilica is constructed in stone, following an essentially neo-Romanesque scheme, and was consecrated on July 4, 1976.

Inside the front doors, look for the two columns dressed with racks of canes—presumably from people cured and no longer in need of assistance—that go 9m (30 ft.) high. There are several masses per day, and in the summer, daily candlelight processions follow the 7:30pm Mass.

Other parts of the shrine complex include the **Scala Santa Chapel** (1891); the **Memorial Chapel** (1878), with a bell tower and altar from the late 17th and early 18th centuries, respectively; and the **Way of the Cross,** which is lined with life-size bronze figures depicting Christ's life. There's also a church store and the **Musée Sainte-Anne,** a small facility housing paintings and sculptures. The church maintains a plot of land along the river for RV campers and runs the **Basilica Inn** for visiting pilgrims; double-occupancy rooms cost C$56 (£28).

The basilica and town are particularly busy on Ste-Anne's Novena and Feast Day, the days of saintly significance in mid- through late July.

Ste-Anne-de-Beaupré. ☎ 418/827-3781. www.ssadb.qc.ca. Admission to basilica and chapels is free; admission to museum C$2 (£1); free for children 5 and younger. Basilica daily 7am–8pm; museum daily 9am–5pm May 4–Oct 12 (open only to groups by reservation the rest of the year).

Other Activities

Just next to the basilica is a building called the **Cyclorama,** which houses a 14m-high (45-ft.), 360-degree painting depicting old Jerusalem at the moment of Christ's crucifixion ("Relive the sight," says the brochure). Open from mid-April until October, admission is C$8 (£4) for adults, C$7 (£3.50) for seniors 65 and older, C$5 (£2.50) for children 6 to 16, and free for children 5 and younger.

Gym rats will want to know about **GymUltra,** 10909 bd. Ste-Anne (Rte. 138; ☎ 418/827-8496), a facility that opened in June 2008. It has workout machines and is open to the public weekdays 6am to 10pm and weekends 8am to 6pm for C$10 (£5) per visit. It's in the Promenades Ste-Anne mini-mall a mile past the basilica.

Where to Stay & Dine

Auberge La Camarine ★ This inn has a kitchen that is equaled by only a handful of restaurants in the region and quirky bedrooms full of personality and bathed in sunny, Provence-style yellows and blues. First, the food: Creative, well-coordinated combinations include smoked salmon and gravlax in fennel and artichoke salad, butternut-squash soup with rabbit and horseradish cream, and lamb shank with a rosemary reduction. Québécois cheeses are offered for the meal's close. Main courses run C$22–C$32 (£11–£16); *tables d'hote* start at C$38 (£19); and a gastronomic tasting menu costs C$55 (£28). Sunday brunch is C$14 (£7). Second, the rooms: Bathrooms are uniformly roomy, comfortable mattresses were new in 2007, and decor blends antique and contemporary notions. Normally, units facing the river would have the most appeal, but given the inn's locale just above busy Route 138, back rooms like nos. 43 and 49, which face quiet fields, can be more relaxing.

10947 bd. Ste-Anne (Rte. 138), Beaupré, PQ G0A 1E0. ☎ 800/567-3939 or 418/827-5703. Fax 418/827-5430. www.camarine.com. 31 units. C$119–C$155 (£60–£78) double. Packages available. AE, MC, V. Pets accepted, C$20 (£10) additional per visit. **Amenities:** 2 restaurants; free Wi-Fi; computer for guest use (free); washer and dryer for guest use (free). *In room:* A/C (some rooms), TV, hair dryer.

4 CANYON STE-ANNE, STE-ANNE FALLS & PARC MONT STE-ANNE

42km (26 miles) NE of Québec City; about 9km (6 miles) NE of Ste-Anne-de-Beaupré

After Ste-Anne-de-Beaupré, you finally enter into thick evergreen woods, and the frenetic pace of urban life begins to slip away. A short drive off Route 138 is Canyon Ste-Anne, a deep gorge and powerful waterfall created by the Ste-Anne-du-Nord River. Unseen from the main road, the canyon and its falls are an exhilarating attraction.

A bit inland is the Parc Mont Ste-Anne, which surrounds an 800m-high (2,625-ft.) peak. In winter, it's the area's busiest ski mountain, while summertime invites camping, hiking, and biking.

Getting There

BY BUS From mid-November until late April, the **Taxi Coop Québec** (© 418/525-5191; www.taxicoop-quebec.com) shuttle service picks up passengers at Québec City hotels in the morning to take them to Parc Mont Ste-Anne, returning them to Québec City in the late afternoon.

BY CAR Continue along Route 138 from Ste-Anne-de-Beaupré. To get to the waterfalls, stay on Route 138 about 5 minutes past the basilica; the marked entrance will be on your left. To get to the park and ski mountain, exit onto Route 360 east. The entrance to the Château Mont Sainte-Anne (p. 280) will be on your left, with the entrance to the park directly after it.

OUTDOORS FUN

Canyon Ste-Anne Waterfalls ★★★ Perhaps it's because these falls are tucked into the woods, but they don't get the attention that the Montmorency Falls do, and it's a shame. They're spectacular and kitsch-free, and count as a must-see. Follow the narrow road from Route 138 through the woods to a parking lot, picnic grounds, and a building containing a cafeteria, a gift shop, and the ticket booth. The falls are less than a 10-minute walk from the entrance, but an open-sided shuttle bus is available to drive visitors; it drops off at the top of the falls. Trails go down both sides to the bottom.

Part of the excitement comes from the approach: You hear the falls before you see them, and you step out of the woods practically beside them. Three (optional) footbridges go directly across the falls. The first crosses the narrow river just before the water starts to drop. The second, and most thrilling, crosses right over the canyon, from the top of the rock walls that drop straight down to the water. Being so close to the thundering, unending force crashing over massive rocks is likely to induce vertigo in even the most stable of nerves. The final suspension bridge starts at the gorge's base, just 9m (30 ft.) above the water where it starts to flatten out again, and ends at an observation platform. The very brave-hearted can also ride a zipline across the canyon directly over the water while harnessed onto a cable wire, for about C$17 (£9).

Along the trails are eight platforms that jut over the water and well-written information plaques. However, management has wisely avoided commercial intrusions along the trails, letting the powerful natural beauty speak for itself.

The falls are 74m (243 ft.) high and at their most awe-inspiring in the spring, when melt-off of winter snows bloats the rivers above and sends 100,000 liters (more than 26,000 gallons) of water over *per second.* (The volume drops to 10,000 liters/2,600 gallons per second in Aug and Sept.) So voluminous is the mist coming from the fall that it creates another wall of mini-waterfalls on the side of the gorge.

From 1904 to 1965, the river was used to float logs from lumbering operations, and part of the dramatic gorge was created by dynamiting in 1917, to reduce the amount of literal log-jams.

Those who have difficulty walking can see the falls without going too far from the bus, and anyone with acrophobia can stay on the side trails, strolling amid the hemlock and poplar trees and away from the bridges altogether. A visit takes about 1½ hours.

206 Rte. 138 East, Beaupré. © **418/827-4057.** www.canyonsa.qc.ca. Admission C$11 (£5.50) adults, C$8 (£4) ages 13–17, C$5 (£2.50) ages 6–12, free for age 5 and younger. May to late Oct daily 9am–4:30pm, and until 5:30pm from June 24 until Labor Day. Hours are subject to change due to weather, so call to confirm on stormy days.

Parc du Mont Ste-Anne ★   The area's premiere wilderness resort surrounds an 800m-high (2,625-ft.) peak and is an outdoor enthusiast's dream. In winter, **downhill skiing** on Mont Ste-Anne is terrifically popular. Just 40 minutes from Québec City, this is the region's largest and busiest mountain; *Ski Canada* magazine named it the best destination in the east for spring skiing. There are 66 trails on three sides, and 35% of the resort is expert terrain. At night, 17 trails are lit. Full-day lift tickets cost C$57 (£28) for adults, C$47 (£24) for seniors, C$44 (£22) for ages 13 to 17, and C$31 (£16) for ages 7 to 12.

Also in the winter, the park offers Canada's largest network of **cross-country skiing** trails—212km (131 miles) of them. A day ticket is C$19 (£9.50) for adults, C$14 (£7) for age 65 and older, C$13 (£6.50) for ages 13 to 17, C$8 (£4) for children 7 to 12, and free for children 6 and younger. There's an inn for cross-country skiers in the middle of the trails called L'Auberge du Fondeur (© **800/463-1568**).

Dog-sledding, snowshoeing, snowmobiling, ice-canyoning, and **winter paragliding** are other options. In summer and early fall, the park also offers **camping, hiking, golfing, in-line skating,** and **paragliding.** A panoramic **gondola** operates daily between late May and mid-October, weather permitting. Details about these activities are listed seasonally on the Mont Ste-Anne website.

Mont Ste-Anne is especially well known for its huge network of trails for both hard-core **mountain biking** and milder day-tripping (bikes can be rented). More than 700 athletes are expected for the 2010 Mountain Bike and Trial World Championships, which will be held here from August 30 through September 6 that year.

From mid-November to late April, **Taxi Coop Québec** (© **418/525-5191;** www.taxicoop-quebec.com) provides daily shuttle service between Québec City and the park.

2000 bd. de Beau-Pré, Beaupré © **888/827-4579** or 418/827-4579. www.mont-sainte-anne.com. General admission to the site is C$9 (£4.50) for a family in a car or, individually, C$3.55 (£1.80) for adults and C$1.75 (90p) for children 7–17 years old. Gondola ticket prices are C$16 (£8) for adults, C$14 (£7) for 65 and older, C$13(£6.50) for ages 7–17, and free for age 6 and younger, with a variety of family rates.

Where to Stay & Dine

In addition to the resort below, **Herbergement Mont-Sainte-Anne** (© **888/827-2002;** www.hmsalm.com) offers condo rentals at the base of the mountain. They run from C$129 (£65) for a studio in summer to C$499 (£250) for a three-bedroom unit in peak winter periods.

Château Mont Sainte-Anne ★ (Kids)   Tucked into the base of its namesake mountain and just next to Parc du Mont Ste-Anne, this resort provides the closest overnight location for all mountain activities. New owners took over in 2005 and have made renovations in the years since, including total makeovers of 47 rooms in 2008 (ask for one of them). The resort's primary identity is as a ski lodge, with ski-in-ski-out accessibility at the base of the gondola lift. But two golf courses and a strong network of mountain biking trails bring summer business. All rooms have either kitchenettes or full kitchens, and 40 have fireplaces. Prices rise and fall depending on occupancy and time of year, so the listings below are a rough guide only.

500 bd. Beau-Pré, Beaupré, PQ G0A 1E0. © **800/463-4467** or 418/827-5211. Fax 418/827-5072. www.chateaumsa.ca. 240 units. From C$249 (£125) double much of the year; from C$99 (£50) double in Apr and Nov. Children 16 and younger stay free in parent's room. Packages available. AE, DC, DISC, MC, V. Pets accepted in some units for an additional C$20 (£10) per night. **Amenities:** 2 restaurants; bar/bistro; indoor and outdoor pools; 2 golf courses; health club; outdoor hot tubs; spa; family programs; free Wi-Fi; 4 computer terminals for guest use. *In room:* A/C, TV, kitchenette, hair dryer.

5 CENTRAL CHARLEVOIX: BAIE-ST-PAUL, ST-IRENEE & LA MALBAIE

Baie-St-Paul: 93km (58 miles) NE of Québec City; St-Irénée: 125km (78 miles) NE of Québec City; La Malbaie: 140km (87 miles) NE of Québec City

The Laurentians move closer to the shore of the St. Lawrence River as they approach the mouth of the intersecting Malbaie River. U.S. President William Howard Taft, who had a summer residence in the area, said that the air here was "as intoxicating as champagne, but without the morning-after headache." Taft was among the political and financial elite of Canada and the eastern U.S. who made Murray Bay, or La Malbaie, such a wildly popular vacation destination in the early and mid-19th century.

Charlevoix first blossomed under the British regime in the 18th century. In 1762, Scottish officers in the British Army, John Nairne and Malcolm Fraser, built sawmills and flour mills here. They attracted French-speaking Catholics, making the region a combination of Old France and Old Scotland.

Grand vistas over the St. Lawrence abound, and there are many farms in the area. Moose sightings are not uncommon, and the rolling, dark-green mountains with their white ski slope scars offer numerous places to hike and bike in the warm months and ski when there's snow. (It's not unheard of, by the way, for it to snow in May.)

In 1988, Charlevoix was named a UNESCO World Biosphere Reserve, which means that it's a protected area for cross-disciplinary conservation-oriented research; development here is balanced against environmental concerns. This was one of the first populated areas to get the designation.

ESSENTIALS
Getting There
BY CAR   Take Route 138 to Baie-St-Paul; turn onto Route 362 to go into downtown Baie-St-Paul. To continue northeast, take either the primary Route 138 or the smaller, more scenic Route 362, which travels closer to the water and lets you visit St-Irénée on the way to La Malbaie.

Visitor Information
Baie-St-Paul has a year-round **tourist office** directly on Route 138 (✆ **800/667-2276** or 418/665-4454) that's open daily from 9am to 5pm, and until 7pm in the summer. It's on a dramatic hill approaching the village and is well marked from the highway (beware, though: it's a sharp turnoff). Stop here for one of the grandest vistas of the river and town below.

There are other tourism offices throughout the region, including one in La Malbaie on the water at 495 bd. de Comporté, Route 362 (✆ **800/667-2276** or 418/665-4454). It's open daily from at least 8:30am to 4:30pm. Regional information is also available at **www.tourisme-charlevoix.com**.

BAIE-ST-PAUL & ISLE-AUX-COUDRES
The first town of any size in Charlevoix via Route 138, Baie-St-Paul is an attractive, funky community of about 7,400 that continues to earn its century-old reputation as an artists' retreat. Some two dozen boutiques and galleries and a couple of small museums show the works of local painters and artisans. Given the setting, it isn't surprising that many of the artists are landscapists, but other styles and subjects are represented, too.

Work runs the gamut from hobbyist to highly professional. Options include the **Maison de René-Richard,** at 58 rue St-Jean-Baptiste (© 418/435-5571).

For **bicycling,** pop off the mainland by taking the free 15-minute car ferry to the small island of Isle-aux-Coudres. Popular paths offer a 24km (16-mile) loop around the island. From May to September, single bikes, tandems, and quadricycles for up to six adults and two small children can be rented from **Vélo-Coudres** (© 877/438-2118 or 418/438-2118; www.charlevoix.qc.ca/velocoudres). The island also has a smattering of boutiques and hotels. The ferry leaves from the town of St. Joseph-de-la-Rive, along Route 362 just east of Baie-St-Paul.

Many of Canada's elite skiers train at **Le Massif** (© 877/536-2774 or 418/632-5876; www.lemassif.com), the area's largest ski mountain. It has a network of 45 trails, many of which give skiers the illusion that they're heading directly into the adjacent St. Lawrence.

There are rumblings of a major project for the area: Daniel Gauthier, a founder of the Cirque du Soleil has been working for years to further develop Le Massif by adding housing and a 150-room hotel. He also has talked about refurbishing a train line to allow travelers to get to the area without driving. A June 2007 fire at the planned downtown location set back plans, but they are reportedly continuing.

Where to Stay

La Maison Otis A central location and a terrific dining room make Otis an easy choice and a good value. A long porch fronts Baie-St-Paul's colorful main street, and rooms in the rambling collection of connecting buildings offer cozy combinations of fireplaces, whirlpools, four-poster beds, and stereo systems. Meals are served in a graceful **dining room** with a stone fireplace and shaded candlesticks. Smoked filet of duck with honeyed figs and leg of lamb steamed with cumin are excellent entrees. Rates listed are for high season and include a five-course dinner and breakfast for two; call to ask about room-only and single-occupancy prices. An adjacent spa has a large menu of massage services.

23 rue St-Jean-Baptiste, Baie-St-Paul, PQ G3Z 1M2. © **800/267-2254** or 418/435-2255. Fax 418/435-2464. www.maisonotis.com. 30 units. C$218–C$320 (£109–£160) double. Rates include 5-course dinner and breakfast for 2. Packages available. MC, V. Pets accepted, additional C$10 (£5) per night. **Amenities:** 2 restaurants; indoor pool; attached spa; free Wi-Fi in reception. *In room:* A/C, TV, hair dryer.

Where to Dine

Foodies will want to consider visits to some of the region's food producers.

La Maison d'Affinage Maurice Dufour, 1339 bd. Mgr-de-Lavel (Rte. 138) Baie-St-Paul (© 418/435-5692; www.fromagefin.com), is a *fromagerie* that makes the highly regarded artisanal cheese Le Ciel de Charlevoix. It offers tours and tastings and serves dinner Wednesday through Sunday in summer. A 4-course meal with coffee runs from C$38 to C$53 (£19–£26).

La Ferme Basque de Charlevoix, 813 rue St-Edouard in St-Urbain, just west of Baie-St-Paul (© 418/639-2246; www.lafermebasque.ca), is a small-scale family farm that raises ducks and makes foie gras sold throughout the province. Tours are offered for C$4 (£2).

Chocolate freaks will want to feed their need at **Chocolaterie Cynthia,** 66-3 rue St-Jean-Baptiste (© 418/435-6060), just steps from the two restaurants listed below. It sells small packets of homemade chocolate, *gelato maison,* and ice cream cones dipped in 70% dark chocolate.

Café des Artistes In addition to its formal restaurant, the hotel La Maison Otis also runs this enormously appealing attached bistro. Pizzas with wafer-thin crusts are exceptional, and there are 15 types to choose from. Other choices include a pâté du jour, Hot-Dogs Français with sauces made in town, salads, and paninis. The cafe does good business with locals and artist types. Because it's small and features a bar, however, it's not open to folks 17 and younger.

25 rue St-Jean-Baptiste, Baie-St-Paul. ✆ **418/435-5585**. Most items cost less than C$12 (£6); *table d'hôte* C$14 (£7). MC, V. Daily 9:30am–midnight.

Le Saint-Pub This casual bistro is part of the town's *microbrasserie*, or microbrewery. The kitchen serves up solid renditions of bar food, done Québécois-style. House specialties include barbecue chicken (C$16/£8) and concoctions cooked with beer (beer-and-onion soup, wild boar burger marinated in beer, chocolate-and-stout pudding, sugar pie with beer). Five brews on tap and four in bottles are all made on-site, and visitors sometimes get to test beverages. There's a patio in summer.

2 rue Racine, Baie-St-Paul. ✆ **418/240-2332**. www.microbrasserie.com. Main courses C$12–C$25 (£6–£13); *table d'hôte* C$23–C$31 (£12–£16). MC, V. Mon–Sat 11:30am–9pm; Sun noon–8pm.

ST-IRENEE

From Baie-St-Paul, take Route 362 northeast toward La Malbaie. The air is scented with sea salt and punctured with gulls' shrieks, and Route 362 roller-coasters over bluffs above the river, with wooded hills and well-kept villages. This stretch of the road, from Baie-St-Paul to La Malbaie, is one of the most scenic in the entire region and is dubbed the *route du fleuve*, which means "river route." (It can be treacherous in icy weather, though, so in colder months, opt for the flatter Rte. 138.)

In 32km (about 20 miles) is St-Irénée, a cliff-top hamlet of just 694 year-round residents. Apart from the setting, the best reason for dawdling here is the 60-hectare (148-acre) property and estate of **Domaine Forget** (✆ **888/336-7438** or 418/452-3535; www.domaineforget.com). The facility is a performing-arts center for music and dance and offers an **International Festival** from late June through August. Concerts are staged in a 604-seat concert hall, with Sunday musical brunches on an outdoor terrace that has spectacular views of the river. The program emphasizes classical music with solo instrumentalists and chamber groups, but is peppered with jazz and dance. Most tickets are C$20 to C$40 (£10–£20).

From September to May, Domaine rents its **student dorms** to the general public. They're clean and well-appointed studios, with cooking areas and beds for two to five people. They start at C$70 (£35) for double occupancy, with discounts for longer stays, and they include access to studio work areas.

Sea-kayaking ecotours from a half-day to 4 days can be arranged through several companies in the area. **Katabatik** (✆ **800/453-4850** or 418/665-2332; www.katabatik. ca), based in La Malbaie, offers trips that combine kayaking with information about the bays of the St-Lawrence estuary. A half-day tour costs C$50 (£25) for adults, C$40 (£20) for children 14 to 17, and C$30 (£15) for children 13 and younger. Tours start in St-Irénée as well as other spots along the coast and run from March through October.

LA MALBAIE

From St-Irénée, Route 362 starts to bend west after 10km (6¼ miles), as the mouth of the Malbaie River starts to form. La Malbaie (or "Murray Bay," as it was called by the wealthy Anglophones who made this their resort of choice from the Gilded Age through the 1950s) is the collective name of five former municipalities: Pointe-au-Pic, Cap-à-l'Aigle, Rivière-Malbaie, Sainte-Agnès, and Saint-Fidèle. At its center is a small, scenic bay. Inhabitants of the region justifiably wax poetic about their wildlife and hills and trees, the place where the sea meets the sky. They also have something quite different to preen about these days: a casino (see below).

A Casino & a Museum

Casino de Charlevoix   The second of Québec's gambling casinos (the first is in Montréal) is about as tasteful as such establishments get. Cherrywood paneling and granite floors enclose more than 800 slot machines, a keno lounge, and more than 20 tables, including blackjack, roulette, stud poker, and minibaccarat. Texas hold 'em mania has finally arrived here (a few years behind the U.S. explosion), with an electronic table and a weekly tournament. Visitors must be at least 18 years old.

183 av. Richelieu (follow the many signs). *©* **800/665-2274** or 418/665-5300. www.casino-de-charlevoix.com. Free admission (18 and older only). Daily 10am–1am; hours are longer in summer and on weekends.

Musée de Charlevoix ★   A terrific little museum. One of the three gallery spaces is devoted to a marvelous permanent exhibition called *Appartenances* ("Belonging") about the history and culture of Charlevoix. Included are photographs from the 1930s of beluga whale-hunting and frontierswomen skinning eels; artifacts from the Manoir Richelieu before its major fire in 1928; folk art from the 1930s and 40s; and engaging descriptive text in English and French.

10 chemin du Havre (at the corner of Rte. 362). *©* **418/665-4411.** Admission C$7 (£3.50) adults, C$5 (£2.50) seniors and students. June to mid-Oct daily 9am–5pm; mid-Oct to May Mon–Fri 10am–5pm, Sat–Sun 1–5pm.

Where to Stay & Dine

Fairmont Le Manoir Richelieu ★★★ (Kids)   This is the region's grand resort. Since 1899, there has been a hotel at the river's edge here, first serving the swells who summered in this aristocratic haven with spectacular views of the St. Lawrence River. After waves of renovations, the decor of the hotel long ago dubbed "the castle on the cliff" is reminiscent of its posh heritage. Many rooms meet deluxe standards, and the Fairmont Gold floor has a lounge serving complimentary breakfasts and evening hors d'oeuvres. A C$15-million project that finished in 2006 molded the golf course into a glorious 27-hole expanse overlooking the St. Lawrence on one side and the hills and mountains of Charlevoix on the other. Guests run a wide gamut, from young couples and families drawn to the resort's many sporting activities for children to gamers from the casino next door and older folks who have been coming here forever.

181 rue Richelieu, La Malbaie, PQ G5A 1X7. *©* **866/540-4464** or 418/665-3703. Fax 418/665-8131. www.fairmont.com. 405 units. Summer from C$269 (£135) double; Nov–May from C$159 (£80) double; suites from C$399 (£200). Packages available. AE, DC, MC, V. Valet parking C$20 (£10) with in/out privileges; self-park for free. Pets allowed. **Amenities:** 4 restaurants; bar; indoor and outdoor pools; golf course; 3 tennis courts; health club; spa w/22 treatment rooms; watersports equipment; children's programs; concierge; room service; babysitting; executive-level rooms; snowmobiling. *In room:* A/C, TV, high-speed Internet, minibar, hair dryer.

La Pinsonnière ★★★   Romance with a princely touch, in 18 pristine rooms, is what's offered here. The 2006 renovation of this luxury inn created six deluxe rooms (up from one) with spectacular views of the St. Lawrence River. Now, too, there are handsome linens, private terraces, and huge bathrooms with oversized whirlpools, private saunas, and/or steam showers. These most expensive units deliver a serious "wow" factor and offer the most transporting visit. Newer rooms have a contemporary, streamlined decor, while older ones are more classic Queen Anne; all have fireplaces, either gas or wood. An indoor pool, unspoiled river beach at the bottom of the property, and attentive service make this tiny resort a regional star. Spot-on dinners featuring extraordinary tartares and local products cost C$68 (£34); menus change daily. Wines are a particular point of pride, with 750 labels in the 12,000-bottle cellar. Taking in the panoramic views is, simply, pure contentment.

124 rue St-Raphaël, La Malbaie (secteur Cap-à-l'Aigle), PQ G5A 1X9. ⓒ **800/387-4431** or 418/665-4431. Fax 418/665-7156. www.lapinsonniere.com. 18 units. C$335–C$485 (£168–£243) double May–Oct and holiday season; C$285–C$435 (£143–£218) double rest of the year. Packages available. Minimum 2-night stay on weekends, 3 nights on holiday weekends. AE, MC, V. Pets accepted. **Amenities:** Restaurant; bar; heated indoor pool; tennis court; 4-room spa for massages and treatments; concierge; free Wi-Fi; limited room service; babysitting. *In room:* A/C, TV, hair dryer.

6 UPPER CHARLEVOIX: ST-SIMEON, BAIE STE-CATHERINE & TADOUSSAC

St-Siméon: 173km (107 miles) NE of Québec City; Baie Ste-Catherine: 207km (129 miles) NE of Québec City; Tadoussac: 214km (133 miles) NE of Québec City.

After visiting La Malbaie, you have several options. You can return back to Québec City the same way you came—it's only 140km (87 miles) along the north shore. To do this, continue up Route 138 for 33km (20 miles) to St-Siméon and cross the St. Lawrence by ferry, landing at Rivière-du-Loup on the opposite shore (this takes a little longer than 1 hr.) and returning to Québec City along the south shore.

But if it's summer or early fall and you have more time—a full afternoon or an extra day to stay overnight—consider continuing on to Baie-Ste-Catherine and Tadoussac. Here at the northern end of Charlevoix is one of the world's richest areas for **whale-watching.** The confluence of the St. Lawrence and Saguenay rivers attracts 10 to 12 species each summer—as many as 1,500 minke, humpback, finback, and blue whales, who join the 1,000 or so sweet-faced beluga (or white) whales who are here year-round. Add to that the harbor porpoises who visit, and there can be 5,000 creatures diving and playing in the waters. Many can be seen from land mid-June through late October, and up close by boat or kayak.

Springtime comes to this area about a month later than, say, Boston and New York—yellow forsythia in May instead of April, or lilacs in June instead of May. Note that in winter and spring, when the whales are gone and the temperatures are lower, most of the very few establishments between St-Siméon and Tadoussac are closed.

ESSENTIALS
Getting There
BY CAR Take Route 138 to reach the ferry at St-Siméon, and continue on 138 to Baie Ste-Catherine. The highway dead-ends at the dramatic Saguenay River, with Tadoussac just across it. There is a free car ferry for the 10-minute passage.

St-Siméon maintains a seasonal **tourist office** at 494 rue St-Laurent, open daily from 10am to 6pm between late June and Labour Day. Visit **www.tourisme-charlevoix.com** for more information.

ST-SIMEON

To get to the ferry that crosses the St. Lawrence, follow the signs directing cars and trucks to the terminal. Capacity is 100 cars and boarding is on a first-come, first-served basis. The daily number and times of departures vary substantially from month to month, so check at ℰ **418/638-2856** or www.traverserdl.com for the schedule. One-way fares are C$38 (£19) for a car, C$15(£7.50) for each passenger age 12 to 64 years, slightly less for folks 65 and older and children 5 to 11, and free for children younger than 5. Arrive at least 90 minutes before departure in summer and on holidays. Voyages take about 1 hour.

Even though this isn't a whale-watching cruise, passengers may enjoy a sighting on the passage from late June to September, when whales are most active. The ferry steams through the area they most enjoy, making sightings an ever-present possibility.

BAIE STE-CATHERINE & TADOUSSAC

The teeny Baie-Ste-Catherine (pop. 260) sits alongside the Saguenay River's estuary. Tadoussac (pop. 913), just across the Saguenay, is the southernmost point of the Manicouagan tourist region.

Tadoussac is known as "the Cradle of New France." Established in the 1600s, it's the oldest permanent European settlement north of Florida and became a stop on the fur-trading route. Missionaries stayed until the middle of the 19th century. The hamlet might have vanished soon after, had a resort hotel, now called **Hôtel Tadoussac** (p. 288), not been built in 1864. Thanks to it, a steamship line brought wealthy vacationers from Montréal and points farther west and deposited them here for stays that often lasted all summer.

Apart from the hotel, just a few small businesses, a whaling educational center, a beach and boardwalk, and some dozen small motels and B&Bs constitute the town. This is raw country, where the sight of a beaver waddling up the hill from the ferry terminal in broad daylight is met with only mild interest. Still, Tadoussac has more to offer than Baie Ste-Catherine for visitors and is the recommended choice for a stopover.

There's golfing at the public, well-maintained, 9-hole, 31-par **Club de Golf Tadoussac** (ℰ **418/235-4306**), which has been in operation since 1890. For 4 days in June, Tadoussac swells to nearly 20,000 when it hosts the annual **Festival de la Chanson,** a festival of French song; check **www.chansontadoussac.com**.

Route 138 dead-ends at the Saguenay River and picks up again on the other side. Passage in between is courtesy of a free 10-minute car ferry (ℰ **877/787-7483**). Departure times vary according to season and demand, but figure every 15 minutes from 8am to 8pm in summer, and less frequently the other 12 hours and in low season. (The ferry is the reason that trucks travel in convoys on the highway, pouring out in groups after each ferry crossing.)

The vista on the crossing is dramatic and nearly worth a trip to Tadoussac on its own: Palisades with evergreens poking out of rock walls rise sharply from both shores. So extreme is the natural architecture, in fact, that the area is often referred to as a fjord.

From mid-May to mid-October, a number of companies offer trips to see whales or cruise the majestic Saguenay.

Cruise companies use different sizes and types of watercraft, from stately catamarans and cruisers that carry up to 500 to powered inflatables called Zodiacs that carry 10 to 25 passengers. The Zodiacs don't provide food, drink, or narration, while the larger boats have snack bars and naturalists onboard to describe the action. Zodiacs, though, are more maneuverable, and dart about at each sighting to get closer to the rolling and breaching behemoths.

Zodiac passengers are issued life jackets and waterproof overalls, but should expect to get wet. It's cold out there, too, so layers and gloves are a good idea. People on the large boats sit at tables inside or ride the observation bowsprit, high above the waves.

Two of the biggest companies are **Croisières AML** (© **800/563-4643;** www. croisieresaml.com) and **Group Dufour** (© **800/463-5250;** www.dufour.ca). Both offer departures from wharves in both Baie-Ste-Catherine and Tadoussac. In high season, they each offer about six daily whale-watching trips. Fares are comparable: 3-hour tours on the larger boats cost C$59 (£30) for adults, C$54 (£27) for seniors and students, C$27 (£14) for children 6 to 16, and free for children 5 and younger. Two-hour Zodiac trips cost C$48 to C$55 (£24–£28) for adults, C$49 (£25) for seniors and students, and C$–2–C$39 (£16–£20) for children 6 to 16. Children younger than 6 are not permitted. Check with each company for exact times, prices, and trip options.

Kayak trips that search out whales are available from **Mer et Monde Ecotours** (© **866/637-6663** or 418/232-6779; www.mer-et-monde.qc.ca). Visitors report that they *felt* the whales before they saw them—imagine being out from the shore and feeling a vibration under the kayak hull! The company is based in Les Bergeronnes, a coastal town 20 km (12 miles) north of Tadoussac, and offers tours in summer that start at the bay of Tadoussac just beyond Hôtel Tadoussac's lawn. A 3-hour trip costs C$40 (£20) for adults, C$31 (£16) for those 15 and younger.

Although the St. Lawrence is a river, it's tidal and often called the "sea" (as in "sea-kayaking.") The waters here are in a marine park, which was designated as a conservation area to protect the whales and their habitat.

A Whale Center

Centre d'Interprétation des Mammifères Marins Start here when you arrive to understand why Tadoussac is such a paradise for whale researchers. At this interpretation center directly on the Saguenay River's edge, there's a small exhibition room (plaques are in French with English booklets for translation), an exhilarating 15-minute video about the whales who visit each summer (in French, with English translation by headphone), and a bilingual expert who answers questions and explains what the team who works upstairs—as many as 50 people in summer—are up to. Its shop sells books, cuddly toys, and clothing. The center is run by the nonprofit GREMM, a scientific research group that studies the St. Lawrence's marine mammals and posts updates about local whale activity at www.whales-online.net.

108 rue de la Cale Sèche (on the waterfront), Tadoussac. © **418/235-4701**. Admission C$8 (£4) adults, C$6 (£3) seniors, C$4 (£2) children 6–12, free for children 5 and younger. Daily 9am–8pm in summer; noon–5pm in spring and fall. Closed mid-Oct until mid-May.

Hôtel Tadoussac   Established in 1864 and now housed in a building from 1942, this handsome old-time hotel is king of the (small) hill that is Tadoussac. A large front lawn overlooks the river and the comings and goings of whale-watching boats. Public spaces and bedrooms have a shambling, country-cottage appearance—there's no pretense of luxury here—and their maple furnishings were made in Québec. If you've traveled far to get here, you'll likely want one of the river-view rooms (there are 51 of them), so book one and pay the worthwhile C$40 (£20) premium. Meals in the large dining room are resort-pricey (C$25 for a cold buffet dinner, for instance) and agreeable enough, though well short of impressive. If you're planning to whale-watch, kayak, or get a spa treatment, check out the many package deals.

165 rue Bord de l'Eau, Tadoussac, PQ G0T 2A0. (℃) **800/561-0718** or 418/235-4421. Fax 418/235-4607. www.hoteltadoussac.com. 149 units. C$204–C$244 (£102–£122) double in peak months; C$154–C$189 (£77–£95) double in low season. Children 17 and younger stay free in parent's room. Packages available. AE, DC, MC, V. Closed mid-Oct to early May. **Amenities:** 3 restaurants when busy, otherwise 1 open; bar; heated outdoor pool; tennis court; spa; children's programs nightly in peak months; free Wi-Fi in lobby; 1 computer for guest use; babysitting. *In room:* Overhead fan, TV, hair dryer.

Where to Dine

Café Bohème   Just a few steps from Hôtel Tadoussac is a cheery 1892 house with a white picket fence and mansard roof. Here, Café Bohème holds court as a dependable stop for healthy food, pastries, good coffee, and groovy world music. This eatery is clean and arty, with wooden floors, benches, tables, and counter seating. Breakfast (served until 11:30am) includes waffles. The *charlevoisien* panini has goat cheese, aged cheddar, pesto, tomatoes, and green peppers; homemade ice creams and sherbets include flavors like mango and chocolate-cardamom. In the busy season, there's an internet cafe, a bookstore, and a free book exchange upstairs.

239 rue des Pionniers, Tadoussac. (℃) **418/235-1180.** Most items cost less than C$10 (£5); *table d'hôte* C$15–C$25 (£7.25–£13). MC, V. Daily 8am–10pm. Closed mid-Oct to mid-May.

Appendix: Fast Facts, Toll-Free Numbers & Websites

1 FAST FACTS: MONTREAL & QUEBEC CITY

AAA Members of the **American Automobile Association (AAA)** are covered by the **Canadian Automobile Association (CAA)** while traveling in Canada. Bring your membership card and proof of insurance. The 24-hour hot line for emergency road service is *©* **800/222-4357.** The AAA card will also provide discounts at a wide variety of hotels and restaurants in Québec province. Visit **www.caaquebec.com** for more information.

AMERICAN EXPRESS In Montréal, 10 travel agencies are licensed to provide American Express Travel Services. One centrally located agency is **Excellent Travel** at 383 rue St. Jacques (*©* **514/345-1121**) on Vieux-Montréal's northern edge; there are no agencies in Québec City. For general information or emergency card service, call *©* **800/668-2639.**

AREA CODES The Montréal area codes are **514** and **428,** and the Québec City code is **418.** Outside of Montréal, the area code for the southern Laurentides is **450** and the northern Laurentides, from Val-David up, uses **819.** The Cantons de l'Est are the same: **450** or **819,** depending on how close you are to Montréal. Outside Québec City, the area code for Ile d'Orléans and north into Charlevoix is **418,** the same as in the city. You always need to dial the three-digit area code in addition to the seven-digit number.

ATMS/CASHPOINTS See "Money & Costs," p. 38.

BUSINESS HOURS Most **stores** in the province are open from 9 or 10am until 6pm Monday through Wednesday, 9am to 9pm on Thursday and Friday, and 9am to 5pm on Saturday. Many stores are now also open on Sunday from noon to 5pm. **Banks** are usually open Monday through Friday from 8 or 9am to 4pm and are closed for the entire weekend. Bankers' hours in Québec City are shorter, from 10am to 3pm. **Post office** hours vary wildly by location, but are generally open from 9:30am to 5:30pm or 7pm on weekdays. Some are open 9:30am to 5pm on Saturdays, and most are closed on Sundays. While many **restaurants** are open all day between meals, some shut down between lunch and dinner; check in advance. Most restaurants serve until 9:30pm or 10pm. **Bars** stay open until 2am or 3am—and sometimes even later.

CAR RENTALS See "Toll-Free Numbers & Websites," later.

DRINKING LAWS The legal drinking age in the province is 18. All hard liquor and spirits in Québec are sold through official government stores operated by the Québec Société des Alcools (look for maroon signs with the acronym SAQ). Wine and beer are available in grocery stores and convenience stores, called *dépanneurs.* Liquor is sold daily in SAQ stores (hours vary depending on location). Bars can pour drinks as late as 3am, but often stay open later.

Penalties for drunk driving in Canada are heavy. New provisions instituted in 2008 include higher mandatory penalties including a minimum fine of C$1,000 (£500) for a first offense, and for a second offense, a minimum of 30 days in jail. Drivers caught under the influence face a maximum life sentence if they cause death, and a maximum 10-year sentence if they cause bodily harm.

DRIVING RULES See "Getting There & Getting Around," p. 31.

DRUGSTORES & PHARMACIES A pharmacy is called a *pharmacie;* a drugstore is a *droguerie.* A large chain in Montréal is **Pharmaprix.** Its branch at 5122 Cote-Des-Neiges (© 514/738-8464; www.pharmaprix.ca) is open 24 hours per day, 7 days per week, and has a fairly convenient location. In Québec City, **Louis-Phillippe & Jacques Royer,** at 57 rue Dalhousie, in Vieux-Port (© 418/694-1262; www.brunet.ca), is open 9am to 7pm on weekdays, 9am to 5pm on Saturday, and 11am to 5pm Sunday, and delivers to hotels in the Old City.

ELECTRICITY Like the U.S., Canada uses 110 to 120 volts AC (60 cycles), compared to the 220 to 240 volts AC (50 cycles) used in most of Europe, Australia, and New Zealand. If your small appliances use 220 to 240 volts, you'll need a 110-volt transformer and a plug adapter with two flat parallel pins to operate them in Canada.

EMBASSIES & CONSULATES All embassies are in Ottawa, Canada's capital. The U.S. has a consulate in Montréal at 1155 rue St-Alexandre (© 514/398-9695) and in Québec City, on Jardin des Gouverneurs at 2 rue de la Terrasse-Dufferin (© 418/692-2095). The U.K.'s consulate in Montréal is at 1000 rue de la Gauchetière ouest,

Suite 4200 (© 514/866-5863), and in Québec City in the St-Amable Complex, 1150 Claire-Fontaine, Suite 700 (© 418/521-3000).

EMERGENCIES Dial © 911 for police, firefighters, or an ambulance. Québec Poison Control Centre is at © 800/463-5060.

FAX Most hotels have fax machines available for guest use (be sure to ask about the charge to use it). Select FedEx Kinko's outlets (© 800/463.3339; www.fedexkinkos.ca) also offer fax services.

GASOLINE (PETROL) Gasoline in Canada is expensive by American standards, even considering the steep rise in costs in the U.S. in 2008. Europeans will not find the prices a shock. Gas is sold by the liter, and 3.78 liters equals 1 gallon. Recent prices of C$1.40 (70p) per liter are the equivalent of about US$5.30 per gallon.

HOLIDAYS Canada's important public holidays are New Year's Day (Jan 1); Good Friday and Easter Monday (Mar or Apr); Victoria Day (the Mon preceding May 25); St-Jean-Baptiste Day, Québec's "national" day (June 24); Canada Day (July 1); Labour Day (first Mon in Sept); Canadian Thanksgiving Day (second Mon in Oct); and Christmas (Dec 25). For more about holidays, see "Montréal & Québec City Calendar of Events" on p. 28.

HOSPITALS In Montréal, hospitals with emergency rooms include **Hôpital Général de Montréal,** 1650 rue Cedar (© 514/934-1934), and **Hôpital Royal Victoria,** 687 av. des Pins ouest (© 514/934-1934), both of which are associated with McGill University. **Hôpital de Montréal pour Enfants,** 2300 rue Tupper (© 514/412-4400), is a children's hospital.

In Québec City, go to the **Centre Hospitalier Hôtel-Dieu de Québec,** 11 côte du Palais (© 418/525-4444).

Also see "Health," p. 40.

HOT LINES **Alcoholics Anonymous** is at ℂ 514/376-9230 in Montréal and ℂ 418/529-0015 in Québec City. The **Poison Control Centre** is at ℂ 800/463-5060 throughout the entire province. **Tel-Aide,** for emotional distress including anxiety and depression, is at ℂ 418/686-2433. **Sexual assault** victims can get bilingual help 24 hours per day at ℂ 514/934-4504.

INSURANCE **Medical Insurance** Medical treatment in Canada isn't free for foreigners, and hospitals make you pay your bills at the time of service.

Check whether your insurance policy covers you while traveling in Canada, especially for hospitalization abroad. U.S. Medicare and Medicaid programs do not provide coverage for hospital or medical costs outside the U.S. Many other policies require you to pay for services upfront and, if they reimburse you at all, will only do so after you return home. Carry details of your insurance plan with you, and leave a copy with a friend at home.

U.K. nationals also have to pay for medical treatment in Canada. Carry a European Health Insurance Card (EHIC), which replaced the E111. More details are at **www.dh.gov.uk/travellers**.

As a safety net, you may want to buy travel medical insurance. Options include **MEDEX Assistance** (ℂ 410/453-6300; www.medexassist.com) or **Travel Assistance International** (ℂ 800/821-2828; www.travelassistance.com).

Travel Insurance The cost of travel insurance varies widely, depending on the destination, the cost and length of your trip, your age and health, and the type of trip you're taking, but expect to pay between 5% and 8% of the cost of the vacation. You can get estimates from various providers at **www.insuremytrip.com**. Enter your trip cost and dates, your age, and other information, for prices from more than a dozen companies.

U.K. citizens and their families who make more than one trip abroad per year may find that an annual travel insurance policy works out to be a better deal. Check **www.moneysupermarket.com**, which compares prices across a wide range of providers for single- and multi-trip policies.

Most big travel agents offer their own insurance and will probably try to sell you their package when you book a holiday. Think before you sign. **Britain's Consumers' Association** recommends that you insist on seeing the policy and reading the fine print before buying travel insurance. **The Association of British Insurers** (ℂ 020/7600-3333; www.abi.org.uk) gives advice by phone and publishes *Holiday Insurance,* a free guide to policy provisions and prices. You might also shop around for better deals: Try **Columbus Direct** (ℂ 0870/033-9988; www.columbusdirect.net).

Trip Cancellation Insurance Trip-cancellation insurance will help retrieve your money if you have to back out of a trip or depart early, or if your travel supplier goes bankrupt. Trip cancellation usually covers such events as sickness and natural disasters. The latest news in trip-cancellation insurance is the availability of any-reason cancellation coverage, which costs more but covers cancellations made for any reason. You won't get back 100% of your trip's cost, but you'll be refunded a substantial portion. **TravelSafe** (ℂ 888/885-7233; www.travelsafe.com) offers both types of coverage. Expedia also offers any-reason cancellation coverage for its air-hotel packages. For details, contact one of the following recommended insurers: **Access America** (ℂ 866/807-3982; www.accessamerica.com); **Travel Guard International** (ℂ 800/826-4919; www.travelguard.com); **Travel Insured International** (ℂ 800/243-3174; www.travelinsured.com); or **Travelex Insurance Services** (ℂ 888/457-4602; www.travelex-insurance.com).

INTERNET ACCESS See "Staying Connected," p. 46.

LANGUAGE Canada is officially bilingual, but Québec province has laws that make French mandatory in signage. About 20% of Montréal's population has English as its first language (about 5% of Québec City's population does) and an estimated four out of five Francophones (French speakers) speak at least some English. Hotel desk staff, sales clerks, and telephone operators nearly always greet people initially in French, but usually switch to English quickly if necessary. Outside of Montréal, visitors are more likely to encounter residents who don't speak English. If smiles and sign language don't work, look around for a young person—most of them study English in school.

LAUNDROMATS Laundromats aren't thick upon the ground in tourist districts. In Montréal, one option is **Buanderie Chez Bobette** in the Plateau Mont-Royal neighborhood at 850 rue Duluth est (✆ **514/522-2612**). In Québec City, try **La Lavandiere,** at 625 rue St-Jean (✆ **418/523-0345**), just outside the Old City walls in the Parliament Hill area. Ask your hotel for options, too—many provide laundry service.

LEGAL AID Your country's embassy or consulate can provide the names of attorneys who speak English. The U.S. Embassy information line ✆ **888/840-0032** works from the U.S. and Canada and costs C$1.59 per minute. See "Embassies & Consulates," above for more information.

LOST & FOUND Be sure to tell all of your credit card companies the minute you discover your wallet has been lost or stolen and file a report at the nearest police precinct. Your credit card company or insurer may require a police report number or record of the loss. Most credit card companies have an emergency toll-free number to call if your card is lost or stolen; they may be able to wire you a cash advance immediately or deliver an emergency credit card in a day or two.

For lost or stolen American Express cards, call ✆ **800/668-2639.** For lost or stolen Visa cards, call ✆ **800/847-2911.** For lost or stolen MasterCards, call ✆ **800/307-7309.** If you need emergency cash over the weekend when all banks are closed, you can have money wired to you via **Western Union** (✆ **800/325-6000;** www.westernunion.com).

MAIL All mail sent through **Canada Post** (✆ **866/607-6301;** www.canadapost.ca) must bear Canadian stamps. That might seem painfully obvious, but apparently, a large numbers of visitors, especially from the U.S., use stamps from their home countries. To mail within Canada, letters cost C52¢ (26p). A letter or postcard to the U.S. requires C96¢ (48p). A letter or postcard to anywhere else costs C$1.60 (80p). **FedEx** offers service from Canada; call or go to its website to find locations (✆ **800/463-3339;** www.fedex.com/ca).

MAPS Good city maps are available for free from the tourist offices (p. 23). The best detailed street guide of Montréal is the pocket-size atlas by JDM Géo published by MapArt (www.mapart.com), which also makes useful maps for all the regions outside Montréal and Québec City that are mentioned in this book. Find them online, and in shops and gas stations throughout Canada.

MEDICAL CONDITIONS If you are entering Canada with syringes used for medical reasons, bring a medical certificate proving that they are for medical use and be sure to declare them to Canadian Customs officials.

NEWSPAPERS & MAGAZINES Montréal's primary English-language newspaper is the *Montréal Gazette* (www.montrealgazette.com). *The Globe and Mail* (www.theglobeandmail.com) is a national English-language paper. The leading

French-language newspaper is *Le Soleil.* For information about current arts happenings in Montréal, pick up the Friday or Saturday edition of the *Gazette* (www. canada.com/montrealgazette). Most large newsstands and those in larger hotels carry the *Wall Street Journal, New York Times,* and *International Herald Tribune.*

PASSPORTS See p. 24 for passport information regarding traveling to Canada.

For residents of the U.S.: U.S. residents can apply for a passport in person or by mail. Applications are available from the U.S. State Department website at http://travel.state.gov. To find a regional passport office, check the aforementioned website or call the **National Passport Information Center** at © 877/487-2778 for automated information.

U.S. residents should allow plenty of time to apply for a passport; processing normally takes 4 to 6 weeks (3 weeks for expedited service), but can take longer during busy periods (especially spring). Keep in mind that if you need a passport in a hurry, you'll pay a higher processing fee.

For residents of Australia: You can pick up an application from your local post office or any branch of Passports Australia, but you must schedule an interview at the passport office to present your application materials. Call the **Australian Passport Information Service** at © 131-232, or visit the government website at www.passports.gov.au.

For residents of Ireland: You can apply for a 10-year passport at the **Passport Office,** Setanta Centre, Molesworth Street, Dublin 2 (© 01/671-1633; www.irlgov. ie/iveagh). Those younger than 18 and older than 65 must apply for a 3-year passport. You can also apply at 1A South Mall, Cork (© 21/494-4700) or at most main post offices.

For residents of New Zealand: You can pick up a passport application at any **New Zealand Passports Office** or download it from their website. Contact them at © **0800/225-050** or 04/474-8100, or go to www.passports.govt.nz.

For residents of the United Kingdom: To pick up an application for a standard 10-year passport (5-year passport for children younger than 16), visit your nearest passport office, major post office, or travel agency. You can also contact the **United Kingdom Passport Service** at © **0870/521-0410** or search its website at www.ukpa. gov.uk.

POLICE Dial © **911** for the police. There are three types of officers in Québec: **municipal police** in Montréal, Québec City, and other towns; **Sûreté de Québec officers,** comparable to state police or the highway patrol in the U.S.; and **RCMP** (Royal Canadian Mounted Police), who are similar to the FBI and handle cases involving infraction of federal laws. RCMP officers speak English and French. Other officers are not required to know English, though many do.

SMOKING Smoking was banned in the province's bars, restaurants, clubs, casinos, and some other public spaces in mid-2006. Most small inns and many larger hotels are entirely smoke-free as well. Check before you book if you're looking for a room in which you can smoke.

TAXES Most goods and services in Canada are taxed 5% by the federal government (the GST, or Goods and Services Tax). On top of that, the province of Québec tacks on an additional 7.5% tax (the TVQ). A 3% accommodations tax is in effect in Montréal.

Nonresident visitors used to be able to apply for a rebate for the GST tax they paid on most items they purchased in Québec as well as on the taxes they paid for lodging, but that practice was eliminated in April 2007. A new Foreign Convention and Tour Incentive Program provides limited rebates on the GST for services used during foreign conventions held in Canada, for nonresident exhibitors, and for the short-term accommodations portion of tour packages for nonresident individuals and tour operators. Details are at **www.cra-arc.gc.ca/visitors**.

TELEPHONES   See "Telephones," p. 46.

TIME   Montréal, Québec City, and all the regions listed in this book as side trips are all on Eastern Standard Time, same as New York. Daylight saving time is observed by moving clocks ahead an hour on the second Sunday in March and back an hour on the first Sunday in November.

TIPPING   Tipping practices in the province are similar to those in the U.S.: 15% to 20% on restaurant bills, 10% to 15% for taxi drivers, C$1 (50p) per bag for porters, C$5 (£2.50) per night for hotel room attendants. Hairdressers and barbers expect 10% to 15%. Hotel doormen should be tipped for calling a taxi or providing other services.

TOILETS   You won't find public toilets on the streets in Montréal or Québec City, but they can be found in tourist offices, museums, railway and bus stations, and service stations. Restaurants and bars in heavily visited areas may reserve their restrooms for patrons. A website called **the Bathroom Diaries** (www.thebathroomdiaries.com) lists facilities by city, along with commentary (for instance, Indigo Books in downtown Montréal gets an "excellent" rating for its free, clean, safe bathrooms with "very pretty white tiles").

USEFUL PHONE NUMBERS U.S. Dept. of State Travel Advisory: ✆ 202/647-5225 (manned 24 hr.)
U.S. Passport Agency: ✆ 202/647-0518
U.S. Centers for Disease Control International Traveler's Hot Line: ✆ 404/332-4559

VISAS   See "Visas," p. 25.

2 TOLL-FREE NUMBERS & WEBSITES

AIRLINES
Air Canada
✆ 888/247-2262
www.aircanada.ca

Air France
✆ 800/237-2747 (in U.S.)
✆ 800/375-8723 (in U.S. and Canada)
✆ 087/0142-4343 (in U.K.)
www.airfrance.com

American Airlines
✆ 800/433-7300 (in U.S. and Canada)
✆ 020/7365-0777 (in U.K.)
www.aa.com

British Airways
✆ 800/247-9297 (in U.S. and Canada)
✆ 087/0850-9850 (in U.K.)
www.britishairways.com

Continental Airlines
✆ 800/523-3273 (in U.S. and Canada)
✆ 084/5607-6760 (in U.K.)
www.continental.com

Delta Air Lines
✆ 800/221-1212 (in U.S. and Canada)
✆ 084/5600-0950 (in U.K.)
www.delta.com

Lufthansa
✆ 800/399-5838 (in U.S.)
✆ 800/563-5954 (in Canada)
✆ 087/0837-7747 (in U.K.)
www.lufthansa.com

Northwest Airlines
✆ 800/225-2525 (in U.S.)
✆ 870/0507-4074 (in U.K.)
www.nwa.com

Olympic Airlines
✆ 800/223-1226 (in U.S.)
✆ 514/878-9691 (in Canada)
✆ 087/0606-0460 (in U.K.)
www.olympicairlines.com

Swiss Air
© 877/359-7947 (in U.S. and Canada)
© 084/5601-0956 (in U.K.)
www.swiss.com

United Airlines
© 800/864-8331 (in U.S. and Canada)
© 084/5844-4777 in U.K.
www.united.com

US Airways
© 800/428-4322 (in U.S. and Canada)
© 084/5600-3300 (in U.K.)
www.usairways.com

CAR-RENTAL AGENCIES

Advantage
© 800/777-5500 (in U.S.)
© 021/0344-4712 (outside of U.S.)
www.advantagerentacar.com

Alamo
© 800/GO-ALAMO (800/462-5266)
www.alamo.com

Avis
© 800/331-1212 (in U.S. and Canada)
© 084/4581-8181 (in U.K.)
www.avis.com

Budget
© 800/527-0700 (in U.S.)
© 800/268-8900 (in Canada)
© 087/0156-5656 (in U.K.)
www.budget.com

Dollar
© 800/800-4000 (in U.S.)
© 800/848-8268 (in Canada)
© 080/8234-7524 (in U.K.)
www.dollar.com

Enterprise
© 800/261-7331 (in U.S.)
© 514/355-4028 (in Canada)
© 012/9360-9090 (in U.K.)
www.enterprise.com

Hertz
© 800/645-3131
© 800/654-3001 (for international reservations)
www.hertz.com

National
© 800/CAR-RENT (800/227-7368)
www.nationalcar.com

Payless
© 800/PAYLESS (800/729-5377)
www.paylesscarrental.com

Thrifty
© 800/367-2277
© 918/669-2168 (international)
www.thrifty.com

MAJOR HOTEL & MOTEL CHAINS

Best Western International
© 800/780-7234 (in U.S. and Canada)
© 0800/393-130 (in U.K.)
www.bestwestern.com

Clarion Hotels
© 800/CLARION (800/252-7466) or 877/424-6423 (in U.S. and Canada)
© 0800/444-444 (in U.K.)
www.choicehotels.com

Courtyard by Marriott
© 888/236-2427 (in U.S.)
© 0800/221-222 (in U.K.)
www.marriott.com/courtyard

Crowne Plaza Hotels
© 888/303-1746
www.ichotelsgroup.com/crowneplaza

Days Inn
© 800/329-7466 (in U.S.)
© 0800/280-400 (in U.K.)
www.daysinn.com

Doubletree Hotels
© 800/222-8733 (in U.S. and Canada)
© 087/0590-9090 (in U.K.)
www.doubletree.com

Econo Lodge
© 800/55-ECONO (800/552-3666)
www.choicehotels.com

Embassy Suites
© 800/EMBASSY (800/362-2779)
www.embassysuites.com

Fairfield Inn by Marriott
© 800/228-2800 (in U.S. and Canada)
© 0800/221-222 (in U.K.)
www.fairfieldinn.com

Hampton Inn
© 800/HAMPTON (800/426-4766)
www.hamptoninn.com

Hilton Hotels
© 800/HILTONS (800/445-8667;
  in U.S. and Canada)
© 087/0590-9090 (in U.K.)
www.hilton.com

Holiday Inn
© 800/315-2621 (in U.S. and Canada)
© 0800/405-060 (in U.K.)
www.holidayinn.com

Howard Johnson
© 800/446-4656 (in U.S. and Canada)
www.hojo.com

Hyatt
© 888/591-1234 (in U.S. and Canada)
© 084/5888-1234 (in U.K.)
www.hyatt.com

InterContinental Hotels & Resorts
© 800/424-6835 (in U.S. and Canada)
© 0800/1800-1800 (in U.K.)
www.intercontinental.com

Loews Hotels
© 800/23LOEWS (800/235-6397)
www.loewshotels.com

Marriott
© 877/236-2427 (in U.S. and Canada)
© 0800/221-222 (in U.K.)
www.marriott.com

Omni Hotels
© 888/444-6664
www.omnihotels.com

Quality Inn
© 877/424-6423 (in U.S. and Canada)
© 0800/444-444 (in U.K.)
www.qualityinn.com

Radisson Hotels & Resorts
© 888/201-1718 (in U.S. and Canada)
© 0800/374-411 (in U.K.)
www.radisson.com

Residence Inn by Marriott
© 800/331-3131
© 800/221-222 (in U.K.)
www.residenceinn.com

Rodeway Inns
© **877/424-6423**
www.rodewayinn.com

Sheraton Hotels & Resorts
© 800/325-3535 (in U.S.)
© 800/543-4300 (in Canada)
© 0800/3253-5353 (in U.K.)
www.sheraton.com

Super 8 Motels
© 800/800-8000
www.super8.com

Travelodge
© 800/578-7878
www.travelodge.com

Westin Hotels & Resorts
© 800/937-8461 (in U.S. and Canada)
© 0800/3259-5959 (in U.K.)
www.westin.com

Wyndham Hotels & Resorts
© 877/999-3223 (in U.S. and Canada)
© 050/6638-4899 (in U.K.)
www.wyndham.com

INDEX

See also Accommodations and Restaurant indexes, below.